Praise for *Brotherhood in R'*

"Stressing the joyousness of their work, ... 't, which makes the book an ideal companion fo .... .c."

—Booklist

"My heartiest applause goes to author Consta............... .or this heart-warming account of my two longtime idols. Fayard and ....id Nicholas had the style, the talent, and the determination to make it to the top of their profession. Needless to say, they inspired me, along with countless others, to reach for the stars."

—BOBBY SHORT

"Most jazz tap dancers stand up and dance. The Nicholas Brothers did that—and then they flew, catapulting themselves over each others heads, step by step down a staircase, or running up a wall and uncoiling backward into thin air. . . . *Brotherhood in Rhythm* tells how they did it. . . . An outstanding researcher, with access to a treasury of home movies owned by the Nicholas family, Hill recreates the theatrical milieus in which the brothers operated: the Standard Theater in Philadelphia, The Cotton Club in Harlem, Broadway, and Hollywood."

—MINDY ALOFF,
New York Times Book Review

"A lovingly researched and thoughtfully created portrait of Fayard and Harold Nicholas. . . . Hill's infectious admiration will inspire even those not well acquainted with the pair. . . . Exceptionally clear and useful. . . . Essential reading."

—Library Journal

"Fayard and Harold brought the energy of jazz to dance. . . . The Nicholas Brothers never failed to invigorate the stage and screen with their awe-inspiring dancing."

—Jazz Times

"A long-overdue appreciation of the team whose fans included Fred Astaire, Bob Fosse, Sammy Davis Jr., and George Balanchine. Constance Valis Hill gives Harold and Fayard Nicholas their proper eminence at last—not as 'daredevils,' 'flash dancers,' or even a 'tap act'—but as two of the century's greatest dancers. Period."

—BRUCE GOLDSTEIN,
writer, coproducer, *Nicholas Brothers: We Sing and We Dance*

"Hill tells the story of the brothers' success, their gigs with Duke Ellington and Cab Calloway, their encounters with racism, their performances in such movies as Stormy Weather, and their innovative response to the advent of be-bop."

—Publishers Weekly

"Hill's book, one of the few sustained analyses of tap, supplies the background— minstrelsy, 'class' acts, swing—and, along the way, a history of American racism. It also tells a love story. Harold was only eleven when the brothers made their Cotton Club debut; Fayard, eighteen, taught him how to shine. . . . For more than fifty years, that dynamic gave their act its emotional fire, and it warms the book as well."

—The New Yorker

To my husband, Stephen,
for your ever-faithful support,

and to my son, Theodore—
sixteen years old and a jazz pianist,
you rocked our house as you played your swinging tunes,
and nightly reminded me why it was so important
to be sitting upstairs, in my study, attempting to write about
the intoxicating rhythms of jazz

Brotherhood
in Rhythm

*The Jazz Tap Dancing
of the Nicholas Brothers*

CONSTANCE VALIS HILL

NEW INTRODUCTION BY JENNIFER DUNNING
FOREWORD BY GREGORY HINES

Cooper Square Press

First Cooper Square Press edition 2002

This Cooper Square Press paperback edition of *Brotherhood in Rhythm* is an unabridged republication of the edition first published in New York in 2000, with the addition of a new introduction by Jennifer Dunning. It is reprinted by arrangement with Oxford University Press, Inc. and the author.

Design by Adam B. Bohannon
Composition by Jack Donner

Published by Cooper Square Press
A Member of the Rowman & Littlefield Publishing Group
200 Park Avenue South, Suite 1109
New York, New York 10003-1503
www.coopersquarepress.com

Distributed by National Book Network

Library of Congress catalogued the previous edition as follows:

Hill, Constance Valis
    Brotherhood in rhythm: the jazz tap dancing of the Nicholas Brothers / Constance Valis Hill
      p. cm.
    Includes bibliographical references and index.
    1. Nicholas Brothers. 2. Dancers—United States—Biography. 3. Jazz tap—United States—History. I. Title.
    GV1785.AI V35 2000
    792.7'8—dc21   99-30917

ISBN 0-8154-1215-0 (pbk. : alk. paper)

⊖™ The paper used in this publication meets the minimum requirements of American National Standard for Information Sciences—Permanence of Paper for Printed Library Materials, ANSI/NISO Z39.48–1992.
Manufactured in the United States of America.

Contents

Introduction to the Cooper Square Press Edition

The Nicholas Brothers were in a league of their own. They glittered. They flashed. "Uncorked genies," as the critic Arlene Croce described them, the brothers flew through acrobatic feats so astounding that projectionists sometimes had to rewind films and replay their dance routines for clamoring audiences.

Categorized by many as a "flash" or acrobatic act, Fayard (1914–) and Harold Nicholas (1918–2000) were instead a sophisticated, stylish "class" act with flash. They never looked less than suave and in total control of their dance and their environment on the screen, even in childhood appearances (though Harold's hair does muss a little, shockingly, as he sails through their signature "Jumpin' Jive" number in *Stormy Weather*).

Other tap greats began performing as children like the brothers, but none were shaped by studying vaudeville regulars from the front rows of theaters that were second homes. Only Bill "Bojangles" Robinson rose as high as the Nicholas Brothers did (though not so quickly) and was, like them, a marquee name who banked salaries comparable to those of the white stars of the day. While Robinson could conceivably be misidentified after a cursory glance, the Nicholas Brothers were immediately and unmistakeably themselves.

Fame made them wiser, perhaps, and Fayard and Harold were more able to roll with every punch than many headliners of their time. The two never seemed to stray very far from the comfortable sidekick siblings that they were in their first film, the 1932 Vitaphone black short *Pie, Pie Blackbird* and countless early home movies: the genial, twinkling-eyed adolescent Fayard and the tiny, irrepressible Harold, who was always simultaneously competing with and dancing for his big brother.

The existence of those home movies suggests something about why the Nicholas Brothers were so different. They came from a stable, middle-class show-business family headed by a professional drummer and a pianist steeped in the New Orleans–style jazz sound of their own youth. There might be no babysitters to see to the needs of their children when Ulysses and Viola Nicholas were at work in the orchestra pits of black theaters in Chicago, Winston-Salem, Baltimore, and Philadelphia, but what could be safer than stowing the infinitely curious Fayard in the empty theater (once he outgrew the bassinet beside his mother's piano in the orchestra pit) to watch as vaudeville acts rehearsed? Fayard must have kept a keen eye on his younger sister and brother once it occurred to him that he could make them dance like the professionals whom he saw perform live and on film at the theater.

Their careful, proud upbringing is the subject of one of the most poignant anecdotes in Constance Valis Hill's vibrant and informative evocation of the lives and artistry of "the brothers," as Fred Astaire called them so simply. Harold was only fifteen when he and twenty-two-year-old Fayard were featured in the Rodgers and Hart musical *Babes in Arms*, their second show with choreographer George Balanchine. Although young and working with theater legends, the brothers knew themselves and their worth well enough to put up a fight over a line in "All Dark People," a song written for them. "All dark people is light on their feet," the line went, much to Fayard's disgust. His mother balked at the grammar, which she perceived rightly as fostering stereotypes about the supposed ignorance of black people. Her sons were never to use improper English in films or on stage, she told them. She and "the brothers" lost the battle eventually, but they fought valiantly.

America has a long tradition of self-taught dancers. Today, as when the Nicholas Brothers were young, there are children who learn to sing, play percussion, and dance on urban street corners for flung coins. That was the time-honored way that the tap greats of the 1920s—Bill "Bojangles" Robinson among them—developed their steps and styles and in turn passed them along to younger generations.

Like the Nicholas Brothers, John Durang trained as a teenager by studying European dancers from the audience in the late eighteenth century, becoming the first native-born American to be recognized widely as a professional dancer and choreographer. Several decades later, George Washington Smith learned enough by watching to become the partner of the famed Austrian ballerina Fanny Elssler and the first American to dance Albrecht in *Giselle*.

One of Fayard's most important early impromptu teachers was his father. Fayard may have gained an extra sense of the thrill of performing by watching Ulysses Nicholas play in drum challenges, ranging his drumsticks along just about every flat surface—just as Fayard would later do with his feet, scaling steps and pedestals, and even venturing a few steps up a wall. In some photographs of the time Viola has the determined look of a genteel stage mother. But it was Ulysses who suggested that his oldest son not copy others in his routines. And look not at your feet but at the audience you are entertaining, a lesson that his son learned well. Fayard should also make more use of his already unusually fluid dancer's hands, and why not incorporate young Harold into your routines?

Dorothy Bernice, the middle child, was enlisted, but danced with Fayard only briefly. In amusing footage of the three children in the Nicholas home movies, Dorothy smiles and covers her face as she walks toward the camera. Fayard appears next, happily striding forward with that distinctively sweet smile of his. Little Harold follows, mugging blithely but somehow all the more enchanting for it.

Fayard gathered an interesting collection of heroes as he studied stage and screen performers in his childhood years. An early one was the nerdy, zany, silent movie comedian Harold Lloyd, after whom Fayard was allowed to name his younger brother. Was it Lloyd's athletic stunts that captured Fayard's attention? Other heroes were less surprising and suggest that the young dancer knew early on that elegance was to be his metier.

Jack Ginger Wiggins caught young Fayard's eye in shows at the

Lincoln Theater in Baltimore, where his parents were playing. Wiggins was an influential innovator, a creator of complex step sequences who stood out for his dignity, authority, and dazzling formal outfits. It was Wiggins who introduced the "class" act to the T.O.B.A. (variously known as the Theater Owners' Booking Association, "Toby," and "Tough on Black Asses"), the black vaudeville circuit that offered national touring shows through the 1920s.

Wiggins convinced the comedian Nipsy Russell that blacks "could have real class in show business," according to the jazz historians Marshall and Jean Stearns. "To southern folk," the Stearns wrote in their 1968 book *Jazz Dance*, "Wiggins transformed the stereotype of 'Darky Dandy' into a high-class gentleman." It was from Wiggins' famous Tango Twist, Fayard said in later years, that he got the idea for a split that went down and rose again.

Leonard Reed was also a hero, a light-skinned matinee idol of a tap dancer who, with his shining top hat and silver-tipped cane, was the Charleston-dancing epitome of polish. Willie Covan, another admired dancer, could do just about every kind of dancing and did, in routines that helped to define the "class" act.

The Nicholas Brothers began to outpace them all, however, not long after they made their formal professional debut in 1931 dancing on radio on The Nicholas Kids on *The Horn and Hardart Kiddie Hour Show*. They had performed several years earlier in a show at the Standard Theater, which had led to appearances at other theaters in Philadelphia and eventually in Baltimore and Washington, D.C. Late in 1931, the brothers accepted a job offer in New York City at the Lafayette Theater in Harlem, where some of the best musicians and bands were playing. Ulysses and Viola left the pit orchestra at the Standard and became the brothers' manager.

The Harlem Renaissance had dwindled—the Depression saw to that—when the Nicholas family arrived in Harlem. But that city within a city still bustled with achievement in the arts and letters, as Hill chronicles so vividly here. The rest of the nation might be staggering dimly through lean years, but Harlem continued to dance and sing and paint and write with nearly unabated energy. And Fayard and Harold would soon be a part of that ferment.

In their well-advertised New York debut, the seventeen-year-old Fayard and eleven-year-old Harold shared the bill at the Lafayette with Eubie Blake and his band and stopped the show again and again. Within a mere five years, they had performed with Blake and the beauteous Nina Mae McKinney in *Pie, Pie Blackbird* and appeared with headliners like Cab Calloway and Duke Ellington at the glamorous Cotton Club for more than two years. That alone would have made them famous in Harlem, recognized on the streets wherever they went. However, by 1937 they had also danced in two Broadway musicals, a musical in London, and some eight short and feature films made in Hollywood and London. In addition, Harold had appeared on his own in suitably cheeky acting roles in two other films.

Remarkably, this early exposure to fame and famous people did not seem to affect the brothers much. They continued to rehearse hard and aim for perfection. They paid attention to their image of well-tailored young men about town, on and off the stage, which must have added extra luster to their status as role models to Harlem youngsters, including Max Roach and Bobby Short. The brothers had proved that not only was making it possible, it was possible to make it big and on one's own terms.

Fayard and Harold were precocious, certainly, and that ingenuous precocity stayed with them, a part of their charm, through their last major film together, the 1948 musical *The Pirate*. True professionals with dancing in their blood, bones, and sinew, they began by dancing through their neighborhood and over the furniture of their childhood homes—anywhere, in fact, where there was a danceable surface.

Their easy naturalness and sharp eye for even remotely achievable effect guided them through the dances in their most famous films, made in the 1930s and 1940s. To perform before cameras or before a live Broadway audience may not have been so terribly different, in the end, from what had come earlier.

Like oil and water, movement and words are unblendable. One of Hill's achievements is to make the greatest Nicholas Brothers dances come alive in words, particularly in her descriptions of the polyrhythmic "Argentina" samba number in *Down Argentine Way*, the sly and high-flying "Chattanooga Choo Choo" dance in *Sun Valley Serenade*, "Alabamy Bound" in *The Great American Broadcast*, and, most brilliant of all, the delicious "Kalamazoo" and "Jumpin' Jive" dances, which explore and utilize just about every unexpected inch of air, floor, and vertical space in *Orchestra Wives* and *Stormy Weather*, respectively.

All but "Chattanooga Choo Choo" were created with Nick Castle, a gifted and sensitive Hollywood choreographer, who not only did not balk at working with black dancers (as some choreographers and teachers of the time did), but was also unassuming enough to be excited at the prospect of drawing on the brothers' prodigious talent. The collaborations were pure Nicholas Brothers, in their smooth blend of tap, eccentric or trick dancing, jazz, Latin, and social dance forms, and in the classical ballet in which Fayard had become absorbed during their first trip to England.

One thinks of Astaire dancing across gleaming ballroom floors and inside romantic hideaways. For Gene Kelly, it was natural settings like urban streets and the equally unbelievable hummocks of Hollywood sets. The Nicholas Brothers seem to dance eternally up and down stairs, with a hurtling grace and impish invention that has nothing to do with the quieter pyrotechnics of Bill "Bojangles" Robinson's famous stair dancing.

The brothers' bodies are much clearer verticals, arms relatively low and close to their sides, in their early film performances (among them the charming "Lucky Numbers" dance from the 1936 *Black Network*.) The sliding feet that were a trademark move, though not at all their invention, may be seen in that dance. Fayard is the perfect suave-but-affectionate straight man to Harold's sweet-singing top banana, a role that he maintained to some extent throughout their career together.

Harold is almost as tall as Fayard in their "Argentina" dance in the 1941 *Down Argentine Way*, a Brazilian-flavored romp that starred Don Ameche, Betty Grable, and Carmen Miranda (in her first American movie). By now, the brothers have adopted their distinctive tilt, which introduced an extra tension and elegance into the mix—their bodies are poised, as if buoyed by air beneath their open high arms. And Fayard is much more clearly "conducting" Harold, his arms and hands seeming to send his younger brother out into space and to draw him back closer. The hypnotic drawing-in or elision is reminiscent of a moment in the second act of the ballet *Giselle*, when Albrecht eases his beloved Giselle into his backward-moving wake with a touch of his hands.

The brothers' legs fly out in a fusillade of sharp taps and rhythms. Even more exciting, in *Argentina* and later films, are the seamless joins that smoothly link unison with solo dancing, debonair floor-bound gliding with sudden explosions of acrobatics, and quick-shifting rhythms with brief pauses and teasing ritards. To see Harold jumping over his large white handkerchief into a split with a perfectly timed rise is to understand immediately the brothers' innately musical phrasing.

The Nicholas Brothers did not dance to music. They danced *inside* it, as symbolized in a more stylized and obvious way by their apposition to the rising trumpet players and riffing pianist in "Jumpin' Jive" in the 1943 *Stormy Weather*. One feasts uninter-ruptedly on the brothers' dancing in that number: on their exqui-site hands, their teasing juxtaposition of plain and fancy, as in the wittily simple step-by-step ascent on either side of a horseshoe-shaped white stairway and in their sudden and exuberant slide down. The actual steps and intertwining of rhythms may be mar-ginally less complex in "Jumpin' Jive," but everything Fayard and Nicholas had become is distilled here.

Stormy Weather and the film musicals that immediately pre-ceded it were the pinnacle of their career. The brothers continued to work, moving on to night clubs, regional theater, and televi-sion as major film and stage opportunities dried up in the late 1940s. They finally received the recognition that they deserved as serious dance professionals during the 1990s, when they received the Kennedy Center Honors award, the *Dance* Magazine Award, and the Samuel H. Scripps American Dance Festival Award, an honor usually given to modern dance choreographers.

A huge, vociferous crowd rose to its feet in "From Harlem to Hollywood," a tribute at Carnegie Hall in 1998. On stage with the brothers were several generations of musicians and a host of young tap dancers. Lena Horne, their old cohort in Hollywood films, presided over the event with the impeccable class that iden-

tified her as well as the brothers. One of the most touching moments in the evening occurred when Savion Glover, preeminent
tap star of the 1990s, performed a solo facing Fayard and Harold,
who were seated at a nightclub table at the side of the stage. It
was time. It was *more* than time to acknowledge the Nicholas
Brothers' role in American dance history, a subtle role for all their
ebullient, gleaming artistry.

Why do we not automatically mention the Nicholas Brothers
in the same breath with Fred Astaire and Gene Kelly in that short,
familiar litany of movie-musical dance greats? The writer Clarke
Peters asks that question in *Nicholas Brothers: We Sing and We
Dance*, a 1992 documentary produced by Bruce Goldstein and
Rigmor Newman. It is hard to answer.

On the most superficial level, the fact that the brothers were
endlessly cast as a specialty act—the popular dance equivalent of
a *divertissement* isolated within a classical ballet narrative—may
have something to do with it. Fayard and Harold Nicholas were
at least as skilled dancers as Astaire and Kelly, but Astaire and
Kelly played roles of sorts and were integrated as characters with
scripted dialogue into all their films. There were also two of the
Nicholas Brothers to make an icon of, and the two formed a be-
lievably loving partnership and a coolly professional small universe
of their own that in many ways shut out the rest of the world.

Did the racial prejudices and stereotypes of their time—and
ours—have something to do with it? That, too, is hard to decide.
Music has tended to take precedence over dance in American culture. Brenda Dixon Gottschild suggests, in her book *Waltzing in
the Dark: African-American Vaudeville and Race Politics in the
Swing Era*, that the names of leading black bandleaders and vocalists of the brothers' time were far more familiar to most Americans
than the names of the great tap artists who also performed then.
Gottschild observes that popular—or vernacular—dances, like
jazz vocalizing, can be discounted easily as "folk art," despite
their considerable formal value.

Still, Astaire and Kelly were kings in that debased country and
the Nicholas Brothers were not. Certainly, the brothers felt prejudice, from the time the two were the only blacks allowed to mingle with the audience at the Cotton Club on nights they were

performing there. For all the brothers' fame, they were acutely aware of the "inconvenience" of being black in America, as the musical-comedy dancer Bert Williams put it. In a profoundly sad moment in the Goldstein-Newman documentary, the otherwise unfazeable-seeming Harold reflects on the pleasure of living and working in Europe in the late 1940s and 1950s. In America, he says, "Your money's not good enough because your color's not right."

In the brothers' occasionally widening eyes and flashing smiles it is possible to see something of the court-jester personae forced on black performers in American films through the 1940s, though Fayard and Harold managed largely to avoid playing the perennial black bellhop. It is also possible to see, in the relentless professionalism and class instilled in the brothers from an early age by their parents, the kind of shield and subversion glimpsed in mainstream black film performances of the 1930s and 1940s. The sly humor of a Fats Waller also subverted stereotype to some extent. One admittedly perilous way of meeting such racism head-on was to embrace the clichés with a passion, wit, and skill that gave them a confoundingly new and rich life. But to look hard into the faces of Paul Robeson and Hattie McDaniel as they sing "Old Man River" in the 1936 film *Show Boat* is to gauge—in their glitteringly angry eyes—the soul-wounding effect of racial stereotype.

In small part, the fascination of the Nicholas Brothers' art lies in the tension of that paradox. As Gottschild suggests, there is additional, though revivifying, tension in the way that jazz dancing like theirs bucks traditional artistic values. The brothers' dances were tightly choreographed, leaving little room for the kind of improvisation inherent in tap. But Gottschild's notion of "high-affect juxtaposition"—the willful breaking up of the continuity and resolution prized in "the European academic aesthetic"—may be found in the relationship between the impulsive-seeming, earthier Harold and the more sophisticated Fayard. It may also be found in the explosive unpredictability and playfulness of their dances.

What will the Nicholas Brothers' legacy be? It is true, as has often been said, that there is a good deal of them in the popular dance that came after them, from tap to breakdancing to Michael

Jackson. It is also just as true that a tap historian might see much of the brothers in the chronicles and images of William Henry Lane, the internationally celebrated mid-nineteenth century minstrel dancer known as Master Juba. In the end, the Nicholas Brothers' legacy may be not just the complexity of their dance, but their ability, to quote the English dance critic Arnold Haskell, to "blend the impossible and create beauty."

> JENNIFER DUNNING
> July 2002
> New York City

JENNIFER DUNNING, a dance critic with *The New York Times* and author of biographies of Alvin Ailey and Geoffrey Holder, lives in New York City.

Foreword

When Constance Valis Hill asked me to write the foreword for this fine book on the life and times of the Nicholas Brothers, I thought to myself, "A piece of cake." Having known and been the number one fan of the Nicholas Brothers for practically all my life, I felt I was the right man for the job.

Yeah. Right.

So here I am, three months later, sitting in front of my computer as intimidated as I've ever been in my life. Constance is calling daily, and I can feel the pressure getting as big as my eyes did the first time I saw Harold and Fayard jump down that huge staircase, step by step over each other into those splits, during their legendary dance number in *Stormy Weather.*

How can I reflect adequately on the greatness of their amazing careers, both as a team and as individuals? Can I paint a picture of them for you to compare with those painted by Fayard's arms and hands while he danced? Is there a way for me to convey to you the ease with which Harold would run right up a wall, into a back flip, into a split, and then pop up as if a puppeteer were above him pulling him up?

No. I can't.

But I can tell you that the dances they performed both on screen and in person were full-fledged art pieces. Death-defying tap-acrobatics that would have required "tap stunt doubles" for anyone else but the Nicholas Brothers. The way they would do the exact same step in unison, as their own uniquely different personalities came through, made us feel like we knew them. The way they would leap into the air and come down into their patented splits and then come up without using their hands. They owned that move. Owned it, I'm telling you. And I know in my heart that there never was a dancer, tap or otherwise, who, upon seeing those "Nicholas Splits," didn't question his or her very own eyes. Could it be? Did they really go down and come right back up sans hands?

Tap dancers were always trying to steal the Nicholas Brothers' steps. Yes, because in the center of all their style was tremendous substance. The steps. The tap shoes hitting the floor. The way they heard rhythms and spaces between beats. The way they would pause and then start again in places that would create a phrase that was so Nicholas Brothers. Believe me, I stole what steps I could from them and even today when I do them, I'll yell out: "This is a Nicholas Brothers step!" Because I feel so good I'm even able to do the step, and I simply have to pay homage to the lasting greatness of what they created.

Look at the films. Look at the fun they were having. They were taking a walk in the park with that dance in *Stormy Weather*. Look at their faces as they dance up that huge staircase, or when they're doing those powerful combinations atop that grand piano, only to take flight and land once again in those splits as if they were two kids jumping into a swimming pool. It was as easy for them as it is for Ken Griffey to make one of his amazing one-handed catches at the wall to take a home run away from some disappointed slugger. Easy for them. Impossible for the rest of us.

That's right, impossible. Hey, if those folks in Hollywood ever do get it in their heads to make the life story of the Nicholas Brothers, the dance numbers would have to be computer generated. Because it would be impossible to find two dancer/actors to play the two starring roles. I mean, maybe, maybe they could find two men who could "act" it, but dance it? Naaa. It ain't gonna happen. It wouldn't even be fair to ask somebody to just try it.

It brings me so much joy to see all the attention the Nicholas Brothers have been receiving over these past fifteen years or so. The Kennedy Center Honors ... the Carnegie Hall tribute ... innumerable lifetime achievement awards ... and now, this book. And what a truly great book it is. Constance Valis Hill has done a fantastic job of telling and blending their story with the story of an era.

There were more than a few times, as I read, that I found myself moved to tears, and then laughing out loud. And all of those emotions came out of me with a great pride. Yes. I felt proud. Proud to be an African American, proud to be a tap dancer, and so very proud indeed to have known and loved Harold and Fayard my whole life.

From the time my brother Maurice and I began dancing as kids, we idolized the Nicholas Brothers. We, like many before us, aspired to be "The Next Nicholas Brothers." Ha! An aspiration unfulfilled. Oh no. Nobody—no tap dance act, no two brothers, no duo—could be "The Next Nicholas Brothers." Better to aspire to reinventing the tap shoe.

So read this book and enjoy. Because we will never ever see the likes of the Nicholas Brothers, Harold and Fayard, dancing on any stage or screen or in person again. The dances they did. The moves they made. The pictures they painted. Well. That's it. Enjoy it. Because, my brothers and sisters: They owned it.

I love you, Harold and Fayard.

— Gregory Hines

P.S. I can't wait for this book to come out, so I can stand in line for an autographed copy, at one of those "in-store" book signings. There's nothing quite like being around Harold and Fayard together. It's so much fun. They still dance together, in their own unique way.

Acknowledgments

In April 1993, I was asked to conduct a public interview with Fayard and Harold Nicholas at the New York Public Library for the Performing Arts at Lincoln Center, for the symposium entitled "Rethinking the Balanchine Legacy: Balanchine, Jazz, and Popular Dance." The Nicholas Brothers had worked on Broadway with George Balanchine in *Ziegfeld Follies of 1936* and *Babes in Arms* (1937), and as a tap dancer and dance scholar, I was to interview them about their collaboration with the great choreographer. As it turned out, Fayard, who lived in Los Angeles, was not able to come to New York for the symposium. I did, however, interview Harold, who lived on West End Avenue in Manhattan. He met me at the Dance Collection of the Lincoln Center Performing Arts Library one afternoon before the event. He brought with him vintage Nicholas home movies, as well as a video compilation of the Nicholas Brothers dance acts from their various musical films. After marveling over the body of jazz dances preserved on film that the brothers had created during their sixty-year career, I selected, for the public interview, a brief dance segment from the 1942 film Orchestra Wives (Twentieth Century-Fox), as an example of classical form in the tap dancing of the Nicholas Brothers. Upon viewing it, the audience—composed of dance critics, scholars, students, and members of the general public—went wild with excitement. They cheered, clapped, stomped their feet, and shouted uncontrollably.

What was it about jazz tap dance as performed by the Nicholas Brothers, I asked myself, that made it so exciting, even intoxicating, to audiences? Put another way, what was it about the Nicholas Brothers *performing* jazz tap dance that made them so immediately appealing?

In the fascinating journey I have taken since first asking that question, I learned that the answers lie (1) in the power of rhythm to communicate swiftly and directly, cutting through divisions of race, class, and gender to unite an audience into a community of active watchers and listeners; and (2) in the bond of brotherhood that enabled two twentieth-century African-American dancers to embody and perpetuate a musical tradition that existed hundreds of years before they were born.

At the core of this work is a comprehensive movement analysis and musical analysis of the Nicholas Brothers' dancing on the stage and screen. Dances and song-and-dance suites have been arranged in a sequence that traces the progression of their choreographic process and the evolution of their performance style. I have had access to almost all of the Nicholas Brothers' films, from their earliest, *Pie, Pie, Blackbird* (Vitaphone, 1932), to Harold Nicholas's latest, *Funny Bones* (Suntrust, 1995), and including those that were filmed abroad, such as *Calling All Stars* (British Lion, 1937) and *Botta e Riposta* (Italia, 1951).

One of the most valuable resources, however, has been the recently discovered private collection of Nicholas home movies, taken by Viola, Fayard, and Harold Nicholas and Lorenzo Hill, with a hand-held 16 mm Bell and Howell camera between 1935 and 1945. One segment of the film is an impromptu dance with Fred Astaire (whom the brothers never otherwise danced with during their career), taken in 1935 on the RKO film lot in Hollywood, where Astaire was setting taps for the film *Top Hat*. Other rarities in the Nicholas home movies are scenes from inside the Cotton Club, taken on different occasions and including Bill Robinson and Cab Calloway in rehearsal with the Cotton Club Girls, and scenes from the Broadway musical comedy *Babes in Arms* (1937), filmed inside the Shubert Theatre on 44th Street.

The New York Public Library and its staff, especially the Dance and Theatre Collection of the Library for the Performing Arts at Lincoln Center, as well as the Schomburg Center for Research in Black Culture, were indispensable to my research. And the staff of the Interlibrary Loan and Lending Services, at the State University at Albany, patiently and untiringly located everything I requested, bringing books, newspapers, and periodicals from across the country to my fingertips. In addition, I have here listed those institutions and individuals who were especially helpful, and apologize if there are any major omissions: the State University of New York at

Albany Library (Greg Barron, director); College of Saint Rose, Music Library, Albany, New York; Museum of Television and Radio (Library, Danny Thomas Console Room, and Edward John Noble Scholars' Room), New York; Hatch-Billops Collection Archive of African American History (James V. Hatch), New York; Elmer Holmes Bobst Library, New York University; Ernie Smith Picture Archive, Smithsonian Institute, Washington, D.C.; New York Film Forum 2 Archive; Harvard University Library (Harvard Theatre Collection); the Museum of the City of New York (Theatre Collection); and the Theatre Museum in London, where dance scholar and Ballet Rambert archivist Jane Pritchard miraculously unearthed programs and other resource materials from *Blackbirds of 1936*.

The Harold Nicholas Archive in New York, curated by Rigmor Alfredsson Newman, contains hundreds of clippings, photographs, videos, and memorabilia. From this I acquired an unpublished interview with Fayard Nicholas that was conducted by Marshall and Jean Stearns on February 6, 1965, at the Knickerbocker Hotel in Los Angeles, and an unpublished transcript of a telephone interview with Viola Nicholas that was conducted by Marshall Stearns on February 7, 1965. Ironically, only a little of this material was published by the Stearnses in *Jazz Dance: The Story of American Vernacular Dance* (1968). The transcripts were valuable in confirming for me many of the theses that I had already formulated about Nicholas dance works.

The most valuable research materials, however, were the dozens of taped interviews and impromptu conversations I had with Fayard and Harold Nicholas, who were always gracious, generous, and candid with me about their lives, their work, their brotherhood, and their creative process.

I would not have been drawn to the subject of this dissertation had it not been for my own rhythmic roots, which I must here acknowledge. It was the Greek folk dances and Turkish belly dances I watched my mother perform with pleasure (before the female members of my Greek family) that initiated me, from childhood, into the sensuous complexities of Middle Eastern rhythms. As a teenager, the keenest memories I have of my father, Sunday Valis, are of us dancing the mambo, cha-cha, and other Latin American dances across the floor of the Roseland Ballroom, in one of our many forays into Manhattan, from Astoria, Long Island City. My husband's Caribbean roots (Trinidad and Granada) and his training as a jazz drummer extended my knowledge of, and passion for, Afro-Caribbean and jazz rhythms. At the Alvin Ailey School of American Dance, as a scholarship student, I studied ballet and modern dance but gravitated to jazz dance. My teachers, Nat Horne and Pepsi Bethel, saw my future as a jazz dancer. And when I studied tap dance with various members of the Copasetics, especially Charles "Cooky" Cook—who would click an intricately timed crossover step with laid-back ease, his worn and floppy hat drooping whimsically over one eye—I was transformed into a jazz tap dancer.

I thank the veteran jazz drummer Stan Shaw, who cajoled me into counting out choruses and identified many of the tunes the Nicholas Brothers danced to in their musical films. I also thank the following colleagues and friends who helped in the conceptualization, research, writing, and preparation of this book: Douglas Ashford, Donald Bogle, Tommy DeFrantz, Lynn Garafola, Martha Goldstein, James V. Hatch, Julie Malnig, Cynthia Novack, May Joseph, Ellen Reed, Martha Rosett, Ernie Smith, Larry Stallman, Sally Sommer, and John Szwed. A special thanks to Film Forum 2 program director Bruce Goldstein, whose clarifications and additions to the manuscript could only have come from years of knowledge about film and a decade of research on the Nicholas Brothers. I am most indebted, however, to my teacher and adviser in the Department of Performance Studies at New York University, Brooks McNamara, who guided me with wisdom and the grace of a dancer through the completion of my dissertation, upon which this book is based.

I offer my deepest thanks to Rigmor Newman, who was an ever-constant resource and spokeswoman for the Nicholas Brothers. Her love for jazz, her faithfulness to the brothers, and her drive to have the story of the Nicholas Brothers written, with a focus on *the dancing*, gave me deep reserves of strength. Finally, I wish to thank Fayard Nicholas and Harold Nicholas, who could not have been better subjects, and whose jazz dancing I never tired of looking at, listening to, and writing about.

Albany, New York   C.V.H
March 1999

BROTHERHOOD IN RHYTHM

Harold and Fayard Nicholas

Preface

Fayard and Harold Nicholas are one of the most beloved teams in dance history. The Nicholas Brothers' exuberant style of American theatrical dance—a melding of jazz, tap, acrobatics, and black vernacular dance—has dazzled vaudeville, theatre, film, and television audiences around the world for more than sixty years. They are most often remembered for the daredevil splits, slides, and flips that were sometimes incorporated into their routines; stuck with the "specialty act" label within otherwise all-white Hollywood films, they were variously labeled "eccentric," "acrobatic," and "flash" dancers. But the Nicholas Brothers were more than a "brilliant swing-era flash act."[1] Their rhythmic brilliance, musicality, eloquent footwork, and full-bodied expressiveness are unsurpassed, and their dancing represents the most sophisticated refinement of jazz as a percussive dance form.

The jazz tap dancing of the Nicholas Brothers extends a three-century-long percussive dance tradition in America that reached its apotheosis in the twentieth century, during the swing era of the 1930s and 1940s, and subsequently matured into a classical American jazz dance form.

Tap dance is an indigenous American dance genre that evolved over a period of some three hundred years. Initially a fusion of British and West African musical and step-dancing traditions in America, tap emerged in the southern United States in the 1700s. The Irish jig (a musical and dance form) and West African *gioube* (sacred and secular stepping dances) mutated into the American jig and the juba. These in turn became juxtaposed and fused into a form of dancing called "jigging," which, in the 1800s, was taken up by white and black minstrel-show dancers who developed tap into a popular nineteenth-century stage entertainment. Early styles of tapping utilized hard-soled shoes, clogs, or hobnailed boots; metal plates (or taps) appeared on shoes around the turn of the twentieth century and became popular in the teens and early twenties on the Broadway stage.

Jazz tap dance developed in direct relationship to jazz music in the twenties, thirties, and forties, sharing rhythmic motifs, polyrhythms, multiple meters, elements of swing (offbeat phrasing and suspension of the beat), and structured improvisation. Swing-style jazz of the thirties emphasized rhythmic dynamics with relatively equal weight given to the four beats of the bar (hence the term "four-beat jazz"), solo improvisation, and a forward propulsion imparted to each note by an instrumentalist through the manipulation of attack, timbre, vibrato, and intonation.

The dance career of the Nicholas Brothers was prefaced by the twenties and launched in the thirties, when they performed at New York's Cotton Club with the Duke Ellington, Cab Calloway, and Jimmie Lunceford orchestras and on the stage and in films with the big bands of Chick Webb, Tommy Dorsey, and Glenn Miller. In the postwar forties, there was a radical transformation in American jazz dance, as the steady and danceable rhythms of swing gave way to the dissonant harmonics and frenzied rhythmic shifts of bebop. Jazz tap rhythms, previously reserved for the feet, were absorbed into the body, and a new style of "modern jazz" dance—less polyrhythmic and performed without metal taps—became popular. With their high-speed and full-bodied style of rhythm tapping that was fast, fluent, and flexible, the Nicholas Brothers endured the radical musical shifts that bebop instigated. They resisted the trend that relegated rhythm to the torso or to the toes, continuing to evolve a style of jazz dance that was as rhythmically nuanced in the feet as in the body, and this they developed into a classical form of jazz dancing.

It is extremely important to examine the relationship between jazz dance and the music of the blues, swing, and bebop, in order to place the dance works of the Nicholas Brothers within the context of American jazz music and dance traditions. For jazz dance cannot and did not exist isolated from its musical counterpart, and the jazz dancing of the Nicholas Brothers demonstrates that jazz swing music was "played" on the rhythmic "instrument" of their bodies.

In locating the links between jazz tap dance and other musical traditions, including Western classical music, jazz's African heritage cannot be overemphasized. Jazz is commonly historicized as evolving from an amalgamation of elements drawn both from European-American and tribal African musics. It is usually seen as the blending in the United States of two great musical traditions—the European and the West African—over a period of three hundred years, through which time European and African strains became entwined and entangled through many stages of cross-fertilization.[2] While it is tempting to characterize one or another aspect of jazz as deriving either from the African or European musical tradition, the question of what is "black" and what is "white" in jazz, and what influences affected which musicians and when, is enormously complex. Jazz, Leroi Jones laments, has become part of "the hopelessly interwoven fabric of American life where blacks and whites pass so quickly to become only grays."[3] But given the representation of both Africa and Europe in jazz lineage, and the contribution of both black and white artists to jazz's development, the incontestable reality is that while jazz did not completely originate with African Americans, most, if not all of its major developments, have derived from them.[4] Emerging as it did from what Houston Baker described as the "material conditions of slavery in the United States and the rhythms of Afro-American Blues," jazz was formed by several patterns of oral and musical performance particular to African-American culture.[5]

In African culture, rhythm permeates all forms of expression; it is "the architecture of being, the inner dynamic that gives it form, the pure expression of the life force."[6] Because West Africans lacked a common spoken language, music and dance served a crucial role as the medium for conveying the history and values of these people who were captured and brought to the New World. Music, in particular, was among the African cultural traditions that were most readily maintained under slavery. The most important musical instrument was the drum, and a variety of other percussion instruments, such as bells, castanets, gongs, and rattles, also figured prominently. These allowed for participatory performance practices that relied on communal creation

and provided the means for slaves to accommodate to the dominant culture without being completely absorbed into it. As Kathy
Ogren explains in *The Jazz Revolution*, it was from the African
participatory heritage of call-and-response experiences and a
strong tradition of improvisation that jazz in America developed
as a "distinctive language" and a unique form of oral performance
that encouraged spontaneity, invention, and the interaction
between performer and audience.7

What culminated as the defining features of jazz performance—
improvisation, call-and-response technique, polyrhythm, syncopation, and blues tonalities—also can be seen as the most dominant
features of jazz tap as performed by the Nicholas Brothers. The
ancient African tradition of the "talking drum," its rhythms "illu-
minating the spirit," seems to be retained in their sensuous embodiment of rhythms; their "drum dancing" confirms the retention of
a West African musical aesthetic.

While the jazz tap dancing of the Nicholas Brothers seems
deeply rooted in African musical traditions, the evolution of their
dance style came not only from what they shared with African-
American jazz artists of their day but from the things that set
them apart from their contemporaries. Although raised in the
black community and deeply rooted in the African-American
vernacular, the young Nicholases never entered tap dance contests. Nor did they perform in talent contests or appear in amateur shows, as was the custom of most aspiring young dancers.
They did not learn to tap dance on street corners, nor did they
perform as "pickaninnies" on the black vaudeville circuit, as did
many young tap dancers—including the great Bill "Bojangles"
Robinson—to launch their careers. Nor did the Nicholases, after
coming to New York in the early thirties, frequent the Hoofers
Club, where many aspiring dancers learned to tap by watching,
stealing from, and challenging each other.

While the Nicholases saw dozens of blackened comedy dance
teams on the vaudeville stage, they did not use blackface makeup,
which was still fairly common in the twenties and thirties; nor did
they incorporate eccentric dance steps and legomania into their
routines. Instead, the brothers drew from two apparently divergent

performance traditions in African-American culture, black comedy dance and the class act. Blending comic quips and bizarre acrobatic feats with virtuosic rhythm tapping, they simultaneously titillated and impressed; their precocious sophistication was appealing and disarming to audiences. In the Depression decade of the thirties, with its notorious blackface stereotyping, segregated audiences, and restricted performance venues for black artists, the Nicholases became the youngest dancers to perform at the uptown Cotton Club and were among a handful of African-American dance artists to achieve "star" status, to work continually in the musical theatre, and to have their work preserved on film. Given the ambivalence of performing before racially segregated audiences, the Nicholases nevertheless transcended the boundaries and limits of their particular historical period, aided by a profound belief that the virtuosity, exemplary professionalism, and integrity of their class-act dancing would dissolve the stereotypes and appeal to a broad American audience.

Because the Nicholas Brothers drew on many varied musical and performance traditions, this study is not confined simply to tracing the evolution of their choreography but also presents a history of jazz tap dance in America.

*Winold
Reiss,
"Inter-
pretation
of Harlem
Jazz I,"
c. 1925.*

One

Born into Jazz

Fayard Nicholas was born in Mobile, Alabama, on October 28, 1914, twelve weeks after the Austro-Hungarian declaration of war on Serbia and amidst the succession of declarations of war by other European countries that exploded into World War I. Harold Nicholas was born in Winston-Salem, North Carolina, on March 17, 1921, in the wake of the Great War. In Paris a year before Fayard's birth, Igor Stravinsky's dissonant and pulsating score for the Ballets Russes' *Le Sacre du printemps* had instigated outraged members of the audience to stomp their feet and beat each other over the head, their strokes synchronized with the beat of the music.[1] Their response to the rhythm-driven syncopations in Stravinsky's jazz-influenced score echoed the volatile predisposition of a people on the brink of war. In the span of time between the Nicholas brothers' births, with its mixed moods of anxiety and optimism over what the future would bring, a new form of music emerged—jazz—that reshaped American culture and influenced European culture with its sudden turns, shocks, and swift changes of pace. English critic R.W.S. Mendl described jazz as being the product of a restless age, "when men and women are still too much disturbed to be content with a tranquil existence . . . America is turning out her merchandise at an unprecedented speed, and the whole world is rushing helter skelter in unknown directions."[2] Symbolic of the new age, jazz served as a reminder, Ralph Ellison wrote, that "the world is ever unexplored, and that while a complete mastery of life is mere illusion, the real secret of the game is to make life swing."[3]

Jazz Music: The Teens Through the Twenties

Jazz invaded Europe on New Year's Day in 1918 when, after the U.S. declaration of war (on Germany, April 2, 1917; on Austria-Hungary, December 7, 1917), hundreds of thousands of black American soldiers were drafted and shipped overseas to France.[4] The American armies brought not only musicians and American recordings but also, as Colonel William Heyward boasted, "the best damn brass band in the United States Army."[5] The 369th Infantry Regiment Band was led by James Reese Europe, who, born in Mobile, Alabama, was a classically trained musician; he had studied violin and piano as a child. In New York in 1910, he had organized the Clef Club, a professional black musicians' association, and in 1913, with his Society Orchestra, he became the first African American to make a recording.

James Reese Europe's 369th Infantry Band, dubbed the Hellfighters, featured Chicago's leading cornetist, Jacon Frank de Braithe, as soloist; Harlem's most beloved tap dancer, Bill "Bojangles" Robinson, as drum major; and a group of multitalented musicians, some recruited from as far as Puerto Rico, who could sing, dance, and perform a number of entertainments.[6] The band prided itself on playing anything—from ragtime cakewalks to novelty music specialties with instrumental effects and "barnyard" imitations to the classics. In the winter of 1918, they traveled two thousand miles throughout France with a program that began with a French march, followed by favorite overtures and vocal selections by a male quartet, and continued with John Philip Sousa's "Stars and Stripes Forever," as well as arrangements of southern plantation melodies. Then came the fireworks, a soul-rousing rendition of "Memphis Blues." Noble Sissle, a drum major in the band, recalls the moment Europe's baton came crashing down on the opening note:

> Cornet and clarinet players began to manipulate notes as the drummers struck the stride, their shoulders shaking in time to their syncopated rags. Then it seemed the whole audience began to sway and dignified French officers began to pat their feet, along with the American general, who had temporarily lost his style and grace. The audience could stand it no longer, the jazz germ hit them and it seemed to find the vital spot, loosening all muscles and causing what is known in America as "an eagle rocking it."[7]

The Hellfighters did not play jazz in the strictest sense, but a rough blend of brass band music and ragtime that James Europe had developed years earlier for the popular American ballroom dance team of Vernon and Irene Castle. With them he had created the fox-trot and many other popular dance steps that had had a major part in initiating the Jazz Age.[8] James Europe's "syncopated music," as it was called, was dance music. Although most of it, like ragtime, was notated—only a few of the solos were improvised—the fiercely insistent beat, built-in syncopation, and deliberately pitched notes of this ragtime-jazz blend were in dramatic contrast to the painstaking formalities of European dance music. The dancing, not simply the jazz music, became the reigning obsession of the Parisian Jazz Age.

After the war ended in 1918, the general public in Paris turned out nightly by the thousands to dance the fox-trot. When the Casino de Paris reopened its doors with the revue *Laissez-les tomber!* (Let them drop!) and with an American band composed of banjos, big nickel tubas, and motorcycle horns, the audience, wrote Jean Cocteau, "rose from their seats and with head, chest and arms, followed the rhythm."[9] No one knew for sure what jazz was, but the music meant dancing that was energetic, with room for full body movement and personal expression. The streets and alleys of Montmartre became the center of Parisian jazz, though everywhere in Paris American bands were playing a rough version of jazz that made people move.

If the boulevards of Montmartre, as the center of postwar Parisian jazz, had become a transatlantic reflection of Harlem,[10] Harlem itself and New York had become the source for "hot" jazz rhythms. "Hot" was the term used in the 1920s to suggest qualities of speed, excitement, and intensity, as well as to distinguish jazz from other music genres.

Jazz had not originated in New York City, but some claim that it was "discovered" there around 1917, when the all-white Original Dixieland Jass [*sic*] Band made its debut at Reisenweber's Cabaret in midtown Manhattan. The group of five New Orleans musicians, which included Nick LaRocca (cornet), Eddie Edwards (trombone), Larry Shields (clarinet), Henry Ragas (piano), and Tony Sbarbaro (drums), played their "jass" by ear and as "hot" as they could; their melodies, *Variety* reported, were "quite conducive to making the dancers on the floor loosen up and go the limit in their stepping."[11] ODJB was at the right place at the right time: the group made the first out-and-out jazz recordings to be issued on the RCA Victor label's popular phonograph-record lists and sold in the millions.

A richer and more developed form of jazz was already being played by black musicians in New Orleans at least ten years earlier. Marshall Stearns reports that the words "jas," "jass," and later "jazz" turned up in Chicago in the middle teens, along with other words like "boogie," "swing," and "rock"; all were descriptive of musical styles with origins in turn-of-the-century Negro slang.[12] And in a Negro cabaret in Chicago, so J. A. Rogers writes, there was a wild and reckless musician named Jasbo Brown who played extravagant and risqué interpretations of the blues on his trombone, to the delight of patrons who shouted, "More, Jasbo. More Jas, more."[13] Still, it was in New York in the twenties where jazz—in its route up the Mississippi River from New Orleans at the turn of the century to Kansas City, Chicago, and points west and east in the teens—heartily took hold. The interesting story is not so much about where jazz was first named or recorded but how it evolved from ragtime.

Although it is difficult to pinpoint exactly when popular tastes turned to jazz, James Lincoln Collier describes the transition as a central rhythmic discovery: "In the first years of the twentieth century, some person or persons in the black and black Creole subculture tried the epochal experiment of making the double speed secondary pulse in ragtime explicit [by] putting a four-beat tap under a two-beat rag."[14] Virtually all rags were written in duple time (or 2/4 time signature), most based on march forms. At some point early in the century, black musicians began to play ragtime in 4/4 time. The rhythmic transition from ragtime to jazz is best understood by listening to a representative sampling of jazz that was recorded over a ten-year period. For example, listen to "Castle Walk," recorded by James Reese Europe and his Society Orchestra in the mid-teens; "Dippermouth Blues," recorded by Joe "King" Oliver and his Creole Jazz Band in the early twenties; and "Sugar Foot Stomp," recorded by Fletcher Henderson and his Orchestra in the mid-to-late twenties. These selections not only present the rhythmic shift from 2/4 to 4/4 time, but underline the salient features of jazz as it was played in the twenties.

If James Reese Europe is a transitional figure in the prehistory of jazz, his "Castle Walk," written with Ford Dabney and recorded in 1914, documents one of the earliest styles of American jazz. Written as a 2/4 time rag, the music was accompaniment to Vernon and Irene Castle's popular ballroom dances, marked by an unmistakable rhythmic excitement and vitality. "Instead of coming down on the beat, as everyone else did, we went up," Irene Castle remembered about the dance. "The result was a step almost like a skip."[15] The instrumentation, which included large sections of violins, banjos, and mandolins, was dominated by the drumming of Buddy Gilmore, whose drum set included not only snare and bass drums but an assortment of cymbals, wood blocks, and cowbells. Though James Europe's pieces were referred to as "syncopated music," the lively and unrelenting tempo smoothed out the more choppy ragtime rhythm. The music was played "as written" but with an unmistakable exuberance, both in the way the instrumental sections "shout" back and forth to each other and in the way the instruments play the lead in unison but then trade back and forth, trying to outdo each other in the variations. The melody was not only doubled for all the melodic instruments but was paralled rhythmically by the snare drum. Altogether, the music expressed a rough excitement and rhythmic momentum that carried its dancers and audience swiftly and merrily along.[16]

In "Dippermouth Blues," recorded in 1923 by Joe "King" Oliver and his Creole Jazz Band, one hears a group of improvising, blues-oriented players who are reflexively attuned both to one another and to the collective power of their instruments. Oliver's jazz band included Lil Harden (piano), Johnny Dodds (clarinet), Honoré Dutrey (trombone), Bill Johnson (banjo), "Baby" Dodds (drums), and on cornet both "King" Oliver and Louis Armstrong (after whose nickname, "Dippermouth," the song was named).

They played in what has been described as a dense, New Orleans polyphonic style, a continuous polyphony in which the wind players were rarely at rest. This instrumental twelve-bar blues featured ensemble passages, as well as the anguished solo of Johnny Dodds for two choruses and the joyous solo of Oliver for three. Between these solos, the ensemble chorus reverberated with Armstrong's horn playing. Unlike the 2/4 ragtime rhythm of "Castle Walk," which gave the music a smooth-trotting beat, "Dippermouth" was written in 4/4 time and played at a far brisker tempo. Oliver's "wa-wa" effects over three chorus solos and Dodds's highly expressive vibrato, which was slightly beneath true pitch, created a deep blues feeling and furthered the music's expressivity.[17]

Twelve years younger than "King" Oliver, Fletcher Henderson grew up in a southern, middle-class black family. He migrated to New York in 1920 and by the late twenties led the most influential black jazz orchestra in the United States. "Sugar Foot Stomp," first recorded in 1925, was based on Oliver's "Dippermouth Blues," which came via Louis Armstrong, who played with Henderson's band in 1925 and 1926. To that composition, arranger Don Redman had added a sixteen-bar secondary theme, altering the structure of the music from ABC to AABBCC, with a concluding chorus of AABA.

Drawing directly from the call-and-response tradition of African-American Protestant churches, Redman fused ensemble work with individual solos, which resulted in an arrangement of driving energy. The opening chorus is a sweeping melodic statement by the saxophones, which is interjected with sharp brass notes. Clarinet trio choruses alternate with sustaining "symphonic" sections; and these in turn are alternated with solo or semi-improvised passages, the most dominant being an extended cornet solo to which the response is laid in by the brass. The drums catch the cornet's spirit and swing with flowing backbeats on the cymbal.

Henderson's band was essentially a "dance orchestra." Setting the framework for future big-band arrangements, it combined the written harmonies of European classical music with the more improvised African-American tradition, harnessing the whole to a swinging 4/4 dance beat.[18] The distinguishing features of jazz, as the music developed from the mid-teens through the twenties, included faster tempos, complex rhythms played against a steady four beat, a move away from New Orleans-style polyphonic playing and toward arranged solo and group passages that were partially improvised, call-and-response between instruments or groups of instruments, and a pronounced instrumental expressivity reminiscent of the human voice—this in large part due to the absorption by jazz of the blues.

The blues took form in the late nineteenth century as a musical synthesis that combined "worksongs, group seculars, field hollers, sacred harmonies, proverbial wisdom, folk philosophy, political commentary, ribald humor and elegiac lament."[19] The "classic blues," which first began to be recorded in the early twenties, crystallized into eight-, twelve-, and sixteen-bar forms, in which singers like Bessie Smith, "in competition with vaudeville acts of dancing girls, freaks and midgets, actors and medicine shows, sang plaintive commentaries on unrequited love and transformed everyday travails into song and poetry."[20] When the vogue for blues reached its height in the mid-twenties, its major market was among blacks and its most important blues singers were black women.

Bessie Smith (1897–1937) is acknowledged to be the greatest of all "classic blues" singers and the first important jazz singer of the twenties to bring emotional intensity and personal expression to blues singing. "St. Louis Blues," composed by W. C. Handy in 1914, sold three quarters of a million records in the first six months after it was recorded by Smith in 1925, and her recording represents the pinnacle of blues performance. The song centers around the wail of a lovestruck woman for her lost man and uses a folk blues three-line stanza to create a twelve-measure strain that combines ragtime syncopation with a real melody in the spiritual tradition.[21]

Smith recorded "St. Louis Blues" with Louis Armstrong, whose sensitive and mournful trumpet playing is heard on the recording and echoes a woman's pain over her man. The sheer weight Smith put on the melody is staggering; taking the song at a slow tempo and dragging out the blue notes on "Feeling tomorrow like I feel today," she got through the entire chorus just once on the two-and-a-half-minute record. The recording demonstrates the absorption of blues musicianship—with its vamps and riffs, breaks and fills, call-and-response sequencing, idiomatic syncopation, and drum-oriented vocals—by jazz musicians, who would also speed up the blues and make the music suitable for dancing.[22]

In the southern jookjoints, or "jooks," where the blues were played in the late nineteenth and early twentieth centuries, the response to the blues included "bumping and bouncing, dragging and stomping, hopping and jumping . . . and shaking and shouting.[23] Even while the blues was being performed as an act in a variety show on a vaudeville stage in the teens and twenties, the most immediate and customary response consisted of tapping feet, clapping hands, rocking, and rolling the hips. Whether played fast or slow, then, twenties blues were stomping blues, with the souls of black folk emanating through the body.

Twenties Jazz and the Harlem Renaissance

The experience of World War I, some fifty years after Emancipation, ushered in an important period of change in the culture and consciousness of African Americans, in which they became self-assertive and socially conscious, many for the first time. They proclaimed themselves deserving of respect, having shed "the costume of the shuffling darky, the uncle or aunty, the subservient and docile retainer, the clown" to become "intelligent, articulate, self-assured" citizens in their own right.[24] Returning from a war that was supposed to end all wars, and that also guaranteed to all the right of self-determination, African-American soldiers paraded up New York City's Lenox Avenue in Harlem after their return, marching to the same syncopated jazz rhythms that had helped them liberate the French during the war. These soldiers sought in Harlem a new capital for their race, a platform from which a new black voice would be heard around the world. The geographical shift in African-American leadership from the Tuskegee Institute in Alabama to New York reflected a transformation from the "old Negro" of the South to the "New Negro" of the northern industrial city. The locus of activity that cradled this symbolic "black rebirth," or renaissance, found its center in New York, with its largest black concentration in uptown Manhattan.

James Weldon Johnson established himself in Harlem in the teens, and in a few short years, after an enormous success in writing songs and plays for the musical stage, he became an organizer and propagandist for the African-American cause and the first black executive secretary of the National Association for the Advancement of Colored People (NAACP). W.E.B. Du Bois also came to Harlem in the teens. As editor of the *Crisis*, a monthly publication of the NAACP, he became identified in the minds of the magazine's wide national readership with the spirit of black protest and self-assertion. In the twenties, Johnson and Du Bois were joined by a group of young intellectuals who thought of themselves as "thinkers, strivers, doers . . . cultured." These men aspired to "high culture," as opposed to the culture of the common man, which they hoped to mine for novels, plays, and symphonies. They put a high premium on "rediscovering" folk materials to document and celebrate their cultural heritage and to use as sources of inspiration and points of departure for artistic creation.[25]

The arts, so it was strategized, would be used as a means of securing economic, social, and cultural equality with white citizens; and once black artists made their mark, equality would emerge on all fronts. At the same time, the black heritage was to remain central to their efforts. To this end, the leaders of the Harlem Renaissance encouraged the adaptation of folk materials to create "high art," with the purpose of replacing existing values with their newly formulated ones.[26] To advance the movement, James Weldon Johnson and Alain Locke issued a call for young artists, "New Negroes," to come to Harlem. The phrase gained currency in 1925, after the publication of Alain Locke's *The New Negro: A Reinterpretation*, and was applied to younger writers, artists, intellectuals, and political activists whose work was seen as creating more positive conceptions of black identity and culture.

The lure of success brought young African-American artists from all over the country to Harlem in the twenties. The young poet Langston Hughes was drawn to the black metropolis after having published his first poem, "The Negro Speaks of Rivers," in the June 1921 the *Crisis*. It resurrected the form, force, and pathos of the Negro spiritual for the modern reader. The writer Zora Neale Hurston, whose collection of folk tales and customs delineated the distinctive features of black folk expression, also came to Harlem in the early twenties. So did the painter Aaron Douglas, whose highly stylized designs—stark black-and-white silhouettes, angular and lithe human forms, and wavelike dancing figures that evoked a kinetic energy—signalled modern black expression in African-inspired art.

Jazz musicians also came to New York in great numbers, if not in response to the "call" of Locke and Johnson, then to that of the city and its exciting creative opportunities. When W. C. Handy came to New York in 1918, for example, he headed straight for Harlem. And what a "big old good-looking, easy-going, proud-walking Harlem" it was. As he tells it:

> I strolled through the principal streets of Harlem and on 135th Street, near the old Lincoln Theatre, I saw a sign on the door. It read: "Harlem Musicians' Association." I paused to listen to a saxophone sextet and walked in, wondering whom I would meet and if anyone would know me. I was instantly recognized.[27]

Eubie Blake and Chick Webb came to New York from Baltimore, Louis Armstrong from New Orleans, Duke Ellington from Washington, D.C., and Fletcher Henderson from Atlanta. These musicians, whose initial rise to fame helped promote the flowering of black expression in the twenties, also translated Negro folk material and drew on black vernacular sources to produce their own original blues compositions and jazz arrangements.

Alone among the forms of African-American expressive production in the 1920s, which included the visual (painting, sculpture, graphics), literary (poetry, plays, novels and short stories, journalism), and performance arts (play production, choreography, musical composition), jazz was treated with a grudging respect by the cultural leaders of the Harlem Renaissance. Nathan Huggins comments that except for Langston Hughes, none of the Harlem intellectuals took jazz seriously. And John Graziano acknowledges that in the 1920s black musical theatre never rose to the "high art" expectations that spokesmen envisioned and was, therefore, not truly accepted by them.[28]

Jazz was popular in design and commercial in intent; it therefore was never intended to serve as "high art" or to develop into a "serious" art form like the other renaissance arts. Nor did jazz project the appropriate intellectual image of the "New Negro." For the renaissance intellectual, who sought to redefine the Negro within America's cultural mainstream, jazz seemed to be the very antithesis of high culture.

The historian Lawrence Levine writes that jazz was the product of a new age, while "culture" was the product of tradition, the creation of centuries; jazz was raucous and discordant, whereas culture was harmonious, embodying order and reason; jazz was accessible and spontaneous, whereas culture was exclusive and complex, available only through hard study and training; jazz was interactive, a participatory music in which the audience played an important role, whereas culture established boundaries that relegated the audience to the primarily passive role of listening to or looking at the creations of "true" artists. While jazz was frequently played in the midst of noisy, hand-clapping and foot-stomping audiences, those who came to witness culture did so in art museums, symphony halls, and opera houses.[29]

Despite its relegation to a "low" art form, jazz permeated Harlem in the twenties and was at the very center of the renaissance movement. Jazz was in the background of, as well as the setting for, the renaissance novels; it was the dance music heard in cabarets, the blues and ragtime music of speakeasies, and the spirituals and art songs of recital and concert halls. Discussing the central role of jazz in the Harlem Renaissance movement with Eubie Blake, Nathan Huggins asked: "You are saying that white people were coming uptown following the music, and it was the sense of the music that was at the center of the Renaissance?" Blake agreed, answering that indeed it was "the music and the entertainment."[30] As the theme of novels, poems, and paintings, jazz performance and its vernacular became evocative of both the modern sensibility, in general, and the black experience, in particular, and provided a general ethos and a style for the intellectual climate of the renaissance.[31] As the metaphor for the fierce independence that defined the "New Negro," jazz was, in Langston Hughes's words, the "tom-tom of the revolt":

> Let the blare of Negro jazz bands and the bellowing voice of Bessie Smith singing Blues penetrate the closed ears of the colored near-intellectuals until they listen and perhaps understand. . . . We younger Negro artists who create now intend to express our dark-skinned selves without fear or shame. If white people are pleased we are glad. If they are not, it doesn't matter. We know we are beautiful.[32]

If there was any one jazz artist who realized the dreams of the renaissance theoreticians, it was Duke Ellington. When Locke was proclaiming the arrival of the "New Negro," and when Countee Cullen and Hughes were publishing their first volumes of poetry, Ellington was honing his skills as a bandleader and gaining a reputation as a gifted young Negro pianist, composer, and orchestra leader. Whether playing "jungle music" at the Cotton Club in Harlem, in which he used blue notes, expressive growls, and animal sounds from muted horns and hot jazz rhythms, or creating for his orchestra soaring harmonies transcribed from the most poignant of

Negro spirituals, Ellington stretched his musicianship to new limits. At the same time, he remained rooted in the fertile artistic soil
of his people.

Writing about Ellington in the late 1920s, jazz critic R. D.
Darrell observed in his essay "Black Beauty" that there was "nothing of the raucous exuberance of the Negro jazz" in Ellington's
music, and that "for all of its fluidity and rhapsodic freedom, it
was no improvisation, tossed off by a group of talented virtuosi
who would never be able to play it twice in the same way."[33]
Darrell's praise, however, belied the musician's deepest source of
inspiration. "The history of my people," Ellington wrote in 1931,
"is a history of a people hindered, handicapped and often sorely
oppressed." He continued:

> The music of my race is . . . the result of our transplantation
> to American soil, and was our reaction in the plantation
> days to the tyranny we endured. Jazz is something more
> than just dance music. We dance it not as a mere diversion
> or social accomplishment. It expresses our personality, our
> souls react to the elemental but eternal rhythm . . . the dance
> is timeless and unhampered by lineal form.[34]

Ellington celebrated Harlem in his music. His compositions
described its echoes ("Echoes of Harlem") and airshafts ("Harlem
Airshaft"), and his songs advised people to stop off there ("Take
the A Train"). These joyous evocations of Harlem's sounds, street
life, and citizens, along with his more than fifty other original
compositions written in the twenties, reflect Ellington's deep
pride in the African-American heritage and prove him to be the
quintessential renaissance artist and jazz pioneer.

Jazz Dance:
From the Teens Through the Twenties

Jazz music and jazz dance developed together along parallel lines
as inseparable agents; performed together, one lent creative inspiration to the other's development.[35] The earliest forms of jazz

music were the spirituals, work songs, and blues—all rooted in both West African and Anglo-American music and dance traditions. They evolved through an amalgamation process that began when the first African slaves arrived in the American colonies.[36] One of the earliest forms of jazz dance was tap dance, which was also rooted in both British and West African music and dance traditions. Tap dance evolved as its own amalgamated form during a period of three hundred years in America.[37] These vernacular music and dance forms, which evolved into what was called jazz in the 1920s, developed directly from ragtime, blues, the brass and marching bands, and the popular dance music of the turn of the twentieth century.

Clorindy or *The Origin of the Cakewalk* (1898) was a musical on the Broadway stage at the turn of the century exemplifying the early style of jazz dance performed by black musical artists. Composed by Will Marion Cook, with lyrics by Paul Laurence Dunbar, it showed how the cakewalk dance came about in Louisiana in the early 1880s. Cook had been classically trained at the National Conservatory in New York, but he also had an intimate knowledge of spirituals and ring-shouts from the black community. He also had assimilated the idioms of popular commercial songs (coon songs and rags) and of sentimental, artistic, and semiartistic songs and marches. In his amalgamated musical product, *Clorindy*, the songs were to be delivered by "heavenly Negro voices."[38] His music was marked by the distinctly syncopated rhythms of ragtime, the general term for turn-of-the-century black popular music, which was distinguished by a rhythmic excitement with offbeat accents. The music was the product of an unprecedented borrowing and blending of melodic and harmonic complexities, which combined syncopation (derived from Africa) and melodic chromatism (derived from Europe).[39]

Clorindy's cast of forty was led by actor-comedian Ernest Hogan, who also staged the dances. Although Hogan's blackface makeup and boisterous physical style were clearly in the minstrel tradition, the eccentric movements that he used to punctuate the lyrics were derived from black vernacular dance. In his extremely

funny delivery of "Who Dat Say Chicken in Dis Crowd," he punctuated Dunbar's lyrics in Negro dialect ("Dam de lan', let the
white folks rule it! / I'se a-looking fo' mah pullet") with offbeat
cocks of the head, shuffling pigeon-wings, and sliding buzzard
lopes, instigated by the ragtime syncopations. Hogan's choreography for "Hottest Coon in Dixie" derived from the dance known
as the strut, a cocky stride created by plantation slaves, who presumably imitated and exaggerated the authoritative gait of the
white master.

Clorindy demonstrates the influence of ragtime on jazz dance,
while *In Dahomey* (1902) shows emerging forms of jazz tap dance
created by the musical comedy team of Williams and Walker. Bert
Williams played the role of a low-shuffling fool in this musical
comedy. Wearing blackface makeup and shoes that extended farther than his already large feet, he shuffled along in a hopeless
way, always the butt of fortune. "My bad luck started when I was
born . . . they named me after my papa and that same day my
papa died," he bemoaned in "I'm a Jonah Man," while interspers-
ing a series of grotesque slides between the choruses and making
an already slouched body look pathetic. His combination of a
lazy grind, or mooche, with swiveling hips introduced an early
style of jazz dance that was comic as well as rhythmically expressive.[40] In contrast to Williams, George Walker played the role of
the high-strutting dandy. He was the "spic and span Negro, the
last word in tailoring, the highest stepper in the smart coon
world" who turned his cocky, striding strut into a high-prancing
cakewalk.[41] After varying the walk more than a dozen times, he
then repeated all the variations to the shrieking applause of the
crowd. In "Cakewalk Jig," these comedians' buck-and-wings,
eccentric slides, twists and rubber-legging cakewalks were danced
to a "ragged" jig that was sped up and syncopated.

Ragtime dancing reached the ballroom in the teens. Its development during this period was accelerated when James Reese
Europe dazzled New Yorkers with his syncopated orchestral
arrangements. Syncopated music, which was played along the
eastern seaboard before World War I, stimulated New York musicians into experimenting with new sounds as public dancing

increased dramatically and black vernacular dances provided the basis for new ballroom fads that swept the dance halls, theatres, and cabarets. The dance-jazz music in this period featured an "ostinato of equally-accented percussive quarter note chords that supported a highly syncopated melodic line,"[42] making the music exciting while regulating the rhythm of the stepping. From 1910 to 1920, Americans went "dance mad" with the fox-trot, that syncopated ragtime dance that bounced couples along the floor with hops, kicks, and capers. At the same time, some hundred black-based "animal" dances, like the turkey trot, monkey glide, chicken scratch, bunny hug, and bullfrog hop, were danced to ragtime rhythms. While dance bands in the downtown New York clubs were "jassing up" by adding speed and syncopation to the grizzly bear and the kangaroo dip for their white clientele, uptown in Harlem the audiences were rocking back and forth with low croons, screaming with delight, waving their hands, and vigorously pounding their palms together in response to jazz rhythms.

Darktown Follies, J. Leubrie Hill's all-black musical revue, which opened at the Lafayette Theatre in 1914, may have been, as Carl Van Vechten writes, an "imitation of the white man's theatre," with its "dash of tenor" voices and "sprinkling of girls in long satin gowns." The greater part of this "Negro ballet in ebony and ivory and rose," however, expressed an inexorable rhythm by its dancers, who "stepped about and clapped their hands and 'grew mad with their bodies' and grinned and shouted."[43]

Once the show was underway, the rhythm spread from one side of the stage to the other; it seemed that even the scenery, stage boards, and footlights flickered to it. The show, which introduced the "Texas Tommy," prototype of the Lindy Hop, also flashed with new styles of tap dancing. One was Eddie Rector's smooth style of "stage dancing"; the other was the more acrobatic and high-flying style of Toots Davis, whose "Over the Top" and "Through the Trenches" were named for wartime combat maneuvers. In the finale of "At the Ball," the entire company spiraled into a stomping circle dance that resembled a coiled serpent.

After watching the fiftieth repetition of "At the Ball," Van

Vechten wrote: "The rhythm dominated me so completely that for days afterwards, I subconsciously adapted whatever I was doing to its demands."[44] *Darktown Follies* began, James Weldon Johnson wrote, "the nightly migration to Harlem in search for entertainment."[45] Florenz Ziegfeld, who night after night "sat admiringly in a box at this show, drinking in the details of the admirable stage direction, the spontaneity of the performers, their characteristic lax ease, and the delightfully abandoned tunes,"[46] bought the show wholesale and moved it to Broadway for his *Ziegfeld Follies of 1914*. Black vernacular dance rhythms were thus transplanted to Times Square.

Twenties Jazz Dance

By the Jazz Age twenties, many dancers had discovered the rhythmic power of jazz. In this decade, in which jazz became a popular nighttime entertainment, performed in the newly designed cabarets and on large stages, the style of tap dance known as "jazz tap" emerged as the most rhythmically complex form. This form of dance, also called "rhythm tap," was distinguished by its intricate rhythmic motifs, the use of polyrhythms, multiple meters, and elements of swing, or offbeat phrasing with a suspension of the beat.

Setting itself apart from all earlier forms of tap dance, jazz tap dance matched its speed to that of jazz music, often doubling it. Here was an extremely rapid yet subtle form of drum dancing that demanded the dancer's center to be lifted, with the weight balanced between the balls and heels of both feet. While the dancer's alignment was upright and vertical, there was a marked angularity in the body line that allowed the swift downward drive of weight.[47] By the end of the twenties, jazz tap dancing would be considered by some as the most "modern" form of stage dance.

Shuffle Along, which opened in New York at the 63rd Street Theatre on May 23, 1921, is said to have single-handedly brought black musical theatre back to Broadway. This all-black musical, with music by Eubie Blake and lyrics by Noble Sissle, introduced

the most exciting form of jazz dancing that had ever been seen on
the Broadway stage. Blake's musical score provided a foot-
stomping orgy of giddy rhythms that spanned traditional and
early jazz styles. From the plantation melodies of "Bandana Days"
and "Oriental Blues" and the ragged "Syncopation Stenos" to the
boogie woogie-style "If You Haven't Been Vamped by a Brown-
skin You Haven't Been Vamped at All" and "Simply Full of Jazz,"
these song-and-dance numbers had audiences shouting for more
tap routines, buck-and-wings, and precision dances. The tap
dancing by the sixteen-girl chorus line, which included the young
Josephine Baker, combined stepping and kicking with stylish
social dances and twisting shimmies. "Every sinew in their bodies danced," Alan Dale wrote in the *New York American*, "every
tendon in their frames responded to their extreme energy. They
revelled in their work; they simply pulsed with it, and there was
no let-up at all."[48]

The jazz dancing in *Shuffle Along* was never specifically referred
to as "tap dance," according to the meticulous research of black
musical theatre historian John Graziano.[49] Various styles of percussive stepping belonging to the genre of jazz tap dance were,
however, often described and singled out as the most exciting
aspects of the dancing in *Shuffle Along*. "Jimtown's Fisticuffs," the
boxing match performed by Flournoy Miller and Aubry Lyles, as
two would-be mayors, had these rivals swinging and knocking
each other down, jumping over each other's backs, and finishing
each round with buck-and-wings and time steps. The title song,
"Shuffle Along," was a song-and-dance number featuring the Jimtown Pedestrians. The Traffic Cop was played by Charlie Davis,
who performed a high-speed buck-and-wing dance that staggered
the audience. Elsewhere in the musical, Tommy Woods did a
slow-motion acrobatic dance that began with time-step variations, which included flips that landed right on the beat of the
music; Ulysses "Slow Kid" Thompson, a well-known tap dancer,
performed eccentric softshoe and legomania.[50]

The most obvious reference to tap dance in *Shuffle Along* is the
"shuffle" of the title, a rapid and rhythmic brushing step that is
most basic in tap dancing. "Shuffle" also refers to the stereotype

of the "shufflin'" old plantation slave who, accused of being lazy and venal, dragged and scraped his feet noisily along the ground. This trait was further exaggerated by white, and then black, minstrel dancers, who, in imitation of the stereotype, shuffled and slid across the stage. While the book in *Shuffle Along* purveyed the old caricature of the black shufflin' fool, the musical part of the show embodied a new image, that of "the black dancer as a rhythmically propulsive source of energy."[51] Tap dance was thus resurrected and re-created from its nineteenth-century minstrel origins. Critics have agreed that *Shuffle Along* "pioneered" jazz in musicals. Musical comedy on Broadway in the twenties took on a new rhythmic life as chorus girls learned to dance to the new rhythms.

The rhythmic revolution that began with *Shuffle Along* in 1921 continued on Broadway with *Strut Miss Lizzie* (1922) and *Liza* (1922), then especially with *Runnin' Wild* (1923), in which a new tap-dancing version of the Charleston was performed while the chorus beat out the time with hand clapping and foot patting. A black vernacular dance originating in the South, the Charleston was learned by Noble Sissle in Savannah, Georgia, as early as 1905; the Whitman Sisters claim to have used the Charleston in their act in 1911; and the eccentric dancer "Rubberlegs" Williams reportedly won a Charleston contest in Atlanta in 1920.[52] But for Broadway audiences, the Charleston was absolutely new in the twenties because the beating out of complex rhythms had never before occurred on a New York stage. The "Charleston" number in *Runnin' Wild*, proclaimed one critic, "pronounced the beat for the lost generation, and liberated the world of jazz movement."[53]

Lew Leslie's *Dixie to Broadway* (1924) featured the singing of Florence Mills and the tap dancing of U. S. "Slow Kid" Thompson, but the high point of the revue was the virtuoso tap dancer Johnny Nitt, of whose performance in "Prisoners Up to Date" the *New York Sun* wrote: "The dark Mr. Nit [*sic*], with a toothful smile slides quietly into the rhythm and gives himself to an artful, beautifully competent soft shoe dance. . . . The lisp of his feet on the floor is rhythm's self."[54] In lauding dancers as "beautifully competent," critics by the mid-twenties showed that jazz tapping was beginning to be perceived as an "artful" form of musical expression. With its distinctive northern and urban focus, *Dixie to Broadway*, in Alan Woll's view, "presented the modern New Negro, the new vision of the Harlem Renaissance." This is evidenced by a publicity release of the revue stating:

> It isn't Africa anymore than it is the South. It is America, jazzing, dancing America. Instead of the simplicity of a backward people, there is the same hard sophistication that is the bone and sinew of every revue.[55]

With eight or more black musical hits on Broadway, from *Shuffle Along* in 1921 to *Dixie to Broadway* in 1924, all stage dancing underwent a change: the steps in jazz tap dancing became more intricate, daring, and perilous,[56] and jazz dancing in general became more rhythmic, with the introduction of inventive and complex manipulations of time.

While jazz tap dancing continued to be singled out and praised in these black Broadway musicals and revues of the twenties, it was not until Lew Leslie's *Blackbirds of 1928* that it began to be distinguished as the most rhythmically complex "cream" of jazz dancing. *Blackbirds* starred Bill "Bojangles" Robinson. Though he was a veteran showman in vaudeville and the most beloved dancer in the black community, the fifty-year-old performer was "discovered" by Broadway audiences when *Blackbirds* opened and was immediately pronounced "King of Tap Dancers."

Born in Richmond, Virginia, in 1878, Robinson had earned nickels and dimes by dancing and scat singing in the street. He had begun his career performing as a member of a "pickaninny" chorus, and by the twenties he was the headliner on both the Keith and the Orpheum circuits, as he was at New York's prestigious Palace Theatre. In *Blackbirds*, Robinson performed his famous "Stair Dance," which he had introduced in vaudeville around 1918. Dancing up and down a flight of stairs in his split-soled clog shoes (the wooden half-sole, attached from the toe to the ball of the foot, was left loose), each step was tuned to a different pitch and used a different rhythm. As he danced to clean four- and eight-bar phrases followed by a two-bar break, Robinson's taps were delicate, articulate, and intelligible. Whether interweaving buck or time steps with whimsical skating steps or little crossover steps danced on the balls of the feet, the dancing was upright and rhythmically swinging. The light and exacting footwork brought tap dance "up on its toes" from an earlier, earthier, more flat-footed shuffling style.[57]

Langston Hughes, describing these tap rhythms as "human percussion," believed that no dancer had ever developed the art of tap dancing to a more delicate perfection than Robinson, who could create "little running trills of rippling softness or terrific syncopated rolls of mounting sound, rollicking little nuances of tap-tap-toe, or staccato runs like a series of gun-shots."[58] Reviewing *Blackbirds of 1928*, Mary Austin observed that the postures of Robinson's lithe body and the motions of his slender cane punctuated his rhythmic patter and restored for his audience "a primal freshness of rhythmic coordination" that was fundamental to art:

> Those swift vanishings from the stage to wipe away the sweat of muscles constrained to their uttermost, and bright returns, all the intriguing quality of bird flight, are as carefully studied as the lifting and placing of the cane are faithfully rehearsed.[59]

Broadway had not only discovered Robinson but had become newly enamored of his strikingly modern rhythm dance.

"In that delicate concealment of effort—the noblesse of the aristocracy of art," wrote Austin, "he offers his audience the great desideratum of modern art, a clean shortcut to areas of enjoyment long closed to us by the accumulated rubbish of the culture route."[60] Like Johnny Nitt and the dancers in *Dixie to Broadway* who presented a modern "New Negro" and a new vision of the Harlem Renaissance, Robinson interpreted Negro folk rhythms, transforming them into a sleekly modern black expression. "A Bojangles performance is excellent vaudeville," wrote Alain Locke. "But listen with closed eyes, and it becomes an almost symphonic composition of sounds. What the eye sees is the tawdry American convention; what the ear hears is the priceless African heritage."[61]

When the tap dancing of Bill Robinson in *Blackbirds of 1928* was being hailed in New York as a delicately perfected art, fourteen-year-old Fayard Nicholas and his seven-year-old brother, Harold, were on the threshold of launching professional careers as jazz dancers in Philadelphia. The dancers were too young to travel to New York to see the great Bojangles in *Blackbirds of 1928*, nor could they imagine that in a few short years they would be head-liners in *Blackbirds of 1936*, in its London revival, or that they would appear with Robinson in the Hollywood film *The Big Broadcast of 1936* and eventually assume his roles at the Cotton Club.

They did know, however, that Robinson was one of the greatest of all living tap dancers. They had seen him perform, along with hundreds of other jazz dancers, singers, and musicians, in the black vaudeville theatres of Philadelphia. Fayard Nicholas, born the year that Florenz Ziegfeld brought *Darktown Follies* to Broadway for his *Ziegfeld Follies of 1914*, was ushered into the Jazz Age listening to the syncopated rhythms, ragtime, and show tunes his mother played on the piano. Harold Nicholas, who was born in 1921, the year *Shuffle Along* opened on Broadway, remembers the rhythms his father played on the drums. As children in the Jazz Age, the Nicholas boys could not help but absorb the music, the dance, and the spirit of jazz, their parents being professional jazz musicians who played in the pit orchestra bands in black vaudeville theatres. Raised on the music of "King" Oliver's Creole Jazz Band, Fayard had heard the recordings of Bessie Smith singing "St. Louis Blues." He knew the sound of Duke Ellington and his orchestra from listening to the radio. And he had seen Louis Armstrong perform; he once shouted to the famous cornetist and trumpeter to play his favorite song, "When It's Sleepy Time Down South." Jazz drew the brothers to Harlem in the early thirties, where they were quickly assimilated into the creative fervor of the Harlem Renaissance as it entered what would be its twilight years.

When the Nicholas brothers arrived, they found themselves collaborating, working, and performing with those musical artists who shaped the elements of folk music into more sophisticated musical forms. Like them, the Nicholases would transform black vernacular dance, with its stomps and buck-and-wing tapping, into a modern black expression. Through their tap dancing, the brothers transposed the syncopated African-American pulse into a modern jazz expression of exquisite elegance, which in time would develop into the classic American jazz dance form.

Ulysses,
Viola,
Harold,
Dorothy,
and Fayard
Nicholas in
New York in
the early
thirties
(Harold
Nicholas
archive).

Two

Brothers

1914–1931

Viola Nicholas always played the piano for her sons, Fayard and
Harold, when they rehearsed their tap routine. Fayard sang, "DEE
bop, deDEE bop, dedeedalee DEE bop," and the muted beats from
the balls of his feet raced up his calves and thighs and through his
bony frame and outstretched arms like an electric current.
Singing and patting, stretching past four bars into six and a two-
bar break, Fayard kneaded out the sounds with his feet. Although
he danced barefoot on the carpeted living room floor, his sounds
were strong and clear. Ulysses Nicholas sat in his armchair, listening to his son's dance. "That's good, do that," he coached,
encouraging Fayard to use his arms and to keep the rhythm in the
body. "Did you see that, Harold?" Ulysses asked one son, as he
pointed to the other. Harold nodded, but he continued to stare
at his older brother pumping away. "Come on!" Fayard shouted
to Harold between breaths, coaxing his brother to do the rhythm,
to try it, lest it slip away. "I don't know if I can do that," Harold
murmured. "Well, why don't you try it and see," Fayard challenged Harold. And getting him up on his feet, they went to
work. Mother fingered the melody on the piano, Father footed

the steady beat, Fayard scatted the offbeat accents, and Harold stamped and shaped. "We can always do it tomorrow," Fayard suggested, when he eyed Harold having trouble with a step.

"No. I want to do it now!" Harold retorted, as he stomped out the two-bar break over and over again. And then the whole family knew he was hooked. They would work for an hour, playing toss and catch with the rhythm, keeping it buoyant. Finally, Harold delivered a cascade of thumping beats that traveled from the feet up and through the body. When the rhythms became visible in the form of small pulses at the elbows, wrists, and fingertips, Fayard knew that Harold had gotten the step. And once Harold got the step, Fayard knew his brother would always have it.

Fayard and Harold Nicholas's brotherhood in rhythm was a family affair. Love and respect, perfection and professionalism had been instilled by parents who not only guided and managed their sons' career but modeled a supreme form of partnership at home that the brothers would celebrate together on the stage. Viola and Ulysses Nicholas were jazz musicians—she a pianist and he a drummer—who during the 1910s and 1920s played in the pit orchestras of black vaudeville theatres up and down the eastern seaboard. They were an extremely handsome couple, "petite and well-built, with a beautiful olive-complexion . . . beautiful people with such personality."[1] Ulysses was "a short man with gusto."[2] Technically, he was not only "a fantastic drummer," but the kind of drummer who was flamboyant.[3] When he performed, one couldn't help watching only him. "I remember him mainly as a drummer, working in the theatre and beating the drums," Harold Nicholas remembers about his father. "And to me, he was special, because he did something I hadn't seen before. . . . He was beating his drums, getting up from the seat where the drums were, and coming out in the audience and beating on the seats that the people were sitting in. I mean, he was really a showman."[4] Harold also remembers that "Daddy was stern. He was the boss," while sister Dorothy remembers her father as being extremely exacting: "He always wanted to look neat. And he always wanted for us to look neat and carry ourselves well, as did Mother."[5]

While Ulysses was the consummate showman, Viola Nicholas was demure and subdued. "She always smiled when she played the piano, and you wondered if she was laughing at you during your dance or whether she was just happy," tap dancer Leonard Reed remembered about Viola. "She was more or less a stride pianist, her left hand flowing all the time, and she was excellent, outstanding. There weren't too many women pianists around in those days in her league."[6] Harold remembers his mother as "being very quiet, going through life and not giving Daddy too much static," and Fayard says that she was extremely versatile: "She wrote music, she played music, she made arrangements for different artists. She could sew and make dresses. She was a great mathematician. You would ask her to add numbers or multiply, and she would do it in her head. She was marvelous."[7] Fayard and Harold's sister, Dorothy, adds, "Mother had a marvelous societal approach to life. She loved life, loved entertaining, loved being with people. When at home or away, there was always that communication, always that give and take from her."[8]

Ulysses Nicholas (c. 1892–1935) and Viola Harden Nicholas (c. 1890–1971) were born in Mobile, Alabama, some 150 miles from New Orleans, the so-called birthplace of jazz. Good railroad lines ran between these cities, and bands from the New Orleans area frequently played in Mobile. From the musicians who passed through Mobile in the 1890s on their way to New Orleans, and from the New Orleans bands that paraded through town on wagons to advertise dances,[9] Ulysses and Viola grew up under the spell of the New Orleans jazz style. They listened to the blues from the Mississippi Delta, to the cacophonous but rhythmically stirring marches, hymns, and popular songs of parading brass bands, and to the waltzes, quadrilles, sentimental ballads, and rags of the dance bands. All these musical styles were being assimilated into the early forms of jazz.

The Hardens were educated, cultured, and musically gifted people. There were teachers in the family, as well as an uncle, Dr. F. W. Wilkerson, who was a renowned physician. From a very early age, Viola was drawn to the piano. "She was a child of the piano," remembers Dorothy. "She had access to a piano, played all the time and was considered a child prodigy. The story I get is that she had gone through the teachers in the little area where she lived, and the next step was to find a teacher out of state. But the family couldn't afford it at the time."[10]

Viola nevertheless kept up with her piano playing, and she is said to have gone to Tuskegee College for a year to study music. Fayard believes that while Viola was in college she met Ulysses, also an aspiring musician and a self-taught drummer. The couple married in the early teens and settled in Mobile, where Viola taught piano and Ulysses worked in a tailor shop. Their first son was born in Mobile on October 28, 1914, just after World War I began. Viola named him Fayard Antonio Nicholas; the unusual and beautiful-sounding French first name, she hoped, would forever distinguish him from all others.

After the war, like the tens of thousands of African-Americans who migrated from the rural South into northern industrial cities in search of work and economic opportunity, Ulysses and Viola moved. They followed the pattern of jazz's diffusion as it spread northward, from its place of birth in New Orleans toward Chicago. The family arrived in Chicago around the same time that Joe "King" Oliver and his Creole Jazz Band arrived there from New Orleans with its "polyphonic" jazz—primarily ensemble music with a series of improvised solos that depended on a thick, melodic texture with a rocking swing for effect.[11]

The black population of Chicago had almost tripled during the Great Migration, from 44,103 to 109,458; this was due in large part to the infusion of New Orleans migrants, who helped create jobs for musicians.[12] James Lincoln Collier writes that in the late teens, jazz spread almost simultaneously with the rise of the dance boom, and that the first jazz musicians to leave New Orleans were those who joined the black vaudeville shows, which passed through Chicago.[13] Like these New Orleans vaudevillians, Viola and Ulysses looked for work in black theatres in Chicago. They soon landed jobs playing in the pit orchestras of black theatres and burlesque houses around the city. Between 1912 and 1920, opportunities increased for work in the pit orchestras having five pieces or more (violin, cornet, clarinet, piano, and drums), especially for those with formal musical training, who could read arrangements and perform in so-called section work, which placed little emphasis on improvised solos.

"Fayard always danced," Viola Nicholas remarked about her son in an interview with Marshall Stearns.[14] Fayard's earliest recollections of his parents, meanwhile, are of listening to the music they played in the theatre: "At the age of three I was hearing music. I'd go to the theatre and hear them play, or be home in the living room listening to music on the radio and just be shakin' in the chair. I'd be moving. So I guess I had this rhythm born into me." He remembers spending all his time as a child in the orchestra pit, where Ulysses and Viola played drums and piano: "I never had a baby sitter, my parents took me everywhere. They'd even take me into the pit, the orchestra pit, where the musicians played for the entertainers onstage. My mother had me in this bassinet right beside the piano, and if I'd cry, she'd take the bottle and stick it into my mouth."[15]

Viola's brother and some other family members from her mother's side had migrated to Chicago. They lived in the industrialized South Side, known as the Black Belt. With the mass migration of many blacks to the city, a large audience for black music developed, especially for the blues.[16] In that city, partly because it was then dominated by criminal gangs, there were many cabarets and dance halls that featured the hot music of the jazzmen.

While it is not certain whether Viola or Ulysses played music in Chicago cabarets and dance halls, they surely listened to jazz in the many clubs on the South Side. They were certainly familiar with the rhythmic lope, or swing, of "King" Oliver's Creole Jazz Band, in which each instrument took a specific role or range in a highly structured but improvisational format. If the Nicholases did find work in Chicago in the late teens and early twenties it was—based on the work they subsequently obtained as musicians in the motion picture and vaudeville pit bands—relatively well paid and provided security and prestige.[17] Such work generally required that the musicians be classically trained, as Viola was, and it had them playing background music for silent films, often from special scores—played not from books but from sides kept in voluminous files by the theatre's musical director.

Wherever Ulysses and Viola Nicholas did find work in Chicago, it was steady work. After their second child, Dorothy Bernice Nicholas, was born on January 8, 1920, Fayard remembers that his mother stayed home for a few days and then "came right back to work in the theatre." But it was not for very long. Soon after Dorothy's birth, the Nicholases moved from Chicago to Winston-Salem, North Carolina, where Ulysses's brother and family had lived. In Winston-Salem, Viola and Ulysses quickly found work as pit orchestra musicians at the Lincoln Theatre, which presented acts on the black vaudeville circuit known as TOBA (Theatre Owners' Booking Association).

Seven-year-old Fayard was soon enrolled in an integrated Catholic school. He went to the theatre every day after school to watch the live variety acts, as well as the silent movies for which his parents played musical accompaniment. At the Lincoln Theatre, Fayard remembers, he saw such silent film stars as Charlie Chaplin, Buster Keaton, Rudolph Valentino, Lillian Gish, John Gilbert, and William Desmond. But his favorite personality was the silent film comedian Harold Lloyd. In March 1921, Lloyd was starring in the Pathé Films hit *Get Out and Get Under*, and the film was being shown in a theatre in Winston-Salem.[18] Fayard loved seeing his favorite silent screen comedian so much that when Viola gave birth to her third child on March 17, 1921, Fayard named his newborn brother Harold Lloyd.

The Nicholases thrived in Winston-Salem, where brothers and aunts and uncles from Ulysses' side of the family provided them with much-needed familial ties and support. Along with playing in the pit orchestra at the Lincoln Theatre, Viola taught piano privately and arranged music for many of the musical stars who worked at the Lincoln. Ulysses, meanwhile, was honing his skills as a showman drummer. "He was sensational," Fayard remembers. "He would have contests with all the drummers who came to town with other orchestras. They would all get together and have contests, and he would win every time. He played on the stage, on the walls, wherever he could beat those sticks. He'd drum down the steps and into the audience, throwing the sticks in the air and catching them when they bounced up from the floor."[19]

Watching his father compete in drum challenges were not the only kind of event that enthralled Fayard, who by age seven was taken with the whole of show business. "I loved all the music and loved all the entertainers onstage," says Fayard. "They looked like they were having so much fun up there." The pair who tickled Fayard's funnybone with down-home, black vernacular humor was the husband-and-wife comedy team of Butterbeans and Susie. Their entrance onto the Lincoln stage, says Fayard, was unforgettable: "They had a screen that had the painting of a record—they sang on the Okeh label, and 'Butterbeans and Susie' was the title of the record. The orchestra struck up, and the master of ceremonies announced 'Here they are! Butterbeans and Susie!' And they walked right through the screen—right through the record! And every show they had to have a new one."[20]

Butterbeans (Henry "Rubberlegs" Williams) and Susie (Jodie Edwards), who were known primarily on the TOBA circuit, acted out the conflicts of marriage in an act that alternated songs, jokes, and dances that were interrupted as each heckled the other. The stout and forthright Susie, in singing "Get Yourself a Money Man," prescribed what she wanted in a man: "He works hard all the time, and on Saturday night when he brings me his pay, he better not be short one dime."

When Butterbeans tried to counter by boasting of treating his women tough, threatening Susie by saying, "I'll whip your head," it was obvious that the short, baby-faced man with the timorous voice was indulging in delusions of grandeur. Between duets, Susie sang the blues and danced a cakewalk, while Butterbeans performed his own style of eccentric movements. At the climax of his routine, he sang "Heebie Jeebies," in which he scratched himself, spasmodically itching and patting his hands over his body, in perfect time to the music.[21]

Around 1924, the Nicholases moved to Baltimore, Maryland. Since Viola and Ulysses were also working in South Carolina and Washington, D.C., during this period, three-year-old Harold, who the family felt was too young to travel, was left in Winston-Salem under the care of a Mama Williamson. In Baltimore, Viola and Ulysses worked as pit orchestra musicians in another black vaudeville house, also called the Lincoln Theatre; this one was located at the corner of Biddle and Pennsylvania Avenue. Fayard was again enrolled in a Catholic school, where he easily adjusted to his new surroundings. "He was a Pied Piper; children always gravitated to him, and he was able to talk to them on their level," remembers Dorothy about her brother, who was declared the fastest runner in the sixth grade upon winning the sixty-yard dash. Not only was Fayard the fastest runner and most popular student, but he was also the favorite of the nuns. Dorothy remembers that when she, the more feisty and outspoken sibling, was later enrolled in kindergarten, the nuns cautioned her to be like the "obedient, young gentleman" that Fayard had been.[22]

If Fayard's teachers were impressed with his manners in school, he was fast becoming impressed with the glittering tap dancing of Jack Wiggins at Baltimore's Lincoln Theatre. "Ginger" Jack Wiggins was the epitome of elegant tap dancing. He was an immaculate dancer with a commanding presence, who served his apprenticeship on the TOBA circuit with blues singer "Ma" Rainey in the teens and later became a headliner in black vaudeville, though he never made it to Broadway. Eccentric dancers on the circuit were known to wear tramp costumes, but the tall and slender Wiggins wore high-heeled patent-leather shoes and a series of dazzling dinner jackets with rhinestones and sequins on the lapels, which sparkled as he danced.

It was not how Wiggins looked but how he danced that impressed Fayard. His softshoe, unlike the slower softshoe (or song-and-dance) of the minstrel stage, had snappy, swinging rhythms and aggressive kicks. He used his whole body when he danced. A "trick" tap step that Wiggins popularized, called "Pull It," ended with his right leg arched behind him as he leaned backward; his "Bantam Twist" had in it an elegant *renverse* turn that was complemented by the full circling of his arms. Wiggins's most famous step, however, was the "Tango Twist," which began with an undulation of the torso; the hips then twisted quickly from side to side, sending the dancer into a floating half-turn that was emphasized by heel and toe taps.

While most tap dancers performed variations on the time step, Wiggins was unique, the most unusual tap dancer Fayard had ever seen. He was so impressed with Wiggins's style of tap dancing that he began to teach himself to tap. "He did a split," says Fayard of Wiggins, "so I went home and I tried it, just going down and coming up. And I found out I could do it better. See, he didn't go all the way down, and I did. I'd go down and put my hands on the floor and come up. Then, I thought maybe I could go down and come up *without* putting my hands on the floor. I discovered I had something no other dancer had; I could go down-and-up without putting my hands on the floor."[23]

Fayard amused himself by walking down the street and jumping over a fire hydrant into a split. And after coming home from the circus, where he had seen a tumbling group called the Cracker Jacks, he tried their acrobatic stunts to music because, he says, "I always wanted to make everything graceful."[24] Not satisfied to do the steps by himself, Fayard began teaching the twists, splits, and whatever else he had seen onstage to Dorothy. They, in turn, showed all their moves to Ulysses and Viola. Says Dorothy: "Fayard was always the active, rhythmical one, who performed for himself and for others at a glance. He loved doing it, and we loved seeing it."[25] Before long, Fayard began enticing his sister to perform with him in school assemblies. He had made up a little act, which he called the Nicholas Kids. Dorothy was not as enthused as Fayard was: "Someone had gotten the idea, and had everybody convinced, that I should be part of the team. So they put together either a song or finale dance, something we prepared, which I feel was a dismal flop. I'm sure it was, because I wasn't excited about it."[26]

Dorothy may not have been so excited about the Nicholas Kids, but others apparently were. Leonard Reed remembered that in 1926, while he was performing on the TOBA circuit with *Hits and Bits of 1925*, he saw the Nicholas Kids perform at the Lincoln Theatre in Baltimore. That act included not only Fayard and Dorothy but also five-year-old Harold, with Viola and Ulysses accompanying them in the pit. "I don't remember how good or bad they were," said Reed. "All I know is they stopped the show, and my partner and I couldn't get on . . . we had to wait. They were applauding for the Nicholas Kids, and then they brought out Harold, who could hardly walk, to do the encore. And that just made it worse. When we did get on, they were still applauding for the Nicholas Kids."[27]

Ulysses frequently traveled to various cities in the East in search of work. In 1926, he and Viola boarded a train to Philadelphia to audition for John T. Gibson, the manager of the Standard Theatre. Gibson promptly offered them the job of organizing and heading the resident pit orchestra at the Standard. The family was moved into a two-bedroom flat in the Gibson-owned apartments on Lombard Street, then Fayard, Dorothy, and Harold were enrolled in the Stanley School, a small, private, integrated school with an excellent academic reputation. The more valuable education for Fayard, however, was gotten by sitting in a front row seat of the Standard, where he saw hundreds of performances by musical artists, whose jokes he repeated, tunes he hummed, and moves he tried on for size, as he absorbed the materials of black vaudeville performance.

There were two general touring circuits for black performers in the 1920s. One was TOBA, which consisted of more than forty-five theatres throughout the South and Southwest, and the other was a smaller, black-owned, independently run chain of theatres in the Northeast, which included the Layfayette Theatre in New York, the Royal Theatre in Baltimore, and the Standard Theatre in Philadelphia. The Standard was owned and managed by John T. Gibson, who, though born in Baltimore, had entered the theatrical business in Philadelphia believing that the city provided the most fertile field for showcasing black theatrical talent.

Gibson subsequently became one of the largest organizers of black talent in the Northeast. "When the rawest and most undeveloped of talent was seeking a foothold, it was Mr. Gibson who encouraged their work and made it possible for some performers to appear . . . before the public where they could grow proficient," wrote the *Philadelphia Tribune* (12 January 1928). Singers like Ethel Waters and comedy teams like Glenn and Jenkins began their careers under Gibson's banner, and most of the renowned black performing artists of the twenties passed through his theatres. "Every black act, every black dancer, every black comic played the Standard," confirmed Leonard Reed. "If you made it in Philadelphia, you felt safe about going to New York. If you didn't make it in Philadelphia, don't even attempt New York because then you were through, you would never make it. Philadelphia, and that particular theatre, was the proving ground. As a matter of fact, that was the *only* theatre in Philadelphia where all the black artists played."[28]

Gibson's first theatre, opened in 1912 and located in the northern part of Philadelphia, was a barnlike structure with a loft used for dressing rooms; it was affectionately referred to as the "North Pole Hole in the Wall."[29] Because of good management, it was possible for Gibson to purchase two more theatres and appreciable real estate holdings in the heart of the city. In January 1914, when Gibson opened the Standard Theatre on South Street and Twelfth, the *Philadelphia Tribune* reported that the city's black population "bristled with enthusiasm of another Negro in the world of the theatre starting for the heights of fame and money."[30]

After opening the Standard, Gibson bought the Dunbar Theatre, located at Broad and Lombard streets, which had belonged to the Layfayette Players. With its massive house, Gibson's New Dunbar Theatre was able to present large-cast musical comedies and revues, many of them black Broadway musicals, such as *Dixiana* (1925), *Runnin' Wild* (1926, 1929), *Charleston Dandies* (1927), *Shuffle Along* (1927), *Gay Harlem* (1927), *Liza* (1928), and *Shuffle Along 1930* (1930). Despite Gibson's heroic attempt to sell tickets and keep the massive house filled, the New Dunbar opened irregularly. The Standard Theatre, however, prided itself on presenting "Supreme Vaudeville—the Biggest and Best of America's Variety Artists,"[31] and it remained a commercial and popular success. In 1928, celebrating its fourteenth anniversary season, the theatre boasted that it had hosted more than seven hundred attractions. In 1932, the Standard Theatre was forced to close, because depreciation followed in the wake of the Depression and forced the loss of all of Gibson's valuable real estate holdings.[32]

At the Standard, Ulysses and Viola organized a highly skilled and musically versatile ten-piece orchestra (bass, guitar, piano, drums, trombone, two trumpets, and three saxophones), which they named the Nicholas Collegians. The band was composed of musicians who could not only read music but interpret to perfection all kinds of show music, popular music, and jazz. "They were good readers, that's why they made good pit," said Leonard Reed about the Collegians. "Because when you're in the pit you had to read the music, you had to know what you were doing."[33] The Nicks, as they were called, dressed like Ivy League college students, wearing white slacks and white sweaters with red trim, with a big letter *N* embroidered on the front of the sweater. Playing a matinee daily, two shows nightly, and a midnight show on Sunday, they accompanied many of the variety acts, musical comedies, and revues that rolled into the theatre for one-week runs. *Dancin' Days*, the "musical comedy supreme" starring Dusty Fletcher and Pigmeat Markham, offered "musical gems by Nick's Collegians" when it played the Standard in 1929, as did *Too Many Cousins*, the "laughing musical tabloid" that played for a week in October that same year.[34] In January 1930, in celebration of the Standard Theatre's sixteenth season, Nick's Collegians were featured in a "special anniversary musical program" billed as *Collegiana*, featuring "50-Celebrated Artists-50 Youth! Beauty! Speed! 15-Caryettes-15" and "World's Fastest Dancing Chorus."[35]

Watching the Collegians perform in the orchestra pit at the Standard in the late twenties, Leonard Reed observed that Viola played outstanding stride piano, a style of playing that developed from ragtime after World War I, distinguished by its fast tempos, full piano range, and a wide array of pianistic devices. Ulysses's style of playing the drums, by all descriptions, was most similar to that of Chick Webb, the drummer and bandleader who was known for his forceful sense of swing, accurate technique, control of dynamics, and imaginative breaks and fills. Reed remembered that almost every drummer in Philadelphia came to the Standard to watch Ulysses,[36] who later gave drum lessons to the vibraphonist and drummer Lionel Hampton.

If one knows anything about the jazz that was played by the

Collegians and other pit orchestra bands in Philadelphia in the late twenties, it is that the music and the accompanying jazz dance, as described in the *Philadelphia Tribune*, were distinguished and admired for their speed and hard-driving energy.

The "Special Jazz Band" of the *Ebony Follies*, which played the New Dunbar Theatre for a week in 1926, was billed as "Brimful of Brown-skinned Beauties" dancing with "Snap, Pep and Ginger"; while *Syncopation*, which played the Standard in 1927, was announced as "The Liveliest, The Tunefullest, the Jazziest, The Dancingest Revue Now Being Offered Anywhere."[37] The musical comedy *My Chocolate Gal*, which played the Standard in 1927, had a "cyclonic" jazz band and "45-Dancing Demons-45"; while *The Tasmanians*, a tumbling trio that performed at the Standard for a week in 1929, specialized in "whirlwind dancing."[38] And the Whitman Sisters' *Dancing Fools*, playing the Standard in 1927, was billed as "The Speed Show That Tops Them All."[39]

Blues singer Bessie Smith performed at the Standard with "35 Cyclonic Speedsters" for a week in 1928; and the musical comedy *Shufflin' Sam from Alabam*, playing the Pearl Theatre in 1928, featured "35 Plantation-Raised Jazz Hounds and a Creole Chorus of Seven Dancin' Streaks."[40] *The Devil's Frolics*, playing the Standard for a week in 1929, had the "World's Fastest Dancing Chorus—Built For Speed."[41] That same year at the Standard, the *Creole Follies* revue, with "more stars than there are in heaven," featured "35-Jazz Mad Steppers-35"; while *Desires of 1930*, at the Standard the following year, had "40-Torpedoes-40 Dancing Creoles."[42]

Although the jazz trumpeter Louis Armstrong had his own bands off and on beginning in the mid-twenties, he did not appear with one of them when he played the Standard Theatre the week of December 26, 1929. In this first Philadelphia appearance, he played with Nick's Collegians. Sitting in the front row seat near the orchestra pit, Fayard asked his father in the middle of the performance if Armstrong would play his favorite song, "When It's Sleepy Time Down South," and Ulysses assured him he would. Armstrong was already a famous musical personality to the black public in the twenties, as admired for his scat-singing solos as for his horn playing. His playing and singing of "Sleepy Time Down

South," which came into his repertory in the mid-twenties and was recorded dozens of times in his career, demonstrated the trumpeter's superior choice of notes and an equally incomparable sense of swing. The way that Armstrong colored and embellished the individual notes of the song—sustaining the word "know," for example, in the line "You didn't tell me because I know when it's sleepy time down South"—with a subtle yet varied repertoire of vibratos and shakes gave his solos a sense of soulfully expressive inner drive and forward momentum.[43] Fayard became so excited at watching Armstrong perform that he sat in his seat, shaking and clapping and bobbing his head, and ultimately broke the seat.

The tap dancer who had most impressed Fayard at the Standard was Leonard Reed. "He was the first great influence on me as a dancer," says Fayard. Born in Lightning Creek, Oklahoma, Leonard Reed (b. 1907) became a dancer at age fifteen, when the Charleston was popular. "Everyone was clapping and doing the Charleston with no music," says Reed, who learned the dance by watching everyone do it in the schoolyard.[44] After winning Charleston contests, his first job, working in a carnival, was to dance the Charleston to tambourine accompaniment on a platform outside a tent show. Reed combined the Charleston with shuffles and struts, twists and grinds, hops, and flat-footed buck dancing,[45] performing it with several partners as he worked his way to New York.

When the tap Charleston hit the New York scene in the mid-twenties, Reed decided to become a tap dancer. He frequented the Hoofers Club, located in the basement two doors down from the Layfayette Theatre, on Seventh Avenue between 131st and 132nd streets, a kind of fraternity of novice and experienced tap dancers who met to trade, improvise and steal each other's steps. By the late twenties, Reed teamed with Willie Bryant in an act they called "Reed and Bryant—Brains as Well as Feet." "It was a classy act. They dressed well and moved with style and grace," says Fayard about the duo, who wore dapper suits for the afternoon performance, beautifully tailored suits for the dinner show, and classic top hat, white tie, and tails for the evening show. Their act opened with a smooth and speedy tap dance, moved to a languid softshoe, and finished with Goofus, or the Shim Sham Shimmy, a one-chorus routine to a thirty-two-bar tune with eight bars each of the double shuffle, crossover, an up-and-back shuffle called tack-Annie, and Falling Offa Log. If Fayard watched the shim sham once, he watched it dozens of times from the wings of the theatre. "Fayard was in everybody's way in the wings, watching everybody he could watch," says Reed about Fayard. "He watched everybody and emulated everything—he could do anybody he wanted to do."

Hundreds of tap specialty acts and musical comedy revues featured tap dancing at the Standard and New Dunbar theatres from 1927 to 1931, and Fayard saw almost all of them. As announced in the *Philadelphia Tribune*, the most notable performers included the "World's Greatest Tap Dancer," Eddie Rector, in *Tan Town Topics*, with singer Adelaide Hall and the Fats Waller Orchestra (1926); the class act of Wells and Mordecai in *Dancemania*; Clarence Robinson's Cotton Club revue, accompanied by Duke Ellington and his Washingtonians (1927); the Berry Brothers, "America's Miniature Williams and Walker," (1927, 1928); Peg Leg Bates in *Dashin' Dinah* (1928, 1931); "The World's Greatest Dancers," U. S. "Slow Kid" Thompson and Arthur Bryson, performing "Intricate Steps and Taps" (1929); "Classy Steppers" Pete, Peaches, and Duke (1931); "Broadway Steppers" Aaron Palmer and Mesa (1931); and Buck and Bubbles (1931). The Whitman Sisters also performed in Philadelphia twice a year in each of Gibson's theatres, often for extended runs, from *Dancing Fools* in 1926 to the *1931 Revue*.

In addition to watching tap dance in live performance, Fayard and Harold saw tap dancing in the films shown at the Standard. Although the policy of mixing film with live stage shows at the Standard was intermittent until 1930, beginning in 1931 the Standard announced a "New Policy of Stage and Screen Shows." The theatre soon boasted an increase in the average attendance by 48 percent in one week.[46] The first time Fayard saw Willie Covan and the Four Covans was in 1929, in the film *On with the Show*. While Covan was known for his pioneering role as an acrobatic tap dancer, his softshoe work was made all the more elegant and distinctive because of the medium of film, which elevated the image of the tap dancer and amplified the sound of his taps. "They impressed me so much the way they danced," says Fayard, "because the four of them looked so great up there on the screen."[47] Fayard was disappointed when he first saw Bill Robinson onstage; it was at a benefit performance at the Lincoln Theatre, and the dancer complained of having a toothache. At the Standard Theatre, Fayard later saw Robinson in the musical revue *Blackbirds of 1930* (playing the week of February 13, 1930) and in the musical comedy *Brown Buddies* (playing the week of April 4, 1931). The young Nicholas brothers, however, became enamored of Robinson only when they saw him in his first film, *Dixiana* (1930), which premiered at the Standard Theatre the week of November 13, 1930. Fayard remembers Robinson's entrance in one scene in the film:

> The orchestra was playin' and all of a sudden he went into his dance. They had a long shot of him and he was way up on the top of a flight of stairs that looked a mile long. And he came down and tapped on each one of those steps. All the way down. As he got down, he did his little break. And then he smiled that wonderful smile. Now, that's Bill Robinson! When I saw him in that motion picture, that did it for me, that's when I fell in love with him.[48]

The tap dancing of the teens and twenties has been variously referred to as "jigging," "jazzing," "hoofing," "syncopated stepping," and "heel-and-toe" dancing. Of all the advertisements for the shows at the Standard Theatre, there are but two specific references to tap dance that actually use the word "tap." The first was a March 7, 1927, review of a musical number by the Harris and Idaho Company, in which performers Carl and Valeska Winters played an odd assortment of musical instruments and wound up with "a tap dancing bit."[49] The only other was the July 16, 1931 performance by Atta Blake, who appeared with "Syncopated Tap Dancers."[50]

Despite the near absence of the word "tap," this dance form was everpresent on the stage and screen of the Standard Theatre. As the *Philadelphia Tribune* confirms, the dance team of Cash and Smith in *Ebony Follies* was billed as "Hoofers That Hoof"; *Dixie*

Revue had a chorus of "16-Heel and Toe Artists-16"; and comedians Sandy Burns and Bilo advertised "Snappy Hoofing" and a great singing and dancing chorus in their comedy revue.[51] The title of the musical comedy revue *Jigfield Follies*, with the "Best Dancing Chorus en Route," was an oblique reference to the jig; and a musical revue featuring Butterbeans and Susie included singer-dancer Baby Cox, billed as "That Syncopated Bundle of Personality."[52] As Leonard Reed confirmed: "They used to say there wasn't such a thing as not having a tap dancer in your show! 'Cause in my day, no matter where you went, you would run into tap dancers. Everything had tap!"[53]

In the wings of the Standard Theatre, or on the carpeted living room floor, Fayard practiced his dancing. He learned to do the time step on both sides, inserted rhythm steps into the Charleston, and practiced squeezing a down-and-up split into the last four beats of a measure. He even somersaulted on the grassy sidewalk and time-stepped with Dorothy on the curb outside his house. Fayard remembers dancing everywhere: "I'd go to our apartment, in the Gibson Apartments, and try to do the steps I saw other dancers do, in the living room. And I would dance from the living room into the kitchen, and from the kitchen onto the fire escape. I was dancing all over the place."[54] Making rhythms with his feet became Fayard's playful obsession:

> If I thought of something, to keep from losing it I'd start performing it. If I had on socks or was barefoot, I'd start doing it anyway, and then when I got it, I'd put my shoes on so I could really hear the sound. I'd even dream about it, and knowing I was dreaming, I'd do the step in my dream and say to myself, 'I gotta remember that.' Then I'd wake myself up and start doing it. Now that's really controlled.[55]

Fayard tapped in hard-soled street shoes; he liked the deep-thumping sounds they made against the wood floor, although it was better at first to improvise barefoot and without music. He says he never named his steps and never counted the rhythm.

He improvised, finding the steps that fit the rhythm he was humming, embellishing with his hands what was sounded through his feet. Because he needed to share what he learned, and sister Dorothy was not an eager participant in his process, Fayard tried teaching tap steps to his little brother.

Harold, though seven years younger than Fayard, was a precocious and quick-witted little guy who could copy whatever he saw, right on the spot. From a very early age, he drew laughs from the family for near-perfect impersonations of Louis Armstrong's grovel-throated singing style. "Harold had a natural facility for languages," said Dorothy. "He had a fantastic ear and sounded out anything he heard."[56] Walking with his little brother down the halls of their school in Philadelphia, Fayard took off his cap and greeted his teachers with "Good morning sisters." Harold would immediately follow, taking his cap off and repeating, "Good morning, sisters," delighting the nuns. "They all thought he was so sweet," says Fayard, adding, "It's lucky I did the right things."[57]

Harold idolized his older brother, trusting him and looking up to him. Awed by Fayard's innate sense of style and grace, he liked to copy Fayard's twirling hand movements, and he liked repeating the rhythms his brother made with his feet. He says his learning to dance was all because of Fayard: "All I did was to follow him," says Harold. "I followed him and tried to do what he asked me to do, what he wanted to teach me to do. When we grew up, I began to think for myself. But at the beginning, it was all him."[58] At age seven, Harold was not thinking about trying to learn to tap dance. While Fayard was in the front row seat of the Standard Theatre, sitting near the orchestra pit and studying all the dancers onstage, Harold was in the wings of theatre, copying the somersaults, cartwheels, and flips that the stage manager was showing him to keep him quiet.

If Fayard fancied putting together a tap routine with his little brother, at first it was not possible because Harold was a lefty, and everything he did was only with the left foot. Only after months of playing at tap dancing with Fayard did Harold experience a breakthrough. "I was standing at the sink, drying dishes, and either some music was on or I was humming to myself," Harold remembers, "and all of a sudden, I started to do the time step on both feet. After I found out I could do that, I had no trouble learning to dance, learning to pick up the steps my brother taught me. I picked it up just like that! He'd teach me a step and bam! I'd have it in a minute. . . . We'd put together a routine very fast."[59]

The story goes that late one evening, when Viola and Ulysses returned from working at the Standard Theatre, the lights were on in the living room. They were greeted excitedly by their sons, who asked them to sit down on the sofa, then proceeded to perform a tap dance routine that they had put together without musical accompaniment. Viola was completely surprised, and Ulysses, who was obviously impressed, said, "It looks like we've got something here!" Around the same time, in 1931, a producer from the *Horn and Hardart Kiddie Hour* radio show, who was scouting talent in Philadelphia, saw Fayard in a school play and invited him to perform on the show. "What do I do on a radio show? I'm a tap dancer," Fayard asked the producer, who told him he could tap and could also sing and tell jokes. Fayard told the man about his little brother. "Bring him on too," the producer said. "That was the first time we danced on the radio," says Fayard, who bought his first pair of tap shoes for the occasion. "We couldn't do any splits because no one could see that. But they could hear those taps. It was the first time we performed for the public."[60]

Ulysses always wanted his sons to follow a strictly professional career. His boys would not be entered in the Tap Dance Contest held at the Standard Theatre every Friday night. Nor would his boys perform for Amateur Night held at the Standard each Wednesday. Instead, Ulysses arranged for an audition for his sons with J. T. Gibson. Viola arranged the music for the audition and accompanied her sons. "He [Gibson] asked us to go onstage and we did a little softshoe for him," Fayard remembers, "and soon after the first number, he said 'That's fine. We'll book you here next week.' We wanted to show him more of our routine, but he told us not to bother, that if the rest of the routine was like the first we'd be great."[61]

The date of the Nicholas Kids' debut at the Standard Theatre is not certain; there are no Standard programs, and the Nicholas

Kids were never announced as an attraction in the Standard's weekly advertisements in the *Philadelphia Tribune*. "We just appeared," says Fayard. "Nobody knew who we were, but after we performed everyone knew who we were." It is likely, however, that one of the first performances of the Nicholas Kids was the week of February 18, 1929, when the Standard offered "The Season's Most Delightful Bill—A Hodgepodge of Jazz, Comedy, Dancing" with "The Best Artists Obtainable."[62]

Within months of that date, the Nicholas Kids were performing in such Philadelphia theatres as the Earle and Pearl, where a one-week engagement was extended to three. And within a year of their debut at the Standard, they were performing in theatres in Baltimore and Washington, D.C. The week of November 2, 1931, Philadelphia's Royal Theatre (South Street at Fifteenth) announced: "On Stage—Flash Dancers of the Age—2 Nicholas Kids."[63] Dorothy remembers that the Kids were an immediate hit with audiences. They were youngsters with a fresh-faced charm, innocent yet optimistic, openly sharing their rhythm dance with each other on the stage. And no matter where they were placed on the program, they always drew tumultuous applause. "People said we looked like kids," says Fayard, "but we danced like men."[64]

In the fall of 1931, the Nicholas Kids were performing at Philadelphia's Pearl Theatre, and the tap-dancing contortionist Jigsaw Jackson was topping the bill. He was expected to receive the most applause, but the Nicholas Kids were "stopping the show"—meaning that the audience clapped so hard and long that the brothers had to return to the stage for an encore, momentarily halting the proceedings and making it difficult for any act to follow. "He killed the people, they loved him," says Fayard about Jigsaw, "but we stopped it more than he did. We killed them."[65] He says that the star came to the brothers' dressing room after the show and told them that they were sensational, that the people loved them. He also told them that he had informed the management that the Nicholas Kids were going to close the show.

Jack Schiffman, the manager of New York's Lafayette Theatre, was in Philadelphia scouting for talent the week the Nicholas Kids were stopping the show at the Pearl. He knocked on the dressing room door after a show, introduced himself to Fayard and Harold, and talked to Ulysses and Viola about letting their sons audition in New York for a job at the Lafayette Theatre. New York had it all for the Nicholases. It was the center of American arts, publishing, music, and theatre and had a large and growing black population, with a long history of black performance. Ulysses and Viola then faced the most crucial decision of their lives, whether to continue their own musical careers as pit musicians at the Standard Theatre or to abandon their plans entirely to properly and efficiently manage Fayard and Harold's growing career. They chose the latter. In December 1931, the Nicholases began preparations to move from Philadelphia to New York City. It was a move they would never regret.

Viola Nicholas and her sons in New York in the early thirties (Billy Rose Theatre Collection, The New York Public Library for the Performing Arts, Astor, Lenox, and Tilden Foundations).

Three

Blackbirds in New York

1932–1934

Pie, Pie, Blackbird (1932), the Vitaphone short subject film featuring Eubie Blake and his jazz orchestra, captures the tap dancing of Fayard and Harold Nicholas when they first arrived in New York in the early thirties. We first see the young brothers peering over the shoulders of a bakerwoman (played by the singer Nina Mae McKinney) in a country kitchen and asking her what she is baking. "Why, that's a blackbird pie," she tells them. "A blackbird pie!" the boys exclaim. "There's no such thing as a blackbird pie," remarks Fayard with skepticism. But she assures them, "It takes a blackbird to make the sweetest sort of pie."

The camera cuts to a closeup of the blackbird pie as it begins to peel open, slice by slice. And out of the pie rise Eubie Blake and the thirteen members of his jazz orchestra, whose instruments include bass, drums, clarinets, trombones, trumpets, saxophones, and two pianos. All the musicians, including Blake seated at the piano, are wearing white pastry-chef hats and jackets. They proceed to "cook" on their instruments, first by playing a "sweet," or melodious, rendition of Blake's "Memories of You," then "hotting" it up by increasing the tempo and adding in expressive

Nina Mae McKinney and Fayard and Harold Nicholas in the opening scene of Pie, Pie Blackbird, Vitaphone 1932 (Harold Nicholas Archive).

growls and whinnies from the brass instruments. McKinney is transported from her sunny country kitchen to a steamy, dimly lit nightclub. Sitting on top of Blake's piano, she sings "Everything I've Got Belongs to You," whining "Ah didn't do no lovin' on no partime plan," with sweet melancholy, and scat-singing one of the choruses in the growling vocal style of Louis Armstrong. Standing at the piano, Blake next sings "I'll Be Glad When You're Dead, You Rascal You," in which he keeps time for the band by swinging a baton with one hand while dancing a sprightly time step.

Then Fayard and Harold enter, on the introduction to "China Boy," a medium-tempo softshoe played in bouncing 4/4 time. Strolling side by side, and in perfect step with each other, they too are wearing white jackets and pastry-chef hats. The first six bars of

their long-striding Walkaround steps move them along the perime-
ter of the giant blackbird pie, and the last two-bar break settles them
in front of the bandstand, where they begin to "cook" with their tap
shoes. Fayard takes the first half of the chorus, leaning forward
into a tap Charleston, in which he alternately crosses and swings
one leg in front of and behind the other. He then varies the step
with a turn and repeats it in double time, breaking with a shuffle-
and-hop onto the tips of his hard-soled shoes. "Perching," or balancing, on the very tips of his toes, he passes the dance to Harold,
who picks it up without missing a beat.

Dancing upright, with close-to-the-floor paddle-and-rolls,
Harold repeats Fayard's Charleston tap, but he adds side-brushing
wings, which take him higher off the ground. He then tilts his
body into a forward diagonal, stroking his legs forward and back
in "Pulling Trenches," and ends by perching on the tips of his toes,
passing the dance back to his brother. Fayard watches Harold
dance and responds to his brother's grunts and squeals of delight
by snapping his fingers and bobbing his head. When he picks
up the dance, it is with a rhythmically elaborate combination of
Charleston steps, crossovers, paddle-and-rolls, and perches; he
then repeats the whole of it in double time. Hunched over his center, arms swinging like a pendulum, Fayard's focus is on his feet
and on the roller coaster of offbeat rhythms he's drumming into
the floor. He tops off his solo with ten sets of one-legged wings,
one leg hopping while the other brushes sideways in circular
motion, that make him look as if he's flying. He finishes the section
with a down-and-up split, with no hands assisting in the recovery,
that fits neatly into the last four beats of the bar.

Harold repeats all of Fayard's steps and variations, but he tilts
his body forward, into a forty-five degree angle to the floor. Hovering over the floor like a hummingbird, he quickens the dance to
such speed that his legs become a blur of fluttering motion. When
Fayard joins Harold in the last chorus, the incinerating rhythms
of their time steps, crossovers, and wings are apparently so "hot"
that they start to burn up the floor. The blackbird pie containing
the musicians and dancers suddenly becomes enveloped in smoke
and then bursts into flame. Through the fire and smoke, and the

whoops and hollers of the musicians, who continue to "cook" on their instruments even as they go up in smoke, Fayard and Harold continue tapping. All that is left of them, in the very last image of the film, is a pair of rattling, tap-dancing skeletons.

Pie, Pie, Blackbird summarized the past and predicted the future of the Nicholas Brothers' tap dancing. The choreography was a distillation of all they had absorbed from listening to jazz and watching jazz dancers. Many of the tap dance steps used in their routine—from the Charleston and splits to the time steps, trench steps, paddle-and-rolls, buck-and-wings, and walkaround—comprised the standard tap vocabulary that dancers had been performing on black vaudeville stages for two decades.

One was buck dancing. Among the oldest styles of percussive stepping, dating back to the plantation days, buck dancing is a flat-footed stepping style in which the whole foot works close to the ground, with shuffling, slipping, and sliding steps and with movement mostly from the hips down. This flat-footed shuffle was captured in a snippet of early film entitled *Child Dancing on a Barge* (1893); it was also demonstrated by the eighty-nine-year-old Horace Sprott in *Buck Dance*, a short 1950s film.[1] Jazz dance historian Marshall Stearns said that buck dancing was a basic blend of the shuffle and tap, and from it developed the time step and the paddle-and-roll, which "King" Rastus Brown is said to have perfected for his famous "Buck Dancer's Lament," which consisted of six bars of the time step plus a two-bar, improvised stop-time break.[2] This flat-footed style of tapping, which is deeply rooted in African *gioube*-stepping traditions, also exists in Fayard and Harold's time steps, especially in Harold's close-to-the-floor paddle-and-roll steps, which use the whole foot to sound out rhythms.

In many instances, however, the brothers lift up onto the balls of their feet and sweep themselves up into the air. The side-brushing, circular sweep of their one-legged wing steps certainly makes them appear to be lighter than old-time "hoofers" from the paddle-and-roll school. The body alignment of the tap dancer in the 1920s was upright and vertical, a posture probably influenced by the Irish jig; it was idealized by Bill "Bojangles" Robinson in his famous stair dance of the teens and twenties, which is captured on *Harlem Is Heaven* (1932), and by the minstrel stage veteran James Barton, whose eccentric legomania dancing was captured in the film *After Seben* (1929).[3]

While Fayard and Harold are upright and vertical in *Pie, Pie, Blackbird*, when they dance the "China Boy" number, they often tilt their bodies forward in their Charleston and trench steps, creating a diagonal line from the top of the head to the tip of the toes. They are also constantly shifting back and forth from the vertical to a slanted diagonal, and the shifting angles create an exciting sense of motion. Buck dancers basically danced in one place onstage, and this was true of many tap dancers in the twenties. Even though the Nicholases are restricted to dancing before a fixed camera in *Pie, Pie, Blackbird*, their circling arms, side-brushing wings, and back-stroking trench steps show them using more areas of space around the body, which adds three-dimensionality to an otherwise flat, presentational performance. While the brothers drew from the traditional lexicon of tap dance and black vernacular sources of movement, their choreography for the "China Boy" number demonstrated a presentation of traditional steps that was quite unusual for the early thirties.

The structure of the tap dance in "China Boy" followed that of the music, which began with an eight-bar introduction in 4/4 time; one chorus containing four sections of music (AABA) followed, each containing thirty-two bars. Rhythmically, there were two ways in which late twenties tap dancers phrased each of the musical sections. The first was to dance to a clean six bars of music, followed by a two-bar rhythm break, which was the traditional form of the time step. This musical structuring of the rhythmic phrasing was best demonstrated in a solo routine by Bill Robinson, as captured in the short subject film *Queen for a Day* (1934).

The second method of musical phrasing was to extend the rhythmic pattern of the phrases beyond the "normal" eight bars of music; this prolonging of the rhythmic line of the taps into a more irregular construction was best demonstrated by John Bubbles in

Varsity Show (1937). In *Pie, Pie, Blackbird,* most of the danced solos are contained within a musical (AABA) section. In only a few instances does Fayard extend beyond the eight bars of music to continue into the next section. This relatively strict framing of musical sections is blurred, however, when his taps play double and triple time against the steady beat of the music in 4/4 time. The speed and rhythmic complexity seen in the Nicholases' syncopated breaks, however, are extremely exciting as danced against the musical beat. This also effects an irregular musical structure for the breaks.

The Nicholas Brothers structured a series of solos for their "China Boy" number, which took the form of a challenge dance; one dancer presents a rhythm or step, and the other dancer repeats and alters it, often making it more complex. Unlike the traditional tap challenge, however, which took the form of a contest or showdown between dancers that was fiercely competitive, the Nicholases' more effusive rhythmic exchange is not confrontational. Fayard claps time for Harold, who in turn responds to Fayard's dancing with affectionate little grunts and squeals. The brothers use the call-and-response mode of the challenge not as a competitive device to drive the dance forward but as their structure for rhythmically developing the "theme" of the tap Charleston and all its variations. The sense of forward drive that is achieved in the traditional challenge dance, as one dancer presents a step that the other betters, is translated by the brothers into a rhythm-driving tapping that has a strong swinging feel. The forward-moving propulsion of their rhythm-driven conversation is extremely musical; it bears a striking similarity to jazz drumming, as the early black dance film historian Ernie Smith confirmed when he commented that the Nicholases "sound like a jazz swing drummer" in "China Boy."[4]

The quality of jazz swing that can be heard and seen in "China Boy" is best demonstrated in Fayard's tap Charleston variations. A syncopated two-step with the accent on the offbeat, the Charleston's basic step was a swinging of the leg, which gave a relaxed and ebullient style of execution to the dance and gave the impression, like the music, of the beat moving relentlessly ahead.[5]

In his Charleston variations, Fayard's legs appear to "fly" in syncopated rhythms, while his body "holds" the fine line of balance, in calm contrast to the headlong rush of the feet. Like the Savoy Ballroom dancers, who infused more of the Charleston swing into their lindy-hopping, there is a rhythmically swinging feel in many sections of "China Boy." Harold's forward-leaning trenches, in the first chorus, whip the four beat into a frenzy of rolling sounds; in the last section, the alternation of lean and vertical time steps with lateral-circling wing steps transforms the dancers' bodies into syncopated swirls of motion.

While Fayard and Harold continued to draw on traditional sources of black vernacular dance, their jazz choreography in "China Boy" suggests that they were moving into a more streamlined style distinguished by lightness, speed, angularity, and swinging rhythms. Their arrival in New York coincided with an extremely rich and stimulating period for jazz, and one that would propel them to explore more "modern" and swinging forms of rhythm dancing.

The Nicholases moved to New York in December 1931. The tap dancer Jennie LeGon remembered that she met the entire Nicholas family on a bus en route from Philadelphia to New York.[6] When the family arrived in New York, they promptly settled into an apartment at 321 Edgecombe Avenue, in the Sugar Hill section of Harlem. Sugar Hill was Harlem's smartest residential area, sloping northward from roughly 145th Street to 165th Street, between Amsterdam Avenue to the west and Edgecombe Avenue to the east. It was home to well-to-do blacks and celebrities of all sorts, from the moneyed and talented to the socially prominent and intellectually distinguished. Ralph Ellison, Paul Robeson, Abbie Mitchell, Billy Strayhorn, Luckey Roberts, Teddy Wilson, and Duke Ellington all lived on Sugar Hill in the thirties, as did W.E.B. Du Bois, Roy Wilkins, Walter White, and Jules Bledsoe. Lined with handsome brownstone houses and expensive apartments, Sugar Hill looked out over the Valley, as central Harlem was called, which contained the neighborhood's churches, shops, restaurants, business places, bookstores, art studios, social clubs, and dance halls. Sugar Hill also provided a wide-angle view of the Harlem theatres and clubs.[7] The two-bedroom, ground-floor apartment at 321 Edgecombe became the Nicholases' new artistic home base. Its large carpeted living room was a family center, where the boys played and the family entertained, and a rehearsal space for the brothers. Viola's piano had a prominent place in the room.

When the Nicholases moved to New York, the country was in the depths of the Great Depression. Business losses across the country had risen to six billion dollars; unemployment had reached thirteen million; national wages were 60 percent less and dividends 5.6 percent less than they had been in 1929. Five thousand banks had failed; thirty-two thousand businesses went bankrupt. The deteriorating economic conditions and dwindling patronage had forced many entertainment establishments to close. Opera houses in Chicago and Philadelphia gave no performances in 1932. On Broadway, there were few hits. "Times were dismal," writes theatre historian Gerald Bordman about the nadir of the Depression. Many of the the best talents on Broadway, if they had not already left for Hollywood, were imprisoned by idleness, and bankruptcy loomed for the likes of Florenz Ziegfeld, Arthur Hammerstein, Charles Dillingham, and the Shubert brothers.[8]

If the country was being strangled by the Depression, Harlem at the time had become a thriving black metropolis wherein an artistic and cultural renaissance had been flowering for more than a decade. "So here we have Harlem, not merely a colony or a community or a settlement—not at all a 'quarter' or a slum or a fringe—but a black city," wrote James Weldon Johnson in *Black Manhattan*, published in 1930. "Located in the heart of white Manhattan, and containing more Negroes to the square mile than any other spot on earth, it strikes the uninformed observer as a phenomenon, a miracle straight out of the skies."[9] After two decades of black migration from the American South and from the West Indies, Harlem by the early thirties had become the perfect community for gathering blacks of the most diverse backgrounds and interests. It had emerged as the social and cultural center of black America. Black cultural expression was flourishing in the Harlem of the thirties, as the "New Negro" artists continued to look to validate the folk, or vernacular, sources, finding new performance venues for their work.

"Occasionally, someone is heard to croon hoarsely that the Negro 'Renaissance' that was launched so bravely in 1926–27 has not continued its voyage on the seas of art," Carl Van Vechten wrote in the *Challenge* in 1934. "On the contrary, I feel the Negro of today to be on a much more solid basis as an artist and as a social individual that he was then." He cited the recent publications of James Weldon Johnson's *Along This Way*, Zora Neale Hurston's *Jonah's Gourd Vine*, and Langston Hughes's *The Ways of White Folks* and the success of Ethel Waters in the Broadway show *As Thousands Cheer* and the national tour of *The Green Pastures* as "much more REAL SOLID evidence of a 'Negro Renaissance,'"[10] because of the added respect and recognition these works brought to black Americans.

Houston Baker, discussing the emergence of a "black modernism" in Harlem in the thirties, concurred with Van Vecten when he wrote: "One of the most obvious culling of fruits occurs in the 1930s and situates itself in accord with the deformative possibilities inherent in the New Negro's validation of the folk, or vernacular."[11]

Just as black writers, such as Hurston and Hughes, continued to create fictional works that were descriptive of the world in which their people lived, so too did jazz artists continue to join together to reflect on and experiment with their musical roots and rhythmic heritage. Jazz historian Gunther Schuller has written that in the early thirties, "true black jazz was bursting at the seams with creativity and new discoveries, especially in New York."[12]

Jazz, after moving up the Mississippi River from New Orleans to Kansas City to Chicago, and settling there for a time in the 1920s, had moved on in the late twenties to New York, which soon became the hot spot. In New York's theatres and ballrooms, big-band jazz orchestras were developed to play a swinging new style of music that drew performers to its stages and social dancers to its dance floors. Bigger bands had become the growing force behind the jazz of the early twenties. From the three to five performers of early jazz to the five to seven of Chicago jazz, the number of players grew to thirteen, thirty, even seventy in a full jazz orchestra—and with the larger numbers came a larger, more managed swing. A new musical sound with a pulsing, unaccented 4/4 time had began to emerge in the early thirties.

In 1932, Duke Ellington's "It Don't Mean a Thing if It Ain't Got That Swing" (Ellington and Mills, 1929), with its forward-pushing beat, could be felt in the elliptical refrain of "Doo-wah doo-wah, doo-wah doo-wah, doo-wah doo-wah, doo-wah doo-wah" that gave the new sound a name. The bandleaders and orchestra leaders of the biggest and best black groups, such as Duke Ellington, Fletcher Henderson, Cab Calloway, Chick Webb, and Jimmy Lunceford, were the developers of the new music that would be called swing.

The notable difference between swing and the earlier jazz forms was a new emphasis on steady and unaccented rhythm sections with harmonious forward propulsion that a jazz player, singer, or band section imparted to each note through the timed manipulation of timbre, attack, vibrato, and intonation. These features gave the music an infectious quality that made dancing to it inevitable. Lindy-hoppers at the Savoy Ballroom delighted in devising furious steps to the music played by big swing bands, and Harlem theatres like the Lafayette, the Harlem Opera House, and the Apollo swelled with the sound, becoming the main theatrical outlets for swing jazz in the early thirties.[13]

The Nicholas Kids made their New York debut in March 1932 at Harlem's Lafayette Theatre, which prided itself on being "America's Leading Colored Theatre Presenting the Finest Stage and Screen Shows." The Lafayette was then Harlem's biggest theatre; the Harlem Opera House and the Apollo Theatre opened later in the thirties. All of the best bands in New York—those led by Sam Wooding, Fletcher Henderson, Earl Hines, Duke Ellington and Cab Calloway, for example—played the Lafayette Theatre in the early thirties.[14] For the black musical artist in New York, the Lafayette was the first and most important stepping-stone to a successful career. "You had to work your way up from the TOBA circuit . . . to Washington," Leonard Reed explained.

"Then you'd go to Philadelphia . . . and when you got to New York you passed through the Hoofers Club on your way to the Lafayette. When I first played the Lafayette, one of the Four Step Brothers was a candy boy, and Fats Waller played organ during intermission."[15]

The week of March 12, 1932, the Nicholas Kids opened at the Lafayette with Eubie Blake "And His Great Band,"[16] making $500 a week in a "Glorious Musical Comedy Revue" that headlined Clarence Hughes and included the 4 Pepper Shakers, Scott and Brown, Straine and McCoy, Sam Paige, B'Way Jones, "Crackshot," the 4 Co-Eds, and Charlie Ray. Viola Nicholas remembered that everywhere in Harlem, prior to the Lafayette opening, there were signs, and that "one signboard was about twenty-five feet tall, and their names [Nicholas Kids] were at the top."[17]

Fayard remembers that he and Harold wore identical three-piece tailored suits for the performance, which Ulysses had had made especially for the stage. Little is remembered, however, about the dancing—only that their number was modeled after the three-part routine they had already rehearsed and performed at the Standard, the Pearl, and the Earl theatres in Philadelphia. It opened with a softshoe in medium tempo, moved into a challenge dance, and closed with an up-tempo dance to "Bugle Call Rag," in which they showed off with flips, splits, and an assortment of acrobatic moves.

While little is known about the content of the act, the audience response has never been forgotten. As the headliner, Clarence Hughes always closed the show. "He was the star of the show," Fayard says, "but we were the show stoppers. And so we closed the show, and he didn't mind."[18] The Nicholas Kids were such a hit with the crowd that by the end of the first week the Lafayette management booked the brothers for another week in April.

A producer from Warner Brothers who saw them perform at the Lafayette came backstage after the show one afternoon to speak to Ulysses and Viola about an all-black musical short film that Vitaphone, a division of Warner Brothers, was making with Eubie Blake and his band. It is quite probable that Blake, after working with the brothers at the Lafayette, brought the

Nicholases to the attention of the producers, who signed them to the project. Filmed in the Vitaphone Studios (formerly Vitagraph) on Avenue A in Brooklyn during the winter of 1932, the film, *Pie, Pie, Blackbird*, premiered at the Regent Theatre in Harlem (the city's first movie palace) on June 29, 1932, and enjoyed a tremendous success with audiences. This "black short" and others of the period represented a new avenue of aspiration for Negro performers, as they brought the best in African-American vaudeville, vernacular dancing, and the more commercial forms of jazz to film.[19]

The Harlem Renaissance had lured an abundance of black performers to New York. In October 1929, *Variety* had counted 300 female and 150 male dancers continuously employed in Harlem's class white-trade nightclubs, with "hundreds more ready for an audition at any time."[20] The black short films soon afforded even more work to black musicians and dancers, despite the encroaching Depression. Although their budgets were low, these films by white directors were well made and suffused with a black ambience, because the loosely scripted vignettes depended on varying degrees of improvisation rather than on narrative or scoring. If some of these shorts still featured "antebellum crooning darkies" who perpetuated southern stereotypes, the new urbane black musical tradition ran parallel to the older images.

Like such black musical short films as *St. Louis Blues* (RKO, 1929), *Barbershop Blues* (1932), and *A Rhapsody in Black and Blue* (1932), Vitaphone's 1932 *Pie, Pie, Blackbird* offered black musicians an opportunity to gain wider popularity for themselves and their music, which was beginning to swell beyond the limits of the record companies' so-called race catalog.[21] Eubie Blake (who with Noble Sissle had written the Broadway musical hit *Shuffle Along* ten years earlier) was a renowned musician in the early thirties, but the film widened the popularity of his trademark song, "Memories of You," and allowed him full range beyond "Everything I've Got Belongs to You," a Tin Pan Alley song he "jazzed up" with speed and syncopation. A number in the film, "I'll Be Glad When You're Dead, You Rascal You," had Blake shouting to his musicians, who answered back, and he danced time steps during instrumental choruses, demonstrating the spontaneous and improvisational quality of his musicianship.

Pie, Pie, Blackbird is also one of the earliest films to document the jazz tap dancing of black artists. The footage of the Nicholas Brothers, for example, shot from one stationary camera, shows their full-bodied tap dancing. Their feet were clearly visible, and the rhythms and sounds of their taps, which were recorded during the filming of the scene, were clearly audible.[22] Though they played the roles of a pair of southern country boys, their characters were not black stereotypes, and the film was devoid of blackface humor. The film's movement of McKinney and the Nicholases from a country setting to an urban nightclub setting may be seen as a metaphor for the "sophistication" of jazz as it was transplanted from New Orleans and the South to New York. The surrealistic final scene has the dancers and musicians burn up, conjuring up racist-fueled images of tambo-and-bones minstrels and lynchings. Yet the "cooked-up" rhythms can also be taken as a witty reference to the flammability of "hot" jazz rhythms. The final image of the brothers, perched on the tops of their toes with arms outspread and looking like a pair of blackbirds in flight, endures long after the whoops and hollers of the musicians all going up in smoke—and longer still after the closing credits.

While theatres offering both live shows and films continued to provide venues for black jazz artists in the thirties, the cafés and clubs in Harlem were nurturing black performers who were to achieve undreamed-of fame. In 1932, in the *New York Amsterdam News*, Lee (Harlemania) Posner observed that Harlem had become a heaven for Negro artists who aspired to be the musical comedy stars of tomorrow: "They sing and dance and play for thrill-seeking whites, whites brings their friends, the place becomes the rage and the particular artist is soon approached by an enterprising [white] producer who sees box office value."[23]

The Cotton Club in particular was hailed as the "alma mater of stage and radio stars." The Nicholases had heard all about the place. After their opening at the Lafayette, agents from all over New York came backstage to sign the brothers, but Ulysses, always the prudent businessman, held them off. He had been advised that the Cotton Club was the best bet. The Nicholas Kids returned to the Lafayette Theatre the week of April 23, 1932, for a show headed by Baron Lee and the Mills Blue Rhythm Band.[24] The band was managed by Irving Mills, manager and collaborator of Duke Ellington, who was then playing the Cotton Club with his orchestra.

It is possible that Mills saw the Nicholas Kids at the Lafayette and brought them to Ellington's attention. Several weeks after the Lafayette engagement, and while Ulysses was in negotiation with the manager of Connie's Inn, Ulysses received a phone call from Herman Stark, manager of the Cotton Club, asking Fayard and Harold to audition for the upcoming Cotton Club Parade. "We got in just about the time they were going into rehearsal for the new show," Viola Nicholas remembered about the Cotton Club. "Stark invited us down and he wined and dined us—of course we didn't drink. And Connie invited us to his place. Each of them was bargaining."[25]

An audition at the Cotton Club was arranged by Stark. When Fayard and Harold arrived, escorted by Ulysses and Viola, Stark introduced them to the African-American choreographer Clarence Robinson, the songwriting team of Harold Arlen and Ted Koehler, and the Cotton Club Girls. Duke Ellington sat at a table with Cab Calloway. Viola handed the musical arrangement for the routine to the rehearsal pianist, then sat down with the others. "We started dancing," remembers Fayard, and with no interruptions, the brothers went through their entire routine. When they finished, Ellington reportedly leaned in toward the others and said, "That was wonderful. They are original." Fayard replied, "Thank you, Mr. Ellington, you are original too!" Everyone laughed, charmed by the teenager's ingenuous remark. "And that did it," says Fayard. "Herman Stark said he was was going to book us."[26]

Stark offered $750 a week, $250 more than Connie's Inn. The Nicholases accepted, and the brothers were immediately installed into rehearsals at the Cotton Club.

The Nicholas Brothers made their debut at the Cotton Club at midnight on October 23, 1932. When Cab Calloway's orchestra opened the twenty-first edition of the Cotton Club Parade with "Let's Put on the Ritz," Harold and Fayard, at ages eleven and eighteen, found themselves in a world where long-legged women shimmied in feathered gowns and men in tuxedos and patent-leather shoes strutted and snapped to the pervasive, insistent rhythms of jazz. The Harlem nightclub served up hot "jungle" music with cool sophistication. The floor shows mixed stateliness with wild abandon, the whole of it having "a primitive naked quality that was supposed to make a civilized audience lose its inhibitions."27

The Cotton Club became home base for the Nicholases in the thirties. It was the "Aristocrat of Harlem," the classy spot on Lenox Avenue and 142nd Street where impeccable behavior was demanded of its clientele. "If someone was talking loud during a show, the waiter would come and touch him on the shoulder,"

Program of the twenty-first edition of the Cotton Club Parade, which opened at the uptown Cotton Club on October 23, 1932 (Harold Nicholas Archive).

Duke Ellington recalled. "If that didn't do it, the captain would come over and admonish him politely and the headwaiter would remind him that he had been cautioned; and if the loud talker continued, somebody would come and throw him out."[28] As the "hangout for the Mink Set, escaping Park Avenue for the earthier realities of Harlem,"[29] the club was frequented by such notables as Lady Mountbatten (wife of the English nobleman who later became First Lord of the Admiralty), the financier Otto Kahn, and Mayor Jimmy Walker.

All the big New York stars, no matter where they were playing, showed up for the midnight performance. After the show, master of ceremonies Dan Healy introduced the celebrities in the audience, who would take a turn: Irene Bordoni sang Cole Porter's "Let's Do It," Tony and Renee DeMarco danced a maxixe (a Brazilian ballroom dance), Walter Winchell showed off with a buck-and-wing, and George Raft trotted to "Sweet Georgia Brown"; and when the singer Sophie Tucker made her way up the floor for a bow, the orchestra stood up in grand style, playing her famous song, "Some of These Days."

Opening nights at the Cotton Club were as exciting and important as any on Broadway. The newspapers sent their top columnists, celebrities studded the audience, and the club was filled to capacity. While in the house the white "elite of society hobnobbed with the elite of the worlds of sports, literature and the arts, and even mobsters and politicians,"[30] onstage all the performers were black. At the Cotton Club, the shows were strictly segregated. No white acts were allowed to perform on the Cotton Club stage, and no blacks were allowed to sit in the audience and watch the shows. Ulysses and Viola Nicholas either observed their sons from the wings or stood in the back by the swinging kitchen doors.

The club first opened in 1926 as the Club DeLuxe, then was sold by the former heavyweight boxing champion Jack Johnson in 1929 to a syndicate led by Owny Madden, who was looking for a suitable entertainment spot for white downtowners, which would also serve as the principal East Coast outlet for "Madden's No. 1" beer.[31] The new management's whites-only customer policy was maintained because of the belief that most white downtowners wanted to *observe* Harlem blacks, not mix with them. Jimmie Durante explained that it wasn't necessary to mix with colored people if you didn't feel like it: "You have your own party and keep to yourself. Nobody wants razors, blackjacks, or fists flying. The chances of a war are less if there's no mixing."[32]

Despite the strict rules of segregation, the Cotton Club was the most prestigious showcase for black musical talent in New York. Duke Ellington rose to national and international fame after he opened there in 1929, largely because his Cotton Club shows were broadcast live by radio, and people across the country could tune in nightly to network affiliate stations to listen to one of the hottest bands on the air. "Some of the proudest Negro musicians in the world played there and adhered to that policy of racial separation," Cab Calloway wrote about the Cotton Club. "The money was good, the shows were fine, and the audiences and the owners respected us for our music. . . . I doubt that jazz would have survived if musicians hadn't gone along with such racial practices there and elsewhere."[33]

The twenty-first edition of the Cotton Club Parade, produced by Dan Healy, with music and lyrics by Harold Arlen and Ted Koehler, followed a formula of fast-paced scenes that centered around a musical number by a featured singer backed by a dancing chorus. Sandwiched between musical numbers were specialty acts by tap, ballroom, and shake dancers, and the whole show was driven by the energy and verve of a sixteen-piece orchestra. Act I opened with "Let's Put on the Ritz," sung by Henri Wessels and Aida Ward and danced by the Cotton Club Boys and Girls. In Scene 2, Leitha Hill sang "Deep Sea Divin' Papa," a shockingly outspoken song in the blues genre. In Scene 3, Ada Ward sang "I've Got the World on a String."

In Scene 4, Cab Calloway sang "Minnie the Moocher's Wedding Day," a specialty number composed for him by Arlen and Koehler. The song capitalized on the popularity of a song that Calloway had written and performed at the Cotton Club in 1931. "Now here's a story 'bout Minnie the Moocher, she was a low-down hoochy-coocher," it began; somewhere in the middle of it, one evening, Calloway claimed to forget the lyrics, so he began to improvise.

"Hi-de-hi-de-hi-de-ho," he sang, and the band answered "Hi-de-hi-de-hi-de-ho" back. He then sounded out the "wah-wahs" of the trumpets by scat-singing "Wah-de-doo-de-way-de-ho," and when the band sang "Wah-de-doo-de-way-de-ho" back, he hollered for the audience to join in. By the end of the song, Calloway was dancing and leading the band as the audience clapped hands, stomped feet, and sang, "Hi-de-hi-de-ho, hi-de-hi-de-hi-de-ho."[34]

The song, "Minnie the Moocher," featured a whole cast of mythical characters that populated an imaginary Harlem, including marijuana-smoking "vipers" and "reefer men." These "moaner" songs derived in type and musical style from the storytelling genre in blues songs, and they were set in minor keys, using slow, somber tempos.[35] Such songs were deeply rooted in African and African-American musical traditions of translating percussion patterns into vocal lines by assigning syllables to characteristic rhythms. Despite its distinctly black musical roots, "Minnie the Moocher" was an amusing lyric with a catchy tune that reached across vast racial and cultural dividing lines to the whites at the Cotton Club, who reveled in clapping to it and shouting back the lyrics.

It was on the wave of the high spirits from "Minnie the Moocher's Wedding Day," which extracted similar call-and-response "hi-de-hos" between Calloway and the audience, that the Nicholas Brothers were introduced, in the last scene of the first act. Dressed in tailcoats and top hats, they dashed out onto the dance floor and opened their act with a smooth softshoe, danced in medium tempo to Hoagy Carmichael's "Georgia on My Mind." The music then accelerated into a lively eight-bar introduction to "China Boy," as they launched into a challenge dance that began with Fayard's tap Charleston, developed by Harold's side-brushing wings and followed by their succession of traded solos. Their finale, danced to "Bugle Call Rag," W. C. Handy's classic composition of 1916 that opened with a high-pitched bugle solo, was an explosion of offbeat rhythms and alternating solos punctuated with superbly timed splits and surprising flips. It left the audience applauding wildly and calling the Nicholas Brothers—no longer the Nicholas Kids—back to the stage for an encore.

The Cotton Club debut had been a complete success. For the next six months, the brothers settled into a strenuous work schedule, performing two and sometimes three shows a night six nights a week. When they returned from the Cotton Club with Viola and Ulysses, at four or five o'clock in the morning, they went immediately to bed, sometimes sleeping until two or three o'clock in the afternoon. On rising, they ate breakfast and were schooled at home by a private tutor, who came every afternoon to the Sugar Hill apartment. They often went to the movies, seeing everything that came out. Harold was crazy about Flash Gordon, and the brothers loved the Western stars. They even created their own "home movies" (one was a Western, shot in Central Park; another was a mystery, "Murder on Sugar Hill"), which they filmed, directed, and starred in. In the late afternoon, they sometimes went back to bed until it was time to eat dinner. After they got up, showered and dressed, and ate, Ulysses and Viola drove them to the Cotton Club for the ten o'clock, midnight, and sometimes two A.M. shows. "We were so wrapped up in our act, we didn't get out and play," says Fayard. "All the kids liked to play baseball, football, and basketball. But our play was onstage."[36]

In whatever spare time was left, the brothers rehearsed in their living room, with Viola at the piano. "I listened to the music and made up the routine to fit," says Fayard. "We never counted it. I don't count, I would just hear the music and go. And that's the way Harold was too, he didn't count anything. I could sing a step to him, and whatever I sang, I did with my feet. I improvised until I found what steps to do. And then I'd teach them to my brother." After the steps were set and the combination sequenced, the brothers worked to synchronize their movements, which was no easy task. Fayard was nearly a foot taller than Harold, so they needed to compromise on the length of their strides and coordinate all the fine details of their gestures. "We worked," says Fayard, "until we got them as perfect as we could."[37]

While Viola sat at the piano, Ulysses watched his sons dance from his easy chair. He recognized the expressive way in which Fayard was using his hands, and he encouraged his son to be aware of them when he danced. Ulysses also recognized Harold's power to charm. So he helped balance Fayard's gracefulness with Harold's comic wit to create their dance performance, which was as pleasing to the eye as it was to the ear.

Perfection of step was mirrored by an impeccable style of dressing. Onstage, the Nicholas Brothers wore full formal dress—custom-made tuxedos, along with tailcoats in a variety of colors, with shoes to match.[38] Offstage, the brothers wore custom-made suits that Ulysses ordered from a tailor in New York almost every week. "They always made sure we were dressed sharp," says Fayard, and Harold remembers: "When we were walking down Lenox Avenue on a Sunday afternoon, everyone was saying how cute we were, dressed up in ties, double-breasted suits, pants with pleats in the back, so immaculate."[39]

As he peeked out into the audience between shows, seeing all the white performers and celebrities who frequented the Cotton Club, Harold slowly realized that he enjoyed performing. He began paying closer attention to what other singers and dancers were doing onstage. He stood in the wings during the shows and began memorizing everybody's routine. He studied the synchronized stepping of the Cotton Club Boys, memorized the words to every featured song, and scrutinized the famous "one-man exit" of Pete, Peaches, and Duke—in which they faced the audience, one man behind the other in precise single file, moving sideways with little tapping steps, looking like a man with three pairs of legs, as they disappeared into the wings.

Then Harold set his eyes on Cab Calloway, who was an irrepressible nightclub personality and a remarkable musical showman. He was witty, well groomed, and dressed dramatically in a white silk suit, which shivered and shook as he snaked back and forth across the stage, setting his struts, glides, dips, knee drops, grinds, and quivers into perpetual motion. He carried on a call-and-response with the band, simultaneously singing, dancing, and stroking out the tempos with his baton. He was also an unusual, broadly gifted singer and improvisational talent who had tremendous rapport with the audience and never sang a song the same way twice. Harold so admired Calloway that he began to imitate his singing, and it was not long before Calloway found a way to use it. At the end of the Nicholas Brothers' dance act one evening, Calloway asked the waiters to set a table under the microphone that hung from the ceiling. He called Harold onstage, lifted him onto the table below the microphone, and asked him to sing "Minnie the Moocher." Harold scatted the "hi-de-hi-de-ho's"; Calloway answered back. The audience loved it so much that he had Harold do it as an encore each night.

In 1933, Harold's masterful impressions of Calloway's singing style earned him a role in Max Fleisher's *Screen Songs* short *Stoop-nocracy* (Paramount), a cartoon with a live-action wraparound (including a "bouncing ball" singalong) and starring the comedians Stoopnagle and Bud. In the film, two reporters from the *Daily Blaze* newspaper are reviewing the newest "inventions" on the market, which include a violin without strings, round dice for people who play marbles, an ashtray with a fan, and fake rubber tonsils. One of the inventions is a Cab Calloway milk bottle, which, when sucked, makes a baby sing. A baby (Harold, dressed in a white baby gown and bonnet) is brought out for a demonstration. As soon as Harold sucks on the bottle, he begins to sing "Minnie the Moocher," with the same intonations and scatted phrasing as Calloway's version.[40]

Harold's singing of "Minnie the Moocher" with Calloway became an expected new feature at the Cotton Club, and it helped to push the Nicholas Brothers' dance specialty act closer to the end of the show. Not all of their material for the act was new. The dances that comprised "Dance Specialty" ("Georgia on My Mind," "China Boy," and "Bugle Call Rag") were basically the same routines that the Nicholas Kids had performed in Philadelphia, although subtle changes occurred each time the brothers performed them. As "professionals," the Nicholases were expected to repeat what had been rehearsed with the orchestra. Yet they were also jazz tap dancers, and jazz is, in very large part, an improvisatory art. The brothers achieved a high level of technical proficiency each night through their repetition of synchronous movement, but they also tried to make the dancing look effortless, as if it were tossed off on the spur of the moment. Their ability to laugh, joke, and sound out at each other furthered the impression of spontaneity.

On the surface, and to the eye of someone who may have seen the Nicholas Brothers several times at the Cotton Club, the routine fundamentally looked and sounded the same. But some subtle shifts in mood caused adjustments to be made to the music each time they performed with a live orchestra. In "China Boy," for example, the sequence of the solos in the challenge dance was set, but there was always the opportunity to improvise within the solo or to respond to each other's solo. While the dances were arrangements of popular jazz standards that Viola had meticulously made, specifying the number of choruses, the tempos, and the musical segues, there were always differences, however slight, in the manner in which the music was played.

Eubie Blake, for instance, played piano in a dominant ragtime style, with prominent "oom-pah" rhythms in the left hand and a syncopated interpretation of melody in the right, even though he introduced a compelling sense of swing and virtuoso improvised breaks into his performance.[41] Blake's "China Boy," as played in *Pie, Pie, Blackbird*, was rhythmically choppy. Although the brothers played their rhythms against Blake's stoutly fingered 4/4 beat by doubling and tripling the time, no strong sense of rhythmic propulsion existed for either the playing or the tap dancing. Yet there was an enormous rhythmic verve in Cab Calloway's band, given the bite, attack, and powerful juggernaut rhythm powered by Leroy Maxey's drums and Jimmy Smith's string bass.[42]

While no recordings were made of "China Boy" by Calloway and his group, the song must have been played for the Nicholases at the Cotton Club with a great swinging energy field, so characteristic of Calloway's organizations. Even though Calloway did not change the tempos as specified in Viola's arrangements, the energy of his players provided a special musical atmosphere. Surely it urged Fayard and Harold into an effusive execution of their routine.

When the twenty-second edition of the Cotton Club Parade opened on April 16, 1933, this time led by Duke Ellington and his orchestra, the Nicholases were exposed to another rich style of jazz musicianship, one that was distinguished by harmony and a "beautiful, jumping, swinging sound."[43] Ellington was a tall, handsome, almost shy-looking man. His hair was brushed straight back, and he had a thin mustache. He wore loose-fitting but suavely styled comfortable clothes, smiled often, and carried himself with an air of assurance that was embodied in his music. The Ellington orchestra had a texture of instrumental sounds, whose expressive powers had been derived from the polyphonic ensemble playing of New Orleans jazz musicians.

Drummer Sonny Greer was a showman who conjured up wildly "primitive" sounds of tribal warriors, man-eating tigers, and war dances on his tom-toms, snares, and kettle drums. He was an adept rhythm man and colorist who responded buoyantly and creatively to fellow musicians.[44] Otto Hardwich and Johnny Hodges played saxophone; Sam Nanton and Juan Tizol played trombone; and Arthur Whetsol, Freddie Jenkins, and Cootie Williams played trumpet, an aggregation of swinging, dissonant harmonies.

But these great musicians, alone or together, could do far more than create the notorious "jungle sounds" for which they were famous while playing at the Cotton Club. The entire brass section could suddenly rise and play an intricately beautiful chorus in unison. They were as adept at playing smooth dance tempos as the most sophisticated of modern New York swing orchestras. During the time Ellington worked at the Cotton Club (steadily from 1927 to 1931, and sporadically from 1931 to 1938), the need for background music for the constantly changing acts required him to investigate composition, rather than merely arranging. In his group he found imaginative musicians who helped him develop a number of distinct musical styles: swinging musical numbers for dancing; "jungle"-style production numbers for Cotton Club tableaux; "blue" or "mood" pieces; and the pop tunes, ballads, and special orchestral compositions.[45]

The twenty-second edition of the Cotton Club Parade, with Ellington and his orchestra, was composed of eighteen scenes, ranging from skits and dance specialties to comedy and songs. On opening night, "Cotton Club Cabin," the last scene in the first act, stopped the show with more than a dozen encores. In it, Ethel Waters sang "Stormy Weather" with George Dewey Washington, who sang responses to her choruses; they were joined by the Talbert Choir and a dancing chorus, which made for a smooth transition to the dance floor.

The Nicholas Brothers performed a new "Dance Specialty" for the twenty-second Parade, choreographed by Fayard to music arranged by Jimmy McHugh. Fayard remembers little about the act, and Harold recalls that "when the show changed, we would get almost the same idea but work it out a little differently." Harold's talent for doing impressions of famous personalities was again put to use in the "Bill Robinson Stomp," in which he captured Bojangles's whimsical style, which combined time steps, skating, and crossover steps, danced on the balls of the feet.

If there was any one style that left an indelible impression on the young Nicholases, it was Ellington's. The brothers did not perform to any of Ellington's compositions. "We'd never say to Ellington, 'Play "Sophisticated Ladies," we'll tap to that.' We'd never do that," says Fayard, who also provided their musical arrangements.[46]

Ellington was the musical artist the brothers most revered. Says Fayard: "He was my favorite. I used to hear his records on the radio, close my eyes and listen . . . the radio announcer didn't have to say it, but I knew it was Duke Ellington because he had a style all his own. He was a master, a genius, and I loved his music."[47] Fayard and Harold often listened to the music that Ellington had most recently composed, including "Mood Indigo," "Sophisticated Lady," "Echoes of the Jungle," and "It Don't Mean a Thing if It Ain't Got That Swing," as well as to such signature pieces as "Blue Tune," "Lazy Rhapsody," "The Mooche," "Double Check Stomp," and "East St. Louis Toodle-oo."[48] Not only did the Nicholases come to know all of Ellington's music, they began to share his musical aesthetic.

Ellington's jazz was not played with the raucous exuberance of a Cab Calloway, nor with the syncopated ragtime rhythms of a Eubie Blake. His orchestra's polyphonic playing of jazz, while suggesting disorder and confusion, also provided reassuring harmonic and rhythmic structures. The brothers, too, preferred to work with structured improvisatory solos that allowed for indi-

vidual expression. As an ensemble—if only of two—they synchronized their movement, harmonized their taps, and played
rhythms against each other to effect a textured blending of tones.
It is possible, furthermore, that the music of the Nicholases'
arrangements influenced Ellington, who recorded a lively stomp
version of "Bugle Call Rag" for the Paramount film *Bundle of
Blues* in May of 1933, a version rearranged from the original 1922
presentation by the New Orleans Rhythm Kings.[49]

Ellington's formal elegance and his fastidiousness in dress and
manner was also admired by the Nicholases, who emulated his
style. Fayard and Harold's outward show of elegance—their donning of tuxedos, or top hats and tails—was not a direct imitation
of Ellington, but it certainly was reinforced by the master's styl-
ishness and superb sense of cool. The Nicholas Brothers neither
feigned elegance nor played the role of urban sophisticates; they
were, after all, only eleven and eighteen years old when they came
to the Cotton Club. What they projected instead—and completely their own invention—was an attitude of precocious
sophistication, which completely charmed and disarmed fellow
musicians and audiences. And in the twenty-second Parade, this
was played to much advantage by Harold, in "Happy as the Day
Is Long," in which he sang and danced with the Cotton Club
Girls. The sight of Harold, barely four feet tall and dressed in a
tailcoat, surrounded by a chorus of glamorous women who were
all uniformly five-foot-six, must have both amused and given
pleasure to the audience. The number began with what was to
become a standard practice—Harold singing and tap dancing in
lavish musical numbers. Around him the Cotton Club Girls
would shimmy and grind, cross their long legs in the Susie-Q,
and sway their hips in the tack-Annie.

There is no visual record of Harold in the "Happy" number
with the Cotton Club Girls, but his performance in the nightclub
scene from the film *The Emperor Jones* (1933) presents a sterling
example of his precosity. In an early scene in the film, in a swanky
nightclub in Harlem, Harold performs a tap dance solo in which
he is backed by a chorus of women not unlike the "Tall, Tan and
Terrific" Cotton Club Girls. This is not the Cotton Club, and the

elegantly dressed guests sitting at tables arranged in tiers around the stage are all black. Yet the set, clearly modeled after the Cotton Club, seats the orchestra on a platform that spills out onto the dance floor. There, a chorus of six women, wearing spangled bathing suits with a flounce of feathers at the hips, strut and kick in line formation. When the line breaks up, the women pair off and stride toward each other, stopping to grind their hips.

We first see Harold flashing a smile and winking at the camera—almost in acknowledgment of the girls' pelvic thrusts. Then the camera cuts to a long shot of Harold doing a split. In the very next frame, with a baton in hand, he leads the orchestra in a swinging musical number to which the girls dance. As the dialogue in the scene starts, Harold joins the girls, who dance a time step in high-heeled shoes. In counterpoint, he taps out paddle-and-rolls, trenches, and wings.

In a publicity still from *The Emperor Jones*, which shows Paul Robeson seated at a table, along with other guests in the nightclub, Harold is onstage, standing in front of the chorus line of six women. He is wearing a tuxedo with white tie, a carnation pinned to his lapel; the women wear one-piece, spangled bathing suits that show off their long legs and blossoming bosoms. Standing tall, with his shoulders pulled back, but no taller than the level of the women's breasts, Harold looks unabashedly into the eye of the camera. His eyes are twinkling, his mouth is wide open, and he appears to be belting out a tune with a big smile on his face. His clean and boyish charm, which contrasts with the sexual maturity of the women, takes the edge off the sensual implications of the scene.

The photo presents an image of Harold as a "little man," small, cute, and innocent; therefore, the scene contains "safe" material. It must have been deemed safe, at any rate, by *Emperor Jones* director Dudley Murphy to have this little boy, who dressed and danced like a man, perform with six half-clothed women—just as it was deemed safe by the management of the Cotton Club to have Harold dance with the Cotton Club Girls.

The Cotton Club management, with its audience-segregation policy in the Depression-era thirties, also thought that it was safe for the two young brothers to go out into the audience between shows and mix with the white guests. Fayard and Harold, in fact, were the only performers given permission by Cotton Club manager Herman Stark to mingle with guests between shows. "We would go right out to the table, say hello and sit down," says Fayard. "And they'd say, 'What would you have?' and I'd say, 'We'd like to have some orange juice.' And we'd talk until it was time to do the next show." The actress Tallulah Bankhead invited the brothers to her table after a show. It was Harold's birthday, and Bankhead asked him whether he would like a picture of her or a new bicycle. Harold answered quickly that he preferred to have *both*. The next morning, a brand-new bicycle—as well as a blown-up picture of the famous actress—was delivered to the Nicholas apartment on Sugar Hill. "I drove that bike all over Harlem," Harold remembers.

The Cotton Club afforded the brothers privileges they did not find elsewhere in New York. It was, they discovered, one of the few places in New York where minors could work. "Once we worked downtown at the Paramount with Duke Ellington, doing five and six shows a day," Harold remembers. "After the first show in the morning, truant officers came backstage to see me, and told me I'm too young to be working, and said, 'Get your clothes and get out of here.' And they took me off the show because I was a minor." The rules differed at the Cotton Club: "I could work because my manager [Herman Stark] ran it, and he was one of the boys. So no one would come up there and tell them I couldn't work. Gangsters ran the Cotton Club," says Fayard. "I guess they were paying off the policemen so we could work there. But I never questioned it."[50]

Nor did the brothers overtly question the Club's whites-only policy. They were, however, quite aware of it. "I was aware of the discrimination policy, but I couldn't understand it," says Fayard. "Bill Robinson would come up there, and Ethel Waters and Jack Johnson, and they would sit them on the side. So I knew there was some kind of prejudice there. But I was so young, I couldn't do anything about it." As a boy growing up in Winston-Salem, Harold remembers not being aware of segregation because "most of the

time I was with my own—our own, you know . . . I didn't go down
into white neighborhoods that much." In Philadelphia in the twenties, the Nicholas children were enrolled in an integrated school,
and Fayard admits: "I didn't know much about prejudice in those
days—I knew it was there, but I erased it from my mind. My parents taught us right from wrong. They never told us about separation and all that. I just got along with everybody."[51]

With their arrival in New York came a searing awareness of the
color barrier, which was undoubtedly heightened at the Cotton
Club, where the great racial divide could be plainly seen. "Black
artists in the 20s and 30s had no options, they had to go along
with the policy," explained the jazz writer Dave Dexter. "If the
'nigger' decided to make his feelings known, destruction of a
career followed. Because the white man was in the driver's seat."[52]

If the brothers did not question the club's strict segregation of
the races, in fact, there were models for them in others who did.
While performing at the Cotton Club in 1933, Harold was cast in
The Emperor Jones. The film, starring Paul Robeson, was the most
revolutionary of its time because it projected an image of the
black man that had never been shown on the commercial screen:
that of a man of strength and dignity, with "brains and nerve," as
the character puts it,[53] and the pride to stand up to the white man
as an equal, if not a superior. When the film opened uptown in
Harlem at the Roosevelt Theatre, in the fall of 1933, it grossed
more than ten thousand dollars in the first week, when more than
two hundred thousand blacks packed the theatre, often with
standing-room-only crowds.

The film traced the evolution of a young black man, Brutus
Jones, from Pullman porter to self-proclaimed king of a
Caribbean island. It mined the deepest level of human character,
exploring the corrupting influences of power and the price it
exacted from those who yielded to it. The scenes of Robeson
confronting the white man and resisting him instilled in black
audiences a pride and dignity they yearned for but could not find
elsewhere on the screen. For Fayard and Harold, *The Emperor
Jones* struck a deep chord of recognition about the racial divide in
America. "I think my brother and I really started something that

was good, even though we were little kids, when we asked Herman Stark to go out and meet those stars [who came to the Cotton Club]," Fayard recollects, "because we could show them that black people had class."

The Nicholas Brothers were installed in the twenty-third Cotton Club Parade, which opened in the fall of 1933 with Cab Calloway and his orchestra. By the time Jimmy Lunceford and his orchestra replaced Calloway in March 1934, the Nicholas Brothers had added "Keep Tempo" (a number developed with Calloway) to their repertoire and were closing the show in a finale with the Cotton Club Girls. When the audience called for an encore and the orchestra played a Lunceford number, the audience insisted the brothers repeat their own number, and Lunceford had to oblige. In this the last show for which Harold Arlen wrote the music, Adelaide Hall sang "Ill Wind," which was an attempt to be a hit sequel to "Stormy Weather." But the talented beauty and former chorus dancer Lena Horne, singing "As Long As I Live" in a duet with dancer Avon Long, was the new rising star.

The stardom of the Nicholas Brothers had already begun to shine throughout Harlem. Harold remembers that he could go anywhere uptown and people would know he was Harold Nicholas from the Cotton Club: "I was too young to go into the Savoy Ballroom by myself, but I went anyway, to watch the lindy-hoppers and hear Count Basie's band having a battle royal with Duke Ellington's band. People liked us, enjoyed us. My Daddy used to buy a new car every six months or so—it wasn't new, it was a used car. And we had a chauffeur drive the car, and people were looking in this huge car going down Seventh Avenue. The car was so big, I could stand up in it and not touch the ceiling."54 The brothers were not destined to drive down Seventh Avenue for very much longer. In the fall of 1934, the comedy tap dance team of Cook and Brown (Charles "Cooky" Cook and Ernest Brown) was hired by the Cotton Club to replace the Nicholas Brothers, who, together with mother Viola and sister Dorothy, boarded the Super Chief for a cross-country train trip to California, where they would make their first Hollywood movie.

Harold dances and Fayard plays guitar in The Big Broadcast of 1936, *Paramount 1935 (Museum of Modern Art).*

Four

All-Colored Comedy

1934–1936

In a scene from *Kid Millions*, the first Hollywood film made by the Nicholas Brothers for Samuel Goldwyn in 1934, an announcement is posted on the cruise ship SS *Luxor*: "Tonight at 8:30 P.M. Ship's Concert: Minstrel Night." The orchestra leader lifts his baton, and Ethel Merman belts out the lyrics to a song that promises a show with "red-hot rhythm" as the camera pans over the smiling faces of the all-white and elegantly dressed audience; at the same time, in the dressing room, Eddie Cantor is putting black greasepaint makeup on his face. He is assisted in blacking up by an elderly black servant who holds the tin of greasepaint. "This is tough to put on and take off," says Cantor to the man. "You know, you're lucky."

"Minstrel Night" opens with a close-up on the clean, bright face of Harold Nicholas, dressed in a white tailcoat and top hat. With a dimpled smile and a twinkle in his eyes, Harold sings:

> I want to be a minstrel man,
> I've always been a minstrel fan.
> I want to dance just like a dandy,
> And sing that song about my sugar candy . . .

I've learned about the minstrel ways,
So bring me back those minstrel days.
I want to be like George M. Cohan,
And be a minstrel man.

"We've always loved a minstrel man/ He thrills us like nobody can," two chorus girls sing. As they continue, the two girls double to four, the four double to eight, the eight to sixteen Goldwyn Girls, dressed in black-sequined top hats, cutaway tuxedo vests, and shorts, marching in long, horizontal rows behind Harold. Stepping in high-heeled shoes, the Girls sing, "The way he dances sure is dandy," as Harold spins, struts, and wags his head. In the third chorus, forty-eight Goldwyn Girls sit on steps in eight vertical rows, striking and passing tambourines, which create pulsating designs in space. Two of the Girls introduce the minstrel show's Interlocutor, who in turn presents the blackfaced Cantor and, in dark makeup, Merman as the minstrel show's endmen. "Ladies and Gentlemen, be seated," the Interlocutor announces, as Cantor and Merman take the end seats in the semicircle of performers and the minstrel show begins.

The minstrel show, a blackface act of songs, fast-talking repartee, and shuffle-and-wing tap dancing, was originally based on the ideas of white men "imitating and caricaturing what they considered to be certain generic characteristics of the black man's life in America."[1] This most popular form of entertainment in the nineteenth century saw white performers bursting onto the stage with burnt-cork makeup on their faces, "contorting their bodies, cocking their heads, rolling their eyes, and twisting their outstretched legs in a frenzy of grotesque and eccentric movements."[2] While intended to amuse audiences—to get them to clap, stomp, whistle, and shout—the minstrel show perpetuated negative stereotypes of African Americans on the later vaudeville stage, in burlesque, and in other subsequent forms of show business in the twentieth century.

As early as the 1720s, the "Negro" was added to the list of American folk characters represented by professional entertainers. By 1810, the singing-dancing "Negro Boy" was established as a dance hall character by blackface impersonators (many of them English and Irish actors who had recently arrived in America) who performed jigs and clogs to popular songs. In 1828, Thomas Dartmouth Rice learned the song and jig dance "Jump Jim Crow" from a black livery-stable boy and used it to become famous in New York City (1832), throughout the United States, and in London (1880). In this period, professional blackface acts multiplied.

But not until 1843, when the Virginia Minstrels (Dan Emmett, Frank Bowers, Dick Pelham, and Billy Whitlock) gave their first full evening of blackface entertainment in New York, did the formal structure of the minstrel show become established. To improve the coordination of the show, they arranged chairs in a semicircle to seat the tambourine and bones (rhythm "clackers" made of rib bones) players, the balladeer (the singer of sentimental love songs), and other members of the minstrel troupe. With the Christie Minstrels by the 1850s came the formal establishment of the endmen—Brudder Tambo and Brudder Bones (named after their instruments)—who sat on each end of the semicircle and were considered the starring comedians. Wearing "fright wigs" and an exaggerated blackface that gave the appearance of popping eyes and gaping mouths, they twisted their words in endless puns in order to keep the audience laughing. Seated in the middle of the semicircle was the Interlocutor, or master of ceremonies, whose precise and pompous command of the language, extensive vocabulary, resonant voice, and dignified mannerisms made the raucous comedy of the endmen seem even funnier.

The first part of the minstrel show interspersed comic repartee between otherwise unconnected songs and dances, sometimes concluding with a "stump speech," a humorous address on a topical subject delivered in a heavy malaprop-laden dialect. The second part's variety section, or Olio, took place downstage in front of the olio curtain and offered a series of specialty acts by song-and-dance teams, acrobats, comedians, and novelty dancers. The concluding Afterpiece, a one-act skit sometimes with a plantation theme, was saturated with songs and early forms of tap dances (jigs, essences, buck-and-wings).

In the walkaround finale, the performers paraded in a circle, stepping and strutting their stuff, challenging each other, and improvising on each other's "darky" steps. When African Americans gained access to the minstrel stage after the Civil War, they inherited blackface conventions set by white minstrels. Applying burnt cork to their faces and painting red gaping mouths over their lips, they too parodied and exaggerated "Negro" life in America—but they also propelled the minstrel show into a vital and "authentic" performance form that was especially inventive in its dance material.[3]

After the Civil War, the minstrel show also underwent a fundamental reorganization in repertory and format in order to broaden its audience base, reach new markets, and enhance its appeal. To do this, minstrel show producers increased the size of their companies, expanded their olios, added new specialty features, and staged lavish production numbers, featuring more "refined" acts. In the transition from small troupes concentrating on portrayals of blacks to huge companies staging lavish extravaganzas that virtually ignored blacks, the practice of caricaturing African Americans faded; but the racist assumptions about them were not lost, and the image of the shuffling plantation darky endured in American popular thought long after the minstrel show disappeared from theatrical circuits.

"Minstrel Night" in *Kid Millions* was not as overt in its racial stereotyping as the minstrel shows of the 1840s. The jokes in the film stayed corny—"Do you know the difference between a horse and a girl?" asked the eye-popping Cantor in a southern drawl. "No," says Interlocutor. "Ooof," says Cantor, "you sure do have some funny dates!" Mild banter aside, in the Depression decade, with its notorious and systematic stereotyping and segregated audiences, blackface performance persisted on the Broadway stage and in Hollywood films and enjoyed a great commercial success. *Kid Millions* was hailed by the *New York Times* (17 November 1934) as a "superior screen comedy" when it opened at New York's Rivoli Theatre. The story of Eddie (played by Cantor), the "pantalooned Cinderella of the Brooklyn waterfront" who falls heir to a seventy-seven-million-dollar fortune, was a lighthearted fantasy into which producer Samuel Goldwyn "poured almost everything that seemed helpful to the cause of pleasure." "Minstrel Night" in the film was a mix of borrowings; its sources ranged from the antebellum minstrel show and Busby Berkeley's choral designs to the lavish floor shows of the Cotton Club. Samuel Goldwyn had seen the Nicholas Brothers perform at the Cotton Club and had personally negotiated their United Artists film contract with the Nicholases' manager, Herman Stark, who was also the manager of the Cotton Club. For his own *Kid Millions*, Goldwyn wanted Harold to replicate with the Goldwyn Girls in the opening of "Minstrel Night" what he had become famous for doing at the Cotton Club with the Cotton Club Girls.

How disappointing, then, that all Harold was given to do in the opening scene was to sing "I want to be a minstrel man" and strut "just like a dandy." Harold was initially cast to play the role of the Interlocutor, the only performer in the traditional minstrel show to appear without blackface. But he has claimed that Cantor objected: "The producer wanted me to play Interlocutor, but Eddie Cantor put a stamp on that. He said no, and to this day I don't know why. But I can imagine." The role was subsequently given to the romantic lead, George Murphy, thus forcing the Nicholases into novelty appearances in the film. The choreographically flimsy opening in the "Minstrel Night" scene was also due to the apparent lack of tap dance expertise on the part of the film's choreographer, Seymour Felix. "He was like Busby Berkeley," Fayard says. "He didn't dance, but he had ideas."4 Obviously, Felix did not know how to utilize Harold's talents.

It was not in the opening of "Minstrel Night" but in the finale, and in a tap dance choreographed by Fayard,5 that the brothers got the opportunity to demonstrate their musical and comedic talents. In the final few choruses of "Mandy" (composed by Irving Berlin), played in a foursquare march, Cantor, Merman, Murphy, and Ann Sothern dance a rather simple combination of walking and crossover steps. These four stars do not execute the steps on the same foot at the same time. Nor can they, after forming a vertical line before the camera, all keep the rhythm of the music. Stepping

*Eddie Cantor
in blackface,
flanked by
Fayard and
Harold
Nicholas in
the "Minstrel
Night" scene
of* Kid
Millions,
Samuel
Goldwyn *1934
(Photofest).*

forward in one line, Murphy, Sothern, and Merman each peel
away from the camera, leaving Cantor bouncing erratically.

With his eyes popping out against the black smear of greasepaint
on his face, Cantor is a comic contrast to the elegant Harold and
Fayard, who, without blackface, are suddenly dancing on either
side of him. Dressed in their sophisticated white tailcoats and top
hats, the brothers perform smooth-bouncing time steps in an all-
too-casual manner. When Cantor attempts to copy their time steps,
Fayard changes up by breaking into a Charleston-and-wing combination in double time. Harold quickly picks up the steps, repeats
them, and passes them back to Fayard.

Cantor tries again to pick up the steps, but he flounders. Trying
to save face, he passes the dance with the wave of a hand to Harold,
who picks it up in a flash with syncopated stomps and wings.

Harold does not even try passing the dance to Cantor on the next round, but instead signals to Fayard, who quickly picks it up with an offbeat combination of double wings and tip-of-the-toe perches. Swinging his leg forward and back as in preparation for a jump, Fayard instead launches into a midair split, drops down into a full floor split, and pulls himself up smoothly, just in time to indicate to Cantor that Harold has already caught the beat.

The brothers continue passing rhythms back and forth to each other. Harold pits his lateral-spinning barrel turns against Fayard's legomania, in which he crosses and recrosses his legs midair; Harold's stomps volley with Fayard's scissor-legs, in which he springs to second position to balance on the tips of his toes before sliding the legs smoothly together. Finally, Cantor begs out of the dance, bouncing backward on one leg, and the brothers slip back with smooth nonchalance to the time steps they began with. But not for very long. Soon, they point their feet and balance on the tips of their toes, turning their soft, white-leather tap shoes into a ballet dancer's pointe shoe. They further their allusion to ballet dancing by executing a "stuttering" *pirou-ette*, in which they turn on one toe while tapping out a synco-pated beat with the other. Fayard then springs onto the tip of his shoe to perform side-brushing wing steps, passing to Harold, who springs onto the tips of his shoes to perform back-clicking cramprolls. They finish with a dual, smooth down-and-up split, recovering to wave gallantly to the Goldwyn Girls, who applaud the brothers on their tambourines. Cantor does not return to the stage, which is reclaimed by the Nicholas Brothers who have ele-vated the minstrel man into an elegant-dancing virtuoso.

There is an important inversion of roles in "Minstrel Night." Cantor is the blackface minstrel man ("imitating" a black man), while Harold wants to be a minstrel man ("I want to dance just like a dandy and sing about my sugar candy," he sings). Although Cantor acts the role of the minstrel man, his impersonation is in sharp contrast to two would-be minstrel boys, who prove to be the superlative singing-and-dancing men. Cantor wears blackface to appropriate "blackness," but the joke is that he cannot repli-cate black artistry. Instead, he has to resort to buffoonery. While

Cantor tries to be one of the boys—or one of the brothers—
he cannot, and the Nicholas Brothers have to play endmen to
the star.

Houston Baker theorized, in *Modernism and the Harlem
Renaissance*, that the "minstrel mask" for the white man represented a "space of habitation for repressed spirits of sexuality,
ludic play, id satisfaction and castration anxiety," and he suggested
that there were two conflicting motives for donning the blackface
mask: one to imitate, the other to demean. Even while blacks in
America were exploited, segregated, and denied access to opportunity by whites, Baker explained, "they nevertheless forged a
mighty identity that forced the white world to stand in awe and,
sometimes, to effect powerful imitation of their signal labors."
Still, within the white psyche, there existed a fear of the black man
and "a deep-seated denial of the humanity of inhabitants of and
descendants from the continent of Africa."[6]

The double impulse is surely visible in the "Minstrel Night"
scene when Cantor, while blacking up, says "This is tough to put
on and take off" to his gentlemanly Negro servant. There is a
wicked irony to that statement: with a stroke, the white man
could don burnt-cork makeup and become what he was not. The
blackface mask effected a closeness, an intimacy with "blackness,"
for it held the key to white-imagined fantasies of what blacks
possessed—spontaneity, carefree ease, happy-go-lucky charm,
childlike innocence, and a natural vitality.

In fact, as easy as it was to put the blackface mask on, it was
also easy to wipe it away and thus regain one's "whiteness." This
was something that blacks could not do—they could not wipe off
black skin and what it signaled. Cantor's remark "You know,
you're lucky" is condescending and cruel. For while Cantor has
the power to put on and take off the black mask when he wishes,
blacks were suspended within the white-made stereotype. This
was perhaps why the Nicholas Brothers were allowed to upstage
Cantor and company in the scene. They might be a pair of tapping virtuosos, but they were also two young black boys who
posed no threat to the white establishment.

Cantor, however, is not the only performer in "Minstrel Night" to wear a mask. The Nicholas Brothers also don a kind of mask, which conceals and obscures deeper emotions and motivations. The Nicholases' "mask" was rooted in American social traditions as well as in minstrel traditions. Black complexity was not permissible for those who served themselves up for white audiences. "We wear the mask that grins and lies, / It hides our cheeks and shades our eyes," wrote the African-American poet Paul Laurence Dunbar. "This debt we pay to human guile, / With torn and bleeding hearts we smile, and mouth with myriad subtleties."[7] For the African American, however painful and deceitful, the mask was an outward accommodation to the rampant bigotry in America and was used as a strategy for survival.

After the Civil War, black tent shows had developed comedians with a more physical and rhythmic style, and the dancing became more formalized. The Dandy strutted, the Plantation Hand shuffled, though each excelled at an inside humor in which they laughed at themselves.[8] Nevertheless, variations on the "masks" of the Shuffling Fool and Strutting Dandy persisted on black vaudeville stages in the twenties and thirties. The Hollywood roles offered most to African Americans during those years were those of maids, butlers, redcaps, handymen, and messenger boys; so most were pushed into wearing the mask of Humble Servant. *Variety* reported that in the 1920s servile roles comprised 80 percent of all black roles.[9] Even the most brilliant performers — such as Bill Robinson, whose renowned dancing was often overshadowed by the type of Uncle Tom character he repeatedly played — were shunted into humble, Old South servant roles. In their entire Hollywood film career, the Nicholas Brothers were spared the roles of simpletons and servants, remaining among the handful of artists who consistently projected a positive African-American image. With the advent of sound films and the recruitment of more professional black entertainers during the thirties, however, the brothers were often cast only in musical specialty spots and were offered little or no development of character. Nor did they escape association with the long-standing, entrenched tap dance stereotypes of the grinning-and-shuffling clown or the strutting dandy.

While the brothers avoided playing most stereotyped roles, they did not refuse the minstrel mask. In *Kid Millions*, Harold's twinkling eyes and dimpled smile when singing "I Want to Be a Minstrel Man" make for a grinning though thoroughly charming disguise that makes one wonder. Fayard too dons a kind of mask in the "Minstrel Night" scene when he plays sidekick to Cantor-in-blackface and smilingly accommodates Cantor's more central presence, only to prevail at the end of the scene through the sheer virtuosity of his dancing. If there was a name for the mask the Nicholases played through, it was that of Precocious Innocent. This mask recalls the West African Yoruba trickster figure Esu-Elegbara; a "master of style," this "jigue" was a highly accomplished dancer who was "swift-footed," "agile and restless," attaining his goals through his wits and deception.[10]

This mask of Precocious Innocent is present in other Nicholas performances. For example, Harold grins and winks right into the camera in the nightclub scene in *The Emperor Jones*, after the chorus girls top their demure promenade with a raunchy bump-and-grind. The wink signals Harold's keen awareness of the girls' sexually provocative moves; the diminutive thirteen-year-old may have been small for his age, but he knew more than most and was bold enough to show it.

In a publicity still from the film *Jealousy* (Paramount, 1935), in which the Nicholas Brothers perform in a nightclub much like the Cotton Club, Harold rolls his eyes, flashing a toothy smile as he stands tall in front of a line of a chorus girls. His big-eyed grimace looks even more bizarre because he is posing before a line of brown-skinned dancers wearing white wigs and black satin gowns. The wide-eyed looks of surprise from this effusive thirteen-year-old might be dismissed as mere mugging—putting on a face to please an audience. In retrospect, Harold says, "It wasn't Uncle Tomming. I was just a kid, bucking my eyes and trying to put some personality into it."[11] Harold's youthful charm is belied by his precociousness; he knows more than what his smiling face reveals, and he acts older than he really is. Instead of projecting the grotesque image of a little boy dressed up in gentleman's clothing, which would make for comic effect, Harold has become

a little man. On the "face" of the mask, then, Harold and Fayard are the "Nicholas Kids," with their sparkling eyes and twinkling feet; behind that mask, they resist being entrapped within the naiveté of the boy-child. "We were kids, but we danced like men," says Fayard, describing what people said about their dancing. Their image (this mask, so to speak) was in reality purposefully projected by the brothers. In their mastering of the form of tap dancing, they surreptitiously undermined the superficial perception that they were merely naive, and ultimately powerless, little black boys.

Harold and Fayard Nicholas in the nightclub scene in Jealousy, *Samuel Goldwyn 1934 (Harold Nicholas Archive).*

The central thesis in Thomas Cripps's history of the Negro in American film, *Slow Fade to Black*, is that all black actors have played stereotyped roles, yet the essence of black film history is found not in the stereotype but in what certain talented actors have done with the stereotype.[12] It is not *that* the Nicholas Brothers don the minstrel mask but *how* they *play through* it that becomes a fascinating example of the way these performers manipulated the seemingly

Fayard and Harold Nicholas in a musical scene in American Wife, *Samuel Goldwyn 1936 (Harold Nicholas Archive).*

intractable rules governing black performance. That the Nicholases "mature" through the mask, until it becomes transparent and finally passes away, is a testament to their development as dance artists and to the integrity of their rhythm dancing.

The Nicholas Brothers' ability to adapt to Hollywood's stringent rules of performance while holding steadily to their desire to develop as jazz tap artists may also be seen in *The Big Broadcast of 1936* (Paramount, 1935). Described by the *New York Times* (19 September 1935) when it was released as "a sprawling potpourri of variety entertainment . . . a goulash of specialty numbers held together by a hare-brained narrative," the film about a troubled radio station on the verge of bankruptcy featured a number of musical and comedy stars, including Bing Crosby, Ethel Merman, Jack Oakie, Amos and Andy, Bill Robinson, and George Burns and Gracie Allen. The Nicholas Brothers, who appeared in several scenes, were cast in the roles of Dot and Dash, two multitalented radiomen working at station W H Y. Their characters were, however, the sheerest disguises of themselves.

In an early scene, Harold teaches a weekly tap dance lesson during a live broadcast. "And now, folks, you've got ten lessons in ten weeks," he announces sweetly into the microphone. "So let's take it right from the first step to the last leap. Will the orchestra please permit?" A recording of "Miss Brown to You," played by Ray Noble and His Orchestra, is placed on the phonograph. With Fayard at the drums, twirling and tossing his sticks in the air while pumping the bass pedal, Harold, wearing tap shoes,[13] proceeds to tap out the lesson on a wooden platform. He clicks out a straightforward combination of time steps and double wings in the first chorus, and in the second chorus, the scene cuts from Harold to a pair of shoes, tapping out the same double wings on the foot support of a barber's chair. The gentleman in the chair, enjoying a manicure and facial steam, is Bill Robinson, who, after a pleasurable sigh, dapperly struts his way from the chair, out the door, and onto the sidewalk. Tap dancing down the street with sprightly little jigging steps, Robinson draws a parade of hat-waving, hip-swaying, black city folk. Following him across city traffc and into a park where he "teaches" tap dance, they copy his steps in call-and-response dialogue.

When the scene cuts from Robinson in the park to Fayard and Harold at the radio station, the tap dancing lesson becomes more complicated. The brothers progress from tapping out six bars of basic time steps and a two-bar break to an offbeat combination of buck-and-wing steps in double time. Then Fayard lifts off, balancing on the tip of one toe, to sweep the other foot sideways into quick-stroking brushes. And next Harold solos, jumping back onto the platform with rambling, triple-time time steps that propel him from a front flip into a full split-and-recover. Fayard joins Harold in the reprise, which sends them striding arm in arm out of the radio station.

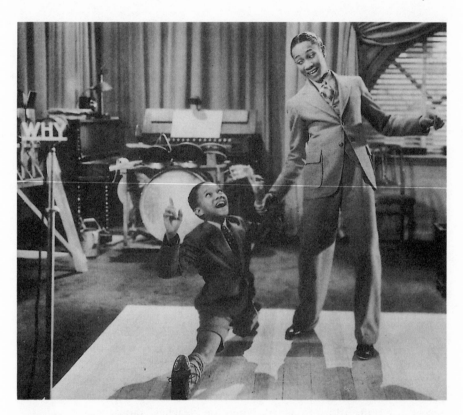

*Harold drops
into a split
as Fayard
cheers
in* The Big
Broadcast
of 1936,
*Paramount
1935 (Museum
of Modern
Art).*

Although the Nicholas Brothers' brief appearances in *The Big Broadcast of 1936* offered little time or reason for the development of character, the brothers managed to express themselves through their dancing. Fourteen-year-old Harold proved himself a master teacher, with a tap lesson of basic time steps that quickly progressed into syncopated, airborne moves impossible for anyone to copy. As Harold promised, the brothers took it "right from the first step to the last leap," turning a simple tap dance lesson into a masterful demonstration of technique and form.

A "mastery of form"[14] is demonstrated again by Harold in a later radio broadcast in the same film, when he sings "Why Dream" (music by Ralph Ranger and Richard Whiting, lyrics by

Leo Robbins, 1935). Accompanied by Fayard at the organ, Harold sings the first chorus with a heartfelt and melodic sweetness, even though he is imitating and embellishing another singer's rendition of the ballad in a previous scene. In the second chorus, when Fayard switches to jazzy, up-tempo, stride-style piano playing, Harold sings scat, putting his more personal style into the song with offbeat accents and squealing end notes. The scene cuts to a black woman listener who, sitting by her radio while peeling a potato, scrapes and bobs her head in time with this more upbeat, contemporary interpretation of the tune. At the song's end, on the last scat phrase, Harold winks right into the camera. His dimpled smile signals his confidence and his mastery of the jazz singing styles of the day.

The Big Broadcast of 1936 was a musical comedy in which comedians other than the Nicholas Brothers played the broadly comic roles. A funny scene involves the white comedy team of Willy, West, and McGinty, who nearly kill themselves for a laugh over plans to build a house: they swing wooden planks, splatter cans of paint, and all fall down over each other. In blackface makeup, the white comedy team of Amos 'n' Andy (Freeman Gosden and Charles Correll) also draw laughs when they try to embezzle money from a cash register: their fingers are crushed, their hands are slammed, and there's plenty of howling. In contrast, the Nicholas Brothers' humor comes from a hip and robust style of rhythm dancing that transforms slapstick comedy into a physically daring, perfectly timed, rhythmically exciting routine.

Between the filming of *Kid Millions* for Samuel Goldwyn and *The Big Broadcast of 1936* for Paramount, the Nicholases returned to New York and "hometown" Harlem, where they were regarded as big-time Hollywood stars. During this transitional period of film contract negotiations and cross-country travel by the family, Ulysses Nicholas suffered a sudden and fatal heart attack as he was being driven across the country by family chauffeur Lorenzo Hill. Although Ulysses had lived long enough to envision and manage the rise of Fayard and Harold's theatrical career, the responsibility of representing the Nicholas Brothers was to become solely Viola's. She continued, with diffculty, to maintain the same standards of professionalism that Ulysses had set.

While in New York, one of the last negotiations Ulysses had handled concerned the filming of two all-black musical comedy shorts for Vitaphone. *The All-Colored Vaudeville Show* (1935), filmed on the stage of a Warner Brothers theatre in Brooklyn, was structured as a variety show, and each of the specialty acts was introduced on a placard carried onstage by a chorus girl. In the first act, the Three Whippets combine flips, cartwheels, and rolls in a fast-paced routine that climaxes with straddling the backs of chairs and stretching into full splits; a series of back flips propels them off the stage. Adelaide Hall, standing sedately before a grand piano in the second act, sings "To Have You, To Hold You," surprising her audience by lifting her long gown in the middle of the song to buck-and-wing in her high-heeled shoes.

Then come the Nicholas Brothers. They plough across the stage on their entrance (to an unidentified tune played in 4/4 time in late Dixieland/early Swing style), moving in single file and in perfect step. With Harold in front and Fayard pressed in close behind, they create the illusion of a one-man machine. Turning to face the audience, they whip their legs like rotary blades in their time steps, then slash their legs open on side-brushing wings. Turning to dance in profile, they step back to drag the balls of their feet in offbeat, back-chugging "moonwalks" that create the illusion of floating backward. Turning again to face the audience, they scissor and slash their legs, then perform sweeping over-the-tops and trenches, arms swinging a full 360 degrees. Joining together again, they cross arms over each other's shoulders and tap in an upright position, gaining a momentum that propels them higher off the ground. Releasing arms, they lean into a forward diagonal with more trench steps, and then yank themselves upright into a flurry of time steps, to finish with a handshake.

The Nicholas Brothers' first dance in *All-Colored Vaudeville* created the illusion of flying and floating; their second (to an unknown tune played in moderate 4/4 time) re-created the Shim Sham Shimmy, a four-part routine from the twenties invented by Leonard Reed and Willie Bryant. It consisted of shuffle steps,

cross-over steps, the tack-Annie, and a half-break with a tagged-on walk-off. The brothers paid homage to this popular routine from the black vaudeville stage, embellishing it with their own rhythm breaks and comic-timed gestures.

Doing the tack-Annie, for example, the brothers lift their pants at the knee, as though they were skirts, making a passing reference to Adelaide Hall's raising her skirts and hoofing in the previous act; and they perform curtsies to each other while stepping daintily on the balls of their feet. Though their steps in the body of the routine reference the shim sham, the "punchline" break is the Nicholases' own eight-bar invention. In the second chorus, the brothers perform the shim sham while wiping a sleeve, fixing a tie, and slicking down their hair. In a light and comic touch in

The Nicholas Brothers shake hands at the end of their dance routine in The All-Colored Vaudeville Show, *Vitaphone 1935 (Harold Nicholas Archive).*

the third chorus, Harold turns round and round for a sixteen-bar tap turn as Fayard, sticking his index finger over Harold's head, mimes turning him under his finger. Another section of the tap dance is punctuated by demure snaps of the fingers and a patting of the knees. At the end of the routine, the brothers leap into the air as preparation for a split, drop down into a full split, and pop up on the recovery to walk off the stage, arm in arm.

Their tap act in *All-Colored Vaudeville* was styled after a vaudeville routine, from its two-man entrance to its fast-paced exit. Far from being broadly comic, the brothers' routine did not detract from their rhythm dancing. It was only later that a group called the Five Racketeers drew laughs through broadly comic means. Singing "Hold That Tiger," they strummed madly on four tiny ukeleles as singer Eunice Wilson did the bump-and-grind and the drummer flipped and beat his drumsticks on the floor, walls, and steps of the stage.

Instead of relying on such sight gags, the brothers had derived their humor from the "comic" timing of their rhythm-driven movement and the fantastic illusions they created of flying, gliding, and hovering over the floor. The camaraderie between Fayard and Harold also makes them delightfully appealing. As they dance, they smile at each other and make what they are doing look effortless. The greatest illusion they create is of two men who dance as one. They exude a joyousness in being in each other's presence and moving together. They are in step with one another, as verified by frame-by-frame analysis of the dance, even though their arms are not quite at the same angle; Fayard looks at Harold nine times, and Harold at Fayard three times.

In their immaculately tailored suits, and with their precision in movement, they present an extremely sophisticated refinement of vaudeville's "two-man rule," which generally restricted African Americans to performing in pairs. What most distinguishes the Nicholas Brothers from other comedy tap teams of the thirties is that instead of playing two contrasting characters in a comically combative relationship, such as Butterbeans and Susie or Cook and Brown, theirs is a more harmonic and symbiotic relationship, one in which they appear, quite naturally, "as themselves."

Thomas Cripps has observed that Ellington also appeared as himself in musical shorts of the thirties.[15] Perhaps the Nicholases were also allowed to appear as themselves because they were perceived as serious jazz musicians with their own following. "We're the Nicholas Brothers," say Fayard and Harold in the Vitaphone short *Black Network* (1936). The scene takes place in a Harlem radio station, where various contestants are competing by showing off their singing and dancing talents live and on-air. Those who sing sour notes or who stutter, as the first couple of contestants do, are eliminated by the sound of a loud gong. "Are you professionals?" the announcer asks the brothers as they step up to the microphone. "Professionals nothing, we're past that stage," touts Harold. The announcer asks what they do, and Fayard and Harold, in unison, reply, "Oh, we sing, we dance." Skipping to the microphone, they share in the singing and dancing of "Lucky Number."

"Lucky number," Fayard croons deeply. "Oh, give me that lucky number," Harold chimes in sweetly. "Hoping that those lucky numbers," sings Fayard (with a "Yeah" from Harold), "will show for me." Harold, in the fill, quickly catches up by singing, "Numbers gonna show for you and me," which lets them finish together on the last note. "Superstition," continues Fayard. "Oh, even makes me suspicious," adds Harold, finishing the thought. And they alternately stagger the lines "Table for thirteen dishes will make me freeze." (Fayard starts with "table for thirteen dishes"; Harold comes in on "thirteen dishes" and continues with "will make me freeze"; both finish on the same note.) They even quibble, in the bridge, over who has the next line: "Having been," starts Harold; "Hey man, that's my *been*," says Fayard; and Harold sings, "Well, all right then," which Fayard rhymes with "Put my trust in." In the last A section of the song, they similarly share and stagger the lines, Fayard finishing with "Lucky number for me" to Harold's "Oh yeah."

They dance the second chorus, continuing the two-as-one theme by trading steps and synchronizing moves. There are some light and airy moves, as when the brothers momentarily flutter on the balls of their feet with running flaps and back-hopping cramprolls, but for the most part the steps are weighted, close-to-the-floor digs, stomps, chugs, slides, drags, and rubbing tack-Annies (with the ball of the foot literally scraping the floor on the crossback).

These create deep-toned sounds and an earthy, aggressive delivery of rhythm. The taps are especially emphatic in the last eight bars of a double-time break, played by the orchestra in stop-time (the musicians repeat in rhythmic unison a simple one- or two-bar pattern, consisting of sharp accents and rests as Fayard and Harold dance). Fayard, after performing Charleston-like flings of the leg, in which he lifts his foot high off the floor, returns to pounding the floor with multiple stomping steps that use the whole foot. The momentum of his stammering forward, in a flurry of taps, makes his feet disappear from the eye of the camera's fixed focus.

The most floor-hungry moves are last in the routine. Return-ing to the rhythmic patterns from the first section of the dance, the brothers add a move in which they spring to second position and pull up into first, pressing the whole foot into the floor. Done very quickly and repeated four times, the eye can view Fayard's long-legged and perfect, X-shaped body line; but even as the eye travels along the exquisite shapes that Fayard creates, the synco-pated ripple of every beat can be heard as well as Harold's squeals of delight. The visual and aural signals that cue the viewer con-firm the absolute control in their choreography.

This "hoofing" combination, with its close-to-the-floor and flat-footed rubs and digs, paddle-and-rolls, and chugging, sliding, and shuffling steps, recalls the early buck style of tap dancing. While the brothers did draw from rural styles of jig and buck dancing, they transformed and elevated these traditional forms into a style that relied on speed, precision timing, and their cool and witty delivery.

In *Pie, Pie, Blackbird* the brothers were transformed from a pair of country boys standing in a southern kitchen to a couple of carefree city kids dancing hot rhythms on top of a giant blackbird pie. In *The All-Colored Vaudeville Show*, in which they danced before a painted backdrop of a brick apartment building in the city, the brothers contrasted earthy buck-and-wing steps with a speedy, light style of tapping that projected an image of transplanted city dwellers. In *The Big Broadcast of 1936*, they were further projected as mature, citified, professional dancers. In their confidently delivered song-and-dance routine in *Black Network*, a hip, urbane ambience flows from their dancing to project their image as urban sophisticates.

Taken all together, these early films of the Nicholas Brothers demonstrate how they transformed and elevated the buck-and-wing tap dancing of the late nineteenth century and black comedy dancing of the early twentieth into the refined and nuanced form of rhythm dancing that bid farewell to the tapping stereotypes of the Shuffling Fool and Strutting Dandy.

The Nicholas Brothers in Ziegfeld Follies of 1936 *(photo by Murray Korman, courtesy of Harold Nicholas Archive).*

Five

Babes on Broadway

1936–1938

By the time they were twenty-one and fourteen years old, Fayard and Harold Nicholas had experienced the glamour of the "Tall, Tan and Terrific" Cotton Club Girls and the glittering charm of the Goldwyn Girls. But before their debut on Broadway in *The Ziegfeld Follies of 1936*, nothing had prepared them for the sheer extravagance of a musical revue that hailed itself as "A National Institution, Glorifying the American Girl."

Produced by the Shubert brothers and Mrs. Florenz Ziegfeld (Florenz Ziegfeld, creator of *Follies*, died in 1932), *The Ziegfeld Follies of 1936* (Winter Garden Theatre, January 31) was one of the most lavish musical revues ever to play the Great White Way. It was staged by John Murray Anderson, with sets and costumes by Vincente Minnelli, music and lyrics by Vernon Duke and Ira Gershwin, and choreography by Robert Alton and George Balanchine. And it starred Josephine Baker, the first black woman to be featured in a Ziegfeld revue, although she and Fanny Brice shared star billing.

As for the Nicholas Brothers, instead of being backed by a chorus of beautiful women, as they always had been, they found themselves playing page boys to Baker in some musical scenes. This they accomplished with such ingenuity and aplomb that they managed nonetheless to distinguish themselves from the female stars who dominated the show.

Josephine Baker, Ernest Hemingway wrote, was "the most sensational woman anybody ever saw. Or ever will."[1] In proportions and curves, her figure was the dream of any painter, sculptor, or couturier. Her singing had a feather-light charm, and her dancing— a series of fast and frenetic changes in tempo and dynamics—was quixotic. She had danced in the chorus lines of *Shuffle Along* and *The Chocolate Dandies* on Broadway in the early twenties, delighting audiences by crossing her eyes and legs in comic distortions of the Charleston. But after her triumphant debut in Paris in *La Revue Nègre* in 1925, she was wholeheartedly adopted by the French and chose Paris as home. Ten years had passed since Baker had last been seen on the American stage, and having engaged her, the *Follies* producers did not know how best to "glorify" this American girl. Torn between presenting her as the exotic "primitive" of the *Revue Nègre* or the sophisticated Parisian songstress of the Folies-Bergères, they presented her as both.

In "Island in the West Indies," in the first act of *Ziegfeld Follies*, Baker was first seen leaping through metallic strips of curtain in a skimpy bikini, with silver, spike-like elephant tusks attached to her bosom; later in the scene, the Nicholas Brothers and eight men were her backdrop as she danced her own version of the conga. The Nicholases figured more prominently in "Maharanee," the next-to-last scene in Act I, in which Baker's svelte figure was encased in a sari, and her face partly covered by a veil. The scene, set at "the midnight races in Paris," opened with Rodney McLennan singing: "Maharanee, oh the gay exotic charm of you/ Oh that leg—Oh that arm of you/ Thrills Paree through and through." Baker strutted and sang in French, with one chorus a wordless coloratura ranging over two octaves, from middle D up to a high B flat. Then she danced a one-step tango and waltz with the Varsity Eight, an all-male chorus dressed in top hats and tails. As Baker danced, one glimpsed the small and sleek figures of Fayard and Harold Nicholas moving swiftly and smoothly around and behind her, shifting the panels of her sari. "She had this beautiful gown on," Fayard remembers, "and we ran around her like page boys, making sure it wouldn't catch on anything. We're running around, and she's singing with these eight guys who surrounded her. They didn't catch her, they just admired her, and she was looking beautiful."[2]

It wasn't until after Baker finished her number and had been escorted offstage by the eight men that the Nicholases took focus. Before commencing with their own dance specialty, however, they could not resist making a reference to the most glamorous woman with whom they had ever shared the stage. Harold began with his own impression of Baker by singing the song she sang in French and gliding across the stage as smoothly as his short legs could carry him. His imitation of the star was so clever that he stopped the show with wild laughter and applause from the audience.

It was on a wave of laughter that the brothers then launched into their own tap dance specialty, which ended with a challenge dance. "For our exit," Fayard remembered, "we did a split, came up together, locked arms, and sort of skipped offstage together, looking at the audience. It was sort of a little strut skip, and our other arm was out to the audience."[3] They left the audience begging for an encore—and one critic comparing Josephine Baker to the Nicholas Brothers. "After her cyclonic career abroad, Miss Baker has become a celebrity who offers her presence instead of her talent," Brooks Atkinson wrote in the *New York Times* (31 January 1936). "She has refined her art until there is nothing left in it." In a double-edged compliment to the brothers, Atkinson added, "When the two Nicholas Brothers follow her with some excellent Harlem hoofing out of the Bill Robinson curriculum, they restore your faith in dusky revelry."

How the Nicholases were recruited as Baker's pages in "Maharanee" is not clear. In the out-of-town previews for the *Follies*, the producers kept switching the sequence of the musical numbers in the show. Where the brothers were going to be placed in the program was fast becoming a problem, because they had quickly gained the reputation as being show-stoppers and nobody wanted to follow them. Fanny Brice allegedly refused to follow the

Nicholases after the Boston preview (December 30, 1935), in which "Maharanee" was listed as the third scene in the first act, and Brice's sketch, "Please Send My Daddy Back to Mother," the fourth.[4] When Brice finally made it to the stage, she reportedly quieted the audience down with the opening line, "Do you think we can talk now?"[5] After several other switches in the sequence of the program, it was finally decided that "Maharanee" would precede "Gazooka," which featured Bob Hope and Gertrude Niesen.[6] Josephine Baker was also a tough act to follow, but the Nicholases found good opportunity in offering to follow her on the program and created a marvelous segue for their dance specialty.

That the Nicholases delivered "some excellent Harlem hoofing" in *Ziegfeld Follies* can only be attributed to themselves. Robert Alton was the credited choreographer of "Maharanee," though the Nicholases claim he never gave them any "steps," only explanations on how he wanted them to handle Baker's gown. It was left up to the brothers to devise how they would move around her. "He didn't show us what to do. In fact, nobody did," says Fayard. "We did our own steps, our own choreography." The brothers do not remember working with George Balanchine in the *Follies*, even though the Boston and Philadelphia preview programs list the Nicholases in "Island in the West Indies," one of the six musical numbers Balanchine staged. Fayard insists that "it wasn't Balanchine we worked with in *Follies*, it was Robert Alton." Balanchine, however, would remember the brothers in one of his next opportunities to work on Broadway.

In the spring of 1936, *Ziegfeld Follies* closed after 115 performances, due to the sudden illness of Fannie Brice. The entire Nicholas family began preparations to sail for London, where Fayard and Harold were to join the cast of African-American singers, dancers, and comedians in Lew Leslie's *Blackbirds of 1936*. Photographs were taken by the Harlem photographers Morgan and Marvin Smith to commemorate the family's momentous departure from New York. One picture shows Viola, in a full-length mink coat, sitting proudly next to her sons, with Dorothy and two friends, Hilda and Vivian Brown, standing behind. Another photograph shows the petite Viola standing between her sons, who

The Nicholas Brothers with Bob Hope in Ziegfeld Follies *of* 1936 *(photo by Murray Korman, courtesy of Harold Nicholas Archive).*

are dressed in matching full-length, woollen-plaid overcoats. These formally posed photographs were taken in New York prior to departure. The more informal snapshots and Nicholas home movies, on the other hand, taken by Lorenzo Hill (the family chauffeur and the brothers' personal valet), capture moments before departing and aboard the liner *Berengaria*, where the brothers are playing shuffleboard, watching an exhibition boxing match, and dancing the Charleston with Jennie LeGon.

Once in London, the family settled into a flat in the West End, and the brothers were plunged into rehearsals for *Blackbirds of 1936*. After producing *Plantation Revue* in 1922 and *Dixie to Broadway* in 1924, Lew Leslie had experienced his first New York success with *Blackbirds of 1926*. It was created as a starring vehicle for Florence Mills, who died shortly thereafter. *Blackbirds of 1928* was Leslie's tribute to Mills, and it became the longest-running black musical of the twenties. The show was so popular that Leslie brought it to London in 1930 and 1933, where it received critical acclaim from the English. Unlike Americans, who thought of black revues in terms of fast dancing, swing songs, and blackface comedians "who played craps and stole chickens," the average Englishman thought of black shows, Leslie claimed, in terms of art and wanted, for example, to hear spirituals sung in the rich and warm manner of a Paul Robeson. "When I put on a revue in England," Leslie told the press, "I have plenty of the 'Old Black Joe' and 'Go Down Moses' type of spirituals. Even the dancing is of the less low-down type."[7]

Blackbirds of 1936, as staged by Lew Leslie, was choreographed by the African-American jazz dancer Clarence "Buddy" Bradley, with music and lyrics by Ruby Bloom and Johnny Mercer, played by the Jack Harris Rhythm Band. It opened at the Gaiety Theatre on July 9, 1936, and was subtitled "A Rhapsody of Blue Notes and Black Rhythm"; and it featured an all-star cast of black musical artists, whose purpose was to show how "Negro Dance-Rhythm of songs in Folk-Lore, Jubilees, Plantation Ballads, Levee Pastimes, Ragtime, Syncopation, Jazz and the Blues" had all begun. James Weldon Johnson wrote the program notes. "In 1619, a Dutch vessel landed twenty African natives at Jamestown, Virginia . . . the beginning of the African slave trade in the American Colonies." He continued:

> These people came from various localities in Africa. They did not all speak the same language. Here they were, suddenly cut from the moorings of their native culture, scattered without regard of their old tribal relations, having to adjust themselves to a completely alien civilization . . . yet it was from these people this mass of noble music sprang; this music which is America's only folk music.[8]

"Negro Cavalcade" opened Act I with mimed scenes of seventeenth-century African slaves cringing under the overseer's lash on the landing stage at Jamestown. It leapt to the cotton-pickers of the 1820s, and a scene where women in bandannas sang "Down on the Oh-i-o," accompanied by straw-hatted men strumming banjos. The show moved forward in time to the twentieth century, with dances that were popular in the teens and twenties, such as the cakewalk, Charleston, shimmy, black bottom, and blues.

Scene 2 took place in the thirties, with Lavaida Carter and Lucille Wilson singing "The Swing is the Thing," and Danny and Edith tap dancing and jumproping. Ensuing scenes criss-crossed back and forth in time to give a taste of black musical theatre in America. "Hot Dogs" introduced the blackface comedians Tim Moore and Gallie de Gaston in a slapstick routine replete with pratfalls and sleight-of-hand. In "Aunt Jemima and Cream of Wheat," the comedy team of Gordon and Rogers (one dressed as a chef, the other as a woman) flipped off the stage and over the heads of the audience to do pratfalls in the aisles. Maude Russell and Emmett Wallace delivered a romantic touch with "Your Heart and Mine," dancing a softshoe; Anise and Aland danced "the Americana," an adagio ballroom dance; Moore and de Gaston returned to the stage with the hilarious lecture "Man's Anatomy"; and barbers, bootblacks, and manicurists sang loudly and lustily as they groomed their customers in "Opera Barber's Shop."

Harold, in the tenth scene of Act I, presented the song and dance "Keep a Twinkle in Your Eye," a vaudeville-inspired routine backed by the Blackbirds Beauty Chorus. Nicholas home movies taken of this number show Harold in a straw hat with black jacket and white pants, singing and strutting before a line of chorus girls in form-fitting gowns with plumed flounces, who fling their legs out in the Charleston and perform time steps. They are a pleasant backdrop for Harold, who inserts kicks, spins, and splits into his close-to-the-floor rhythm tapping. At the close of the first act, "Akosiah's Wedding" told the story, based on African legend, of Akosiah—the "Princess of the Nimble Feet" who danced at her wedding feast not blessed by rain. The "Happy-Hearted Minstrel Man" opened Act II with the characters of Interlocutor, Mr. Ham, and Mr. Bones, in a minstrel show that culminated in a walkaround dance

Harold Nicholas dancing before the Blackbirds Beauty Chorus in Lew Leslie's revue Blackbirds *of 1936 (Harold Nicholas Archive).*

by the Four Bobs, a precision tap dance team. Then Lavaida Carter sang "Dixie Isn't Dixie Anymore," and the cast performed "She Done Me Wrong," an adaptation of the Frankie and Johnny story set in a speakeasy in Harlem.

In the fourth scene of the second act, the Nicholas Brothers performed their tap dance specialty in "A Few Minutes With." Though neither of the brothers remembers the music or the choreography for the act, Nicholas home movies catch them onstage, in top hats and tails, moving together and sportily breaking off into individual solos. *Play Pictorial* (15 September 1936) reported: "One of the cleverest turns imaginable is provided by Fayard and Harold Nicholas, with their astonishing dancing and infectious high spirits." The final scene, "Professional Night at the Ubangi Club," set in a cabaret in Harlem, led the entire cast and chorus into a smooth-turning walkaround finale.

"Intoxicating rhythm, sweet singing, dazzling dancing, ripe humor, and a dash of barbaric splendor—there you have Lew

The Nicholas Brothers in Lew Leslie's revue Blackbirds of 1936 *(Harold Nicholas Archive).*

Leslie's *Blackbirds of 1936*," wrote the *London Times* (10 July 1936) after the opening. Described as "the gayest, liveliest, cleverest" show in town" by the *Era* (15 July 1936) and "an amazing show of breathless virtuosity, bewildering range, and bountiful measure" by *Sketch* (22 July 1936), *Blackbirds of 1936*, with its "miracles of acrobatics in star-spangled brassieres, and prodigies of rhythm in evening dress" (*Tatler,* 29 July 1936), was praised as the most spectacular of all the editions that played in London.

New *Statesman and Nation* (18 July 1936) complained, however, that the revue lacked cohesion and arrangement (18 July 1936), while *Saturday Review* (12 September 1936) thought that it was

Harold and Fayard Nicholas combining tap and acrobatics in the scene "A Few Minutes With," in Lew Leslie's revue Blackbirds *of 1936 (Harold Nicholas Archive).*

too noisy: "After having been blared at and tap-danced at for a whole evening at colossal speed, I feel a little weak." The *Dancing Times* (7 October 1936), headlining its review with "Noisy but Vital Show," wrote: "It may be that these Negro singers and dancers can only reach the high pitch of excitement at which their performance is carried on by kicking up a hullabaloo. It comes hard on the ears, though. Mine are still ringing." The *London Times* (10 July 1936) reported that "when the chorus, the principals, and the brass are in high competition, one remembers with longing, gunnery exercises of which were mitigated by cotton-wool. Here there is no cotton-wool."

Harold believed that the cast of *Blackbirds* was a novelty to the English because "they hadn't seen so many black people in one show."[9] Several comments by the critics, however, demonstrated a blatant misconception of African-American performance and jazz culture. "These colored people can certainly dance," wrote *Saturday Review* (12 September 1936), while the *Sunday Times*

(12 July 1936) reported: "These black dancers do not need to assure me that their feats are incredibly difficult, but they seem to take to it as ducks to water." The *Observer* (12 July 1936) noticed "a fierce (almost maniacal) physical energy about them, that comes into the least thing that they do," while the *Sunday Times* (12 July 1936) asked, "Is it a trifle noisy? Yes, but these are the children of noise."

Only *Sketch* (22 July 1936) understood and appreciated how well these musical artists balanced spontaneity with technical control:

> They are spontaneous as children, and their exuberance, their utter lack of self-consciousness, their sincerity of emotion, gay or grave, bring something irresistible into the theatre. To this natural endowment must be added the disciplined control and technique acquired by training. The speed, precision, and accuracy of their dancing are something to marvel at.

At its best, *Blackbirds of 1936* was judged by *Saturday Review* (25 July 1936) as a well-balanced mix of "excellent dancing, a good deal of humor, singing that was beautifully harmonized and music that is tuneful all the time"; and the *Tatler* (29 July 1936) found it to be a show whose performers were "more concerned to interpret the spirit of modern Harlem—with the flick-flicker of iron-tapped, patent-leather shoes in the quickest tap-dancing you ever saw."

While Lavaida Carter was consistently singled out as a versatile singer, Moore and de Gaston were marveled at as cross-talking comedians, and Jules Blesdoe was praised for his hearty baritone voice, the Nicholases came away with the most favorable critical notices. "The two brothers Nicholas always have something spirited to add," wrote *Sketch* (22 July 1936): "Their sense of rhythm is so marked that it seems impossible for these dancers to go wrong, and it is always so alive on stage that the impression is of energy let loose in a kaleidoscopic whirl which sweeps us from the cotton plantations to Harlem." And the brothers were declared "outstanding" by *Saturday Review* (25 July 1936).

The *London Times* (10 July 1936) wrote: "The elder is the more accomplished dancer . . . the younger has an impish self-assurance and a compelling joy in life which immediately captivates his audience." Harold was exceptionally favored by *New Statesman and Nation* (18 July 1936) as "an engaging young man" and by *Illustrated London News* (18 July 1936) as a young man who was "precociously adult in manner." Wrote the *Sunday Times* (12 July 1936): "He is unique among infant phenomena in that he is both a tot and an artist, and his turns were the smash hits of the evening, the audience not knowing which to admire most, twinkling feet or slow, baby smile." The *Tatler* (29 July 1936) added: "I suppose he was a pickaninny once upon a time. . . . But it is difficult to believe when you see him: four-foot-nothing of a little man-about-town, ogling the chorus and telling them in song how to keep a twinkle in their eye." And the *New Statesman and Nation* (18 July 1936) said: "With all the assurance of Miss Shirley Temple, and a slice that rivals Master Locke, he struts his stuff with infinite charm."

The dancing of the Blackbirds Beauty Chorus in *Blackbirds of 1936* was consistently cited by reviewers as being "the best, for work and looks" (*Era*, 15 July 1936). This was due in large part to the choreographer, Clarence "Buddy" Bradley, whose fluency in a variety of jazz dance styles sustained the historical theme of the revue. Born in Harrisburg, Pennsylvania, the African-American dancer moved to New York in the twenties, where he learned to tap dance by frequenting the Hoofers Club in Harlem and performed as a chorus dancer at Connie's Inn. He rechoreographed the *Greenwich Village Follies* in 1928 (for which he received no credit—Busby Berkeley's name remained on the program), and at the Billy Pierce Dance Studio off-Broadway, he created dance routines for such white stars of Broadway musicals as Gilda Gray, Jack Donahue, Adele Astaire, and Ann Pennington.

On Broadway in the twenties, musical comedy dancing, whose simple walking steps were reserved for ingenues, was the lowest common denominator in show dancing. Uptown, African-American tap dancers were inventing intricate steps with complex rhythms. Bradley's formula for creating dance routines for white dancers was to simplify rhythms in the feet, while sculpting the body with shapes from black vernacular dances. He used the body to express, rather than accompany, the music. Even though he simplified rhythms, he never sacrificed the syncopated accents of jazz, and he used the accents of jazz improvisations to shape new rhythmic patterns in the body.[10]

In 1930, Bradley arrived in London to choreograph *Evergreen*, the Rodgers and Hart musical that catapulted him onto the English musical stage. In it, he was to transplant American vernacular dance into the English soil. In "Dancing on the Ceiling," a softshoe dance choreographed for the English dancer and actress Jessie Matthews in the film version of *Evergreen* (1934), Bradley's "polyrhythmic" style of jazz dancing is seen in the way Matthews bobs her head in one rhythm, while shimmying her shoulders and stepping in counterpoint to the head.

In *Blackbirds of 1936*, this style of moving is also seen in the finale of Act I, as the chorus of male dancers step forward on the 4/4 beat, while doffing their hats in slow, sustained time and bobbing their heads in double time. As the men move forward in line, they create a weaving pattern with the women, who, stepping back on the beat, wave their arms in slow, sustained time and twist their torsos. The loose, fluid quality of Bradley's jazz choreography, punctuated with small pulses of the head, wrists, and knees, made the movement vibrate with rhythm. The dancing of the female chorus in Harold's number, "Keep a Twinkle in Your Eye," which is recorded in Nicholas home movies, also demonstrates how the smooth-twisting motion of the torso worked with and against the shimmying shoulders.

Bradley did not choreograph "A Few Minutes with the Nicholas Brothers," but he did stage the brothers, along with the entire cast and chorus, in the first- and second-act finales of *Blackbirds*. Because the brothers were receptive to all styles of jazz dancing, they certainly observed and absorbed Bradley's approach to working rhythms into the body. There is some evidence of this in the film *Calling All Stars*, which the brothers made for British Lion films in 1937 prior to returning to the United States. Harold, in one scene, scat-sings "Smokey Joe," one of the "moaning" songs Cab Calloway made famous at the Cotton Club. While Harold did most of the singing, both he and Fayard "danced" the song, not so much with actual dance steps but with subtle undulations of the torso, arms and legs. "Here's a very entrancing phrase," Harold sang; "What about it?" Fayard quipped, filling in the last two beats of the measure. "It will put you in a daaaaze," sang Harold, to Fayard's double take; "It may not mean a thing," crooned Harold, with Fayard pointing a finger, "But it's got a peculiar swing." Harold moaned the chorus, scatting "Sa si SAH si SAH si SAH si," and the members of the band repeated back, "Sa si SAH si SAH si SAH si," as Fayard did a slow and sinuous worming movement with his torso that looked as if the rhythm of Harold's scat had made its way slowly up his trunk. With and against this sinuous torso movement, Fayard snapped his fingers and rolled his shoulders, all the while grinding his hips slowly to the beat. The Nicholases were already full-bodied rhythm dancers before coming to London. But their playing of rhythmic textures in the body, which Bradley's polyrhythmic style reinforced, had never before been as prominent as in this scene.

The year 1936 was a period of full creative bloom for Harold. At the age of fifteen, he was being touted as the youngest and most shining of stars in *Blackbirds*. "Keep a Twinkle in Your Eye" was such a hit that he recorded it, along with "Your Heart and Mine," on the HMV label in London, on September 15, 1936. If the crooning of his boy soprano voice was sweetly infectious, so was Harold's bright face and dimpled smile, which appeared in full-page pictures in such London tabloids as the *Bystander* (29 July 1936), along with the caption HAROLD NICHOLAS—YOUNGEST BLACKBIRD:

> Small but shining star, little Harold Nicholas smiles irresistibly, dances nimbly, and sings, in his metallic boy's voice, with the greatest confidence and not a trace of conceit. He appears twice in *Blackbirds*. . . . The house roars with joy at him, and welcomes him back like a long-lost darling when he reappears in the second half, this time with his elder brother who is two years [*sic*] his senior and just that much a better dancer.

London was Harold's oyster, and he seemed to excel at anything he set out to do there. Nicholas home movies taken during this period show him playing tennis in a double-breasted suit and riding on horseback with Viola and Dorothy. Equestrian sports became one of Harold's favorite pastimes in London, and he even dreamed of becoming a professional jockey. "But Mother said she couldn't have me falling off any horses," Harold later recounted, and the idea was quietly put aside.[11]

By the age of fifteen, Harold was beginning to test his independence. He left London by himself one afternoon in December 1936, and traveled by train to Edinburgh to see a young lady friend, Miss Elisabeth Bergner, an actress who was performing in the play *The Boy David*. He never made it back to London the next day for his own performance, and shortly before the curtain was due to go up on the production of *Blackbirds* at the Adelphi Theatre, it was announced that the performance would not take place. "Everybody thought I was kidnapped," said Harold. "The headlines in the papers read, 'One Blackbird Missing!' And when I came back the next morning, the taxi had an accident. The police looked in the cab and said, 'Aren't you one of the Nicholas Brothers?' They took me home and, oh man, it was a big thing . . . reporters were all in the house." Catching "a slight chill" from his adventure in Edinburgh, Harold was unable to perform, and *Blackbirds* had to be canceled the second evening in succession.[12]

If the Nicholases' claim is correct, they stayed in England through at least part of the reigns of three kings (George V [1910–36], who died on January 20; Edward VIII, the Prince of Wales, who abdicated the throne on December 11, 1936; and George VI [1936–52], father of Elizabeth II). They probably returned to New York around the late winter of 1937, after having been abroad for over ten months. When the family returned, the Depression had deepened. In the midst of national and international turmoil—marked especially by Hitler's and Mussolini's geopolitics that led to the onset of World War II—violence in Harlem had increased dramatically, with more than 80 percent of its population on public relief. The pride and cultural flowering of the twenties had begun to give way to a new militancy and antiwhite resentment that had escalated on March 19, 1935, into a race riot. "It got to a point where newspaper men and radio people were telling whites not to go to Harlem because it was too dangerous," Leonard Reed remembered. "Cab drivers started not taking white people to Harlem. They had a fear, there was no reason, but they just had a fear."[13] On February 16, 1936, on the heels of the Harlem race riot and with the repeal of Prohibition (ratified in December 1933) having seriously cut into its profits, the uptown Cotton Club closed its doors. With the hopes of transplanting its glamour and its roster of black talent to a safer and more accessible location, the Club was relocated to the famous old Palais Royale, on Broadway and 48th Street, in the heart of the theatre district.

The Nicholases were in London for the September 24, 1936, grand opening of the downtown Cotton Club. But they were immediately installed into the second edition of the Cotton Club Parade, which opened on March 17, 1937, with Duke Ellington and His Orchestra. With the Cotton Club as their home base, Herman Stark as their manager, and the William Morris Agency as their agent, the brothers were booked into several theatres and clubs in and around New York. "The Cotton Club was home," says Fayard. "We'd do a show here, a show there, go to L.A. and do a film, and then come back. Even if we didn't start in a new show, our manager would put us in it."[14]

While the Nicholas Brothers were performing at the Cotton Club, *Babes in Arms*, a new Rodgers and Hart comedy that was soon to open on Broadway, had out-of-town previews in Boston. It became clear to the producers there that the two young men who were playing the role of brothers in the previews would not follow the show to Broadway. George Balanchine, the show's choreographer, asked that they be replaced by the Nicholas Brothers. Production supervisor Dwight Deere Wiman remembered being dispatched to New York to see the brothers perform at the Cotton Club and recruiting them.[15] Says Fayard: "He [George Balanchine] wanted us, so we decided to do both—the Cotton Club and *Babes in Arms*." This meant that after performing Tuesday through Sunday in the eight P.M. show of *Babes in Arms* (with matinees on Wednesdays and Saturdays), they shot over to the Cotton Club for the midnight and two A.M. shows.

The brothers began rehearsals in New York. "We went to the Shubert Theatre, where we met Richard Rodgers and Larry Hart. Balanchine was sitting in the audience. And he asked us to show him a little something, and so we did," Fayard remembers:

We started tapping, and my brother did a thing where he'd go through my legs in a split, and I'd jump over him into a split. And then Balanchine suddenly got excited—he said he had an idea for a big production number, an Egyptian ballet, he was working on. He said, "Here's what I want you to do. I'll arrange the whole thing but this is what I have in mind. . . ."16

Balanchine's idea for the so-called Egyptian Ballet was for Fayard to jump over a line of chorus girls and for Harold to slide through the girls' legs. First two girls stood together and hunched over to make a bridge, with Fayard jumping over the backs of the girls and Harold sliding through their legs. Then another girl joined the line, and the brothers repeated the jump and slide; one by one, girls were added until there was a line of eight girls, pressed together and bent over with legs straddled. Fayard timed his jump over the backs of the girls and into a split so that on his recovery, Harold's slide under could be extended through Fayard's legs. "He didn't show us anything," says Fayard about Balanchine. "He just told us what he thought would be sensational for the number. And it was—the audience went wild."

Babes in Arms, a musical comedy in two acts and fourteen scenes, projected a youthful, contemporary vitality when it opened at the Shubert Theatre on April 14, 1937. The musical was filled with young and relatively unknown performers and charming songs, such as "My Funny Valentine," "Where or When," "The Lady Is a Tramp," and "Johnny One-Note." These became classics of American musical theatre. The story was simple: To avoid being sent to a work farm, children of traveling vaudevillians pool their talents and present a show, "Lee Calhoun's Follies." The show fails financially, and the kids are hustled off to the farm but are rescued by a French aviator who makes an emergency landing on the field, befriends them, and takes them on an around-the-world journey. "Calhoun's Follies," the show-within-a-show in Act I, allowed for ample display of the talents of Wynn Murray as the Singer, Douglas Perry as the Child, Alfred Drake and Eleanor Tennis as the High Priest and Priestess, Bobby Lane as the Acrobat, and specialty dancers Mitzi Green and Duke McHale.

The Nicholas Brothers played the roles of Nubians in "Calhoun's Follies," dancing Balanchine's so-called Egyptian ballet dressed in costumes that replicated those of Egyptian deities. Nicholas home movies (taken by Viola Nicholas during a performance at the Shubert Theatre) show them leaping over the heads and through the legs of Egyptian priestesses and exiting in mock-Egyptian style with bodies in profile, arms bent at the elbows and wrists, and heads jutting forward and backward. *Variety* (21 April 1937) reported that "the colored Nicholas Bros. from the niteries proved socko with their terp taps and blended well throughout."

Fayard remembers that George Balanchine once, after a rehearsal, asked the brothers if they ever had any training in ballet. Fayard answered that they had not. "Well, it really looks like you did, because you look like ballet dancers," Balanchine replied. Fayard says, "That's when I had a serious talk with him. I said I'd like to work for him again, and that I hoped we would do another Broadway show with 'the great George Balanchine.' And he told me he was the one to be proud of working with 'the great Nicholas Brothers.'"[17] Balanchine was not the only one who was perceptive in identifying certain elements in the Nicholases' dancing which were similar to classically trained ballet dancers. "Everybody who saw the show asked us if we ever had any ballet training," Fayard remembered.[18] The proportioned carriage of their arms, for instance, certainly resembled ballet *port de bras*, and their fully extended splits, slides, and splay of the legs in their tap Charleston variations were similar in form to the *jetés*, *sissonnes*, and *rond de jambes en l'air* of ballet. Fayard and Harold, of course, had never had any formal training in ballet; their only direct means of learning about ballet dance had been watching Balanchine work with other dancers. ("Maybe it comes natural, from watching you," Fayard remarked when asked by Balanchine if they had ballet training.) Fayard observed, for example, how

Balanchine, in working with Duke McHale on a tap dance number, asked the ballet-trained dancer to "tap *as* he did the turning step, so the tapping and turning could blend together."

Furthermore, there was a certain aesthetic to Balanchine's Russian-styled classical dance, with its bravura display of steps, vertical alignment and elevation, elegant symmetries of the arms, and precise footwork, that the brothers both aspired to and identified with in their own dancing. Perhaps Balanchine's greatest contribution to the Nicholases—more than the routine he contrived for them in *Babes in Arms,* which was used throughout Fayard and Harold's dance career—was his reinforcement of certain elements in the Nicholases' style that had already been developing, such as their full-bodied extensions, air work, gracefulness, speed, and precision.

The interesting question is not what the brothers gained from observing and working with Balanchine but what Balanchine absorbed by working with the Nicholas Brothers. Jazz was not new to Balanchine; several early works from his Russian years testify to his fascination with jazz rhythms and black dance. One of his earliest choreographies was a ballet to Igor Stravinsky's *Ragtime*, for a school concert in 1920; in 1921, he created *Foxtrots* for his company, Young Ballet, as part of a demonstration concert in Petrograd, and in 1923, he devised movements to poems set to music for cabaret entertainments. The next year, when the Young Ballet went on tour to Germany, the company decided not to return to the newly established Soviet Union and went to London to perform in popular music halls.

For the Opera de Monte-Carlo in 1925, Balanchine choreographed *L'Enfant et les sortileges*, with a score by Maurice Ravel that is usually cited as the composer's first use of ragtime jazz. In *Jack in the Box* (1926), ballerina Alexandra Danilova was cast as the Black Dancer in an acrobatic adagio. Balanchine himself donned blackface to dance the role of Snowball in *The Triumph of Neptune*, with choreography described by Cyril Beaumont as being "full of subtly contrasted rhythms, strutting walks, mincing steps and surging backward bendings of the body, borrowed from the cakewalk."[19]

Between 1929 and his arrival in the United States in 1934, Balanchine had several opportunities to take his jazz inspiration in new directions. "What Is This Thing Called Love," for C.B. Cochran's *Wake Up and Dream* (1929), was choreographed to music by Cole Porter; and a short jazz number for *Stoll's Variety Shows* (1931) used the recorded music of Jack Hilton and His Dance Orchestra. In *Cochran's 1931 Revue*, Balanchine worked with co-choreographer Clarence "Buddy" Bradley, and from him observed how simplified rhythms in the feet and black vernacular dance steps could reshape musical theatre dance. Balanchine was also a great admirer of Josephine Baker: he may have given her private ballet classes and staged some numbers for her in Paris, and staged some dances for her in *Ziegfeld Follies of 1936*.[20] But aside from Baker, the Nicholas Brothers were the first African-American jazz dancers with whom Balanchine worked intimately after arriving in the United States in January of 1934.

Working closely with the young Nicholases must have been extremely exciting for Balanchine, who, says dancer Fred Danieli, "was fascinated with American rhythms. Absolutely loved tap. Tried to learn it."[21] Even without a working knowledge of jazz tap dance (Johnny Pierce, a white tap dancer, assisted Balanchine in staging the tap dances in *Babes in Arms*), Balanchine was able to absorb this new material into his own classical idiom. "Just as folk and ballroom steps have been classicized," wrote Edwin Denby in 1953, "so Balanchine has been classicizing movements from our Negro and show steps."[22] This observation is verified by what Sally Banes has described as "speed, broken lines, off-center weight placement, intertwining bodies, and syncopated accents" in the "Rubies" section of Balanchine's three-part ballet *Jewels* (1967); and dancer Edward Villella has noted that one step in "Rubies," in which the man does four steps to the woman's one, is "all thirties jazz."[23]

Elizabeth Kendall has also observed the influence of jazz tap dance on Balanchine, writing that his "love for tap dancing shaped his choreographic style in the most fundamental way, generating intricate, syncopated rhythms, with a relatively understated *port de bras* that at the same time allowed for a flexible torso."²⁴ Perhaps the most direct evidence of the influences of the Nicholases on Balanchine is seen in Balanchine's 1946 ballet *The Four Temperaments*, which he choreographed to Paul Hindemith's "Theme with Four Variations." The three thematic duets that form the opening suite, and the following "Melancholic," "Sanguinic," and "Phlegmatic" variations, contain what Brenda Dixon Gottschild describes, in her lengthy analysis of the ballet, as an "Africanist-inflected vocabulary," which includes the displacement and articulation of hips, chest, pelvis, and shoulders, leg kicks attacking the beat, and angular arms and flexed wrists.²⁵ In the final recapitulation of the themes, one also sees the "Egyptian arms" exit (from *Babes in Arms*) and the "Charleston-variation" kicks in the second duet, as well as the "scissor-legged" split-lifts in the third duet, which are all direct references to the Nicholases' style of jazz dancing.

In *Babes in Arms*, Fayard and Harold were featured in several other scenes that were designed to draw on not only their talents but all of those of the cast. Nicholas home movies that were taken out of sequence of various scenes in *Babes in Arms*, as it was being performed at the Shubert Theatre, show the sheer number of softshoe dances, ballroom adagio dances, and tap dances that filled each musical scene. These not only demonstrate Balanchine's fluent drawing from several forms of dance, from ballet and ballroom dance to jazz and popular dance forms, but they also show the singing demands on this cast of talented performers, with the best songs going to the strongest voices and personalities.

Richard Rodgers and Larry Hart wrote a specialty song for the Nicholases called "All Dark People." While the brothers were duly impressed with the efforts of Rodgers and Hart, one of the lines in the song read, "All dark people is light on their feet." The line offended all members of the Nicholas family. "I hated it," says Fayard. "With all those wonderful songs in the show, that one got nowhere." Viola Nicholas objected the most strongly to the grammatical construction of the line "All dark people *is*," because it fed the conception of blacks as ignorant and unable to speak proper English. "She never allowed us to use dialect in movies or onstage," says Fayard about Viola. "She was always conscious of that and always wanted us to speak well." Fayard remembers a brief moment in a scene from the film *Kid Millions* in which Harold as a messenger boy asks Eddie Cantor if he can keep the tip. The line originally read, "Can I keep the quarter?" Viola instructed Harold to say, "*May* I keep the quarter?" Harold obeyed his mother's instructions and changed the line.

While they were rehearsing "All Dark People Is," Viola continually warned her sons not to sing "is." On opening night, Fayard and Harold followed their mother's instructions and sang, "All dark people *are* light on their feet." The stage manager barged into the brothers' dressing room after the show, ordering them to sing the song as written. "Mother was mad," says Fayard, "but we went back to singing the lyrics as they were given to us—though sometimes we would just forget, and the stage manager would get mad again, and come right back to our dressing room."[26]

"All Dark People" was a reminder to the Nicholases that black stereotypes persisted on Broadway and that black performers were expected to perpetuate them. The Nicholases prided themselves on being among a handful of African Americans who achieved fame on the Broadway stage in the thirties. But it was as performers—not black performers—that they wanted to be recognized. And while they could not extinguish the rampant stereotyping of blacks on the Broadway stage or in Hollywood films, they did continue to fight against them by directly refusing to play blackface comedy or to sing songs in "Negro" dialect. There were also other, more subtle means. "Where there was something that we had to fight for, we fought for it, but we didn't constantly dwell on it," Dorothy Nicholas remarked about the "All Dark People" incident. "I think that what has been one of the most sustaining things for us—and not only us, I mean most black people—is our ability to find humor in everything."[27]

For the Nicholases, perhaps the most effective strategy for breaking through the race barrier was to demonstrate exemplary professionalism, virtuosic rhythm dancing, and the highest degree of musicianship in their work. Their jazz dancing would not be the embodiment of the Russian-derived classical ballet of

Balanchine; Fayard and Harold had no aspirations as art dancers. The elegant long lines and asymmetrical forms that marked their jazz dancing, which would become more pronounced after they worked with Balanchine on Broadway, would be translated not into another form of classical ballet but rather into a more refined style of jazz dancing that was a purely American "class" act.

The expressive elegance of the Nicholas Brothers captured in James J. Kriegsmann's photograph in the late thirties (Photographs and Prints Division, Schomburg Center for Research in Black Culture, New York Public Library, Astor, Lenox and Tilden Foundations).

Six

Class Act and Challenge

1938–1945

Home movies taken of the Nicholas Brothers performing at the Cotton Club in the late thirties show them looking smartly streamlined in black tailcoats and dancing with such swirling speed that their tails are flying out behind them. The hand-held camera cuts from the jazz orchestra, playing on a raised platform at the rear of the stage, to a flight of stairs curving down onto the dance floor, where Harold is turning and tapping, brushing and patting the floor with the tip of his patent-leather shoe. With arms sailing, he waves the dance to Fayard, who strokes the floor with velvet-smooth glides; and together, they traverse the stage with slides and traveling crossover steps. As they move side by side and in perfect step with one another, their kicks and struts etch double-image designs in space. Whether leaping onto the platform, step-clapping down the stairs, or leaning into smooth-tapping *renverse* turns, the brothers retain their composure while exuding a cosmopolitan cool, right through to their exit—which has Fayard walking closely behind Harold, the two of them looking like one man with four legs. Sweeping back onto the stage for another bow, they simultaneously turn, bend, straighten up, and swoop off, their eyes never leaving the audience.

Then Fayard returns to the microphone and introduces a song, which both brothers sing; Harold cocks his head, rolls his eyes, and scats the lyrics, while Fayard conducts the orchestra by striking out the tempo with his hands, elbows, and buttocks. The song moves into another tap dance and flash finale in which Fayard, followed by Harold, runs across the stage and flips into a split, then jumps onto the platform into a split and off the platform into a split-and-recovery that sends them both spinning and strutting off the stage. Fayard, who is the last to exit, runs, slides, and salutes the audience before disappearing into the wings.

By the late thirties, on a number of New York stages, the Nicholas Brothers had formalized and perfected a tap dance act that combined singing, softshoe dancing, acrobatics, and rhythm tapping with precision movement and meticulous dress. "I don't want to use the word 'flamboyant' because they were too talented for that. They were born tap dancers with a lot of flair, a lot of style and just enough flash, which was very popular in those days,"[1] said Bobby Short about the brothers, whose dancing epitomized the most sophisticated jazz performance style in the Swing Era, known as the "class act."

At the turn of the century, concurrent with musical comedy dance teams working in the blackface tradition, there was an elite group of black performers who rejected the minstrel show stereotypes of the grinning-and-shuffling blackface clown. Clean-faced and well-dressed, these performers who insisted on the absolute perfection of sound, step, and manner were the forerunners of what developed in tap dance as the class act. While they eschewed the stereotype of the lazy, ignorant, incompetent Fool, they imitated and embellished the formal elegance and sophistication of certain white acts and ran headlong into the stereotype of the high-strutting Dandy, who "thought only of flashy clothes, flirtatious courting, new dances, and good looks."[2] These performers nevertheless aspired to a purely artistic expression that was driven by the desire for respectability and equality on the American concert stage.

When Bob Cole and John Rosamond Johnson began their partnership at the turn of the century, coon songs were the rage on the musical stage. Cole and Johnson decided not to write and perform songs that presented repellent portraits of black life, but instead to present themselves in a quiet and finished manner that was "artistic" to the minutest detail. The two entered, handsomely dressed in evening clothes, and talked about the party they were about to attend. They played Ignacy Jan Paderewski's Minuet in G, sang classical songs in German, as well as songs of their own composition, and fast became a success with the white theatrical elite.[3] Cole and Johnson were a far cry from the minstrel Dandy, who nurtured the white perception of the northern Negro, newly arrived in the big city, and illustrated just how ridiculous and ludicrous Negroes could be when they tried to live like "white gemmen." These parodies neatly reinforced what whites wanted to believe about northern Negroes and became permanent stereotypes of the urban black. Though Cole and Johnson abdicated playing such minstrel fops as "Count Julius Caesar Mars Napoleon Sinclair Brown," or other dandy Broadway swells who "preened and pranced across the minstrel stage on their way to 'De Colored Fancy Ball,'"[4] they were inextricably tied to the nineteenth-century tradition from which these characters sprang. Donning the attire of gentlemen—which their performance proved they were—Cole and Johnson touched on the role of the Dandy ever so gracefully, while ridiculing those aristocratic whites who aped European manners and cultivation.

At the turn of the century, the pioneering class-act team of Charles Johnson and Dora Babbige Dean billed themselves as "Johnson and Dean, the King and Queen of Colored Aristocracy," establishing the roles of the genteel Negro couple on the American stage. Dean was not a singer; she "talked" her songs and "posed" in fancy dresses. Johnson was not a tap dancer; he was a strutter in the cakewalk tradition, which he claimed to have introduced on Broadway. Together, they appealed to audiences through well-dressed elegance and impressive personalities. Johnson, who always presented himself in full evening dress—top hat, tailcoat, monocle, gloves, and cane—attributed his stage success to the inspiring stories of his mother, a former slave, who told him to always be "a real gentleman."[5]

After touring Europe with Johnson and Dean, dancers Rufus Greenlee and Thaddeus Drayton returned to New York and in 1914 formed an act that was influenced by Johnson. They matched formal dress with an elegant style of dancing in which strutting, ballroom dance, and cakewalking were combined with percussive stepping. In 1923, at the height of their career, Greenlee and Drayton opened at the uptown Cotton Club with a graceful dancing act that was described as "Picture Dancing," every move making a beautiful picture. Strolling onstage, they sang "You Great Big Beautiful Doll," doffing their hats and making sweeping bows; and in "Virginia Essence," a softshoe danced to stop-time, they filled in the breaks of the music with conversation in various foreign languages.

"With the partial exception of Charles Johnson, this was probably the first occasion that any pair of Negroes, *not* clad in overalls, performed the Soft Shoe on the American stage," writes Marshall Stearns, who claimed that it was in the early twenties, and chiefly in reference to Greenlee and Drayton, that the phrase "class act" came into general use among black dancers.[6]

Developing within the creative atmosphere of the Harlem Renaissance, the class-act dancer made further renovations to the minstrel show Dandy by presenting an image of the "New Negro" who knowingly established his own culture's standards of class. Such elegant tap soloists in the twenties who prepared the way for the dozens of class acts in the thirties and forties included the handsomely dressed Maxie McCree, who ended his act with a drop-to-the-knee bow, and Aaron Palmer, who strutted, sang, and tapped with impressive ease to slowed-down and soft music. Jack Wiggins wore high-heeled patent-leather shoes as he performed refined translations of the Argentine tango. And Eddie Rector wore a top hat, spats, and tails in an act that emphasized clean and precise footwork; his "stage dancing," as it was called, dovetailed one step into another to create a seamless flow of sound and movement.

Dancing at the Cotton Club in the thirties, and often on the same bill as the Nicholas Brothers, were Pete, Peaches, and Duke (Pete Nugent, Irving Beaman, and Duke Miller), who further defined the class act through their precision-styled dancing. Dressed in yachting costumes, they opened with a military drill, tapping as if they were glued together; they closed with a one-man-exit, all three facing the audience in single file, doing a tricky step together while disappearing into the wings as though they were one man with three pairs of legs. Also at the Cotton Club in the late thirties, the Cotton Club Boys, whose dancing was captured on Nicholas home movies, wore Foreign Legion-style suits and tapped out military drills in precision style.

"What one remembers about dancers of that era was their immaculateness—not just the way they danced, because all of it was crystal clear, but the way they looked," says jazz singer Bobby Short. "It was the style of the 1930s, if you were in vaudeville, to be dressed to the nines. And the Nicholases were always dressed beautifully. Everything was taken care of, from the nails and shave to the clothes they wore—that's what gave them the overall style they had."[7]

More than any outward show, it was the way the Nicholas Brothers moved and used the stage that distinguished them as class-act dancers. "They just didn't stay in one spot and dance like Bill Robinson, they were all over the stage," the drummer Max Roach observed.[8] And as tap dancer Pete Nugent once said, "I'm a tap dancer first, last and always, but if you have to make a choice, I prefer all body motion and no tap to all tap and no body motion."[9] Like Nugent, the Nicholas Brothers were often praised for their full-bodied dancing, Fayard especially for his expressive use of the hands. "Fayard has something no other dancer has, hands!" says Leonard Reed. "He has the greatest hands of any dancer I've seen. . . . There's flair in the way he uses his head, his eyes. . . . When they hit the stage and Fayard makes one move, they've got their eyes on him."[10]

The Nicholases' impeccable dress was matched with impeccable tap execution. Their insistence on perfection, that every move be synchronized to fit with the music, and that their every sound be clean and clear, gave them purity and integrity. Various segments of Nicholas home movies, shot by Lorenzo Hill in the late thirties from the wings and front rows of an unidentified theatre, illustrate

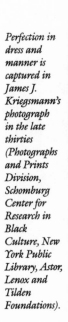

*Perfection in
dress and
manner is
captured in
James J.
Kriegsmann's
photograph
in the late
thirties
(Photographs
and Prints
Division,
Schomburg
Center for
Research in
Black
Culture, New
York Public
Library, Astor,
Lenox and
Tilden
Foundations).*

the smooth precision with which the brothers moved. In one section, the brothers spin to the right and left while brushing the toes
or digging the heels; they shuffle sideways, with their arms placed
over each other's shoulders; and they snap their fingers and pat
their legs in the walkaround, shuffling lightly on the tips of their
toes, always in synchrony. In another dancing section, the degree of
every turn, the timing of every arm gesture, and the length of every
step give the appearance of sameness—even though Fayard is taller
and has longer legs.

Their exacting standards of precision dancing, which challenged them to execute the highest degree of control and nuance in technique, could only be achieved through constant practice and the repetition of steps. Then, of course, it was made to look as though it could be tossed off effortlessly. "We always liked to go onstage, know what we were going to do, and do it the same way every time," says Fayard. The formal repetition of their routines was largely due to the fact that the brothers were performing with big swing orchestras, which sometimes numbered as many as thirty musicians who played off written arrangements of the brothers' music. Little room was allowed either the dancers or the musicians for improvisation, except in previously arranged solo spots. "The only time we'd improvise is *after* our act," says Fayard. "People would want more and more, so we'd go back onstage, and my brother and I would improvise for the ladies. . . . But that's not our act, improvising."[11] Said Leonard Reed: "They did the same thing the same way each time they performed. That's what made them such perfectionists. This is the only way in show business you can become a perfectionist—to do the same thing the same way until you've accomplished what you have. And when that exhausts itself, you have to replace it with something, and do *that* over and over and over. . . . That's where professionalism comes from—work.[12]

Work they had. When Fayard and Harold returned to New York early in 1937, after almost a year in London, the brothers immediately began rehearsals at the downtown Cotton Club. "It was more glamorous," said Reed about the new Cotton Club. "The girls were pretty, they were dressed up and didn't have bandannas on, and there weren't cotton bales laying around."[13] And it was at the Cotton Club, while doubling at several other New York theatres, that the brothers refined their dancing into a sophisticated and aurally complex jazz form. By the spring of 1937, the swing era was at its peak, and the second edition of the Cotton Club Parade (March 17–June 13), as advertised in *Variety* (24 March 1937) was "Rockin' in Rhythm to the Musical Magic of Duke Ellington and His Famous Orchestra." From the joyous and relaxed sound of Ellington's "Rockin' in Rhythm," danced by

Bessie Dudley, to "Chile," a Cuban-styled rhumba sung by Ivy Anderson and danced by the ballroom teams of Anise and Aland and Renee and Estela, the rhythmic moods at the club ranged from celebratory to mysterious.

The second edition of the Cotton Club Parade, "Cotton Club Express," with an opening set that featured the rear observation platform of a speeding train, had fast-paced songs and dances staged by Clarence Robinson, with specialty numbers by "Tap Mathematician" Bill Bailey, the Three Giants of Rhythm ("tall and husky legomaniacs"), and Kaloah, whose "rippling rump and tremolo tummy" did "Afro-Harlem gyrations" to Ellington's "Black and Tan Fantasy." "There's plenty of dancing via the Nicholas Brothers in combo," wrote *Variety* (24 March 1937), and the "Young Harold whams 'em with his Taps is Tops solo as the single outstander of the proceedings." Wearing formal white tailcoats to perform their dance "Specialty" in Act I, Fayard and Harold donned feathered costumes in Act II to introduce "Peckin'," "The New Dance Craze," which combined imitations of farmyard chickens pecking at food with "shuffling in hybrid Truckin' and Susie-Q." The music for this dance number, introduced by Mae Diggs and backed by the chorus, was based on Cootie Williams's solo in "Rockin' in Rhythm."[14]

The third edition, which opened on September 22, 1937, was to headline Bill Robinson with Cab Calloway. Because of the unexpected cancellation by Robinson, who went to Hollywood to film *Rebecca of Sunnybrook Farm* with Shirley Temple, the Nicholas Brothers were pressed into service, co-starring with Calloway. They had one week in which to rehearse the show, and Harold handled the routines abandoned by Robinson with such aplomb that he received tumultuous applause from the audience on opening night. "The 16-year-old tapster of inherent cute personality is a precocious trooper," wrote *Variety* (29 September 1937), "and save for the fact that he's been around these parts a bit too much—lacking the vintage qualities which makes such vets as Bojangles acceptable at any time—he sustained his end hardily."

The third edition of the Cotton Club Parade, "Tall, Tan and

Terrific," which was praised by *Variety* (29 September 1937) for its "frenzied . . . fast-dancing pace" but slighted for being "overboard on hoofing," was staged by Leonard Reed. He also gathered much of the dancing talent, including Tip, Tap, and Toe, who tapped on top of a large, wooden drum; the Chocleteers, a comedy dance trio; Dynamite Hooker, an eccentric dancer who vibrated his body while dancing at frenetic speed; George "Shorty" Snowden and his Lindy Hoppers; Cuban rhumba dancers Pete and Company; and cooch dancer Tondelayo. Reed remembered that the Nicholases "were sensational in the Cotton Club" and that he scattered them liberally through the show, staging them in both the opening and the finale.[15] One number, the "Bill Robinson Walk," featured Harold doing an outstanding Bojangles impression. And in a number with June Richmond, Harold jumped into the singer's arms and was carried by her offstage.

Harold was coming into his own by the fall of 1937, and he was revealed as a particularly creative performer, reminiscent in many ways of a young Bill Robinson; columnists such as Walter Winchell, Louis Sobel, and Ed Sullivan were beginning to single him out.[16] Fayard meanwhile, who was ever the prolific choreographer, created his first solo work in collaboration with the composer and arranger Chappy Willett. Fayard had originally conceived of this long, complex tap dance as a duet but says Harold was not interested in learning it. ("He knew it was going to be a little difficult," remembered Fayard of Harold, "so I said okay, I'll do it by myself.") Working with Willett in his Harlem studio, Fayard danced the steps and hummed the accents of rhythms as Willett, on piano, improvised the melody.

"It was like we were in a rehearsal hall with mirrors and everything," Fayard recalls. "He wrote down everything I said and showed him—I even sang some of it to him—Da da, dat-da dee do dee daa, like that. That would be the introduction. No music." Unlike the thirty-two-bar musical structure the brothers most often used when working with big bands, Fayard's more openly structured solo "was more like a classical thing,"[17] he says, and it stretched past the eight-bar phrase. Instead of being episodic,

with the B section following A, and so on, there was a more continuous weave of sound and movement. The resulting tapwork
not only dovetailed with the melody but also included special
accents that were reinforced by the accompaniment. Fayard did
not have a name for it, so he called it "Dance Specialty," and he
performed it after his and Harold's "Specialty" act at the Cotton
Club. Willett's formal, written arrangement of the music for big
band enabled Fayard to perform the dance not only in the intimate setting of the Cotton Club but also on bigger stages and
with other big-band orchestras.

After the closing of the Cotton Club's third edition in March
1938, the William Morris Agency booked the brothers on a
South American tour, which settled them into a two-month
engagement at the Club Utto in Rio de Janeiro, following a performance there by Josephine Baker. In Brazil, the brothers
learned some songs in Portuguese as well as many popular social
dances, including the samba. When the Nicholas Brothers
returned to the fifth edition at the Cotton Club in the fall of
1938 (opening September 28), again to share top billing with
Cab Calloway and His Orchestra, they could not have arrived in
New York at a more opportune time. Afro-Cuban dancing (cha-
cha-cha, rhumba, conga) had become the rage and, as ever,
reflecting *au courant* style, the Cotton Club featured a new dance
band, the Tocares Orchestra, with which Mae Johnson sang and
the Nicholases danced to "Congo Conga." Nicholas home
movies of their performance during this period show how the
brothers inflected their movements with sexy but subtle isola-
tions of the hips and shoulders that they had incorporated from
Afro-Brazilian dance.

Swing had also captivated the public taste by the late thirties,
with major white bands and swing orchestras overshadowing all
but the most successful black bands and orchestras, such as
Calloway and Ellington. The Cotton Club had reflected this
trend in a grand redecorating effort by Julian Harrison, former
scenic designer for film producer Cecil B. De Mille. Murals were
installed in the bar and entrance lounge that depicted the evolution of swing, in which such white bandleaders as Benny

Goodman, Tommy Dorsey, Gene Krupa, and Larry Clinton were seen—with a "sepian-twist," in blackface.[18]

In keeping with the swing spirit, Calloway led the number "A Lesson in Jive," and the Nicholases sang and danced with Whyte's Lindy Hoppers. They also introduced and popularized "The New Boogie-Woogie," a swinging version of an old step associated with the early style of piano playing. Boogie-woogie, a percussive style of piano blues characterized by the use of blue chordal progressions combined with forceful, repetitive left-hand bass figures, was recorded in the twenties; in its brief vogue in the late thirties, it was linked to the swing craze.

There was a new singing act in the fifth edition that riveted Harold's attention. The Dandridge Sisters—Dorothy and Vivian Dandridge and Etta James—had just arrived in New York after playing small parts in several Hollywood films. Singing "A-Tisket A-Tasket," "Swing Low, Sweet Chariot," and "Madly in Love," their delicate harmonies sweetened the show, while Dorothy's soprano rang clear into Harold's heart. Dorothy was fourteen years old when she first saw Harold, who was in rehearsal at the club, but he eyed her as he was tapping. "I had heard of him, had seen photos of him, and I knew that he and his brother were already famous and money-making entertainers," Dorothy later wrote. "I learned that they had a big car and a chauffeur, and that their mother, who traveled with them, had a mink coat. All of which was impressive to a fourteen-year-old suddenly in the company of big-timers."[19] The seventeen-year-old Harold courted her, and their ensuing romance culminated in marriage in September 1942.

While performing in the midnight and two A.M. shows at the Cotton Club, the brothers also performed, or "doubled," in the matinees and evening shows of several New York theatres. They had a successful three-week engagement at the Paramount with Mitzi Green and the Clyde McCoy Orchestra, which their manager, Herman Stark, announced in *Variety* (9 March 1938). They also played the Roxy, Loew's State, the Capital, the Strand, and the Palace; but if ever they had a second home, it was the Apollo. From its opening in 1935 on 125th Street between Seventh and Eighth Avenues, the Apollo featured more dance acts than any other New York theatre. As many as fifty top dance acts played there regularly. The Apollo also had the toughest audience in New York. "If you got past that audience you were really good. If they didn't like you, they let you know," says Marion Coles, a member of the Apollo's famous "Number One Chorus," which was the finest female tapping line in town.[20]

Shows at the Apollo were designed to appeal to the common folk of Harlem, who relied on it "to provide a little elegance . . . and generate some excitement."[21] Doors opened at ten in the morning and closed past midnight, with each of the five shows a day comprising a short film or cartoon, then a newsreel followed by a feature film, and then the stage show, when the master of ceremonies would announce, to the rising applause and screams of the audience, "Ladies and Gentlemen, it's showtime at the Apollo!" After a band's number with the chorus, the emcee brought on a "sight act,"—such as a tap dancer, an acrobat, or an animal act—then a singer, followed by another chorus number and a comedy act, and finally the featured attraction.

When the Nicholas Brothers performed at the Apollo with the big jazz bands and swing orchestras of Duke Ellington, Jimmie Lunceford, Don Redmond, Floyd Ray, Claude Hopkins, or Count Basie, they were always booked as the Apollo's featured attraction. "They were screaming from the rafters, as they later did with the Mills Brothers, Teddy Hale . . . and Baby Laurence," said Leonard Reed about Apollo audiences.[22] This raises the question of how the Nicholas Brothers, who were in marked contrast to the blackface comedians and black comedy dancers with whom they shared the Apollo stage, were able to draw similar responses, in the form of loud whistles, cheers, and stomps. Their act, curiously enough, was not so very different from the one performed at the Cotton Club; from choreography to costumes and musical arrangements, it could be repeated in or adapted to any venue in which the Nicholases performed. How was it that with roughly the same act, the Nicholases received as tumultuous a response from largely black audiences uptown as they did from mostly white audiences downtown?

The answer has much to do with a key component in the

structure of the Nicholases' tap choreography, which transformed their performance from one that was merely presentational to one that actively engaged its audience, as well as giving it the look of being improvised when it had been carefully rehearsed. A re-examination of a segment of home movies taken of the Nicholas Brothers performing in an unidentified New York theatre in the late thirties reveals what made their performance universally appealing.

The film segment (without sound) shows the brothers in the midst of performing their act, and as usual they look elegant, in white suits with black ties and with handkerchiefs tucked neatly into their jacket pockets. Dancing side by side, they beat out a fast, rhythm-driven combination that progresses from close-to-the-floor time steps and pullbacks to lateral-splaying Charleston variations and wing steps. Fayard solos with a flurry of back-running flaps; when he perches on the tips of his toes at the end of a phrase, his side-brushing wings lift him farther up in the air. Harold joins Fayard. Fayard steps aside, and then Harold solos, repeating Fayard's running flaps but adding cramprolls and heel-drops; he repeats the toe perches and wings but then transforms them by leaning forward on the diagonal to deliver a succession of his trademark trenches.

One brother steps aside as the other solos, directing his focus to the sounds, steps, and patterns the other is performing (Fayard looks and claps, Harold points and sounds out). They join together in a synchronized rhythm-tap and softshoe dance that summarizes what they have already done. On the second round of solos, they trade eights (each dancer takes eight beats of the measure and passes back the next measure of eight), passing back and forth the moves and rhythm patterns from the previous solos, but varying and/or one-upping on them. In one sequence, the brothers trade glides, which extend into lengthier slides, which in turn are further extended into splits.

In another sequence of trades (that looks as though it is being improvised), cramprolls and hops progress to perches on the tips of the toes, and these in turn are taken into hopping perches; two-legged wings are added, and then finally the more difficult one-legged wings (in which the standing leg balances with foot in full point while the working leg brushes laterally sideways). The Nicholases build the combinations with increasingly more daring and unexpected moves. In the exciting finale, Fayard, followed in direct succession by Harold (which gives the image of a double-exposed picture), runs across the stage, flips onto an upstage platform to land in a split-and-recover, jumps off the platform into a split-and-recover, and soars off the stage.

The concluding section of the routine, in which the brothers repeat and vary, trade and one-up on each other's steps, is based on the structure and form of a challenge dance. It is the challenge, with its dynamic exchange of rhythm and movement, which gives the brothers a structure for building their routine to a climax, while also giving their performance the look of being improvised.

The oral and written histories of tap dance are replete with challenge dances, from jigging competitions on plantations staged by white masters for their slaves to challenge dances in the walkaround finale of the minstrel show, showdowns in the street, displays of one-upmanship in the social club, and juried buck-and-wing contests on the vaudeville stage. Motivated by a dare, focused by the strict attention of one's opponent, and developed through the stealing and trading of steps, "challenge" is the general term for any competition, contest, breakdown, or showdown in which tap dancers compete before an audience of spectators or judges. Fiercely competitive, the challenge was the dynamic and rhythmically expressive engine that drove the tap performance, setting the stage for a "performed" battle that engaged dancers in a dialogue of rhythm, motion, and witty repartee.

Tap dance, as mentioned earlier, evolved from the fusion of Irish and West African musical and step-dancing traditions in the Caribbean and through three hundred years in America, in which time the Irish jig and African *gioube* (secular and sacred step dances) were fused with juba, buck-and-wing, and jigging dances, all early forms of tap. The congruence of the belief systems and the shared competitive traditions of the indentured Irish and enslaved West Africans also contributed to both the development of tap dance and its perpetuation of the key features of the challenge.

Both the African myths of the Oriki-Esu and the Gaelic legends of Airthirne were described by an oral tradition of folk tales and songs of slander that shaped an "insult" tradition of verbal abuse and satire. (Esu-Elegara, the trickster figure of Yoruban mythology, was a "divine linguist" who spoke all languages and was known for his powers of magic, parody, and satire; Airthirne, whose exploits are recounted in ancient Gaelic manuscripts, was a divine poet feared for his "word magic" and so powerful in his poems of slander that he could demand the single eye of a king.) The "Song of Marvels," or Lying Songs of the Irish, were sung in competition using fantastic inventions of lying, boasting, and verbal trickery to amaze, dumbfound, and entertain. The West African "Songs of Derision" were so powerful that an intended victim paid griots (African storytellers, keepers of the family history) not to sing them. These musical forms and expressive traditions were brought to the United States and to the Caribbean by slaves and indentured servants. Sung in fields, danced in slave quarters, recited to fiddle tunes, they cast satirical aspersions on masters and became the basis for blues songs, calypso "cutting" contests, and jigging competitions in which insults added ammunition to the trip-hammering of feet.

Because tap dance is learned by watching people dance—its "technique" is transmitted visually, aurally, and corporeally through a rhythmic exchange between dancers and musicians—mimicry is necessary for the mastery of form. The Irish-American actor Thomas "Daddy" Rice reportedly stole the song and jig "Jump Jim Crow" from a black stable boy in the 1820s; he also replicated the black's ragged clothes and worn leather boots and used burnt cork to make up his face. Rice's success led to the development of the minstrel show, a blackface act involving singing, fast talking, and shuffle-and-wing dancing. The African-American dancer William Henry Lane, who was hailed "King of All Dancers" after beating the champion white minstrel John Diamond in a series of challenge dances in the 1840s, was crowned "Master Juba" because he could skillfully imitate all the reigning white minstrel dancers of the day, after which he would execute his own specialty steps that no one could copy. One important aspect of Lane's challenge was his "signifying"—an aggressive style of joking in which one puts down, berates, sounds on, or pulls rank by referring to an aspect of an opponent's behavior. Lane signified on Diamond by masterfully duplicating his steps, then one-upped the challenge by showing off his own specialty. After the Civil War, African-American minstrel performers mimicked, stole, and signified on each other in minstrel show challenge dances with improvisatory sections that brought new steps and styles into tap dancing. They soon incorporated an entirely new vocabulary of black vernacular social dances and steps, from rubber-legging, shimmies, and animal dances to wings, slides, chugs, and drags.[23]

Around 1895, black musical comedy burst onto the American stage with the vigorous duple-metered, syncopated music of ragtime. African-American performers coming from the black touring circuits of the South were making their professional debut on the Broadway stage during this period, as tap dance developed as a musical form that paralleled jazz. In the Jazz Age twenties and swing-era thirties, tap dance was "refined" into a concert form by the two-man class act that "tamed" the challenge with performance-level duels, thereby softening the edge of fierce competition.

Instead of being pitted against each other, class-act "challengers" were partners who were often billed as "Brothers." Instead of one-upping each other, they combined their specialties in building to a climax a routine in which structured improvisation was reserved for some sections of the dance; most often these were solos during which each dancer demonstrated specialty steps and traded on them. Instead of mimicking the other's steps, as in the traditional challenge, the two moved as one, each a mirror image of the other. The practice of signifying further evolved the repetition of rhythmic phrases into paragraphs of sound and movement that, when traded back and forth, became a lively and witty dialogue between dancers, enabling a development of complex rhythmical ideas.

The most traditional identifiers of the challenge—the use of insult and praise, the mimicking and mocking of steps—were not immediately recognizable when watching a performance by the Nicholas Brothers or by the dozens of other class acts of the thirties. Yet the challenge was very much alive and thriving on the stage. It sometimes took the form of a separate dance section within the framework of the dance act; it might be a call-and-response exchange that gave formal structure to the sequence of rhythmical ideas. "Most of the class acts," says Honi Coles of the class act team of Coles and Atkins, "opened with a flash number, followed with a softshoe and inevitably led to some form of a challenge, in which partners would do some competitive dancing among themselves."[24]

In the swing-era thirties, there were contests of all sorts, from the swinging "battle of the bands" at the Apollo to lindy-hop competitions at the Savoy Ballroom. Veteran hoofers confess to sitting in the front row of the Lafayette Theatre to watch the opening of all new tap dance acts, only to rush back to the Hoofers Club, where there was one unwritten rule: "Thou Shalt Not Copy Anyone's Steps—Exactly!" "Black performers didn't have the easy way, to go and let somebody teach them," explained Leonard Reed. "They had to do like I did, and like everybody else. It's called stealing. You go to a theatre and you see somebody do something, and you say 'I like that—I'll do it, but I'll do it a different way.' They eliminate the bad by watching other people."[25]

Fayard and Harold Nicholas were too young to hang out at the Hoofers Club—and with the high "professional" aspirations that Viola and Ulysses Nicholas had for their sons, they would not think of allowing them to hoof at the club anyway. Performing at the Lafayette Theatre in the early thirties, it was the Nicholas Brothers from whom would-be tap dancers attempted to steal, although the brothers tried desperately to avoid it. Reed said that in the days when the Nicholases got themselves together, very few people actually saw them in rehearsal: "They were doing their own thing and it was a closed shop. They wouldn't let anybody watch what they were doing because they didn't want you to steal it before they had done it."[26] While there were few who could steal from the Nicholas Brothers, there were some who challenged them, as did the Berry Brothers at the Cotton Club in the fall of 1938.

The Berry Brothers—Ananias, Jimmy, and Warren—were members of an acrobatic, flash dance team that first performed at the Cotton Club in 1929. Dressed in tailcoats with top hats, they began their act with one brother doing an elegant, high-kicking strut, a cane under his arm, while two brothers sang and posed; then they all strutted together, stopping and starting in sudden contrasts of tempo to end with an explosion of acrobatics, precisely timed splits, jumps, and somersaults—all while passing the cane. For the fifth edition (fall 1938) of the Cotton Club Parade, which the Nicholases co-hosted with Calloway, the Nicholas Brothers were scheduled to perform their specialty near the middle of the production.

Herman Stark, who was in charge of programming, scheduled the Berrys to close the show. "He also happened to be the personal manager of our rivals, the Nicholas Brothers," Warren Berry later told Marshall Stearns, "and he put us on last so we had to top the preceding acts or die." When Ananias, the eldest of the Berrys, questioned Stark about the order of events, Stark reportedly cut him short with "You're the Berry Brothers! Let's see what you can really do."[27]

Cab Calloway's orchestra was playing on an elevated platform at the rear of the stage, and about twelve feet above and behind the platform, there was a balcony with stairs on each side. The Berrys performed their dance act as they had been performing it for years. To challenge the Nicholas Brothers, in an obvious reference to their signature slides and splits, the Berrys devised a new and more exciting ending to their routine. Ananias and Jimmy jumped up on the band platform, then sprinted further up a flight of stairs to leap over the heads of the musicians, twelve feet through the air; they landed in a split on both sides of Warren, who at the same time snapped out of a twisting back somersault into a split on the last note of the music.[28] Though the Berry Brothers were the victors in this tap challenge, their performance was regarded as a publicity stunt by the Cotton

Club management. The Berrys, who compressed jazz dance and acrobatics into a brilliant theatrical style, were flash dancers. The Nicholases were jazz tap dancers.

Where the Nicholas Brothers more veritably engaged in a challenge was not with other dance teams but between themselves. From the beginning of their professional career as the Nicholas Kids, there was always some form of a challenge incorporated into a Nicholas tap routine. In "China Boy" from *Pie, Pie, Blackbird* (1932), the choreography was structured as a series of solos that took the form of a challenge dance; it developed from a call-and-response repetition of toe-perches to one-up variations on wings and culminated in the brothers "flying" with one-legged wing steps. "Yes, we did a challenge," says Fayard. "We'd start out together and do a little chorus together, and then I would back away and he would do a step. And when he'd finish his step, then I would do one." Fayard adds that it was "not to see who was the better dancer," but instead to get together with Harold, to praise him and direct the focus to what he was doing. "He would do it and look pretty, and I'd admire him doing it. Then I'd do my step, and he'd look at me and admire me. Then we'd get back together and finish the routine."²⁹ There is also a challenge dance in *Kid Millions*, in the last two choruses of the musical number, not so much between the brothers and Eddie Cantor but as between the brothers themselves. In it, side-brushing wing steps and back-sliding trenches are passed back and forth, and these in turn progress into tip-of-the-toe wings. In *Big Broadcast of 1936*, in the last section of solos at the end of their routine, the brothers also trade off on one-legged wing steps, which lead the musical number to an exciting climax. Similar exchanges of wing and air steps can be seen in various brief sections of Nicholas home movies.

The challenge was one of the few opportunities the brothers had to improvise before an audience. "The only time we'd improvise," says Fayard, "was after we did our act, and we could have some fun. We'd go back onstage and I'd go to the mike and say, 'Thank you very much, ladies and gentlemen, and now we're going to do a little challenge for you.' And my brother and I would improvise for the ladies." The brothers learned about challenge dances, both fierce and frivolous, early in their development as dancers. An advertisement in the *Philadelphia Tribune* (13 February 1930) for Bill Robinson at the Pearl Theatre reads: "You haven't seen dancing until you've seen the challenge between Bo Jangles and his 15 Girls." Though it was hardly a traditional challenge, it testifies to popular references to challenge and competitive dancing in this period.

A sublime example of the way the Nicholas Brothers both used the challenge dance as a resource and extended its traditional form can be seen in one scene in *Down Argentine Way*, their first film for Twentieth Century-Fox (1940). Fayard and Harold are performing in a swanky nightclub (nearly identical to their performance at the Cotton Club in the late thirties). Inside the club, the Latin orchestra plays the eight-bar introduction to "Argentina" as Fayard and Harold, dressed in tailcoats, enter the club and hand their top hats and canes to a pair of doormen. Harold opens by singing the title song in Spanish as Fayard shakes a pair of maracas; they come together on the last four beats of the bar to tap dance.

The second chorus begins with slipping and sliding steps and a rhythm break in double time. Because of the inherent "slippery" nature of the slide, these steps add exciting offbeat accents and elongations of the beat; they comprise the "theme" of the choreography. Harold solos with cramprolls and back-slipping chugs; as a variation on the slide, he rubs the whole of the foot along the floor. Fayard adds skidding steps and a double-time break. When he passes the dance to Harold, he tries to take it back by waving his hands toward Harold, who mimes being stretched and released like a rubber band. When Harold snaps free, he dives into six rounds of his own signature trenches, which he then repeats with a surprise ending—a split propelled by a front flip.

When Harold struts away, waving the dance to Fayard, it is clear that he has challenged Fayard to come up with a better split than the one he just did: the challenge has begun. Fayard jumps into the air and, with legs splayed, drops right down to the floor

into a full split. From that position, he makes eight half-turns on the ground, then pulls himself—with no hands to assist—up to a stand. Harold answers by diving into a forward flip, which takes him into a full split; on the recovery, he does a one-arm flip and split, then repeats the entire flip-split-rhythm phrase, walking away by sending Fayard a cocky "Top that!" salute. And Fayard does: holding the ends of a white handkerchief he has gallantly unfurled from his breast pocket, Fayard jumps over the handkerchief to land in a split; he then pulls himself back up to jump back over the handkerchief again to land in a split. While Fayard stands proud with legs outspread, replacing the handkerchief in his pocket, Harold, who has been standing behind him, takes a running slide through Fayard's legs. He pulls himself up just in the nick of time to finish the last four bars of music; after a slip and a slide and a fast rhythm break, the brothers bow and exit.

Fayard jumps over his handkerchief to Harold's surprise in the challenge sequence of their dance routine in Down Argentine Way, *Twentieth Century-Fox 1940 (Harold Nicholas Archive).*

Perhaps the most exciting elaborations on the idea of the challenge dance can be seen in this performance by the Nicholas Brothers, as slides are extended into slip-sliding glides, which in turn are pushed to their farthest extension with splits, which in turn are translated into a dazzling variety of acrobatic maneuvers. Drawing on two distinct African-American expressive traditions, the Nicholases fused the elegant and highly stylized movement of the class act with the dynamic, rhythmic drive of the challenge. While one tradition aspired to the attainment and display of physical perfection—to achieve through synchrony, precision, balance, clarity—the other was driven by competition toward the more inward-focused rhythmic exchange between dancers and musicians. One gave a beautiful form and shape to the "body" of the dance, while the other gave the dance its breath, dynamism, and driving beat.

"We were little gentlemen, and talked well to all the people, from Harlem to Broadway. And in that way, we showed them that black people had class," Fayard remarked, his sentiment expressing the belief that equality and respectability could be achieved through the professional manner in which they presented themselves. "They were pushing those people," Harold added about Hollywood producers and their stars. "But we had to push ourselves. We pushed us."[30] While the Nicholases' aspirations for respectability and equality were never completely realized within the commercial realms of white Hollywood and Broadway, they were in the black community, among those who deeply acknowledged how the brothers had transformed the minstrel-rooted Dandy into the supreme refinement of dance artist.

"The Nicholas Brothers were household names in the black community when I was growing up during the 1930s," said drummer Max Roach. "They were the heroes of young people." Jazz singer Bobby Short confessed: "I wanted to be like the Nicholas Brothers. I wanted their success, I wanted to look like them, act like them, and make that kind of money." Roach believes the Nicholas Brothers were role models: "We couldn't afford to dress like them because this was coming out of the Depression. But they were big stars. They were the ones who inspired us, and who we looked up to in those hard days in this country. They went outside of the art for us, they were symbols, and they meant a great deal to our community." Dorothy Nicholas confirms simply: "They were asked to sing and to dance. So they sang and danced as best they knew how, which was their way of bringing dignity to their race."[31]

The Nicholas Brothers singing the title song in Down Argentine Way, *Twentieth Century-Fox 1940 (Harold Nicholas Archive).*

Seven

Forties Swing, Hollywood Flash

1940–1945

When the Twentieth Century-Fox musical *Down Argentine Way* was released in 1940, one scene triggered a vociferous response from audiences across the country. That scene, just three and a half minutes long, featured the Nicholas Brothers, singing and tap dancing with lightning speed to a swinging samba. Audiences watching the scene would not stop whistling, clapping, and stomping their feet. Some even shouted up to the operator in the projection booth to stop the film, rewind it, and show the scene again. In the South, where it was the custom to censor segments of a film that contained scenes with black actors, *Down Argentine Way* was shown uncut, and both black and white audiences in their segregated movie houses screamed in excitement over the tap dancing of the Nicholas Brothers.

In a small town in Texas, the local newspaper informed its readers of how many minutes into the film the Nicholas Brothers appeared; townsfolk arrived at the theatre minutes before the scene, stood and cheered while watching it, and left soon after it was over. In Brooklyn, the marquee of a movie theatre announced, "Nicholas Brothers starring in *Down Argentine Way*," even though that was the one and only scene in which they appeared. Even on Hollywood Boulevard in Los Angeles, the starring names of Betty Grable and Don Ameche were dropped from the marquee of the Hollywood Theatre, which instead announced, "Nicholas Brothers in *Down Argentine Way.*"

This scene—which director Irving Cummings initially wanted to cut away from, but which by persuasion of choreographer Nick Castle was left in for preview audiences—opened with the Nicholas Brothers entering the Club Rendezvous, a swanky nightclub in Buenos Aires. Dressed in their classic black tailcoats, they hand their top hats and canes to a pair of doormen and move out onto the dance floor as the eight-piece band plays the eight-bar intro-duction to "Argentina." The film's title song was already familiar. In an earlier scene, Don Ameche had introduced it in Spanish. "Flo-recerá un querer, se llega usted ir a ver, Argentina," he sang smoothly while playing the piano at a dinner party. Looking hand-some in his black tuxedo as he crooned, Ameche brushed lightly over the duple-time samba he played (ONE *and* TWO *and*) on the piano. He captured the samba's characteristic "bounce" action that occurs over two beats of the bar (counted as ONE *and*), which gave the song a feeling of gay affection.

When Betty Grable repeated the song, in the same scene, she sang it in English and ironed out the bounce: "You'll find your life will begin, the very moment you're in Argentina," she sang serenely to Ameche. The smooth 2/4 rhythm in the song was only broken after "Argentina," sung not with words but with a subtle clicking of the teeth in a syncopated rhythm:

(and)	2	(and)	1	(and)	2	(and)	1
click	click	click		click		click	

She continued to sing, "You'll be as gay as can be, if you can learn to sí sí like a Latin/ And mister soon you will learn, you may never return to Manhattan," moving her way through the tables of guests onto the dance floor. Swinging her arms and swaying her hips in a midriff-baring top and flounced gown, Grable delivered a swirling tap dance in high-heeled shoes, in which she clicked out the rhythm of a Cubanola and brought all the guests and partners to their feet.

In the final chorus, the ballroom was filled with formally dressed couples, bouncing elegantly to the ONE *and* TWO *and* rhythm of the samba. The whole of the musical number was made ever more exciting when, near the end of the last chorus, six drummers pounded out a ONE *two* THREE *four* rhythm on the tocare drums as couples danced a square, closed-partner samba (to the dance rhythm of slow-slow-QUICK-QUICK), punctuating their social dance from time to time with the side-tapping rhythm of "and one TWO and THREE and FOUR." As the camera panned over the ballroom of shimmering figures, it pulsated with the rhythm of the samba.

The romance in *Down Argentine Way* between a wealthy American woman (Grable) and an upper-class Argentinian horse breeder (Ameche) was enhanced musically with Latin American folk songs and dances, Tin Pan Alley tunes, and American jazz standards that had been arranged and orchestrated for both Latin percussion ensemble and swing orchestra. At the Club Rendezvous, the Nicholas Brothers' scene combined the best of Latin American and swing rhythms for their rendition of "Argentina."

Harold opened by singing the song in Spanish: "Florecerá un querer, se llega usted ir a ver, Argentina," he sang, enunciating the foreign words percussively; and in the style of a scatsong, he retrieved the lively ONE-*ee and a* TWO-*ee* beat of the samba. As Harold "sang" the rhythm, translating the rhythmic bounce of "Delatará su vivir al contestar con sí sí dulcemente/ Un amorcito tendrá que con carino dira lo que siente" into eye winks and shoulder shrugs, Fayard shook out the rhythm on a pair of maracas. Both brothers came together after "Argentina," clicking their teeth in percussive imitation of Spanish castanets.

The Latin-flavored arrangement of the song for the brothers featured the 2/4 rhythmic ostinato of the samba, played by the band's rhythm section, and the employment of various Latin percussion instruments to accent different beats—such as a triplet figure (ONE *two* THREE—) on the wooden clave, and the duple (ONE *and* TWO *and*) rhythm on the guira, a gourd instrument.

While Harold and the orchestra held the Latin beat in the AA sections of the first chorus, they shifted to a swing arrangement of the song in the bridge, with Harold singing, "Cuando digo que yo te amo, no diga usted que no/ Porque de cualquier modo un beso le dara y usted lo aceptará" to the musicians' steady 4/4 beat. In a surprising introduction to the second chorus, Harold scatted the rhythm that was a classic swing anthem: "va VA va VI – VI – VA – VA VI vi VAH VAH –." This was his clarion call for the orchestra to break into a purely swinging arrangement of the song. "Argentina" had a tightly structured written arrangement; each chorus contained four sections of music (AABA) with eight bars of music to a section, totalling thirty-two bars of music. In the tap dance that followed in "Argentina," the brothers played their movement rhythms over and against the alternating 2/4 and 4/4 time feels of the orchestra.

The brothers launched into the AA sections of the second chorus with a combination of rhythm time steps and sliding steps (chugs, slips, and drags) that elongated each measure of music and added exciting off-the-beat accents to the phrase. As the band played the bridge with a 4/4 swing feel, Harold soloed with cramprolls and back-slipping chugs in the time feel of the samba. In the last A section of the chorus, the band returned to the 2/4 samba feel as the brothers performed back-skids and lengthy slides, topped by a swinging rhythm break in which their taps played double and triple time against the band's samba-beat.

Building the excitement by cross-playing their rhythms against those of the band, Fayard (in the third chorus) paired comical back-crossing walks (that he accented in the rhythm of ONE *and* TWO *and*) with his signature Charleston variations and one-legged wings. Harold continued the rhythm with whisking trench steps that sounded like whisk strokes on the hi-hat of the drums, his flip-into-a-split timed with the four beats of the measure. Harold's trenches and flip-splits then instigated a challenge dance between the brothers in the last chorus, which had Harold slip-sliding forward and back (his slides sounding like pressrolls on the drum), and Fayard diving into splits that spun him around in circles on the ground. Harold delivered a no-hand flip that landed in a split, and Fayard one-upped by pulling out his hand-kerchief and springing over it to land in a split. In the end, Harold took a running slide through his brother's legs, and on the pop-up recovery the brothers took a bow and swept them-selves away.

Slip-sliding to the swinging rhythms of the samba, Fayard and Harold had been transformed into two bolts of lightning on the dance floor of the Club Rendezvous. Their performance in *Down Argentine Way* was so electrifying that soon after the film was released, Twentieth Century-Fox awarded them a five-year con-tract. And no wonder. The swing era was at its peak by the dawn of the forties, and its spirit had completely enraptured the Amer-ican public; in three and a half minutes, Fayard and Harold had captured the spirit and tempo of swing and transferred its wildly infectious energy to the movies.

Swing, in its simplest manifestation, was about rhythm: it excited and made people want to move. It propelled its listeners to inadvertently start tapping their feet, snapping their fingers, and bobbing their heads to the beat of the music. Swing, as in the verb "to swing," was not really new in jazz. The forward-driving propulsion of swing, produced from the conflict between a fixed pulse and wide variety of duration and accents played against that pulse,[1] was a quality attributed to all styles of jazz performance, from ragtime (1890–1900) and "sweet" music (1900–1915) to "hot" early jazz (1917–25) and semisymphonic sweet (1925–32) jazz. And even though the steady 4/4 time marches played by turn-of-the-century New Orleans bands did not really "swing," those who stepped and strutted behind and alongside the band did,[2] by playing their body rhythms with and against the steady pulse of the band to propel the rhythm.

Swing, the name given to the jazz style and related popular music—characterized by written arrangements with solo impro-visations, a repertory based largely on Tin Pan Alley songs, with an equal weight given to the four beats of each bar—began to emerge in the early thirties. Duke Ellington's "It Don't Mean a Thing if It Ain't Got That Swing," recorded in 1932, was probably the first famous song to have the word in its title. The elliptical roll of the lyrics, "It don't mean a thing if it ain't got that swing," had a "Doo-wah doo-wah, doo-wah doo-wah, doo-wah doo-wah, doo-wah doo-wah" response, sung by vocalist Ivie Anderson, "vocalized" by the brass section and embellished by the "talking" plunger solo on the trombones and florid arpeggios on the saxophones. The song was one of the earliest to offer both a working definition and whimsical demonstration of swing. Just exactly what "that swing" was eluded explanation. In this period, when this kind of music was played both by black and white bands and was danced to and listened to by teenagers and young adults, swing "knew no class, no age, no boundary lines."[3] It was the music featured on the new radio programs, and it sold dance records by the millions, but it was not strictly defined.

Swing was something all good jazz musicians did but few could adequately describe in words. For Fats Waller, swing was "two-thirds rhythm, one-third soul." For the trumpeter and bandleader Wingy Manone, it was "feeling an increase in tempo, though you're still playing at the same tempo." Swing, said Louis Armstrong, was "my idea of how a tune should go."[4] It was less a specific style of music, more the way jazz was performed. Glenn Miller believed swing was achieved in his orchestra by the "solidarity and compactness of attack by which rhythm instruments combined with the others," and it was always performed for the sole purpose of creating within the listener a desire to dance.[5]

Compared to the polyphonic, collectively improvised music of New Orleans and Chicago jazz, swing was tightly structured through written arrangements. With relatively little room for spontaneous improvisation, even solos tended to be worked out in advance and performed with little variation. The twelve-bar blues and other, more complex forms that provided the framework for much earlier jazz were largely supplanted in swing by popular songs written in the standard thirty-two-bar-AABA structure of Tin Pan Alley songs. As dance music, the smooth swing replaced the choppy two-beat "bounce" that characterized early jazz. Swing's more flowing, streamlined four beat was partly due to a change in instruments, register, and range. The tuba was replaced by the string bass, the banjo was replaced by the guitar, and the basic pulse was transferred from the snare drum to the hi-hat or ride cymbal in the rhythm section.[6] The result was a lower, smoother sound.

Rhythm was a central component of swing, but it was not enough for the regular and reiterated 4/4 time to be present, either explicitly or implicitly. Swing needed to be felt. "It's something that you feel," said Glenn Miller, "a sensation that can be conveyed to others." Frank Froeba explained it as "a steady tempo causing a lightness and relaxation and a feeling of floating." Fats Waller offered the best demonstration of "feeling" swing when he played the second line of a setting of Shakespeare's "The Lover and His Lass" this way: "With a hey (beat beat) and a ho (beat beat) and a hey (beat) nonni (beat) no."[7]

Swing became such a phenomenon in American culture that a lexicon of swing—words and phrases—developed from the music. The *New York Times* (12 July 1942) reported that in Gene Krupa's twenty-five-page lecture on the "Lexicon of Swing," the drummer defined the phrase "out of this world" as "something completely original," and he traced the use of "solid" to "the excellent playing of the drums and rhythm instruments." The most notorious authority on the language of swing, or jive, as he called it, was Cab Calloway, who published two editions of his *Hepster's Dictionary*. A "cat," in Calloway's dictionary, for instance, was "a musician in a swing band"; a "growl" was "a vibrant note from a trumpet"; and "to lay some iron" was "to tap dance."[8]

If there was a variety of opinion as to what swing was, there was great agreement as to its effect: swing produced unmitigated excitement in listeners. Writing in *Collier's* (25 February 1939), Virgil Thompson noted the "high degree of intellectual and nervous excitement" in audiences listening to swing music:

They sit up straight, their eyes flash, they applaud the licks. They occasionally jerk on the absent downbeat, but on the whole they seem to be enjoying one of those states of nervous and muscular equilibrium that render possible rapid intellection.

Swing was as exciting to dance to as it was to listen to. In contrast to the bouncy vertical steps of earlier jazz dances, the Lindy Hop—the dance counterpart to swing—flowed horizontally with a smooth, rhythmic continuity. Unlike the Charleston, whose 4/4 beat was jerky, the swing beat in the Lindy Hop never missed. "It was right there, 'da da da da,'" says Savoy dancer Norma Miller.[9]

The Lindy Hop incorporated the "swing" characteristic from the Charleston's basic step, the Charleston swing. This "swing" infused the Lindy Hop's basic step, a syncopated two-step with the accent on the offbeat, with a smoothly propulsive quality that gave the impression of the beat speeding ahead. The fundamental innovation of the Lindy Hop was the "breakaway," often performed during an instrumental solo, when dancers spun away from each other to improvise a dance break. By the late thirties, lindy-hoppers at the Savoy Ballroom incorporated acrobatic "air steps" which had men flipping their partners over their backs, thrusting them upward, and balancing them from hip to hip. The jitterbugs—white dancers whose version of the Lindy Hop was fast and swinging but less smooth—jumped, bounced, twisted, shivered, and shook to the rhythm.

In fact, the Nicholas Brothers danced neither the Lindy Hop nor the jitterbug, though their moves recalled the air and breakaway steps of the Lindy Hop, and their tap Charleston was descended from it. Like these social dances, their tap choreography was the aural and visual embodiment of swing music. This is seen and heard most clearly in the "Chattanooga Choo Choo" number in the film *Sun Valley Serenade* (1941), which shows the brothers stretching the social dance form of the Lindy Hop into a staged dance form, reshaping their tap dance into a most rhythmic personification of swing.

The Twentieth Century-Fox film starring Sonja Henie and John Payne and set in a ski resort in Sun Valley, California, centered around a big band's attempt to get a recording contract. The big band was played by Glenn Miller and his orchestra; instead of making brief and improbable cameo appearances, which was the custom during World War II, they appeared in several scenes of the film. Miller was already a well-known trombonist and band-leader in 1940, famous for his orchestra's full, ultrasmooth, and readily accessible four-beat rhythm, its distinctive woodwind and brass sound, and its rich harmonies. When the film was released, at the peak of the swing craze, Miller was propelled to Hollywood stardom, largely because of his "Chattanooga Choo Choo"; the song, written by Mack Gordon and Harry Warren, was such a gigantic hit that it sold a million records in the first six months of being issued.[10]

In *Sun Valley Serenade*, the scene in which "Chattanooga Choo Choo" is performed is also the one scene in which the Nicholas Brothers appear. In a ski lodge, Miller and members of his orchestra are anxiously awaiting the arrival of their lead singer. They are asked to "play a little something" to stall for time for an audition. Miller counts out a moderate four beat with his baton and leads his orchestra into the song, which is written in a thirty-two-bar AABB structure. The theme of the music is introduced and repeated by various sections of the orchestra—first by muted trumpets in the first chorus, then by the saxophones, who stand in unison to answer the theme. The music builds through the addition of trombones and trumpets; and each succeeding chorus is connected by the rhythm section's piano and guitar, bass, and drums. While the tempo remains steady, with its strolling and unaccented 4/4 beat, the music builds to a crescendo through the accumulation of instrumental sections, which stand in succession to answer the preceding sections.

The second chorus opens with one male vocalist (Ten Beneke) who, casually whistling, walks over to a table where four other vocalists (the Modernaires) are sitting. He sings: "Pardon me boys, is that the Chattanooga Choo Choo/ On track twenty-nine? Boy, will you give me a shine?" The group responds, "Can you afford to board the Chattanooga Choo Choo?" He answers, "I got my fare, with just a trifle to spare." In double time, against the steady four-beat played by the band, they all sing the succeeding BB sections in four-part harmony: "You leave the Pennsylvania Station 'bout a quarter to four/ Read a magazine and then you're in Baltimore. . . ."

In the last sixteen bars of the chorus, the singers are joined by the orchestra in a crescendo of brass instruments, which draws the song to a climax and near closure. But on the last eight bars of the measure, the orchestra continues to segue into a third chorus, as the camera shifts to another part of the ski lodge and a cardboard set of the back of a train, attached to which is a platform and railing. Standing beside the train and waiting to board is Dorothy Dandridge, dressed in a black satin dress with matching parasol; she is trailed by Fayard and Harold, sportily dressed in matching plaid suits, snazzy bow ties, and straw hats.

Against the strolling tempo and a steady four-beat, Fayard, Harold, and Dorothy begin the third chorus by sharing, trading on, and adding on to one another's lines. "Pardon me boys," Dandridge sings (on beats ONE *and* TWO *and*) to Fayard and Harold's "yes yes" (on *and* THREE of the measure). "Is that the Chattanooga Choo

Dorothy Dandrige with the Nicholas Brothers in the "Chatanooga Choo Choo" number in Sun Valley Serenade, *Twentieth Century-Fox 1941 (Harold Nicholas Archive).*

Choo?" she asks (on *and* FOUR *and* ONE *and*), and they finish (on TWO *and* THREE *and* FOUR of the measure) by answering, "That's the Chattanooga Choo Choo." Then Harold continues, "On track twenty-nine." "Twenty-nine?" Dorothy interjects. "Uh huh!" Fayard answers. "Right on the Tennessee line," sings Dorothy, as Harold echoes "She said" and Fayard repeats "the Tennessee line." Fayard sings, "She said that she can't afford," and Dorothy echoes, "I can't afford to take the Chattanooga Choo Choo"; and after Harold (on counts three and four of the measure) suggests, "Why can't you jump on in back?" Dorothy answers, "I'll have to pay for my fare." "You will?" asks Fayard. "Uh huh! Without a nickel to spare," answers Dorothy, as Harold squeezes in, "Well I do declare!"

The fourth chorus doubles the tempo, and the Nicholases and Dandridge perform a tap dance that begins with the succesive stomps and slides that sound out the locomotion rhythm of a train. They continue with smooth and sassy stamps and heel-digs that are both traded off and performed synchronously, ending with the brothers following Dandridge until she boards the back of the train. The tempo picks up, and the brothers trade steps on each succeeding two beats of music (a variation on the locomotion sound); their solos are interspersed with both of them walking a circle and turning. By the sixth chorus, the orchestra is playing at top speed and the brothers take to more daring air steps. With high and side-swinging "bells" (a tap step where toes or heels click together) in which the legs are raised to ninety degrees off the floor, the brothers soon descend into backward slides that make them look as if they are skating. After they toss off their hats, Harold performs back flips, and Fayard does a one-armed cartwheel that catapults him into a midair split. They turn and slide together, then Harold steps back, runs toward Fayard, places his foot on Fayard's bent knee, and back-flips off that knee to land in a split. Harold's recovery is timed to coincide with Fayard's (who has also dropped into a split); sliding backward, they take a one-handed jump over the railing and onto the train platform to land in a deep knee bend, which springs them up, legs splayed, into a midair split.

Harold and Fayard's breakaway moves in the "Chatanooga Choo Choo" number in Sun Valley Serenade, *Twentieth Century-Fox 1941 (Harold Nicholas Archive).*

The tap choreography in "Chattanooga Choo Choo," as performed by the brothers in their duet, was beautifully shaped and styled after the Lindy Hop. Unlike earlier dances in which, for the most part, the brothers moved side by side facing the camera, they now were in the "open facing position" of Latin American social dancing.[11] This partnering position had a strong resemblance to the breakaway move in the Lindy Hop. Harold's back flip off Fayard's knee, which was one of the few times the brothers made physical contact while dancing, resembled the air move in the Lindy Hop when the man flips his partner over his back. Harold's running slides through Fayard's legs, though not in "Chattanooga," were also reminiscent of a move in the Lindy Hop, in which the male slides his partner back and forth through his legs.

More important, all the moves in the choreography—from the forward and back swinging of the legs and back flips into splits to

springs from second position *plié* into slides in all directions—had
a certain momentum. There was a pronounced diagonality, both
in the body line and in the lateral splay of arms and legs that had
always marked the brothers' style. One move in "Chattanooga,"
however, looked totally new—jumps with legs angled in *attitude*
and arms lifted and outspread *à la seconde*—and appeared at first to
be influenced in form by ballet. But these moves were accomplished
with such acrobatic ease that they seemed instead to be a response
to the buoyancy of the swing beat.

In the swing orchestra, the unvarying four-beat from the
rhythm section was the pulse that made possible the complex,
ornamental, expressive structure of the brass and woodwind sections. Like these sections, the brothers were able to "play" their
complex tap structures, to create more swinging extensions on
the unvarying four-beat rhythm. From the double and triple

*Nicholas
Brothers'
jump-split
finale in the
"Chatanooga
Choo Choo"
number in
Sun Valley
Serenade,
Twentieth
Century-Fox
1941
(Harold
Nicholas
Archive).*

time-step breaks against the unaccented four-beat to aerial moves that both coincided with and moved past the measure, their rhythms catapulted the momentum of the dance forward.

Hollywood's representation of swing in *Sun Valley Serenade* was twofold: the neatly dressed white musicians of Glenn Miller's swing orchestra, sitting in a symmetrical arrangement on the bandstand and playing the unvarying four-beat and glossing harmonies, projected an image of straightness and sobriety. This image was enhanced by the bespectacled Miller, who looked like a college professor and played his muted trombone unpretentiously. Dandridge and the Nicholases, on the other hand, were effusive in their performance. They demonstrated an incomparable sense of swing, both vocally and in their tap dancing, in a number of ways: propulsion of the beat (by trading, doubling up on, and repeating each other's words and steps); shifting and accelerating speeds; dividing quarter notes into eighth-note beats of varying and unequal duration; and displacing the accent of both step phrases and vocal phrases so that it would alternately move toward and away from the listener.

The difference in swing styles between Miller and the Nicholases was the rhythm. Miller admitted that his orchestra's forte was not rhythm but harmony. "The years of serious study I've had with legitimate teachers finally is paying off in enabling me to write arrangements employing unusual, rich harmonies, many never before used in dance bands," he told *Down Beat* (1 February 1940), making no pretense of musical "authenticity," which he implicitly associated with rhythm:

> I haven't a great jazz band, and I don't want one. Some of the critics among us . . . point their fingers at us and charge us with forsaking the real jazz. Maybe so. Maybe not. It's all in what you define as "real jazz." It happens that to our ears harmony comes first. A dozen colored bands have a better beat than mine.

While it is pointless to argue who represented "the real jazz," or who swung more in "Chattanooga Choo Choo," there are two groups of performers in the scene with distinctly different styles of swing. One group is white, the other black, and neither group interacts with the other. They remain separated, not only by race and by musical style but by class. The racial divide is most obvious; the members of Miller's band and the vocalists are all white. But class differences are more subtle.

Dandridge, for instance, boards at the back of the train; and she sings, "I can't afford to board the Chattanooga Choo Choo." When Harold suggests, "Can't you jump on in back?" she says she'll pay the full fare "with not a nickel to spare." The male singer in Miller's band could afford the fare, "with a trifle to spare"; he certainly had enough money to ask, "Boy, will you give me a shine?" The more insidious inequality in the scene is that while the groups are separate, they are not equal. Dandridge and the Nicholases are introduced in the scene almost as an afterthought. They have no lines in the film and are not connected to the plot; their costumes look out of context with the period and the design concept; and they never appear in any other part of the film.

Their "scene," of course, was designed to be cut out of the film when it was shown to white audiences in the South. Leonard Reed, however, remembered seeing *Sun Valley Serenade* in an all-white theatre in Birmingham, Alabama, and being surprised that "Chattanooga Choo Choo" remained in the film: "For some reason, they did not cut the Nicholas Brothers out, and the people were screaming. You couldn't hear the rest of the picture when they finished their dance."[12]

Hollywood producers, unwilling to go beyond the prevailing norms, and buying into the double standard of racial segregation, were free to keep the scene or to detach it from the film, as needed. While the Nicholases were among the handful of blacks to gain access to Hollywood, they had no artistic control. Even a deep sense of pride in their work and respect for each other were not enough to break the persistent racial segregation in Hollywood. It was only their consistent return to the big swing bands and to performing live on the big stage that assured them their audiences were still thrilled.

At the height of the swing craze in 1938, the William Morris Agency touted itself in *Variety* (5 January 1938) as "the preeminent managing and booking agency for talent in motion pictures, radio, vaudeville and legitimate theatre." But it had no serious band department, and the agency found itself lacking in organization to handle the swing craze. Duke Ellington, Louis Armstrong, and Cab Calloway had all signed with them in 1929. In the mid-thirties, when the Nicholas Brothers were signed, a variety unit was organized to book them with comedy teams and stage shows in movie theatres between picture presentations.

In April 1939, after William Alexander, a leading executive from MCA, joined the Morris office and began booking some of the top swing bands (among them Artie Shaw and Glenn Miller), the agency launched an aggressive campaign to book the Nicholas Brothers for live performances with big bands in theatres across the country.[13] From 1938 to 1945, the brothers played such theatres as the Roxy, Loew's State, RKO Palace, RKO Vaudeville, Paramount, and Keith's Palace, performing with the big bands led by Duke Ellington, Count Basie, Cab Calloway, Jimmie Lunceford, Louis Armstrong, Glenn Miller, Tommy Dorsey, and Artie Shaw. It was in these venues that swing expanded, visually and acoustically, into panoramic proportions.

The Paramount, for example, the Times Square entertainment palace at Broadway and 43rd Street, with an ornately curved and garishly lit marquee, was housed in a building that was thirty-three stories high, with a seating capacity of 3,600.[14] On the big stage, measuring 100 feet long, musicians were lined up in ascending height to create an effect of perfect symmetry. In contrast to the "hot jazz" band musicians of the 1920s, who clowned and mugged as they played, swing musicians were inscribed with the look of the art moderne. Streamlined sections of instruments, in standing solos, made gleaming geometric parallelograms; the musicians played their instruments dramatically at oblique angles; and symmetrical arrangements of rhythm, brass, and woodwind sections were played in harmony and with syncrony.

Bands costumed their musicians in resplendent, identical uniforms, with new costumes for different engagements. A sideman, for example, recalling Ellington preparing for an important engagement at New York's Roxy Theatre, remembered the sketches of the stage set, which Ellington scanned for days. Musicians were scheduled for fittings of new uniforms for the show: cinnamon-brown slacks, chocolate-brown jackets, billiard-table-green shirts, pastel yellow ties. At the Roxy's dress rehearsal, Ellington thought the shirts muddied the musicians' features under the lights, so he rushed to the phone to order shirts of a different color.[15]

Each big band had its own distinctive look and sound. Duke Ellington's orchestra was the epitome of black, urban sophistication. Count Basie's big band, whether playing a slow blues or exploding over a charging rhythm, appealed to people's sense of excitement. At the center of the Basie band, drummer Jo Jones was "ever musical, ever pushing the beat with a touch here, a bomb (a well placed accent) there, or a highly relevant break, in

The Nicholas Brothers working with Count Basie in the forties (Harold Nicholas Archive).

addition to his beautiful high hat and cymbal playing."[16] His style was in fact an update of New Orleans rhythm. "You could march on it, dance on it, because it was so swinging," said trumpeter Joe Newman.[17] While Jones's concept of drumming was light-footed, drummer Jimmy Crawford of the Jimmie Lunceford band featured a strong, pulsating quality that could be open and very swinging, yet it could run down the scale to quiet and subtle.

These jazz swing drummers, along with Sonny Greer from Duke Ellington's orchestra, opened Fayard and Harold to unfathomed modes of rhythmic expression. A 1940 booking at New York's Paramount Theatre with Tommy Dorsey and His Orchestra introduced the brothers to yet another drumming man they would have the greatest admiration for, Buddy Rich. Dorsey's allstar band also included vocalist Frank Sinatra, trumpeters Ziggy Ellman and Sy Oliver, and pianist Joe Bushkin. Fayard remembers that when he first handed the huge suitcase of musical arrangements for his act over to Dorsey before a rehearsal, Dorsey remarked, "Hey, this is like a symphony." He then proceeded to distribute the arrangements to all his musicians and rehearsed each of the musical numbers several times with them. "Just one song, ten times, and with all of the musicians. He wanted to get it to the best," says Fayard. Buddy Rich put the arrangement aside. "He didn't read music at that time, but he'd listen," says Fayard. "And the first time he heard it, he had it."[18]

Buddy Rich was both a showman and a superb technician who was known for his speed, dexterity, and ability to spark a band. Early training as a singer and dancer, and experience performing in vaudeville in the twenties, where he had the opportunity to observe the best drummers of the time playing in pit bands, had made him an extrovert and a showman in everything he did. There was a strutting feeling to his playing that brought strength to the brass and ensemble figures, heightened the snap and crackle of accents, and enhanced the flow and impact of group notes and phrases within the arrangements.

His left hand played rhythm, and his right hand stroked the snare drum with tart crispness. The right bass-drum foot was his greatest strength and the center around which his hands evolved drum patterns. His single-stroke-roll ending was so fast and furious that his sticks became a blur.

In the tradition of the great swing drummers, Rich held the beat and never sacrificed rhythmic continuity for brass explosions; his accents and fills functioned to move the music forward. "When one heard him play breaks and solos," Burt Korall observed, "the picture emerged of a highly inventive tap dancer; and that picture constantly reappeared on stage, as Rich created hand and foot patterns behind the ensemble and individual sections, cleverly translating what he learned from dancers to the drums."[19]

Rich had a rapport with dancers; he could catch every accent and add dimension to what they did. "He was a sensitive drummer," says Fayard. "He'd play every beat. I'd say, 'Buddy, just go, catch us! Chuk! Catch that with your hand!' And he did." The brothers found out Rich could tap, so for an extra encore, they called him down from his drums. "We'd say, 'Take it, Buddy,' and he could really go," says Fayard. "And there was one step he'd do and we'd say, 'That sounds good, Buddy. Let's see you do it on the other foot.' And he'd turn around and do it again! That thrilled the audience. He was the best. Of all the drummers, he was the one."[20]

While performing with a swing band at the Club Zanzibar (with Bill Robinson, Louis Armstrong, and the Peters Sisters) in New York in the mid-forties, the brothers were doubling at the Roxy Theatre, two blocks away, with Carmen Miranda and her Latin Band. "We were doing two different acts with different costumes," Fayard remembers. "Five acts a day at the Roxy, and two at the Zanzibar."

From Miranda and her band, the brothers absorbed the Afro-Brazilian rhythms that were translated into their swing repertoire. Born in Portugal, Miranda migrated with her family to Brazil in the twenties, and there absorbed the country's traditional folk songs and rhythms, particularly the samba. Drawing directly on the Brazilian folk materials, she created a repertory of songs (with the Brazilian composer Sylvan Silva), which she sang in Portuguese, accompanied by an ensemble of guitarists and percussionists. Wearing a colorful draping of beads down her bodice and her trademark turban of fruit on top of her head (an idea she

The Nicholas Brothers onstage with Carmen Miranda at the Roxy Theatre in 1940 (Harold Nicholas Archive).

adapted from the Bayana folk of Bahia), Miranda sang the lyrics of her songs with such a whisking speed that the lush, sloshing sounds of her beautiful language washed over the melody while accenting the duple-time rhythm of the samba. After being spotted by the Shuberts at the Casino da Urca in Rio de Janeiro, she went to the United States in 1939 to make her first Hollywood movie, *The Streets of Paris*.[21] During the filming of *Down Argentine Way*, in which she also performed, she met the Nicholas Brothers and developed a close bond with them.

A silent home movie taken of the Nicholases in 1942 shows the marquee of the Roxy Theatre and its announcement: "On Stage in Person: Carmen Miranda and Nicholas Brothers." Inside the theatre the brothers, wearing Spanish-style full-sleeved white shirts, black-appliquéd toreador pants, and cummerbund sashes, perform onstage with Miranda, backed by three guitarists.

Harold sings "Mama Yo Quiero," the song Miranda introduced in the opening scene of *Down Argentine Way*,[22] and Fayard and Harold perform a tap dance containing their signature splits, trenches, and Charleston variations. When Miranda joins them for a song in which hips swerve, arms undulate, and hands and wrists flutter ever so subtly to the beat of the samba, it is clear that the brothers have been opened to a more sensuous though subtle style of rhythmic movement that is Afro-Brazilian.

While the brothers were absorbing these dance rhythms from Miranda, a choreographer at Twentieth Century-Fox was broadening their dance vocabulary and embellishing their tap routines with balletic moves that they had never before imagined being able to perform. Nick Castle (Nicholas John Casaccio), the noted Twentieth Century-Fox choreographer, who staged dances for stars like Bill Robinson, George Murphy, Ann Miller, Shirley Temple, and Bert Lahr, was assigned to work with the Nicholas Brothers through their five-year contract. Fayard created the choreography for *Down Argentine Way*—much of it drawn from their act at the Cotton Club in the late thirties—but the tap choreography for the films made by the Nicholas Brothers while under contract with Twentieth Century-Fox was developed with Nick Castle.

"The only time we worked with someone who gave us something was with Nick Castle," says Fayard candidly. He remembers that the very first thing Castle said to the brothers when he first met them was "I'm so happy to meet you guys. Now there's somebody here who can do my ideas." Harold remembers Castle as a man who was great fun to work with, and who "was all the time laughing, and playing a lot of jokes on us." Says Fayard: "We'd all think up ideas. The three of us would get together and he'd show us something, and I'd say 'How about putting this step to that?' And he'd say, 'Yeah, that's it, that's great.'"

Nick Castle, who started his career in Hollywood in 1935 as Dixie Dunbar's tap teacher and was known in vaudeville as part of a dance act with Frank Starr, was not a rhythm tap dancer per se. In *How to Tap Dance*, a tap dance instruction manual he published in 1948, the five "Basic Tap Steps" that Castle notates—

single tap, brush, shuffle, flap, and triple tap—are all executed on the balls of the feet. These make for a light-footed, elevated style of tap dancing with less emphasis on the heels to syncopate and accent off the beat.

Given the "Famous Tap Dance Steps" of the movie stars that appear in the manual, it appears that Castle was a master at creating the dance steps typical of the characteristic style of the stars with whom he worked in Hollywood. The "Bill Robinson Step," for instance, is an Irish-style shuffle-hop-step combination that captures Robinson's jigging style, arranged to fit into six measures of music and a two-bar break. The "George Murphy Step" is in the softshoe mode, while the "Shirley Temple Step" is a traditional waltz clog, and the "Carmen Miranda Step," subtitled "Samba Boogie Tap," has simple lunges and hip thrusts in 4/4 time. The "Nicholas Brothers Step," which Castle suggests should be danced to "Chattanooga Choo Choo," is a rather simple routine incorporating the Nicholases' signature back-slides, stomps, and lunges; it is one of the few combinations in the manual danced to syncopated rhythms with the heels.[23]

Castle's strong suit as choreographer to the Nicholas Brothers was not so much his invention of rhythmically complex combinations but his imaginative extending of their performance skills into musically and visually succinct tap-dancing extravaganzas. In *Down Argentine Way*, for example, he added the jumps Fayard does over his handkerchief, as well as back-sliding splits. In their dance scene in *Tin Pan Alley* (1940), Fayard and Harold are two marble figures who come to life in a harem, where women in midriff-baring saris lounge beneath lush groves and fountains bursting with fruit. Bare-chested and bare-legged, the brothers are swathed in gold-brocaded briefs and turbans with gold snake bracelets wound around their wiry arms and gold knee pads wrapped around their bony legs. If the costumes are the most bizarre things one has ever seen on these dancers, their steps and rhythms are still the same blazing assortment of slides and wings, splits and jumps. *The Great American Broadcast* (1941), another Castle collaboration, showed them dancing on suitcases while the Ink Spots, dressed as redcaps, sang "Alabamy Bound"; as the

The Nicholas Brothers dancing in the harem scene in Tin Pan Alley, *Twentieth Century-Fox 1940 (Museum of Modern Art).*

song ended, they jumped through the window of a moving train into midair, 180-degree splits.[24]

Harold thought Castle was kidding when he told the brothers that, for their scene in *Orchestra Wives* (1942), he wanted them to run up walls and do backward flips into a split. "Are you crazy? Let me see you do that!" Harold remembers telling Castle when he first heard the idea. But Castle just laughed and said that

The Nicholas Brothers tap dancing on suitcases in The Great American Broadcast, *Twentieth Century-Fox* 1941 *(The Ernie Smith Collection).*

although he could not do the move, he knew that Harold could. "Look, I'll fix it for you; first, we'll put a belt on you," Castle told Harold, who was convinced. Harold remembered trying it:

> I went up and slipped the first two times. But he said, "Don't worry, I'm not gonna let you go." So I did it again and bam! I did it. I went into a split and everything, and Nick said, "That's great." Then, he went over to the guys and said, "The next time he does it, don't hold him—but make him think you're holding him." So they did. I ran up and jumped over, and boom! Perfect again. And old Nick said, "Oh, great, Harold, that's great. Okay, you've got it." And I said, "Well, er—good thing they're holding me." And he said, "They weren't holding you that time." And I just went to my knees![25]

Splashy costumes and flashy acrobatics would have expired all too quickly in Hollywood if they were the only building blocks in a Nicholas routine. The infusion of Castle's bright ideas into the brothers' rhythmically complex repertoire transformed their routines into spectacular musical performances. Castle was not all flash; he incorporated ballet, modern dance, and ballroom dance movement into the Nicholas lexicon, and he shaped their dancing. Greatly influenced by African-American social dance styles, which he blended and "whitened" for Hollywood starlets (as well as for such major stars as Judy Garland, Mickey Rooney, Ann Miller, Gene Kelly, and Fred Astaire), Castle had also worked with black dancers in Hollywood (dancers with whom choreographers like Hermes Pan did not care to work). As an admirer of the Nicholases' broad talents, he was respectful and inquisitive about black culture. Castle was well aware, as he devised extraordinary feats to challenge the brothers, that he, as well as they, drew on American vaudeville traditions and black comedy dance.

The most tantalizing of the Nicholas-Castle collaborations for Twentieth Century-Fox was the last. In 1942, the brothers were performing on the East Coast when they received a telegram from Fox executive Darryl F. Zanuck, who ordered them to return to Hollywood for the filming of the musical *Stormy Weather*, which starred Lena Horne and Bill Robinson. The film, directed by Andrew Stone—with songs by Ted Koehler, Andy Razaff, Fats Waller, Dorothy Fields, Jimmy McHugh, Harold Arlen, James P. Johnson, Irving Mills, and Cab Calloway—was choreographed by Nick Castle and Clarence Robinson. The brothers returned, and with only a week to rehearse before filming, they immediately went to work.

Stormy Weather was a musical extravaganza that featured an all-star black cast—in addition to those mentioned were Dooley Wilson, Nicodemus Stewart, Babe Wallace, Ernest Whitman, and Mae E. Johnson—but not much of a plot. The story was about a backstage romance between two entertainers, one a rising star, played by the twenty-six-year-old Horne, and the other a burned-out dancer, played by the sixty-five-year-old Bill Robinson. They fall in and out of love, their story loosely based on the careers of

Jim Europe, Noble Sissle, and Adelaide Hall. In the film, Robinson performed a lively riverboat tap, displaying his cool, copasetic style, and Horne sang "I Can't Give You Anything but Love," and "Stormy Weather" (the song Ethel Waters had made famous at the Cotton Club ten years earlier). Katherine Dunham's dancers presented a moody, mist-filled ballet to the title song; Ada Brown belted out heart-wrenching blues; Flournoy Miller and Johnny Lee did a classic black comedy skit of "indefinite talk," in which the two men spoke to one another, each one never letting the other complete a sentence, yet understanding each other perfectly well. And Fats Waller appeared briefly, playing his own "Ain't Misbehavin'." But it was Cab Calloway's swinging "Jumpin' Jive," in the last scene, the only one in which the Nicholases appeared, that swept the film to the highest peak of excitement.

Set on a stage in a ballroom, the scene opened with a drum roll and a quick pan over the orchestra playing a brassy and upbeat introduction, as Calloway, in a shimmering white tuxedo, bounced up and down with baton in hand to the swinging four-beat rhythm of "Jumpin' Jive." Turning to the camera, he called out: "Oh boy!" And all the musicians in the band stood up and answered, "Whatcha gonna play, that game?" "Oh boy!" Cab repeated. "Whatcha gonna play, that game?" they answered back and sat down. "Palomar, Shalomar, Swamee Shore; Let me dig this jive once more," Cab rhymed and scatted. "Oh boy!" he called again. "Gotta get down to the game," they replied. "Oh boy!" Calloway told them. "Gotta get down to the game," they repeated. And Calloway continued:

> When you hear that hep cat score;
> Come on boys, let's jive once more.
> The Jim Jam Jump is the jumpin' jive;
> Jim and jam on the mellow side,
> Hep hep!

This time, the muted trumpets shouted back the response. "Hep, hep," Cab repeated, and the trumpets honked back again. "The jim jam jump is the solid jive/ Makes you feel nine feet tall when you're four foot five/ Hep! hep!" sang Calloway, and the trombones stood up and roared back. "Hep! hep!" Cab scatted back, and the brass roared back again. "Then don't you be that ickaroo/ Get hep, come on then, and follow through," sang Cab, suddenly doubling the steady four-beat with "And a jug and a jump and a jug and a jive" in double time. "Jim jam jump is a jumpin' jive/ Makes you like your eggs on the Jersey side/ Hep! hep!" rapped Calloway. And the camera cut to the audience, whose snapping fingers and bobbing heads proved that indeed they were ("hep" is Calloway's jive lingo for being "hip" or "cool"). Smooth as a roller coaster, Calloway rode the rhythm, scatting, "Bibipity boppity hippity hoppity/ bippity boppity hippity hop hop / BANG BANG BANG," strutting back and forth along the front of the bandstand.

He moved to a corner of the stage, near a cluster of tables where the guests were seated, and sang, "Boogally boogally boogally BOY!" And the Nicholas Brothers, who were seated at one of the tables, stood and answered back, "Boogally boogally

Cab Calloway scats the Nicholas Brothers onto the stage in the "Jumpin' Jive" number in Stormy Weather, *Twentieth Century-Fox 1943 (Harold Nicholas Archive).*

boogally BOY." "Biggity BOY, biggity BOY," Cab called out again, and the brothers, dressed in tailcoats, jumped on top of their table and answered, "Biggity boy, biggity BOY." Cab scatted, "Oh, riggity raggety rah rah," as the brothers jumped from table to table, then over the railing separating the audience from the stage onto the stage floor. Stepping and sliding across the floor, they followed Calloway to center stage and began their tap dance.

Spins, cramprolls, turns, and crossover steps were woven into an intricate pattern of sound and movement, as the brothers spun out back-sliding rhythms that slipped them smoothly from place to place on the stage. In the second A section, the brothers repeated and varied these step patterns in alternating solos and duets. Then, with a back-slide split that sprang up into a jump-split, the brothers landed on the platform where the first row of musicians in the orchestra were seated. In the bridge (the B section), the brothers jumped onto round pedestals that looked like the tops of large drums, positioned in various places among the five rows of musicians. Drumming the rhythms with their feet, they sprang from one pedestal to another, moving higher and higher up past the rows of musicians, and criss-crossing each other midair as they jumped. Drum-dancing their way to the highest pedestal, they were welcomed by two trumpet players who stood like pillars while blasting their horns. Then the brothers jumped over the heads of the musicians, skipping lightly from drum to drum until they landed once again on the stage floor.

The second dancing chorus, which repeated the steps and rhythms of the first A-section chorus, ended with the brothers jumping three steps at a time up a flight of stairs that curved up and around the five rows of musicians onto a long and narrow platform crowning the rows of musicians. Dancing along the platform, the brothers alternated turns with slides, splits with pullups, then sprang onto the top of a grand piano—one row below them—to trade fours with the pianist. From the piano, they took a long leap over the heads of the musicians onto the stage floor, their split-and-recover a visual counterpart to the sliding sound on the trombone.

The Nicholas Brothers jump over the orchestra in Stormy Weather, Twentieth Century-Fox *1943 (Harold Nicholas Archive).*

Jump-turning and figure-eighting around each other, they danced their way across the floor, then paused again at the bottom of a curved flight of stairs. Together they leapt, three stairs at a time, all the way up the stairs. Their slipping around each other, in figure-eights at the top, was prelude to a breathtaking series of descents down the stairs: Fayard jumped down one step and landed in a split, and Harold leap-frogged over Fayard and landed on the next step into another split. Fayard recovered and jumped over Harold's head to land in yet another split. They alternately recovered, then jumped over each other and onto the next step into another split, until they reached the bottom of the stairs. Skidding victoriously across the floor, they were suddenly halted by the piercing wail of a trumpet, which spun them around and catapulted them up the flight of stairs—Harold on one side, Fayard on the other. Jumping three steps at a time up the stairs, they turned around at the top and slid, in full split, down each of the curving ramps and pulled up, just in time for Calloway to shout out, "Everybody dance!"

Fred Astaire told the brothers that the "Jumpin' Jive" number in *Stormy Weather* was the greatest number he had ever seen on film. He would have been more impressed had he known, Harold admits, that "when it was time to do the jumps over each other's heads into splits in the routine, we never rehearsed it." Fayard adds: "It came nice and easy. Nick Castle said not to rehearse it, that we knew what to do, so we did it like a rehearsal. And in one take!"[26]

Reviews of the Nicholases in *Stormy Weather* were all raves. *Metronome* (July 1943) reported that *Stormy Weather* presented the "Nicholas Brothers at their brilliant best in a tap and acrobatic dancing solo." And Donald Bogle wrote: "This highly demanding performance is so perfectly executed—splendidly styled yet seemingly spontaneous, too, without any sign of strain or sweat—that it truly commands our respect and inspires awe." It was the spirit of the brothers, he added, that communicated a joy and pleased the audience and that framed the movie, "bringing it to an almost intolerably pleasurable peak."[27] Several critical comments, however positive, reveal a general misunderstanding of the Nicholases' style of jazz tap dancing. In the view of film historian Thomas Cripps, the three highest moments in *Stormy Weather* are Horne's "Stormy Weather," Dunham's "Diga Diga Doo," and "the adolescent Nicholas Brothers in a flashdance that Robinson could no longer do."[28]

In fact, Fayard was twenty-eight and Harold twenty-two when *Stormy Weather* was released; and the sixty-five-year-old Robinson *never* did acrobatics in his routines, so that comparison of these two generations of tap dancers is flawed. Then there is the "flash" label. In the public eye, tap dancing at its best was flash—the catchall term for "wildly exciting dance movements incorporating acrobatics, often used to finish a dance."[29] For the rest of their dance career, the Nicholas Brothers were stuck with the flash label. "Flash dancers didn't do too much, just flips and turns and spins," said Leonard Reed. "And there were a lot of great flash dancers, like Jack Wiggins, Johnny Nitt, and Blue McAllister, who played the Standard, and that I'm sure is where Fayard saw them. But Fayard and Harold were not flash dancers."[30]

Although there were acrobatic moves in the "Jumpin' Jive" number in *Stormy Weather*, the masterful musical fusion of the Nicholas Brothers' steps and rhythms made their drum dance brilliant. Acrobatics was merely one small part of that choreography. "If they were gonna just stand in one place and dance, they would have been in the same category with everybody else," said Leonard Reed. "The Nicholas Brothers became great because of their acrobatics and because of their exploiting the *action*, that's the word, *action* in their dancing."

While the Nicholases, from *Stormy Weather* on, continued to be given the flash label, the more appropriate description of their dancing was that they were swing dancers. A jazz swing drummer exploits the action of his rhythmic expression by playing the various instruments in his drum set—hi-hat, cymbals, and bass drum; these instruments comprise his "palette" of sounds. So too the Nicholases, with their palette of jazz steps and swinging rhythms, exploited the action of their musical expression. How ironic that the brothers were labeled "flash dancers" and never called swing drum dancers. In fact, it was the music of jazz swing, with its forward-moving propulsion, of which the brothers became personifications.

*An example of
the airborne
vertical stance
of Harold
Nicholas,
performing in*
Free and
Easy,
Amsterdam,
*1959 (Harold
Nicholas
Archive).*

Eight

Converging Styles

1942–1945

Orchestra Wives, Twentieth Century-Fox's swinging musical romance of 1942, followed the musical highs and marital lows of jazzmen in a traveling big band. True to life, the film featured Glenn Miller and his orchestra. Miller plays a famous big-band leader who embarks with his group on a whirlwind national tour, during which lead trumpeter Bill Abbott (George Montgomery) impulsively marries one of his many ardent fans, a naive young woman named Connie (Ann Rutherford). At first, the new bride is more than willing to put up with infrequent time with her husband and listening to the malicious gossip of the other wives, but the strain of life on the road threatens to end both the new marriage and the entire band. In the end, both are saved by the intoxicating powers of swing, which draws the jazzmen back to their rhythms and rekindles the romance between them and their mates. The film included such popular Miller compositions as "Serenade in Blue," "At Last," and "Kalamazoo," the last receiving a 1942 Oscar nomination for Best Song.

The Nicholas Brothers appeared in the last scene of *Orchestra Wives*, singing and tap dancing to "Kalamazoo," a three-and-a-half-minute routine that was choreographed by Nick Castle in collaboration with the brothers. Though it was short, structured as an afterthought, and not integrated into the plot of the film, the routine was a superbly crafted choreography, demonstrating the convergence of a number of dance and performance traditions that distinguished the Nicholases' unique style of jazz dancing in the early and mid-forties. Fayard describes the style of the Nicholas Brothers as "classical tap": "When we tapped, we added a little ballet, a little eccentric, a little flash, and we used our hands a great deal. With style and grace, we used the whole body from our heads down to our toes."[1] Perhaps Fayard was prompted to describe his tap dancing as classical because of George Balanchine's acute observation that the brothers looked ballet trained.[2] As demonstrated in the choreography for "Kalamazoo," the Nicholas style is "classical" not because of its resemblance to Western classical ballet but because of its evolution within and alongside the classical forms of jazz, blues, and swing. Furthermore, this black American dance form that the Nicholases and other jazz tapsters evolved in the thirties and forties swing era was distinctly modernist in expression.

Like the "Chattanooga Choo Choo" number in *Sun Valley Serenade*, "Kalamazoo" opens with Miller, the orchestra, and a harmonizing quintet of singers. Just as the music reaches its crescendo and the orchestra is soaring smoothly to a close, the camera shifts to a small stage at the far corner of the ballroom, and the band makes an awkward-sounding transition into a second musical introduction. The velvet curtains of the small proscenium stage split open to reveal the silhouetted figures of Harold and Fayard, who, dressed in white ties and tails, are bouncing ever so subtly to the 4/4 time vamp. Strutting out onto an extended platform of the stage, they quickly peel away from each other and stop to pose, arms open and legs straddled, at the top of a small flight of stairs. Fayard jumps two steps at a time down the stairs, making one and a half turns on the descent, then opens his arms wide to introduce Harold, who, from the top of the stairs, sings: "A! B! C! D! E! F! G! H! I've got a gal!"

"Where?" Fayard interjects, sliding his legs smoothly together as Harold skips down the steps. "In Kalamazoo," Harold answers; "Kalamazoo!" Fayard repeats in disbelief. Harold continues, "I don't want to boast, but I know she's the toast of Kalamazoo," as he strolls downstage and Fayard fills out the bar with "zoo zoo zoo zoo zoo zoo zoo." They stop short. "Years have gone by; my, my, how she grew," Harold sings, turning dreamily away from Fayard. "Man, did she grew," Fayard repeats, capping his aside with a smooth sliding-together of the legs, which propels him into a spin-turn. They began to stroll. "I liked her looks/ When I carried her books/ In Kalamazoo," sings Harold, and Fayard echoes, "zoo zoo zoo zoo zoo."

Though the brothers are as handsome and debonair as ever, they look older and more mature in the film. Harold, with barely a shadow of a mustache over his lip, is almost as tall as Fayard, who is squarer in the jaw and more statuesque. Standing wide-legged, with their chests open and shoulders broad and straight, the brothers look self-assured. From head to hips, their torsos are pulled up, though tilted slightly backward; the placement of their arms, raised chest-high and slightly bent at the elbows and wrists, helps lift the torso and frees the legs to extend into long, diagonal lines. What is immediately apparent from the entrance is the way the brothers have refined working together as an ensemble. There is not one line that they do not share; Fayard has become a master at filling, completing, or continuing Harold's lines with a look, a quick-stroking gesture, a slide, or a spin.

"I'm gonna send a wire," Harold sings; "Pop it on a flier," Fayard continues; "Lea-ving today," Harold croons, as Fayard repeats his second-to-first sliding spin. On the upbeat beat of the next measure, both dart sideward to tap out the six clear beats of a Maxie Ford (a side-hopping tap step consisting of a stomp, shuffle, pullback change, and toe-tip), landing with the feet in neat fifth position. "Am I dreaming?" Harold asks himself; "I can hear you screaming," Fayard answers, and assures his brother that "Everything is Oh—"; "Kay!" finishes Harold, "A!" snaps Fayard, "L," shouts Harold, "A," adds Fayard, and they alternately spell out *K-A-L-A-M-A-Z-O-O*. When Fayard gets to "O," Harold adds, "Oh, what a gal/ She's a real piperoo," and Fayard interprets

*The Nicholas
Brothers
performing
their on-the-
toes knee
swivel in*
Orchestra
Wives,
*Twentieth
Century-Fox*
1942
*(Harold
Nicholas
Archive).*

that jive expression by singing, "She's a fine chick!" while miming
the shape of that gal's hourglass figure. "I'm gonna see that freck-
led-face kid I'm hurrying to," Harold sings, promising he'll go to
Michigan "to see the sweetest gal in Kalamazoo."

The brothers' shared singing of the song in the first chorus
leads in the second chorus to a synchronized jazz tap dance. They
begin by tip-toeing downstage, knees pressed together and shifting from side to side, as the toes tap out a dainty "daDA da da da,
daDA dada dada da" beat. Then arms and legs are suddenly
splayed open into an asymmetrical stance (in which the weight is
shifted over one bent leg, the other leg extended), from which
they click out military cramprolls with their toes and heels. Sliding their legs back together, they repeat the tip-toeing and knee-

swiveling in double time, and they break with a syncopated "dit dit DOT di DI dalee DI dalee" beat. The second (or B) section of the chorus shifts the attention from the whole body to the feet, from big shapes to intricate foot rhythms. Though the brothers are dancing in hard-soled character shoes (they would later dub in the sound of the taps), their feet are as pliant as their points and perches. During turning movements, their legs are placed in a position that resembles ballet's *sur le coup de pied* (one foot is placed on the ankle of the other foot). Other steps also resemble ballet, such as a *coupé*-like cutaway step and a *coupé jeté* springing step from the position of *sur le coup de pied*. Some steps mix ballet and tap: spins (with feet in *sur le coup de pied*) that are halted with offbeat stomps and *attitude* turns (the body is supported on one leg with the other lifted behind, the knee bent at ninety degrees and higher than the foot) that extend into one-legged pullbacks.

In the bridge section of the chorus, the brothers cover the space with tapping *chassés* (gliding steps in which one foot "chases" the other out of its position), which are followed with grapevine steps (side-traveling steps in which the foot crosses in front and behind the other foot) accented by stomps and claps. They have many new steps, as well as stylistic variations on familiar ones: the Charleston swing, a trademark Nicholas step, has lost its "flung" quality and is now executed with more control; with more of a sense of the leg being "placed," the step resembles ballet's *ronde de jambe en l'air*.

In the slow-moving adagio section of the third chorus, the entire stage is dark except for a spotlight on the brothers, whose slow-developing extensions cast long dramatic shadows across the floor. They lunge sideways, falling into a deep second position, and twist their upper bodies around to face upstage; reversing the twist, they continue to spiral upward in the opposite direction as their legs, entwined into a tight fifth position, bring them to the balls of the feet. With a small hop onto the tips of the toes, they lift arms above their heads while circling a leg on the floor. This unusual spiraling movement gives the look of being turned on a pedestal. Closing the legs into tight fifth position, they turn to face the camera in a beautiful suspension, which is suddenly broken with a backward slide that stretches into a down-and-up split that fits perfectly into the last two beats of the measure.

On the recovery from the split, the lights brighten and the tempo quickens as Fayard takes Harold by both hands and flings him halfway across the stage into another split-and-recover. In this section, the camera shifts back and forth from one brother to the other, reinforcing cinematically the ensuing challenge dance. Fayard leaps high into the air, extends one leg in front of him, whips it to turn once around, then lands in a split-and-recover. Harold returns by lunging forward and jumping in the air, turning around one and a half times, and landing in a split-and-recover. Fayard challenges that move with back-sweeping trenches and a barrel turn, in which he rotates his body while keeping it suspended midair, to land in a split-and-recover. And Harold returns with a jump that darts straight up and turns around one and a half times, landing in a split-and-recover.

Then the music speeds up to an exciting climax as Fayard bolts across the stage, jumps up onto a square marble pillar, and pushes backward off the pillar to land in a split-and-recover. Harold's bravuric answer to Fayard's pillar-jumping move is to sprint with lightning speed across the length of the stage floor, then continue to "run" halfway up the square pillar and push off into a backflip that propels him into a series of slippery back-sliding steps that return him to Fayard. In the air-defying finale, both brothers turn and run upstage to jump onto a "trampoline" platform, which bounces them up and onto the small stage they first entered. Turning around, they run and jump once more onto the springing platform, which sends them soaring through the air like rockets into a split-and-recover landing. They bow and exit.

"Kalamazoo" was a breathtaking routine, but it was not the product of working with one choreographer on one particular film. Despite the tremendous influence that Nick Castle exerted over the brothers as their dance director at Twentieth Century-Fox from 1940 to 1945, "Kalamazoo" was a fluent blending of a number of dance styles and movement vocabularies that Fayard and Harold had been observing and absorbing for over a decade. The smooth-

flowing and open-partnered synchronization of adagio ballroom dance, the Africanist-inflected stage and social dance styles of the teens and twenties, the flash and acrobatics of turn-of-the-century black comedy dance, the formal elegance and fastidious movement rhythms of the class act, and the rhythmic drive of the challenge dance—all were absorbed by the Nicholases and then distilled into their own distinctive style of American jazz dancing.

Still, meticulous footwork, virtuosic aerial jumps and turns, vertical deportment, and the formal ordering of their bodies—all movement qualities traditionally associated with ballet—are also in evidence in "Kalamazoo." This explains why "classical" defines the elegant deportment and fastidious stepping style that people often associate with the Nicholases. "Fayard was absolutely the epitome of classical dancing," said Geri (Pate) Nicholas (who married Fayard in 1942), explaining that Fayard memorized scores from symphonies, practiced tap dancing from those scores

The Nicholas Brothers in Orchestra Wives, Twentieth Century-Fox 1942 (Harold Nicholas Archive).

he could remember, and liked to conduct. In addition, he was totally the graceful dancer: "Fayard danced with his eyebrows, he danced with his hands, every single thing was movement, beautiful movement."[3] Here, the word "classical" refers to beautiful, graceful movement.

To discern what is "classical" about the Nicholas Brothers' dancing, it is first necessary to inquire about the nature of classical dance, the term designating traditional ballet technique, a style of concert or theatrical dance that prevails in the Western world. Ballet was developed from the Renaissance festivities of the Italian courts and the efforts of sixteenth-century French neoclassicist academicians to reestablish the basic relationship among poetry, music, and dance as epitomized in the classical Greek theatre.[4]

In the seventeenth century, ballet developed into a social dance form practiced by the French nobility in the court of Louis XIV. In the eighteenth century, ballet became a codified theatrical dance form taught by French, Italian, and Russian dance masters who proposed a formal ordering of the dancer's body according to geometric principals of alignment and proportion. Even as the *ballet de cour* (court ballet) of the eighteenth century gave way to the still very formal nineteenth-century *ballet d'action*—which told its story through the marriage of dance steps and mimed gesture—classical technique continued to dramatize "the open, physical and graceful attitudes of the marble Greek gods."[5] Vertical deportment, "the upward-aspiring straight line that aspired to purity, honesty, and . . . [the] heroic," became the fundamental principal of classical dance.[6]

Other qualities became distinguishable in classical dancing. What the critic Castile-Blaze observed as being "eminently classical" about the dancing of the renowned ballerinas Marie Taglioni and Mlle. Saint-Roman in 1825 was that "the whole body moved."[7] André Levinson, in the early twentieth century, further developed the notion of the classical body as "ex-centric": "The arms and the legs stretch out, freeing themselves from the torso, expanding the chest,"[8] paying great attention to turnout of legs and feet, which extended the dancer's range of motion and offered a centrifugal presentation of the body. Adrian Stokes pointed out that the bearing of the classical dancer was characterized by lightness: "Every bend, every jump of the classic dancer was accomplished with an effect of ease and lightness."[9] In 1944, composer John Cage added that classical ballet demonstrated not only lightness and grace but "clarity of rhythmic structure."[10]

Ballet dancers were not the only dancers capable of demonstrating the principles of grace and clarity. Lincoln Kirstein's description of classical dancing, in "Classic Ballet: Aria of the Aerial," invites comparison to the Nicholas Brothers when he describes ballet training and performance as accentuating "the area of air," in its "denial of gravity by leg-work in beats and jumps; brilliant multiple turns; speed in the stage-traverse; *pointe* [toe]-shoes; and virtuoso acrobatics."[11] Although the brothers' black-leather tap shoes replaced the ballerina's pink-satin pointe

The Nicholas Brothers' extension of wings into high kicks en pointe (Harold Nicholas Archive).

shoes in "Kalamazoo," the brothers mastered "the area of the air" with their jumps, backflips, and brilliant multiple turns, with their speedy flight of steps across the space, and with their rhythmically clear "beats" that are produced not through *petite batterie* but by their bells, cramps, and paddle-and-rolls. From the geometry of their bodily forms to their gravity-defying acrobatics and aerial steps, much in the "Kalamazoo" number follows the principles of classical dance. It may be seen in their unwavering control of grace and elegance, their rhythmic clarity of the feet and bodily motions, their opened-up "lift" in the torso that allows the legs to extend fully (not into *grande jeté* but into full splits), and their full-bodied expressivity. "We didn't want them to just take our feet, even though we may have been doing a lot of tapping, because we'd be missing something," Harold has stated about the Nicholases' film dancing. "We wanted them to take our body, the whole body, because you can always hear the taps."[12] Taken altogether, Nicholas dancing was performed in what Levinson called the classical spirit—its generative reinforcement of aesthetics, elegance, brilliance, *ballon*, and virtuosity, plus its precision of step execution.

While the Nicholases' tap dancing reflects the classical aesthetic, in the main, theirs was not derived from that tradition of Western classical dancing. Fayard and Harold claim, and there is no reason to doubt them, that they never received any formal training in ballet. Their musical orientation, rooted in African-American folk traditions, came largely from their parents, professional jazz musicians. From a very early age, Fayard and Harold's dance "training" was gotten largely by watching hundreds of African-American tap dancers, singers, and comedians perform on the stage and in film.

Because they modeled themselves after the African-American dance and musical artists they had seen in black vaudeville and the jazz musicians whose music they had heard on record and in live performance, the Nicholas Brothers' performance seems, for the most part, to be "Africanist," the term that has been used by contemporary African-American scholars Joseph Holloway, Toni Morrison, and, most recently, Brenda Dixon Gottschild to refer to the African-American resonances, presences, trends and phenomena in American culture. These include the influences, forms, and forces—both past and present—that arose as products of the African diaspora, as well as the wealth of African-based American traditions and genres such as blues, jazz, and the dance forms that moved from the ballroom and nightclub floors to the popular and concert stages.[13]

While synchronized precision movement, one of the signatures of the Nicholas dance style, is equivalent to the *pas de deux* in classical ballet, this form of movement, for the Nicholases, was derived from the class-act tradition, which, like ballet, challenged its partners to execute the highest degree of controlled precision while moving together with smooth effortlessness. The Nicholases' virtuosic aerial steps—the jumps, splits, flips, and multiple turns that, like ballet, proclaimed "capacity in flexibility, lightness, power, [and] brilliance *off the floor*"[14]—were also rooted in black performance traditions, specifically black comedy dance, which prompted its performers to perfect their own eccentric specialties to wow vaudeville audiences. If the Nicholas Brothers were at all influenced by ballet, it came from their watching of ballroom adagio dancing, which may have informed the smoothly synchronous Nicholas routines.

Exhibition ballroom dance, later enriched immeasurably by African-American and Latin American influences, was introduced in the teens by Vernon and Irene Castle. Though they may not have been the first, the Castles took such popular black social dances as the fox-trot, two-step, turkey trot, black bottom, Charleston, Argentine tango, and Cuban rhumba, and presented them publicly to largely white audiences. Working with James Reese Europe, their composer and orchestra leader, the well-dressed Castles brought fluidity, elegance, and sophistication to these social dances that were performed to the syncopated rhythms of ragtime, jazz, and Latin music.

In the twenties, while such white Broadway stars as Gilda Gray, Ann Pennington, and Adele Astaire were learning "marvelous, new, dirty steps" from black dance instructors like Buddy Bradley, African-American dancers like Harold Norton and Margot Webb

studied ballet, toe, and white ballroom styles, soon gaining a reputation for their smooth and sustained dancing supported by a
strong foundation in ballet technique.[15] Thus opportunities
abounded for the Nicholases to absorb the synchronous partner-
ings of such African-American ballroom dance teams as Anise and
Aland, who appeared with them in the London production of
Blackbirds of 1936, and Norton and Webb, who toured extensively
on the East Coast and in the Midwest, on the black vaudeville
circuit. On tours from New York to Philadelphia, to Baltimore to
Washington, D.C., it is possible that Norton and Webb may have
first demonstrated to the Nicholases ballet movement and technique.

While the Nicholases admired and absorbed the elegant tap-
dancing styles of such black class-act dancers as Jack Wiggins, Pete
Nugent, and Eddie Rector, little evidence exists to show that the
brothers emulated the most elegant of white tap dancers, Fred
Astaire, who has been called "a genius . . . a classical dancer like I
never saw in my life" by Mikhail Baryshnikov. Astaire was con-
sidered by many, including Rudolf Nureyev, to be "the greatest
American dancer in history."[16] A remarkable segment of the
Nicholas silent home movies taken by Viola Nicholas is of Fred
Astaire doing an impromptu tap dance with her sons on the RKO
Studio film lot in Hollywood in 1934.

Astaire, at the time, was starring with Ginger Rogers in *Top
Hat*, which he choreographed. In the movie, released in 1935, the
filmgoer saw Astaire in formal wear, with top hat, brushing off his
tails with white gloves and singing, "I'm stepping out, my dear,
to breathe an atmosphere that simply reeks with class" in the
number "Top Hat, White Tie and Tails." His dancing was a fusion
of ballet jumps (complete with beats of the legs), ballroom dance
(with strutting, lunging, and turning movements), and tap
rhythms.

The home movie allows a rare and side-by-side comparison of
these dancers' styles, both of which have been described as classical. The Nicholases and Astaire are looking cool and casual on this
afternoon, with Fayard and Harold in three-piece suits and
Astaire in loose-fitting white slacks, an open shirt, a sport jacket,

and a hat. Wearing soft-soled shoes, the three are seen dancing double time steps, smiling at one another and the camera while dancing. There is a sense of pull-up in Astaire's torso as he dances, and his knees lift higher off the ground than the brothers'. While the brothers dance the time steps in vertical alignment, their arms swing more naturally than Astaire's and follow the momentum of the movement, which is motivated by the foot rhythms. After several repetitions of the time steps, the brothers step aside for Astaire, who continues an impromptu dance. With a snapping of his fingers to keep time, he leans sideways into side-brushing grapevine steps, then "places" his arms in preparation for inside turns; he springs to second position for a smooth transition into a *renverse* turn and finishes with a flourish of toe taps.

This brief segment of silent film confirms Astaire's smooth elegance and demonstrates the dominance of form over rhythm in his dance style. It confirms what class-act dancer Honi Coles once said of Astaire, that he was not a tap dancer so much as a dancer who used tap steps.[17] While Fayard and Harold were less than smooth, and considerably more angular in form than Astaire was, they integrated the tap rhythms into their bodies. And these rhythms, in turn, determined the form of the movement. But while the Nicholases admired Astaire, they neither copied nor coveted his dancing style. "My brother and I, we were doing our thing long before we saw Fred Astaire, and long before there was a Gene Kelly," Fayard remarks. "I think they [Fayard and Harold] considered Fred Astaire the best ballroom dancer in the whole wide world," said Geri Nicholas. "But when he started to tap, he wasn't really dancing, like all over."[18]

Neither ballet nor ballroom but the classic American forms of jazz, blues, and swing exerted the greatest influence on the Nicholas style. "Jazz is the spirit child of the Negro musicians, and its artistic vindication rests in its sound development by these musicians," wrote the Harlem Renaissance theoretician Alain Locke, who distinguished a "jazz classic" as a work which, "rising from the level of ordinary people, usually in the limited dance and song-ballad forms, achieves creative musical excellence." He called "classical jazz" that which "successfully transposes the elements of folk music, in this case jazz idioms, to the more sophisticated and traditional musical forms."

Locke cited both as examples of the "serious Negro music" that was contributing to "the new modernistic music of our time."[19] Equating American swing with classical European music, Benny Goodman argued that swing jazz could elevate its audience to an appreciation of concert music by training its fans actually to listen to music: "A youngster reared on the rhythmic patterns of a Jo Jones, a Lionel Hampton, a Dave Tough or a Gene Krupa would hardly find Stravinsky's *Sacre du Printemps* perplexing," Goodman wrote. "And the contrapuntal interweavings of a first-rate jam session had more relationship to a Bach fugue than even the musicians would consider possible."[20] Goodman's hopes were not unfounded; the *New York Times* reported in 1938 that 70 percent of swing record buyers also purchased classical recordings.[21] By the same token, Alain Locke believed that Duke Ellington, in addition to being one of the great exponents of "pure jazz," was one of the persons most likely to create "classical jazz," because he transposed the elements of Negro folk music into sophisticated American musical forms, which he gave symphonic proportions. Paralleling Ellington's music, considered a classical American musical form, would be the Nicholases' tap dancing.

Jazz tap dance, like jazz music, was created by the fusion of European melodic and African rhythmic sensibilities. That is why certain aspects of jazz dancing can be compared to Western classical dance forms. Yet jazz dance, like jazz music, is, in many ways, quite distinct from its European counterparts. While the body in Western classical dance is distinguished by its verticality, the body of the (black) jazz dancer is distinguished by its diagonality, as epitomized by the aerial breakaway moves of Savoy Ballroom lindy-hoppers in the swing era. While Western classicism tends toward a geometric formula and the symmetrical and formal ordering of the body, the corporeal forms of the jazz dancer are asymmetrical. The center of gravity for the ballet dancer is as high as the solar plexus, but the center of gravity for the jazz dancer is lower, at the base of the torso, which opens the region of the pelvis to flexibility and mobility of the legs. The body of the

ballet dancer is made to be fully dilated, based on years of training that distort the legs into full turnout, while the legs of the jazz
dancer extend into parallel lines that are broken only at the
elbows and knees, thus turning curves and circular shapes into
angled forms. While the arms of the ballet dancer are formally
"placed," the carriage of the arms in jazz dancing naturally follows
the momentum of the movement.

Perhaps the greatest difference between classical American jazz
dancing and Western classical dance is that in the former, energy
situates and determines form,[22] and in the latter, energy is sub-
ordinated to form—"the dancer's energy is shown channelled
through systems and forms and designs."[23] Western classical
dance follows the traditional musical structuring of classical music
(beginning-middle-end; theme and variation; development and
resolution), but jazz music and dance are structured after the call-
and-response pattern of twelve-bar blues and the thirty-two-bar
AABA structure of Tin Pan Alley songs.

In ballet, the male will support and frame his female partner;
in traditional forms of jazz tap dancing, the duet is democratized
to present the two-man team in an equal partnership (synchronous movement), with dancing that is rhythmically driven by the
competition of the challenge.

The Nicholas style has been referred to as looking classical,
with the underlying assumption that they appropriated ballet
steps, styling, and grace. But there has been little discussion until
very recently on the reverse—how Western classical dance appropriated and absorbed aspects of classical American jazz dance and
music forms. Classical theatrical dancing, with whatever formal
technique it possessed, first appeared in the United States in the
late eighteenth century.[24] But by the twentieth century, it had
become profoundly influenced by jazz rhythms. In the Jazz Age
twenties, ballerinas dancing *en pointe* performed black American
social dances on the concert stage, such as the Shimmy (the torso-
shaking dance that isolated body parts), the leggy Charleston
(which tilted the torso to the horizontal to splay the arms and
legs), and the Snake Hips (which dropped the center of gravity
into the pelvis).

This period saw ballet become an American dance genre, distinguished by angularity and a downward drive of weight and speed, a fracturing in the timing of the phrase, and a turning in of the feet—thereby modernizing classical form. "The strongest exterior influence on the development of the academic dance has derived from jazz rhythm, beat, the shifting pulse and syncopation of styles and steps from ragtime to rock," wrote Lincoln Kirstein, adding that the classical line of the thirties and forties was at once "rangy, athletic, modish," the prototypes being more Ginger Rogers and Fred Astaire than former imperial Russian ballerinas.[25]

Kirstein mistakenly failed to include the Nicholas Brothers and other jazz tap dancers of the thirties and forties as "modernizing" influences on classical balletic form. Jazz tap dancing, as it developed in the Swing Era, became an expressive form with a thoroughly "modern" sound. In his book *Modernism and the Harlem Renaissance*, Houston Baker proposed that it was the simultaneous "mastery of form" and "deformation of mastery," or the filtering of Western standards in art through African-American cultural expression, that led artists of the Harlem Renaissance to an African-American modernism.

Baker used Booker T. Washington's oratory as an early model of the African American's mastery of white Euro-American rhetorical form. Washington was an educator and reformer who advocated a philosophy of social advancement for African Americans through self-help, racial solidarity, accommodation, and the cultivation of the virtues of patience, enterprise and thrift, which would with the respect of whites and lead to being fully accepted into all strata of society. The oratorical "mastery" of Washington was countered with the writings of W.E.B. Du Bois, who, in urging the retention and preservation of African cultural traits, such as folk culture and the blues, advocated transforming European models to draw out an authentic African-American folk "sound." The simultaneous "mastery of form" and "deformation of mastery," a creative blending of class (mastery) and mass (deformation), produced in the early twentieth century distinctly "modern" African-American forms of expression.[26]

Baker, furthermore, gave the examples of Billy Kersands, who stretched the minstrel mask to a successful black excess, and Bert Williams and George Walker, who converted nonsense syllables and awkward minstrel steps into pure kinesthetics. These turn-of-the-century artists stretched the contortions of eccentric dance into black artistry.

Like these artists, the Nicholases absorbed and "mastered" a variety of American dance forms and performance traditions, simultaneously "deforming" or filtering them through their particular Africanist sensibilities. They extended (or "deformed") *jetés* into full split-and-recovers, for example, which they further "distorted" into fantastic splayed movements of the limbs. By combining these full-bodied extensions with complex beats of the feet, the brothers created a superlative form of rhythm dancing that became a masterful black artistry. Baker did not cite jazz among the black modernist expressions emerging from the Harlem Renaissance; yet jazz tap dance may well be the quintessential "modern" African-American sound, the inheritor of the legacy of the African drum. Jazz tap dance embodies the spirit of drummed rhythms, the mother tongue of the African gods. It uses the dancing body in its sounding out of a fiercely modernist expression. It is resonant of what Amiri Baraka, in his poem "Return of the Native," wrote:

> Harlem is vicious
> modernism. Bangclash
> Vicious the way it's made.
> Can you stand such Beauty?
> So violent and transforming?

Jazz tap dance, like the tradition of American modern dance that also evolved in the early decades of the twentieth century, plays with weight distribution, both giving in to it and resisting it. A fusion of Irish jig and African *gioube*, early forms of jigging combined close-to-the-ground shuffling steps with lighter and speedier winging steps. The quintessential embodiment of that vertical-stanced, up-on-the-toes style was Bill "Bojangles" Robinson. But as tap dancing developed, paralleling jazz in the twenties, the up-on-the-toes jigging style gave way to syncopated heel-drop-ping rhythm tap, whose primary exponent was John Bubbles. There also developed a vocabulary of steps exhibiting a downward drive of weight (stomps and heel-digs) and the giving in to and resisting of weight. In it, jumps were performed not to emphasize the going up but to punctuate the going down—"to highlight rhythm and percussion rather than melody and ethereality."[27] The Nicholases absorbed both the light-footed jigging style of Bill Robinson and the heel-dropping rhythm tapping style of John Bubbles; when dancing to thirties swing and early forties forms of bebop, they combined these older styles of rhythm dancing into their own uniquely modern expressions.

Marshall Stearns wrote that "tap dancing for its own sake lost ground the moment it set foot on the Broadway stage [because] Broadway did not encourage plain hoofing," meaning that in the 1920s, tap dance was inextricably linked to black musical theatre and therefore incapable of expression without the resources of mimetic and symbolic conventions.[28] Whereas the popularity of black Broadway musicals declined at the end of the twenties, jazz tap dancing continued to be performed on the big-band stage during the Swing Era and was found to be thoroughly expressive—but without the various traditional resources of mimetic and symbolic conventions. With neither a story line nor a character on which to hang a routine, rhythm dancing succeeded with no need to represent anything but itself—that is, it was rhythm for the sake of rhythm. It came to demand the exclusion of every element that veiled, muted, or distracted from its basically "pure motion and sound."[29]

Ironically, this is why so many of the Nicholases' tap dance routines were able to be inserted, almost arbitrarily, into Holly-wood musical films; in fact, sometimes the same routine appeared in more than one film, although filmed from new angles. The Nicholases' movement rhythms could be enjoyed just for the sake of the dancing, and not where they figured in the plot.

The dictionary tells us rhythm is inherently "abstract," in that it creates and mirrors movement, tension, and emotional values, "through the pattern of regular or irregular pulses caused in music by the occurrence of strong and weak melodic and harmonic beats." In rhythm tap dancing, even the so-called break, which is the most basic way of punctuating the movement phrase, is essentially abstract in its radical juxtaposition of one rhythm phrase against another. Jazz tap dance, then, as the premier popular dance expression of the thirties and forties, must have been seen as a distinctly modern expression, with its emphasis on speed, attack, and force, the employment of angular and asymmetrical formations, the succession, repetition, and juxtaposition of movement rhythms, and the playing with weight as formal modes of expression. Nowhere is this better demonstrated than in Harold Nicholas's tap solo in *The Reckless Age* (1944, Universal). Choreographed and performed by Harold after Fayard was drafted into the army, Harold's solo demonstrated the purely modernist style of jazz dancing.

The Reckless Age starred the singer Gloria Jean and featured Harold in one scene with the star, singing "Mama Yo Quiero" in Portuguese while moving a piano in a storage room. At the end of the song, Harold scats "mamamama, mamamama" and springs to the edge of the piano, then repeats "mama mama mamamama" and springs to the top of the piano. The 2/4 time samba then changes to a tune with a swinging four beat, as Harold leaps from the top of the piano to the floor where, with a spin and slide, he proceeds to tap dance. The storage room is filled with large pieces of furniture covered in white sheets. Even before the start of the dance that moves him past the abstract furniture forms, the shape of Harold's sustained leap off the piano signals how his body's geometrical form will interplay with the abstract forms of the furniture, and how gravity-defying aerial moves will interplay with his close-to-the-floor rhythm tapping.

Harold's first dancing chorus combines taut-legged crossover steps and wide-circling kicks, providing swift transitions into inside turns, back-crossing steps, and a rhythm break (dada da DA dit DOT/dada da DA dit DOT da DA), which Harold taps out on top of a small, square table onto which he has sprung. Chugging the balls of his feet, digging his heels into the tabletop, and turning while shuffling his feet, Harold then leaps from table to floor and taps out a rhythm break on the landing. Not only the rhythm of his feet but also the shape of his body midair creates percussive transitions in the dance. The angular shape (resembling an isosceles triangle) that Harold strikes in the air when he jumps off the table, for instance, becomes beats one and two of the last measure, with beats three and four of the measure taking him to the floor. Harold's body melds with the tap rhythms to create a full-bodied rhythm dance.

In the bridge of the first chorus, Harold creates transitions from intricate rhythms of close-to-the-floor steps to larger, across-the-floor movements as he skids, slides, and leaps through the maze of odd white shapes. He travels along a diagonal path with tapping crossover steps, dives forward into barrel turns, and darts sideways with slip-sliding steps. He then pauses to tap in place between two long parallel tables positioned to create a long, narrow pathway. Tapping down that pathway, Harold springs onto the tops of the tables, and with legs straddling them, he circles his hips to fill out the rhythm pattern that was started by the jump. He then leaps off the tables, tapping the rest of his way down the aisle.

No music accompanies the next section, as Harold's close-to-the-floor tapping focuses the audience on the purity of the rhythmic expression. This passage, with a variety of shapes and sounds, takes the form of a drum solo, in which Harold alternates hard-hitting "sock" sounds with less intense "click" or "swish" sounds. When the musical accompaniment returns, the dance stretches again through the space as crossover steps, back-slides, and Charleston variations carry Harold laterally through the maze, his twisting turns constantly changing his line of direction.

After he jumps over a long table into a handspring somersault and a split, a smooth recovery moves Harold from one beautiful shape to another; body-curving crossovers melt into circle kicks and turns, heel-clicking bells descend into lunges, and multiple turns (with the hands placed neatly on the hips) blossom into scissoring sidesteps. In the final chorus, Harold climbs up a six-step ladder, tapping out a rhythm on the third and fifth steps, and dives backward from the top step into a backflip. He lands just in time, on the last two beats of the measure, to deliver a triple turn, jump-split, double turn, and bow.

"That's wonderful," the mink-coated Gloria Jean exclaims at the end of the number. "Thank you, just a little warmup for the job," Harold answers with an understated cool as he proceeds to move the piano. In his melding of opposites—hot rhythms and cool integrity of form—the rhythmic excitement builds in his dancing to stimulate pure audience intoxication. He stretches out and opens up the rhythmic flow, but he never becomes overly assertive; grace and subtlety predominate in his performance. He remains consonant with the feeling of the arrangement, playing the flow of the rhythm.

The speedy, swinging rhythms of Harold's drum dancing— dissonant in the clatter of metal tapping, yet exciting in the offbeat, rhythmic propulsion—not only "sound" out a new breed of black American jazz artists who might finally "shed the costume of the shuffling darky."[30] More surely, they shaped a style, a "classical" American style, of jazz dancing that in sound and shape was purely modernist.

*The Nicholas
Brothers flying
high in Paris,
1947 (Harold
Nicholas
Archive).*

Nine

Swing to Bop

1945–1958

Despite the unanimous critical praise that the Nicholas Brothers received for the film *Stormy Weather* (1943), in which their jazz tap dancing, as one critic wrote, brought the movie "to an almost intolerably pleasurable peak,"[1] their five-year contract with Twentieth Century-Fox was not renewed in 1945. The reasons, ironically, had as much to do with Fayard and Harold's maturation as jazz dance artists as with shifting racial politics in Hollywood during the postwar years.

The bombing of Pearl Harbor on December 7, 1941, had unleashed a terror of the Japanese that shook America; within weeks, wartime mobilization set in motion developments that were to transform American society for generations to come. With World War II, which precipitated massive political and social change for all Americans, came conditions that aided black Americans in their long struggle for civil rights. In 1940, about 70 percent of African Americans were living in the rural South; during the next decade, more than two million moved to northern and western industrial areas in order to gain employment in the war effort. While the accelerated migration to northern urban centers created urban ghettos, resulting in overcrowded housing and hard-pressed social programs, blacks gained a new independence from the overwhelming social constraints of small, rural southern communities; in addition, they gained some new freedom in the expression of civil rights.

Black determination to fight racism first became obvious in 1941, when the March on Washington Movement, led by A. Philip Randolph, insisted that black Americans challenge the employment policies of the federal government and demand equal treatment in the work force. This led to the establishment, in June 1941, of President Franklin D. Roosevelt's Committee for Employment, and very soon black employment increased dramatically. Nevertheless, jobs failed to address the promise of equal opportunity because most were at low levels, with blacks hired as unskilled labor, janitors, or scrubwomen rather than as technicians, skilled craftsmen, or secretaries. At this time, the ever-present Jim Crow laws still maintained "separate but equal" segregation in the South for transportation, education, and public accommodation—and even in some states of the Midwest. The country's simultaneous postwar optimism, prosperity, and ongoing oppression spawned anger and frustration in black Americans; soon a new spirit of militancy and assertiveness became part of the new protest movement.[2]

During the war, the all-black musical *Stormy Weather* was produced. "Culturally black in roots, and wearing its black patriotism on its sleeve,"[3] the story—recounting the life of a veteran hoofer (played by Bill Robinson)—was told through a series of flashbacks from the Jazz Age through the Swing Era. It simultaneously drew on the lives of James Reese Europe, Noble Sissle, and Eubie Blake; their images were intercut with newsreel footage of the 15th National Guard marching up Fifth Avenue in New York, its Croix de Guerre ribbons flying on its guidons, and with footage of Harlem, the Fisk Jubilee Singers, the Pekin Theatre in Chicago, and other sites of African-American performing culture.

The film addressed growing ideological tensions between integration and cultural uniqueness, and it produced in the minds of many black activists an anxiety over the implied retreat from integration in Hollywood films. To further complicate the debate, *Stormy Weather* was released during the summer of 1943, as "race riots" broke out in Harlem and Detroit and as "zoot suit" riots hit Los Angeles. The riots drew attention to the persistence of racism in America and indicated that movies—which had added to the pressures for the enhanced status of blacks in films—were a factor. Twentieth Century-Fox considered pulling the movie; the decision to release it earned praise from blacks from all political sectors. Walter White, director of the National Association for the Advancement of Colored People (NAACP), praised Fox president Darryl F. Zanuck for refusing to permit the race riots to change Fox's plans, suggesting that the resulting tension required "affirmative prevention plans," which movies might provide, if "getting along together" was ever to come about.[4] *Stormy Weather*, like most wartime movies, made a profit, with long runs in key cities and southern towns; more important, the film spoke to the conscience of liberals, while signaling a general retreat from producing all-black Hollywood musicals.

Perhaps this was one of the reasons Twentieth Century-Fox let the Nicholas Brothers' contract lapse in 1945: the studio saw no commercial advantage in retaining a pair of African-American specialty dancers. Fayard insists, however, that the Nicholases refused to renew with Fox, largely because they had never been fully employed by Fox during their five years under contract. In all seven of their contract films, the Nicholas Brothers made only brief appearances in the musical scenes, which could easily be edited out, if desired, for distribution purposes.

They were never integrated into the plots of these films. Furthermore, while the brothers were under contract with Fox, they continued to be booked by the William Morris Agency in New York, the implication being that Fox could not or would not find work for them. How was it, then, that the more renowned the Nicholas Brothers became, the less aggressive Fox was in casting them? "As gifted as they were," Dorothy Nicholas has explained, "it was a time when . . . a lot of people didn't feel that they [blacks] should get too far. And I hate to put it on that basis, but . . . if you get too good, they won't hire you."[5]

*Harold,
Viola, and
Fayard
Nicholas in
Los Angeles in
the mid-forties
(Harold
Nicholas
Archive).*

Perhaps the most pressing reality to confront Fox executives in any consideration of contract renewal was that in June 1943, Harold was twenty-two and Fayard twenty-eight. Sporting a wisp of a mustache over his lip, Harold was a dashing figure on film, and Fayard was unabashedly sexy, especially in the way he stroked his fingers and swerved his hips while singing a song. It seemed as if the brothers had, all of a sudden, grown from boys to men. No longer were they the cute youngsters who had charmed and disarmed audiences with their dimpled smiles and jubilant rhythm dancing. Precocious sophistication had given way to a mature sexuality.

Historically, the black man's dancing body on the concert stage aroused for white audiences deeply entrenched fears of power and sexual potency. The concert stage became the arena for controlling and subduing that threat. Minstrelsy had "fixed the tradition of the Negro as only an irresponsible, happy-go-lucky, wide-grinning, loud-laughing, shuffling, banjo-playing, singing, dancing sort of being."[6] Black Broadway musicals in the teens and twenties only hardened the stereotype of black male dancers as easygoing innocents, whose dancing abilities could be fully appreciated in the simple delight they provided.[7] As long as the Nicholases projected the image of bright-faced innocents who were devoid of any sexuality (as the "eunuchs" they had played in the harem scene of *Tin Pan Alley*), they presented no challenge to white authority. In their films, the Nicholases would appear in few scenes with women, unless of course an all-female (black or white) chorus, with whom they never exchanged a line of dialogue, backed them up.

The only woman with whom the Nicholases ever danced in a Fox film was Dorothy Dandridge, in the "Chattanooga Choo Choo" number in *Sun Valley Serenade*. "They never saw us dance with a lady before, and that was different," says Harold about Dandridge. And Fayard remembers that the William Morris Agency told him that the reason the Nicholas Brothers were never cut from *Down Argentine Way* when it was shown to audiences in the South was because the brothers had no verbal or physical contact with the film's blond star, Betty Grable: "They told me it was because we did our thing and we were by ourselves, not surrounded by anybody, so the people were just looking at us."[8]

When the brothers were on tour with Carmen Miranda in 1940, Harold remembered, white Southerners in the audience expressed their displeasure at seeing a white woman touch the brothers onstage. "She'd just grab us, grab us both and tickle us," said Harold. "And once during a performance, a man in the audience hollered, 'Hey, what are you doing?' And she shouted back jokingly, 'What's the matter, are you jealous, yeah?'"[9] Miranda had been able to quell with humor the sparks of hostility that were ignited in the audience over seeing a white woman playfully touch a pair of black teenage boys. But what was Fox do with the Nicholas Brothers in 1945? Now too old to be cast as a pair of carefree teenagers, and too talented and proud to accept roles as tap-dancing shoeshine boys, Fayard and Harold were still too young (and sexually potent) to play the role of veteran hoofers past their prime, as had Bill Robinson in *Stormy Weather*. It was only a matter of time before the brothers would be doomed to experience the same restrictions and taboos as any other African-American man living in the generally segregated American society of the 1940s.

During the war years, Twentieth Century-Fox was also confronted with another problem, the constant hassle to keep the Nicholases from being drafted. Until the middle of 1943, Fox had successfully done so by telling the California Draft Board that they were needed for films currently in production. The studio must have been forced to act on its word, however. Late in 1942, the Nicholases were working on the East Coast when they received an unexpected telegram from Darryl Zanuck, ordering them back to Hollywood to film *Stormy Weather*. They had not initially been cast in the film, which had already been in production for several months. Fayard's new bride, Geraldine Pate Nicholas (they married in January 1942), remembered that soon after receiving the telegram, they were visited by what she describes as "gangsters":

> This guy, with his hat pulled down low over his eyes, came there and let us know that he was armed, and said, "Get your things together." . . . He got two other guys and they put all the bags together, and they were marched out to the post to finish the film.[10]

In July 1943—one month after the release of *Stormy Weather* and with no talk from Twentieth Century-Fox about any future film projects for the brothers—Fayard got his notice to appear for a physical from the California Draft Board. He was immediately inducted into the army and sent to a boot camp in Gloucester, Mississippi. Geri recalled that "Fayard, who had never washed a sock in his life, was put in a quartermaster unit . . . a laundry unit that was going to be sent overseas."[11] He subsequently managed to get a transfer into a United Service Organization (USO) unit in Fort Hunchia, Arizona, where he was stationed for thirteen months.

Harold, too, got his notice from the California Draft Board, but when he reported for his physical, he was found, at five feet two inches, to be one inch short of the minimum height requirement, and thus he was never drafted. Without Fayard, and "relieved" of his contract with Fox, which had specified *both* Nicholas brothers, Harold began to look for work in Hollywood. He was quickly cast in Universal Pictures' *The Reckless Age* (released on October 26, 1944). Then Columbia Pictures cast him in a leading dance role in *Carolina Blues*. The film starred Kay Kyser, Ann Miller, and Victor Moore, and it told the story of two young entertainers trying to join Kyser's big band as they raised money for war bonds. It also featured an all-black dance troupe, and the musical scene in which Harold appeared was a throwback to the Cotton Club of the thirties.

At the opening of the scene, the master of ceremonies announced, "We'll have some more of that stuff and that's for certain. So, Mr. Man, open that curtain." The curtains part, revealing Kyser's gleaming big band. Ann Miller (in dark makeup, bearing an uncanny resemblance to Lena Horne) strides onstage, her gown sparkling: "I've just come from Harlem, from the land of Hi-de-ho, and it's not the Harlem I used to know," she sings, telling of meeting "a cat named Lucius, Beebee is his name," a man "quoted more than Confucius, whose clothes brought him fame." The orchestra splits in half and slides offstage, right and left; another curtain parts in front of a huge movie screen, onto which is projected the giant-size shadow of that stylish Harlem man. The shadow jumps off the screen and onto the stage; it is Harold, wearing a cutaway with tails and top hat, a gold watchchain hanging from his waistband. The tempo accelerates from a slow blues to a medium swing,

Harold Nicholas and Marie Bryant in the "Mr. Beebee" number in Carolina Blues, *Columbia Pictures 1944 (Harold Nicholas Archive).*

and Harold sings: "Mr. Beebee, he's the man who knows, Mr. Bee-bee, sets the style in clothes/ Fancy cravats and those turn-out spats, Beebee's the man who knows."

In this long and lavish production number, which includes the Four Ink Spots and the Four Step Brothers, Harold sings with June Richmond and dances with Marie Bryant. But he is at his best in a quick-stepping solo that refers to several "classic"

Nicholas Brothers steps—Charleston variations, one-legged wings, slip-sliding chugs—as well as his signature long-sliding split through the legs of the chorus girls. Despite the retro-thirties design of the scene, Harold's asymmetrical forms—particularly a wide-stanced lunge, with one leg bent (the weight over that leg, and the other leg extended into wide second position)—are more modern; this is the stance that became the signature "modern jazz" dance pose that was replicated by many jazz dancers of the forties and fifties.

In September of 1944, after being released from military service with an honorable discharge, Fayard returned home to California, where he was reunited with his brother and other members of his family. Still officially under contract to Twentieth Century-Fox, but with no assignments promised or projected, he and Harold headed back to the William Morris Agency in New York with the intention of picking up where they left off. They soon realized that the Morris agency's representation of them during the postwar years was not to be as it once had been. "They took advantage of the Nicholas Brothers," says Geri Pate Nicholas about the agency, which got fees for white acts like the Williams Brothers that were triple what they could get for the Nicholases. Fayard's wife said: "They put them on one of those slave contracts, where you have to do anything at their will." Fayard, she added, never complained about the pay; instead, "he would finish the day and go in, turn the records on and start improvising. It was just his life. You've never seen such dedication. He had no bitterness about what was not done. He just went on."[12]

If the postwar forties ushered in a period of bittersweet change for the Nicholases, these years also delivered a blow to the owners of nightclubs, ballrooms, and theatres across the country. After the war, the federal government imposed a 20 percent tax on all public entertainment—to be paid in addition to the usual city, state, federal, and alcohol taxes. The federal "entertainment tax," as it was called, was a factor in the closing of many of the big ballrooms. The big swing bands that played these ballrooms soon found themselves out of work, as did the singers and tap dancers who performed with them.

This, along with the wartime recording bans of 1942 and 1943 and the postwar 1948 ban, brought less work to jazz dancers and musicians. What was left of vaudeville by the end of the thirties began to die. "Vaudeville went down the drain," Max Roach remembered of the period. "The Paramount Theatre, the biggest theatre in the United States for vaudeville, disappeared, as well as public dancing—people couldn't dance together—and there was even a tax for singers. Everything fell out of sync during that period."[13] Vaudeville houses increasingly were turned into movie theatres; television began to increase in popularity; and popular tastes on Broadway turned from tap dance toward ballet. About that time, small groups of jazz musicians began playing small clubs. In a shift away from the big bands' steady and danceable swing rhythms, the new groups played the angry, dissonant sounds and frenzied rhythm shifts of a new style of jazz—bebop.

More than a new style, bebop was a revolt by young black jazz artists who were asserting a new artistic independence. This came partly as a reaction to the swing band boom, which had brought huge financial success mainly to the white bands, while it segregated black musicians. Bebop, radical and abstract, shorn of pop melodies, and played at a tempo fast enough to to keep older and less informed musicians out of jam sessions, denied jazz as background entertainment. It rejected all uses for jazz except that of an object of aesthetic appreciation.[14] Bebop was to be a listening experience for those willing to learn the new vocabulary.

At the core of bebop, or bop as it was soon called, was a new set of social ideas. If jazz performers of the twenties and thirties considered themselves public entertainers, the bop musician made a deliberate attempt to avoid playing the role of "the flamboyant black entertainer which whites had come to expect."[15] In the eyes of the young musicians, bop stood for an assertion of black dignity, which had been submerged in show business. "The music of bebop," Ralph Ellison wrote,

> was itself a texture of fragments, repetitive, nervous, not fully formed. Its melodic lines underground, secret and taunting; its riffs jeering—"Salt peanuts! Salt peanuts!" Its

timbres flat or shrill with a minimum of thrilling vibrato. Its rhythms were out of stride and seemingly arbitrary, its drummers frozen-faced introverts dedicated to chaos.[16]

Bebop, like all styles of jazz, did not emerge suddenly, from nowhere. By the late thirties, rhythmic changes began to be sounded by musicians like the guitarist Charlie Christian. In the forties, saxophonists Lester Young and Coleman Hawkins and pianists Nat "King" Cole and Art Tatum were working toward the territory that would finally be established after the war by Dizzy Gillespie, Thelonious Monk, Bud Powell, and Charlie Parker.

Whereas swing was played at medium tempos, bop was played very fast or very slow. In swing, pairs of notes were played and stressed unevenly; bop musicians played notes with almost equal stress. While choirs of instruments harmonized in big bands, bopists played in unison. Swing, said Lennie Tristano, "bumped and chugged along like a beat and wornout locomotive,"[17] while bebop could be cool, light, soft, with a more subtle beat that became more pronounced by implication; and at a low volume level, many more interesting and complex accents could be introduced. Bop could also be hot, strident, idiosyncratic, bold, and challenging. In time it would split into hot and cool—or modern—jazz.

Bebop drastically reduced the size of the ensemble back to the five pieces typical of early jazz and reinstated extended improvisation, now sequential rather than collective. While most bebop compositions were drawn from the repertoire of popular songs, familiar melodies were discarded in favor of underlying harmonic structures. "The sharp contraction of the ensemble in Bebop, together with the emphasis on individual virtuosity and dissonant (to swing-attuned ears) sonorities," wrote David Stowe, "suggested the heroic alienation of the postwar individual at loose from Depression-era modes of commitment, or the racial militancy taking root among African Americans in the late forties."[18]

Bop began to dominate the musical scene after the war. After attending a concert by Dizzy Gillespie, music critic George Simon exclaimed, "It's getting too frantic for me." He lamented the band's constant repetition of overcute, multinote phrases, the trumpets that sounded as if they rehearsed in a soundproof room, the loud and boisterous drumming, and too many musicians' infatuation with the sound of their own notes. "With all this disintegrated stuff going on," he wrote, "it's little wonder that the band swung very little."[19]

By the late forties, lindy-hoppers at the Savoy Ballroom danced the jitterbug in open-partnered formations to the frenzied tempos of bebop-styled swing, called the bebop lindy. In order to deal with the schizoid-seeming tempos of bop, the Savoy dancers slowed to half-time undulations and incorporated rubber-legging, slides, and spins, as well as full-bodied movements that absorbed rhythms up into the body.[20] Only a handful of jazz tap dancers were able to make the transition from swing to the newer bop. "Baby" Laurence Jackson, for example, matched the speed of bop with taps that were like explosions, machine-gun rattles, and jarring thumps; he then "moved" these rhythms from the feet up, playing his body as though it were a percussion instrument. But for the most part, the frenetic tempos of bebop made dancing to the music too restrictive.

In January 1945, the Nicholases were presented with the opportunity to experience the new jazz firsthand when the Morris agency proposed organizing a tour for them through the southern states (from North and South Carolina to Georgia, Alabama, Tennessee, Mississippi, Louisiana, Arkansas, and Texas). *Hepsations 1945*, as it was called, would include Dizzy Gillespie's new bebop big band. "They thought he was gonna be big," says Fayard about Gillespie. "And so we said, 'Sure, why not, we love Dizzy's music. That would be beautiful.' This was, you see, Dizzy's first break, being in our show." *Hepsations 1945* headlined the Nicholas Brothers and featured comedians Patterson and Jackson, vocalist June Eckstine (wife of Billy Eckstine), shake dancer Lovey Lane, and Dizzy Gillespie's first "modern jazz" big band, which included Charlie Parker (saxophone), Leo Parker (baritone sax), Leo Williams (alto sax), Freddie Webster (trumpet), Kenney Dorham (trumpet), Fats Navarro (trumpet), Benny Harris (trumpet), and Max Roach (drums).

The show was booked in theatres, auditoriums, and ballrooms in cities across the southern belt, and it consisted of two parts. The first was a stage show, hosted by the Nicholas Brothers and featuring their dancing. Then came separate acts, all of which were accompanied by Gillespie's band playing from written arrangements of the performers' music. The stage show also featured Gillespie's band playing such original compositions as "Blue 'n Boogie," "Salt Peanuts," "Shaw 'Nuff," "Night in Tunisia," and "Bebop," arranged by Walter Gilbert Fuller from records that Gillespie had made. The second part of the show consisted of a public dance, with Gillespie's band playing for the members of the audience.

"I'll never forget it, never forget it," says Max Roach about the *Hepsations* tour. Most performers and musicians traveled by bus, the Nicholas Brothers rode in a limousine, and no one stopped to use the segregated public facilities. The performers usually stayed in the homes of local families, sometimes their own, in the South, because they were not welcome in hotels in the cities along the so-called chitlin circuit. "Everything was segregated at that particular time, before the 1954 Supreme Court decision, and racism was rampant," says Roach, who remembers that in one city in the Deep South, a valet named Mississippi was pulled off the bus by the police because he did not say "Yes, sir" to a white man. "We were stopped for something, and he happened to be the one they approached," says Roach. "We saw him a couple of days later when they released him. They put him in jail and roughed him up a bit."[21]

Because segregation was strictly enforced in the South, the same show was performed in the same theatre at different times for different audiences. The show might first be performed for an all-white audience, with the band playing for a whites-only dance. Then, the management took an hour to clear everyone out of the house before the all-black audience entered. In some states, the theatre might be booked for two nights, one night for blacks, the other for whites. "But it was never integrated, never integrated," says Fayard. "The only way you might say it was integrated is when black people were downstairs enjoying the show, and the white people were in the balcony, looking down. Then the next night, the whites would be downstairs and the blacks upstairs."[22]

In his autobiography, *To Be, or Not . . . to Bop*, Gillespie wrote: "To attract a mass audience to bebop, we had to first establish a feeling for the music among the large black population of the South. . . . But things didn't work out the way I'd hoped, and that first big band exists as a blur in my mind. I'd prefer to forget it."[23]

Hepsations 1945 opened in North Carolina in June; the audience was all black, and the public dance preceded the stage show. "Everybody was there, the place was packed," says Fayard. The band was onstage and the curtains were closed when a voice from backstage introduced Gillespie and his big band. When the curtains opened, the audience rushed up to the bandstand as Dizzy struck up "Bebop," one of his new compositions. "They were playing like mad," says Fayard about the band, "and everybody was listening. They were dumbfounded at first. And then they said, 'Oh, man, you a drag!' And walked away! They were ready for him, but they couldn't understand this bebop music."[24]

"People wanted to dance," explains Roach. "And the reaction was, they'd stand around and look at us kind of blankly. . . . They couldn't dance to it. With this modern music, the tempos were much faster, and it was just a different kind of thing." Arranger Walter Fuller recalls that during the public dance in Bluefield, West Virginia, someone hollered out, "Can't you nigguhs play no blues!" And the musicians worried that the audience would start throwing bottles or shooting in its frustration with the music. Gillespie explained:

> This orchestra and our style of playing was geared for listening, and nearly all of our arrangements were modern. So imagine my chagrin and surprise when I found out all we were playing was dances. Jazz should be danceable. That's the original idea. . . . Even when it's too fast to dance to, it should always be rhythmic enough to make you wanna move. . . . So my music is always danceable. But the unreconstructed blues lovers down South who couldn't hear nothing else but the blues didn't think so. They wouldn't even listen to us.

Fayard thought audiences might be more receptive to the new jazz if Gillespie mixed the program with blues and swing:

I told him, I said, "Diz, why not play something that they're familiar with?" He said, "Aww, no, no . . . this is my music!" I said, "I know it's your music, but slip a little bit of that in too. Make them happy! Then go back to your thing. Kinda compromise with them." I said, "Play a little 'Stormy Weather,' or something they're familiar with. Give them a little bit of jazz that they know. Then come on out with your bebop, your modern jazz." But Dizzy didn't care, he played it anyway.

Fayard believes that, ultimately, southerners rejected bebop because they didn't understand it; the music was ahead of its time: "Down South, they wanna hear the blues, get with it. And when you bring them something that's outta their class . . . it was way over their heads. But we understood it, the musicians understood it, and so we were having a ball."[25]

While both black and white audiences rejected Gillespie's music for dancing, they loved the stage show. "We'd bring them on," says Fayard, with:

"Now, ladies and gentlemen, Miss June Eckstine." And she looked good. Aww, that girl looked good! And before she started singing, all the boys were ready to say, "Yeah!" She sang modern, and they couldn't understand her either. Brought in our little dancing girl, Lovey Lane, shake dancer, see—oh, they liked that—right on down with it, and they liked our two comedians, Patterson and Jackson. Both of them weighed three hundred pounds, and they'd sing and dance. Oh, they were beautiful, yes. And then we closed the show. And after that, we'd do a little finale with everybody on. We'd do "Salt Peanuts," or something like that. We all did that with Dizzy.[26]

Max Roach said the Nicholas Brothers did not sing in *Hepsations 1945* but "did what they usually did, they danced." In contrast to Bill Robinson, whom Roach describes as a "standup" dancer (meaning that he danced with a vertical deportment and usually in one place), Fayard and Harold used the whole stage.

"They did acrobatics, they did ballet, and you could hear the taps going on at the same time. They were unusual in that respect. I would describe them as musicians, because you listened to them. You looked at them and you listened to them."[27]

While Gillespie's musicians played the swing arrangements the Nicholases provided them for "Jumpin' Jive" and "Kalamazoo," there was certainly a different feel to the execution of the music, as played by young jazz musicians oriented to bebop. Gillespie's musical style excited Fayard: "Every night, instead of going to our dressing rooms, we'd come out there and just watch him and listen to him. Because there was something different every night. He never played the same way twice, and each time it seemed greater, which was remarkable."[28]

The Nicholases did not think of themselves as bebop dancers. "We never did get into bebop," says Fayard, "though I would have liked to. We were doing our own thing with jazz and swing music, and working all the time."[29] In 1945, however, the transition from swing to bop was far from complete; nor would it ever be, some argue. For instance, there were bop "licks" (a short motif inserted into an improvisation) being played by Cab Calloway's band back in the "Jumpin' Jive" number in *Stormy Weather*.

And the Nicholases—if only for the speed of their jazz dancing and the shifting rhythm fields they employed in their arrangements—certainly had a penchant for what came to be called modern jazz. "I first heard Dizzy's music in the forties," Fayard remembered, "and right away, as we say, I dug his music, I loved his style. It was different. It had something that was all his own. And I would listen to this bebop music, and I tried it— I would create different steps to it to fit the music. Then I would try and do something that I'd been doing before, and see whether I could fit that to it."[30] Although not self-proclaimed bopists, Fayard and Harold had the musicality of bop musicians. Like Gillespie, they were adaptable and open to change. "It's funny about artists, the great artists, it makes no difference what the environment is," says Roach about the Nicholases. "We worked on that *Hepsations* tour every night, and every night the stage would be different. . . . But they would improvise or devise a way to do just what they were known for doing."[31]

One possible explanation for the brothers' openness to bop was their incorporation of rhythm changes in their own dance routines. "Their music had to be especially arranged for them because the tempos were constantly changing," says Roach about the Nicholases' music in *Hepsations 1945.* "It wasn't just steady, rhythmic things. It would go on to bolero, to ballet, to ballads, to bolero-styles that were fast and slow during the course of a performance. The music was constantly shifting to accommodate the things they did."[32] The shifts in tempo and rhythm in the Nicholases' dance routines was not new; the style of these musical arrangements dated back to the mid-thirties, when Fayard created "Dance Specialty" with arranger Chappy Willett. What might have been new to bop-oriented musicians was something the brothers had been doing for nearly a decade.

Honi Coles goes even farther to claim that it is the constant shifts in rhythms by jazz tap dancers which, in fact, influenced bop musicians. "If you notice the orchestrations of the early twenties, all you heard the drums doing was chi-chi-dum. You never hearn ka-didji-bop-wop-dible-dable-didji-kawop-wop. But at some point the drummer in the dance would start to listen to what the dancer was doing—you know, shagadi-dooga-diga-daga-skippidy-diga-bippidy-boom-shaga-daga—and he'd come up with something like it for himself on the drums. Then the horn player would listen up . . . and then he'd start working the melody that way, and they were off and running."[33]

The tour of *Hepsations 1945* lasted until August 9, 1945, the day the Japanese surrendered to the United States. The company was getting ready to perform in Pine Bluff, Arkansas, when news of the Japanese surrender came over the radio. The police asked the company not to perform because of the excitement that had been generated across the city over the news that the war had finally ended. The company packed up and the brothers headed back to Los Angeles. While for Dizzy Gillespie *Hepsations 1945* was an event worth forgetting, it was an artistic triumph of sorts for Fayard, who says:

My brother and I handled ourselves very well, even there. After the show, people would be coming backstage, and the whites would come and hug us, and kiss us. And I'd say to myself, "Is this the South?" It wasn't a black and white thing, it was like, "These are the Nicholas Brothers and I like them." They weren't looking at us like we were the *black* Nicholas Brothers, but like, "These are guys with talent, they made us happy, they performed for us." That's when I really knew they didn't cut us out in the films we played in the South.[34]

By choosing music that was danceable, Fayard and Harold committed the ultimate act of generosity. They pleased audiences, black or white, and they awarded them the greatest gift of which they were capable: in watching these two brothers perform, audiences were able to surrender preconceptions of race and, perhaps for a moment in time, achieve universal understanding.

Dixieland Jamboree, a Vitaphone black musical short featuring Cab Calloway, Louis Armstrong, Adelaide Hall, and the Nicholas Brothers (in a routine pulled from a previous film), was released on April 24, 1946. By that time, Fayard and Harold were back again on Broadway in *St. Louis Woman*. Most commentators agree that *Oklahoma!*, the 1943 Rodgers and Hammerstein musical, choreographed by Agnes De Mille, marked a major turning point for dance on Broadway with its use of ballet to express moods and feelings. No blacks were in that production, which was hailed as "one of the milestones in American musical theatre."[35]

The Broadway revival of *Show Boat* three years later did provide opportunities for black dancers to work. Choreographed by Helen Tamiris, the production included Pearl Primus, Talley Beatty, Joe Nash, Claude Marchant, and Laverne French. But *St. Louis Woman*, which opened on March 30 of the same year, provided the only sustained black artistic presence on Broadway. Lauded by the *New York Daily News* (1 April 1946) as "the best Negro musical in many seasons, and the best new musical of this season," the show featured Harold in the starring role of a jockey, with Fayard in a smaller role, playing his rival.

Based on the Arna Bontemps novel *God Sends Sunday*, which Countee Cullen adapted for the stage, *St. Louis Woman* was directed by Rouben Mamoulian, and its music and lyrics were by Harold Arlen and Johnny Mercer. Set in St. Louis at the turn of the century, it starred Ruby Hill as Della Green, the fancy girl-friend of local bar owner Bigelow Brown (Rex Ingram), who attracts the admiring eye of Little Augie (Harold Nicholas), a "cocky" and "high-riding jockey such as never was in Missouri, 1898" (*Herald Tribune*, 1 April 1946).

In a tense barroom scene, Augie confronts Bigelow over his harsh treatment of Della, and the bar owner is shot. Bigelow, believing that Augie has killed him, curses the jockey with his last dying breath, though it was his former mistress Lila (June

Harold Nicholas, Ruby Hill, Fayard Nicholas, and Pearl Bailey in St. Louis Woman *(Billy Rose Theatre Collection, The New York Library for the Performing Arts, Astor, Lenox and Tilden Foundations).*

Hawkins) who shot him. Augie feels cursed, and his luck goes from bad to worse as he loses races. Della, believing herself to be the source of the jinx, threatens to leave him. At the climax, Augie enters a race, believing that if he loses, he will lose Della forever. In a spectacular staging of the scene, with the onstage crowd watching the offstage race from outside the fence, Augie wins the race. Jumping into Della's arms, he sings "Ridin' on the Moon," which, along with "Come Rain or Come Shine," established Harold as one of the finest singers in musical theatre.

Despite Harold's starring role in *St. Louis Woman*, he refused to accept individual credit, and both Fayard and he were listed in the program as "Nicholas Brothers."[36] In one scene, cited as "the show's brightest hoofing,"[37] Fayard as the rival jockey Barney did a challenge dance with Harold's Little Augie, who, according to the *Herald Tribune* (1 April 1946), "scampered to the top of a piano and did a fabulous split to the center of the stage." Fayard was praised by the *New York Sun* (1 April 1946) for his "magic feet"; and the *Daily News* (1 April 1946) called the Nicholases' dancing "unrivaled in precise agility." Both Harold and Fayard were grateful for the opportunity to develop their skills as actors and to stretch beyond their solid reputation as musical perfor-mance artists.

St. Louis Woman is memorable not only for its remarkable cast, which also included Pearl Bailey and Juanita Hall, but because of the unusually bold act taken by its members in stopping rehearsals temporarily in protest over the offensive stereotypes in the show, specifically the bawdy character and loose morals of its female leads. "Blacks were getting to the point where they didn't want to portray their women as prostitutes all the time," Harold explained about the cast's objections.[38] Mamoulian staged a funeral sequence in which June Hawkins, having killed her lover, was to fall on her knees and raise her hands to heaven, and every-one else was do the same. The performers felt the gesture was "too Negroid" but were reluctant to discuss the matter with Mamou-lian. Pearl Bailey formally acted as negotiator to help smooth out the differences. Although rehearsals thereafter proceeded amiably, the episode suggested that changes might be coming in black-performed Broadway musicals, and that stereotypical roles, which were once tolerated by blacks as part of appearing on Broadway, might not be accepted so willingly in the future.

In Hollywood in the forties, by the same token, there were individuals who were set on finding roles for black artists that did not fit into the black stereotype. One such person was the dancer Gene Kelly. "Gene always wanted to dance with us, but he could never find the right story," says Fayard. "He didn't want us to come on like we were servants, and all of a sudden I'm whistling and tapping a little bit, and he says, 'That's nice, how do you do that?' He didn't want to do that."39

In early 1947, after the brothers returned from an ambitious tour that carried them to Mexico City, Panama City, Havana, and Kingston, Jamaica, Metro-Goldwyn-Mayer producer Arthur Freed called the Nicholases with an idea for a story set in the Caribbean. "There was nothing American in it, so you couldn't think about prejudice and all that jazz," says Fayard about *The Pirate* (1948, MGM), directed by Vincente Minnelli, with songs by Cole Porter. The film starred Judy Garland as Manuela, a fanciful maiden who falls in love with Serafin (Gene Kelly), the leader of a circus troupe who, she believes, is really a Caribbean pirate. Fayard and Harold were cast as performers in the circus troupe, which lands on the Caribbean island, and they appear in a few scenes. In one scene, however, in which Serafin spares himself from being hanged, by entertaining his captors with a performance, the Nicholas Brothers formally danced with Gene Kelly. "You may give your show," says the Viceroy to Serafin at the opening of the scene. "It would be a pleasure to be executed by a man of such charm," Serafin replies, and orders his troupe to "prepare the proscenium, so that I and my two brilliant colleagues will entertain you."

Before the Viceroy, Manuela, the Mayor, and members of the town, Kelly sings the advice his mother always gave him: "Be a clown, be a clown/ All the world loves a clown." Walking through a set of double doors, wearing a black shirt and pants, Kelly reemerges moments later dressed in bright turquoise trousers and a yellow dunce cap. "Act the fool, play a calf, and you'll always have the last laugh," Kelly sings proudly, with his legs placed wide apart. Fayard suddenly comes sliding through Kelly's legs and pulls himself up into an open-legged stand, followed by Harold, who slides through both men's legs and pulls up to an open-legged stand. In the ensuing routine, all three—step for step—perform somersaults, one-arm handstands, barrel turns, and Russian-style kazotsky kicks, and finally climb on top of each other, only to collapse into a mound of brightly colored body parts.

While the synchronized dance routine that Kelly choreographed required pinpoint timing and sinuous acrobatic skills, the material seemed all too easy for Harold, who tells this story:

> We were rehearsing one day, and naturally, I don't put my heart and soul into rehearsals and I'm doing it just like a day in school. And Gene Kelly looks at me and says, "Harold, what's the matter with you? You're not doing the routine." They were doing it like, like the cameras were rolling, you know? And they were perspiring, and carrying on. And he said, "Man, we're working our heads off, and you're just moping along." I said, "But I know the routine." And Gene says, "You don't know it. How can you know it if you're doing it like that?" So Gene Kelly talks to Fayard and says, "Let's sit down and watch him do the routine. He says he knows it but I bet he doesn't. Let him do it." So I says, "Oh, man, okay, I'll do it." Bam! Music strikes up, and I go through the routine, bang, bang, bang, bang, bang, bang, bang, whack! And I finish, da da! And I said, "How's that?" And Gene Kelly was so mad, he didn't know what to do![40]

Fayard was pleased with the way audiences responded to *The Pirate*: "When people saw the film, some of them didn't know they were looking at the Nicholas Brothers. They thought they were looking at somebody else. They weren't thinking about two black guys dancing with this white man."[41]

What is disappointing about the *The Pirate* is that the Nicholases neither created the choreography nor collaborated on it, to any great extent, with Kelly—the first time the brothers were not performing their own material. Perhaps this explains Harold's ennui during the rehearsal process: Kelly's clown routine was not very challenging. Also, despite Kelly's best intentions of casting the Nicholas Brothers in nonstereotyped roles, there was neither character development nor spoken lines for the brothers in this film, in which Kelly and Garland were clearly the stars. The "Be a Clown" number reached its climax not in the scene in which the brothers danced but at the very end of the film, when Kelly and Garland, in tattered hobo clothes (and with charcoal rubbed on their faces), sang the same song. Even sadder for their fans is the image of the Nicholas Brothers piled onto each other and Kelly in a colorful heap at the end of "Be a Clown"—the last image audiences would have of them in a Hollywood film for the next twenty-two years.

Through the forties, in Hollywood, social life was marred by consistent segregation. African-American stars, such as Duke Ellington and Count Basie, lived almost exclusively at the Dunbar Hotel on Central Avenue in Hollywood. And clubs such as the Plantation Club in Los Angeles both catered to and featured such black celebrities as Art Tatum and Paul Robeson. Yet there were places where blacks were sure to be excluded. Geri Nicholas remembered going with Fayard, Harold, and Dorothy to the Hollywood Palladium to see Tommy Dorsey and His Orchestra in concert. The Nicholas Brothers had toured with Dorsey and knew him well.

"There was always a huge audience, about fifteen hundred people, and they heard the Nicholas Brothers were outside," Geri remembered. "The doors opened and everybody rushed ... When all that died down, the band was about to start playing and we wanted to go in ... and the men who were standing at the door said we couldn't come in because they didn't allow black people."

Someone apparently informed Dorsey, who stopped the band, walked through the house and into the lobby, and ordered the management either to let the Nicholas Brothers enter the theatre or give the audience its money back and send them home. The

Nicholases were finally ushered to front row seats, and Frank Sinatra, who was the soloist with the band, invited Fayard and Harold to sing with him. "Tommy was thrilled," said Geri. "He was really quite a good man."[42]

"It was going on all over," said Harold about the pervasive racism, recalling an incident that happened while he and Dorothy were in their own apartment:

> I'm lying on my back with my wife . . . with my head on her lap, and a policeman stopped us. And he started asking questions . . . and he got mad at me because I didn't jump up when he came to the window. . . . It was a pretty bad scene for a while, but nothing happened really. It was just the atmosphere, the feeling. The tension was bad.[43]

Living in Hollywood for Harold was a paradox. While he was regarded as a star, there were places he was not admitted. One of the passions he had acquired while traveling abroad was golf. He had a set of custom-made golf clubs, and he could easily afford to belong to a golf club like other Hollywood golf aficionados, but he was never allowed to join. The only day he could play was on Monday, "Caddy Day," when the clubs were closed and a friend who was a caddy invited him to make up a foursome.

The persistence of racism in the United States as well as the paucity of work for tap dancers prompted the Nicholases, by the late forties, to consider working in Europe. From the early twenties, when Josephine Baker and Florence Mills became the idols of Paris and London, black musical artists were continually drawn to Europe's stages. "A Negro will find it exceedingly difficult to land an ordinary job in England or on the Continent," the *Philadelphia Tribune* (28 July 1927) wrote, "but if he is a good comedian, musician or dancer, he usually has little trouble getting an engagement in theatres, clubs, or fashionable restaurants. All Europe is crazy over Jazz." In the postwar years, this enthusiasm had not wavered. In 1948, the Nicholases left for Europe, where, Geri says, they were received beautifully. They wound up working there for three years.

At the London Palladium in 1948, the Nicholas Brothers, with Duke Ellington, Pearl Bailey, and Danny Kaye, gave a Royal Command Performance for the King of England. In Sweden, some appreciative members of the audience who had never seen African Americans up close and in person, brought chocolates to the Nicholases' dressing rooms after the show. In Paris, at the Cirque Midrano, the Nicholas Brothers were such an immediate hit that a special stage was built and carried out for them to dance on. In Italy in 1951, the Nicholas Brothers performed in a musical segment for the film *Botte e Riposta*, which had them jumping over each other and down a flight of stairs before a painted backdrop of New York City skyscrapers hung with "Broadway" street signs. The brothers returned to the United States in 1951, hoping for the same successes at home that they experienced abroad. The work they found, however, was neither on Broadway nor in Hollywood film.

At the end of World War II, radio and movies constituted the principal forms of entertainment, and television represented an eccentric idea offered by a few esoteric inventors. Fifteen years later, 75 percent of all American families owned their own televisions. The number of stations steadily grew, from six in 1946 to 442 in 1956. Seven thousand television sets were sold in 1945; three years later, the figure had leaped to seven million.[44] Every other form of popular culture paled in comparison to the astonishing growth of television, which ultimately reshaped American culture by bringing people from the most disparate backgrounds together in a common viewing experience.

Ed Wynn's The All-Star Revue, one of a series of comedy/variety shows popular in the early fifties, was one of the earliest television shows on which the Nicholas Brothers appeared after returning from Europe in 1951. The sixty-minute show, which also included guest stars Ray Bolger and Bob Hope, is a good example of how the variety format from the vaudeville stage was adapted for television. "Aren't you the Nicholas Brothers?" Wynn asked when the handsomely suited Fayard and Harold, sporting thick mustaches, walked onstage to the loud sounds of studio applause.

Wynn asked the brothers if they needed to use the phone—it hung from a cord in a cardboard telephone booth as a leftover prop from a previous comedy routine. "No, no, we would just like to dance," Harold answered. "Well, that's an honest answer. You very rarely hear that on television," quipped Wynn. "But listen, fellas, I can't have two great artists like you dance in this sort of atmosphere." He asked them to picture in their minds the magnificent Palace, before which they would dance. When the curtains opened, instead of the Palace, there was the painted backdrop of a brownstone brick building. "You'll just have to dance in front of this crummy storefront," said Wynn, "but picture the Palace."

The live but unseen studio band struck up "Argentina," and the Nicholas Brothers—looking more at ease once the music began—returned to their virtuosic choreography from *Down Argentine Way*. As exciting as their dancing was in that film, this performance on television was disappointingly flat, due largely to the long, narrow studio dance floor, so unlike their original set, the film's Club Rendevous. Harold's sliding split-and-recover through Fayard's legs, originally performed directly to the camera, had to be performed along the horizontal, thus losing the thrilling immediacy of having the dancers move straight through the line of vision. Moreover, the clarity of the rhythmic patterns in the tapping was seriously hampered when the orchestra played too loud; nor did the television orchestra—which had altered the original arrangement of the music to avoid paying royalties—swing the arrangement.[45]

In 1951, during the Korean War, the Nicholases traveled to Korea to help entertain the United Nations forces in *The Bob Hope Christmas Show*, one of many USO Christmas tours Hope presented from 1941 to 1972. The show, broadcast from the top deck of a U.S. aircraft carrier, was performed for American naval troops. "Here's two wonderful friends of mine who are really mad about the navy," Hope announced, as the brothers strode onto the deck of the ship in navy uniforms, their bell-bottomed pants flapping in the wind. Les Brown and his twelve-piece "Band of Renown" accompanied a fast-paced tap routine that began with close-to-the-floor paddle-and-roll tapping and built to a crescendo with a challenge dance, in which Fayard's half-turn splits on the floor were answered by Harold's triple-turn drop-splits. While the dancing was in good form, the band was loud and brassy, and it overpowered the details of the phrasing of the rhythms. Nor was the band particularly inventive when trading eights with the brothers; by the last four measures of the chorus, the sounds of their feet were completely muddied. The sailors were nevertheless pleased; they responded to the Nicholases' tap dancing with loud whistles, stomps, and claps.

As the brothers strode onto the deck of the ship in the opening of this act, Harold became distracted by several bits of white paper that littered the area where he was about to dance, because the confetti posed the potential hazard of making him slip. Though he whisked the paper off the floor through most of the eight-bar introduction, and just in time for the opening of the dance performed in stop-time, the opening was flawed.

Hope later called the Nicholases out for an encore, and he joined them in trading steps and in tossing off variations of the Cubanola rhythm. By the finale, the three performed double time steps; Harold slid from second to first; Hope flew over his feet with over-the-tops; and Fayard pulled them both into forward-leaning trenches.[46]

The *Colgate Comedy Hour*'s "Abbott and Costello Show" interspersed slapstick routines with songs by Margaret Whiting, ballroom dancing by Buster Shaver and Olive, and tap dancing by the Nicholas Brothers. After being introduced as "some of the finest dancers in our Hollywood area ... the very famous Nicholas Brothers," and accompanied by a twenty-piece orchestra, they opened their act by dancing tacit, moving into a chugging combination in stop-time. By having the orchestra come in late, the brothers' rhythmic themes were clearly stated. Even when the orchestra grew increasingly loud, in the second chorus, their synchronous movement of chugging steps, accented by hand gestures and full-bodied stomps, maintained the clarity of the rhythmic flow. Still, it was only a matter of time before the tapping was again blunted by the orchestra. At one point, the sounds of their feet were overwhelmed by a drummer bearing down too strongly on the tom-tom and bass drum. The brothers could not beat them, so they joined forces with the rhythm section and, with splayed hands, struck the air as though their hands were percussion instruments.

Another dance in the routine, to medium-tempo swing, was an almost pat repeat of the slipping-and-sliding steps from "Argentina," though translated as a more skipping softshoe. Harold's forward-leaning trenches and Fayard's one-legged wings were delivered with a smooth nonchalance. There were also refinements of classic Nicholas steps: Harold's virtuosic triple-turn split-and-recovers and Fayard's split-jumps over the handkerchief were unusually swift and light. The most flashy steps, such as Harold's slide-and-recover through Fayard's straddled legs, predictably were the most exciting and drew wild applause. Nevertheless, something was still missing in their televised dancing. And it was not the dancing that seemed to be at fault.

Television, despite the adjustments the Nicholas Brothers struggled to make, was simply not the best medium for presenting their—or any other performers'—dancing. The studio orchestra was too loud, and it did not swing; the camera work was crude, and it usually captured only the tops of the dancing bodies; and the studio's acoustics were abysmally insensitive to the sophisticated sounds of their rhythm dancing. The brothers looked shrunken on television. Their dancing had lost its clean-cut edge; their facial and bodily effervescence was lost in the black-and-white dots and lines of the television screen.[47]

By the mid-fifties, vaudeville was dead, and many of the big ballrooms that once thrived on the big-band sound were closed down. Fred Astaire, Gene Kelly, and Donald O'Connor were tap dancing their way through movie musicals, but there were no great black tap dancers to be seen on the silver screen. Work had become alarmingly scarce for the Nicholas Brothers. "There was a change in the whole entertainment structure," Dorothy Nicholas explained. "You began to have intimate rooms, with intimate rooms you needed intimate performances. . . . Dancers would have to dance in a small cubicle, and they [Fayard and

Harold] were used to spreading it."[48] By the mid-fifties, the Nicholases also began to split away from the William Morris Agency, and with that came the trouble of finding another agent. "We worked here and there, but it was not constant like before," Harold recounts, "and to fight that and the racism was heavy."

Around 1956, when the brothers were offered a chance to return to Europe, they jumped at it. "It was fantastic, especially for me," says Harold, "'cause nobody said, 'Your money's not good enough because your color's not right.'" Harold also always had the desire to do things other than tap. He wanted to sing but had rarely been given the opportunity. In Europe, he was able to sing as well as dance. The brothers worked hard and traveled all over Europe. By 1958, however, Fayard suddenly became homesick.

"I wanted to come home and see my family," Fayard recollects. "I didn't want to come back right away," says Harold, who told his brother to go home and take care of the business—he would return later. "So I went back home," says Fayard. There was no argument. There was no bitter talk of breaking up. The brothers just decided, by mutual consent, to let each do what was best for himself for a while. In 1958, Fayard left Paris and returned home to his family in Los Angeles. Harold remained in Paris. The Nicholas Brothers would not perform together for the next seven years.

The Nicholas Brothers in the early seventies (Harold Nicholas Archive).

Ten

Nostalgia and All That Jazz

1964–1989

On the evening of July 31, 1964, on ABC-TV, the marquee of the Hollywood Palace pulsated with thousands of flashing lights as show host Ed Wynn announced: "And now, the Nicholas Brothers, Harold and Fayard." The studio audience burst into applause. "I'm glad you feel that way, because I feel that way," said Wynn. "They were one of the greatest dance teams of all time, and the *Hollywood Palace* has brought Harold back from Paris, just for one occasion. So here they are, ladies and gentlemen, dancing together again, the Nicholas Brothers!" The curtains parted on a gigantic flight of stairs with ramps down each side. Harold entered from one side of the stage, Fayard from the other, and as they approached center, they stopped short and stood motionless, facing each other. Harold was the first to break the stillness by thrusting his arm up and around Fayard's shoulder, then the two shook hands and broke into unrestrained laughter. As the brothers' hands pumped up and down and the audience clapped heartily, their seven-year separation seemed instantly to dissolve.

"Welcome back. How was it in gay Paree?" asked Fayard; "Oh, it was very good," answered Harold, in a slight French accent.

Courtesies aside, Fayard got down to business. "Do you remember this step?" he asked, moving away to demonstrate. "Wait a minute, not too much," Harold warned, stepping back. "Seven years is a long time, take it easy." Ignoring Harold's hesitancy, Fayard tapped out an eight-count riff of flaps, cramprolls, and a Maxie Ford. His long fingers, stroking over the beats while he danced, worked magic to change Harold's mind. "Hmmm, I think I can get into that. Let's try it again. Are you ready?" asked Harold. "Are *you* ready?" Fayard countered. Harold counted "A ONE uh, a TWO uh," and they were off, repeating the riff. Then Harold struck out his own rapid-stomping solo and triple turn. "Wait a minute, hold the phone! Now what was that?" snapped Fayard, stopped dead in his tracks. "Same step, with just a little French accent," said Harold, puckering his lips and kissing his brother on the cheek. "Ah, mais oui," squealed Fayard, snapping his fingers to signal the band to get on with the dance.

Moving side by side and in perfect step with each other, the brothers lifted up into hop-shuffling riffs and slip-sliding chugs, which were repeated in double time. Then Fayard thumped out, "Ba doopa doopa DA/ Ba doopa doopa DA/ Ba doopa doopa DA/ Doopa doopa DA DA" and, with Harold looking on, clicked toes-and-heels as he circled clockwise. In the second chorus, the medium swing tune changed to the instantly recognizable "Jumpin' Jive," from the film *Stormy Weather* (1943), as the brothers brushed gracefully into their signature *rond de jambes en l'air* and one-legged wings, while moving closer to the giant flight of stairs. Edging nearer to the first step, they teased the floor by tapping:

> DAH dah DAH dah—DAH di DAH DAH
> DAH dah DAH dah—DAH di DAH DAH
> DAH dah DAH dah—DAH di DAH DAH.

After breaking with the rhythm of "DAH dah DAH dah" and a back-slide into a split-and-recover, the audience could guess what came next. They danced their way up each of the six giant stairs, pausing on steps three and five for rippling paddle-and-rolls, and when they got to the top step, they clicked out a variation on the theme:

Dida la dee DOT DOT DOT DOT da dee dee,
Dida la dee DOT DOT DOT DOT da dee dee,
Dida la dee DOT DOT DOT DOT da dee dee—

breaking with "Dida la dee DOT DOT" and step-glide-turn. The drums rolled. From the top step, Fayard jumped into the air with spread legs to land, one step down, in a held-split. Then Harold sprang into the air with open-spread legs, leaping over Fayard to land on the third step down in a held-split. Fayard popped up as Harold landed, leapfrogging over his brother to land on the fourth step down in a held-split; then Harold popped up as Fayard landed, jumping over his brother to land on the fifth step down in a split. Fayard split-jumped over Harold onto the floor, Harold followed suit, and both recovered simultaneously. It was not yet over. The trumpets screeched a high-pitched wail, which shot the brothers back up the flight of stairs. Spinning around to face the audience at the top, Fayard and Harold slid down each of the ramps that framed the stairs. And the momentum of the slide shot them like bullets across the floor into full splits, from which they recovered with open arms to welcome the applause from the audience.[1]

Fayard was fifty years old and Harold forty-three when they were reunited to perform on *Hollywood Palace* in the summer of 1964. And more than twenty years had passed since filming "Jumpin' Jive." To ensure that television audiences would remember them, after having been out of the mainstream of American public entertainment for well over twenty years, the brothers thought it necessary to repeat their famous stair routine from the film that many regarded as their greatest hit. Copied from the big-band ballroom setting in *Stormy Weather*, the flight of stairs that was built for the set of the *Hollywood Palace* took on surreal proportions. And the playing of "Jumpin' Jive" on television was not as swinging as Cab Calloway's had been in the film. Nevertheless, it was felt that reconjuring their images in that fantastic stair dance was necessary to reestablish their reputation as renowned jazz tap dancers.

This strategy was a success, but Fayard and Harold soon discovered that the audiences of the sixties wanted continual
reminders of those golden flashbacks from their past. Referencing
past works while continuing to develop as "modern" jazz dancers
would be the greatest challenge to the Nicholases for the next
twenty years of their dance career. The more personal task for the
brothers, meanwhile, was to recapture their brotherhood in
rhythm: seven years away from each other had eaten away at their
ensemble dancing.

For Harold, the years spent in Europe as a soloist had made
him more confident and self-sufficient. He remembered his initial
separation from Fayard, however. "At the beginning, it was hard for
me to be onstage [in Europe], doing a dance and not looking over
and seeing him, because when I was a kid, I used to bump into
him all the time when we were dancing. But after a fashion, you
get used to it, which I did. I started doing the whole tour by myself,
and the people accepted me by myself. They didn't ask, 'Where's
your brother?'"[2]

In Europe, Harold had become recognized as a singer and an
actor, as well as a dancer. At the Carré Theatre in Amsterdam, in
1959, he starred in *Free and Easy*, Harold Arlen's blues adaptation
of *St. Louis Woman*. He recorded two albums for Mercury, *Harold
Nicholas* and *Harold Nicholas: New York-Paris*, and he co-starred
with Eddie Constantine in the French film *L'Empire de la nuit* (1963,
UFA-Comachio). He also performed in his own nightclub act in
casinos in France, Spain, Italy, and the Middle East, becoming
fluent in several languages and even learning to sing in Turkish.
Divorced from Dorothy Dandridge in 1949, Harold married a
French woman, Elayne Patronne, with whom he lived in Paris. And
like Josephine Baker, with whom he performed at the Olympia
Theatre in 1959, Harold says he was idolized by the French: "I was
the American dancer, and I taught the French how to do certain
dances. It started with the Cha Cha, then the Madison, Hurley
Gurley, and the Twist—everybody was twisting—and the Swim."
Although Harold had always had a sense of self-esteem and self-
respect, he says he found that in Europe "I began to feel that even
more because the people over there were so wonderful to me,

particularly in the Scandinavian countries where they weren't used to seeing black people."[3] The work in Europe apparently furthered Harold's technical skills, for he returned to America looking svelte, with added speed and suppleness to his dancing.

Fayard, in the years from 1958 to 1964, had returned to California to live with his family in Hollywood, nearer to his mother and sister. He too was divorced from his first wife, Geri, and was remarried to the Mexican dancer Vicky Barron, with whom he performed in South America and in various nightclub acts in Hollywood. He also performed as a single in Las Vegas, toured Mexico, and did summer repertory work at the University of California at Los Angeles. From the late fifties to the early sixties, performance venues for jazz tap dancers had reached their lowest ebb in America, and

Harold performs with Josephine Baker at the Olympia Theatre in Paris, 1959 (Harold Nicholas Archive).

Fayard's idleness became debilitating. "He had that marvelous personality for being able to withstand all kinds of pain, physical and
emotional, and not let it get him down," his sister, Dorothy,
remembered of Fayard during this period. "But what happens emotionally is that all the aches and pains that accumulated over the
years in dancing hit you—Fayard developed arthritis when he was
with us, and it really began to develop so that he was hardly able
to work at all."[4] The severity of Fayard's arthritic condition was
not apparent in his performance on *Hollywood Palace* in July of
1964, but in subsequent television performances the length of his
strides began to shorten, his famous "no-hands" split needed the
assistance of the hands on the recovery, and his elegant gestures
became exaggerated and were distracting.

Fayard was not the only jazz tap dancer to find himself idle in
the sixties. Charles "Honi" Coles, for example, took a job as the
production stage manager of the Apollo Theatre in what he called
"the lull," when there was no call for dancers.[5] Other hoofers took
jobs as bellhops, elevator men, bartenders, and carpenters. Television had come into almost every American home by this time,
but the regular weekly variety shows had become the more infrequent "television special." Except for those specials, with an occa-
sional performance by a Ray Bolger or a John Bubbles, little or no
tap dance was to be seen. The situation became even worse for tap
on Broadway after the success of *West Side Story* (Winter Garden
Theatre, September 27, 1957). A new style of jazz dance—the
Jerome Robbins style—had become popular, with bits of ballet,
exotic, acrobatic, and abstract modern movement. Writing in
Dance Magazine, Marshall Stearns bemoaned the alleged use of
jazz movements in this so-called modern jazz dance, in which the
arms, legs, and pelvis flew out in different directions, seemingly
without regard to the rhythm in the musical accompaniment.
Stearns conceded that *West Side Story*, with music by Leonard
Bernstein and dances by Jerome Robbins, was a milestone in theatre, and that the choreography was being hailed for "its splendid
use of jazz dance." But there was a fatal flaw. Stearns argued that
Bernstein's music was not jazz and that the dances employed only
one "ancient" jazz movement—"the finger-poppin' hipster's

hunch, arms swaying, shoulders down, and knees up" movement known as the Pimp's Walk, derived from the Strut. The mambo-style dances, moreover, lacked "the rhythmic fire" of those that were being danced just around the corner from the theatre, at the Palladium Ballroom.[6]

"It's gone silly!" Broadway jazz choreographer Jack Cole commented in 1963 about the "modern jazz" dance. Cole tried to explain in a *Dance Magazine* interview that jazz was an urban folk music, and jazz dance was the movement corresponding in style to the music. When Cole, in auditions, asked young, ballet-trained dancers to simply snap their fingers in rhythm (it was "invaluable in detecting true jazz feeling," he explained), they did the whole thing from the outside: "They assume feeling. It requires a less formal person—by that I mean someone who is more concerned with individual expression, rather than one who sees himself as part of a tradition."[7]

In the sixties, while tap dance was beginning to be notated and "modern jazz" dance was being discussed in public forums (such as the Dance Notation Bureau–sponsored "What Is Jazz?" in 1961, which included panelists Mura Dehn, Al Mimms, Billy Taylor, Matt Mattox, and Walter Nicks), jazz tap dance was being treated as if it were dead. "For many of us, tap dance never did 'die,'" Billy Mahoney wrote in her article "Did Tap Ever Really Die?" She cited the few dancers in the early sixties who persisted in keeping tap active. They included Eleanor Powell, in her 1961 "comeback" appearance at the Latin Quarter in New York, who was a dazzling hit despite preopening questions about how "pure tap" would go over with nightclub patrons accustomed to "modern jazz" dance; John Bubbles, who performed once in 1961, and eight times in 1965, on *American Musical Theatre* on CBS-TV; and Jackie Gleason, who, each week for ten years (from 1953 to 1963), danced with the sixteen June Taylor Dancers in a tap dance number that opened his show.[8]

The one event that brought life back to tap dancing took place on July 6, 1963, when Marshall Stearns, at the Newport Jazz Festival, presented Honi Coles, Chuck Green, Charles "Cooky" Cook, Ernest "Brownie" Brown, Pete Nugent, Cholly Atkins, and Baby Laurence in a show entitled *Old Time Hoofers*. These "seven virtuoso tap dancers of the old-fashioned pounding school of hoofing who drew their strength from the floor," wrote Leticia Jay in *Dance Magazine*, "reminded an enthusiastic audience at the Newport Jazz Festival of what this much neglected, American ethnic art form of exciting rhythm has to offer." The overwhelming response to these dancers had Jay pondering why tap dancing was so seldom seen or studied by young dancers. "Surely, someone will sponsor them in this coming season, and let more people make the joyous discovery of what we have in this remarkable American ethnic art form."9

By the summer of 1964, when Harold returned to the United States to perform with Fayard on *Hollywood Palace*, the popularity of jazz tap dance was on a sluggish upswing. Fayard had earlier been contacted by a promoter for the Palace Theatre in New York who was interested in bringing back "the old vaudeville," or variety theatre. "My brother called me from California," Harold remembered, "and asked if I would come back for just two shows. I hadn't planned to come back and I didn't have to stay." When Harold did return to the States with his French wife, he says, he noticed a big change in the mood of the country: "When I walked down Hollywood Boulevard with my wife, no one was turning their heads, looking out the window, or peeping and carrying on. I said, 'Hey, they must have gotten cool.' So I decided to stay and get something going here like I did in Paris."10

With the passage of the Civil Rights Act in 1964, attitudes toward the black performer were slowly beginning to change. "No longer just an 'entertainer,' the Negro dancer is now well accepted as 'artist' in the mainstream of dance," Harriet Jackson commented in *Dance Magazine*. Tracing the roots of the black American concert dance to William Henry Lane ("Master Juba") and Bill "Bojangles" Robinson, she cited Arthur Mitchell, Donald McKayle, and Alvin Ailey as the young black artists "emerging from the minstrel-vaudeville cocoon" and making room for "the Negro dancer and choreographer who no longer feels he must be confined to dancing 'Negro roles' and to expressing 'Negro themes.'"11 While the dance artists that Jackson named may well have been striving to overcome the old stereotype of black minstrel performer, the old guard of black jazz tap dancers from the thirties and forties were beginning to come back strong. As keepers of the faith and still proud to call themselves entertainers, they were eager to show that the tradition of rhythm dancing had not lost its fire.

When the Nicholas Brothers returned to *Hollywood Palace* for a second performance in 1965, they were introduced by Dale Evans as "one of the greatest names in entertainment." And when the curtain parted, there were Fayard and Harold standing at the top of a grand flight of stairs. The stair motif was repeated in a starburst of wood slats suspended above the stairs. For their entrance, Fayard stepped down one of the curved flights that flanked the central stairway and Harold stepped down the other, and they met at the bottom. Harold opened by scat-singing "Old Black Magic," and Fayard moved to his brother's bongo-like vocalese. They stomped, single file, across the stage in the second chorus, splaying their hands in front of them as if they were palming an invisible drum. Chugging forward and hop-shuffling back, the pattern of their movement and the rhythm of their steps must have sounded a familiar ring to those who knew their dancing. While some of their steps were direct quotes from their routine in *The All-Colored Vaudeville Show* (1934), their wide-eyed pleasure in performing them made the choreography look as though it were being performed for the first time. In the last chorus, Fayard pulled a handkerchief out of his pocket and jumped back and forth over it, and Harold took a running slide through Fayard's legs, as they had done in *Down Argentine Way* (1940).[12] They finished with a bow. Perhaps no one realized that the giant flight of stairs that the brothers had been standing on at the opening of their act was never danced on. No matter, the stairway served only to reference the Nicholas style. Following in the tradition of Bill Robinson's famous stair dances in the twenties and the pedestal dances incorporated into the class acts of the thirties and forties, for the Nicholases the stairs were a grand salute to the stepping traditions of the past, and the quintessential symbol of their unique style of jazz tap dancing.

A variation on their stair-and-ramp routine was presented by the Nicholas Brothers on a 1964 *Hollywood Palace* hosted by Victor Borge and featuring singer Nancy Wilson and comedian Pat Morito. After a sweeping orchestral introduction, the curtains parted on the brothers standing before a set of various-sized boxes and platforms—some stacked into staircases and ramps, others assembled into skyscrapers. In the first chorus, Harold sang, "My kind of town," and with the wave of an arm illuminated one of the boxes; Fayard finished Harold's line with "Manhattan is," and with a wave lit up another box, until the entire set was lit up like a city skyline. In the second chorus, this cityscape became the brothers' playground. Tossing off a swishing softshoe on one box and darting across another, they alternated athletic jumps, flips, and spins with rhythmically smooth "SLIDE digaty digaty dee/ SLIDE digaty digaty dee" rhythms, to end by jumping off a seven-foot-high platform and landing in a split-and-recover.[13]

While the repetition of material from past routines may be seen as an unimaginative return to the tried-and-true, the vintage steps—the dancing up the stairs, the sliding down the ramps and through each other's legs—were what audiences wanted to see. Were not television hosts, when introducing "the very famous Nicholas Brothers," already setting up the expectation that the brothers would be doing what had made them so famous? And the brothers, who saw themselves as entertainers—performance artists of the highest octave—were obliged to deliver. It was for television that they began to shape their dance material to accommodate that expectation. In general, although they opened with new tap choreography—new combinations of steps danced to a contemporary tune—they then slipped, in the second and third sections of the dance, into direct citations of vintage routines, with a flashy ending: the slides down ramps, the jumps over and under each other, the synchronized splits and recovers.

Through the device of repetition—the repeating of steps, movement forms, and rhythmic phrases that deliberately referenced past works—the brothers were, in essence, emphasizing their own virtuosic style of jazz tap dancing. This device, moreover, enabled them to effectively codify their own dance technique. Jazz tap dance, like jazz music, must establish aurally its own grammatical patterns in order to be comprehended. Each successive repetition of a rhythmic phrase, in turn, emphasizes the structure of the musical form. Repetition is one of the most important elements in jazz performance; hearing the theme, the repeat of that theme, then all its variations enables the listener to comprehend the original musical idea.

Given the narrow range of "basic" tap steps (shuffles, slaps, riffs, rolls, pickups, hops, and slides) that comprise the lexicon of tap dance, the repetition of steps and rhythm patterns is inevitable. With the reality of the way jazz music is structured, moreover, it can be argued that Fayard and Harold were not literally repeating steps but instead enumerating and formalizing the step combinations, step patterns, and movement forms that they had established as their own unique style of jazz dancing. The repetition of certain clusters of rhythmic movement, then, enabled audiences to immediately comprehend the signature style of the Nicholases' jazz dancing. The brothers were in essence interpreting and reinterpreting their own jazz dance, as jazz musicians do when playing, in their own signature styles, a standard jazz tune.

That, by the mid-sixties, the Nicholases had effectively codified their own form of jazz dance can be seen in their performance on *The Bell Telephone Hour*'s "The Song and Dance Man." Broadcast on NBC-TV (January 16, 1966), this mini-musical history of tap dance in America saw the Nicholases and Donald O'Connor demonstrating a tap dance challenge. The performance was less a challenge dance and more a brilliant demonstration of signature Nicholas jazz tap combinations, which O'Connor was able to absorb and perform as the third member of the team.

"The Song and Dance Man" began with O'Connor dancing an Irish jig, followed by a Scottish reel, Spanish *zapateada*, and German *spatlasse*. "Out of a little of this, and a little of that, came buck dancing," Anthony Newley, who hosted the show, explained, as O'Connor danced a buck-and-wing. "From this, some ingenious men got the idea of adding little metal plates to the soles and heels of their shoes, and tap dancing was born." After whisking through a softshoe, to "Tea for Two," and sand-dancing, Newley's tap history jumped to the 1930s and 1940s when, he said, "a bit of ballet, a touch of jazz and interpretive, and imaginative jumps, spins, grace, and humor" were infused into tap dance. Only then, Newley reasoned—all too simplistically—did it become an exciting challenge for dancers to outdo each other in a challenge dance. Enter O'Connor with the Nicholas Brothers.

With O'Connor in the lead, all three were in line, stomping out a "DAH di DAH di DAH/ didalee didalee dee dee" rhythm in their feet as their splayed hands palmed invisible drums. O'Connor then dropped out of the line, leaving Fayard and Harold to turn around and retrace the line of direction on which they had entered with offbeat running flaps. They moved backward along the line of direction in circling *ronde de jambes en dehors* with upright torsos as their arms extended into long and graceful lines, and their feet shuffled a profusion of chugging and digging steps. Harold turned and sprang out of line, his legs in a well-shaped *attitude*, to pass the dance to Fayard, who shaped the space with long-gliding slides.

O'Connor rejoined the brothers on the musical segue to "Cute," a medium-tempo swing tune by Neal Hefti with a repeating A chorus of thirty-two measures, in which the dancers traded four-and-eight bars of music with the band. Then, with lightness and ease, all three dancers performed the Nicholases' smooth slides, crossover steps, and one-legged wings. In the best dance television camera work to date, the dancers' X-shaped arm-and-leg splays were captured in full-bodied motion, filling the television screen with triple-X designs. O'Connor tapped out a fluent "ZIPpity DIPpity DIP dah dah dah" riff that was punctuated with feather-light shuffles and heel-clicks. Fayard repeated O'Connor's ditty in double time, adding side-traveling stomps that replaced O'Connor's high-pitched clicks, then passed to O'Connor, who tapped a variation of his first riff. He passed to Harold, who repeated O'Connor's steps with added speed and his own winging embellishments. Harold next passed to O'Connor, who repeated the first riff on the other leg and passed the dance to both brothers, who mirrored each other with crossing-back steps in the delightful rhythm of "dee DAH DAH DAH dee/ DEE da lee DEE da lee DEE da lee dee."

Step for step, all three turned and walked upstage and leapt on top of square, stool-high pedestals. Hopping up and off them in perfect time with the music and with one another, they finished this vaudeville-inspired section of the dance by sitting on the pedestals and faking Russian-styled kazotsky kicks. Rolling into the final chorus, all three hoofers were hooting and hee-hawing one another. After twirling through sets of barrel turns, sweeping the legs backward in trenches, and spinning out double and triple turns, they finished with a decelerated ending—a salute to the class-act finale—in which they strode upstage, turned around, and sat back down on their pedestals with folded arms.

Although it lacked the sharply competitive edge of most challenge dances, this performance drew directly, in step and style, from the Nicholas Brothers' repertoire to demonstrate superb jazz ensemble dancing. The brothers were fully mature artists, and O'Connor was a proficient technician, able to absorb the Nicholases' choreography with ease, thus proving himself as an equal member of the trio. Something about these three dancers moving together, three men as one, was transcendent. Without letting their own personalities distract from the performance, and totally absorbed in their efforts to meld with one another, they projected almost no awareness of differences in race or in technique. Under the influence of the rhythms, the spectator relinquished the thought process; the handsome forms and synchronous movement produced a sense of total fulfillment. O'Connor did not smile, nor were the brothers their usual effusive selves in this performance. By concentrating on the details of choreography and giving up to the shapes and rhythms of their full-bodied movement, they exuded a supreme mastery and a generosity of performance that was rare in television, given the constraints of the studio stage and the small screen. "The Song and Dance Man," as it was performed by O'Connor and the Nicholases on this 1966 *Bell Telephone Hour*, seemed to mark yet another upturn in popularity for jazz tap dancing, even if it was still generally relegated to nostalgia.

Beginning on April 7, 1969, Leticia Jay presented her *Tap Happenings* at the Bert Wheeler Theatre at the Hotel Dixie, on West 43rd Street, off Times Square in New York. There, for several successive Monday evenings, such out-of-work and underemployed hoofers as Lon Chaney, Honi Coles, Harold Cromer, Bert Gibson, the Hillman Brothers, Raymond Kaalund, Baby Laurence, Ray Malone, Sandman Sims, Jimmy Slyde, Tony White, Rhythm Red, Derby Wilson, and Chuck Green participated in "jam sessions of traditional tap dancing."[14]

Writing in *Dance Magazine*, Patrick O'Connor described the performance he saw as "the scene of a wake, a farewell ceremony for departing giants." The experience was one of "watching powerful men, none of them young, making an electric connection mostly with each other and incidentally with the audience." After interviewing some of the dancers, asking them why they thought tap dance was dead, O'Connor reported:

> What killed tap dancing, Mr. Malone? "Agnes De Mille." What killed tap dancing, Mr. Chaney? "Dope." What killed tap dancing, Rhythm Red? "Kids won't take the trouble to learn, can't discipline themselves." What killed tap dancing, Mr. Green? No answer. For Mr. Green, tap dancing is still alive.[15]

Tap Happenings later reopened as *The Hoofers* at the Mercury Theatre off-Broadway, where it played for two months and became the toast of the dance world. Nevertheless, O'Connor's commentary reflected the attitude, which continued to prevail during the next ten years or so, that tap dancing, if not already dead, belonged only to veteran hoofers aged sixty and more.

After the new production of "The Hoofers" and the 1970 Broadway revival of the 1925 hit musical *No, No Nanette* (choreographed by the seventy-five-year old Busby Berkeley and starring the sixty-year-old Ruby Keeler), tap dance more than ever remained identified as nostalgia. In this period, there developed "a kind of archeologist interest in rhythm tap dance,"[16] and all New York dancers wanted to learn it.

"I would think that with nostalgia, and everybody craving to return to the thirties and forties, the old-time Vaudeville hoofers would be right up there on the Great White Way making hordes of money," tap dancer Jane Goldberg wrote upon discovering a group of grand masters tapping away in the bowels of an old, musty church, St. John the Apostle, on Columbus Avenue in upper Manhattan. "It occurred to me as I watched them reminisce about the old times that somebody should grab them fast and learn their special brand of tap dance." Goldberg described the style of these hoofers as a listener's dance that was "all in the feet, as they produce millions of different sounds."[17] The Nicholas Brothers at the time were enjoying a much more commercial success, however, and they were using all of the body in their more classical style of jazz tap dancing.

Record cover for the Nicholas Brothers' We Do Sing Too, *recorded for Mercury and distributed in Europe (Rigmor Newman).*

A television special in the early seventies presented the brothers in quintessential seventies costume: light-blue and brown polyester suits with large-collared shirts and wide ties, their long hair brushed into Afros. Looking fashionably hip and with the times, the brothers fed the public hunger for jazz nostalgia. "We'd like to do a little medley from a couple of movies we made with the Glenn Miller Orchestra," Harold announced into the hand-held microphone, while standing in the middle of a bright-yellow sunburst that was pasted on the stage floor. The brothers sang bits of "Kalamazoo" and "Chattanooga Choo Choo," and Fayard urged Harold to "talk to the people, brother, tell 'em how you feel" between songs; then they slipped into a languid softshoe dance.

Even while the overly amplified television studio band drowned out the sound of the taps, the rhythm dance became visible as it moved from the brothers' black patent-leather tap shoes up the body. Stepping and turning with legs in *attitude*, sliding with outspread arms, twisting in the shim sham, tilting sideways in grapevines, flicking the legs in triple-time step-wings, it was all jazz tap dance—minus the sound of metal taps—and so fully corporeal that it mattered little that the taps were not the solo voicing.[18]

The Nicholas Brothers crisscrossed the United States in the seventies, sang and danced on television, played the casinos and clubs, and acted in films, though not always together. Fayard played a dramatic role in William Wyler's film *The Liberation of L. B. Jones* (1970, Columbia), a tale of militant racism in the South. Harold played the gangster Little Seymour in the Sidney Poitier film comedy *Uptown Saturday Night* (1974, Warner Brothers). The brothers came together to perform in Las Vegas with Redd Foxx and to appear in *Sammy on Broadway* (Uris Theatre, April 23, 1974), a one-man show by Sammy Davis Jr., with assists by a handful of other artists. In 1974, Metro-Goldwyn-Mayer released *That's Entertainment*, a nostalgia bash with introductions by MGM stars of scenes from nearly a hundred MGM musicals. The "Be a Clown" number from *The Pirate* (1948) was included in the compilation, and movie audiences were again stunned by the dancing of the Nicholas Brothers from some thirty years past.

On many occasions throughout the seventies, the veteran hoofers inspired the young with their masterful dancing. One of the best moments was during the last three days of 1979, with the Brooklyn Academy of Music's *Steps in Time: A Tap Dance Festival*, reported Susan Reiter in *Dance News*, in which "a dazzling collection of tap-dance veterans, joined by a few of their present-day heirs, took to the stage to display their undiminished prowess." The four-hour program included an hour-long musical section by Dizzy Gillespie and his band, performances by members of the Copasetics, and "the act that was saved for last—the Nicholas Brothers, who specialized in flashy, acrobatic dancing and were featured in several films 40 years ago."[19]

In the eighties, there was a renaissance of interest in tap dancing that began to grow and spread. James "Buster" Brown remarked, "It's satisfying to know tap didn't die," and Howard "Sandman" Sims commented, "Tap dancing never got lost, the people just lost dancing," in George Nirenberg's film *No Maps on My Taps* (1980), which documented the hoofers who helped keep tap alive through its lean years. In Michael Blackwood's documentary film *Tapdancin'*, also released in 1980, the Nicholases were tracked offstage in a Las Vegas engagement, where they hinted at what held hoofers to the art form for so long. The off-camera interviewer asked, "Why do you do it, do you do it for the applause?" "Yeah, the applause, that's what you want to hear, and if you don't hear it, you must be slipping," answered Harold breathlessly. Sally Sommer wrote in response to seeing the *Tapdancin'* clip, "These dancers build their routines to irresistible climaxes, and they want to arouse the audience to high response."[20] She suggested that the resurgence of interest in tap dance was motivated, perhaps, by audiences who hungered once again for the call-and-response between performer and spectator—applause being the sign of approval for dancers, whose desire it was to energize their audiences.

Through the eighties, the Nicholas Brothers continued to titillate audiences with their rhythm dancing. It was very much appreciated, and it was rewarded. In March 1981, they performed, presented awards, and were themselves honored with a retrospective of their works on film during the *Academy Awards*.

The honors continued. In April of 1981, in San Francisco, Harold won the Bay Area Critics Circle Award for Best Principal Performance for *Stompin' at the Savoy*, a musical set in Harlem in the thirties, in which he had provided a six-minute turn on "Lady Be Good," "singing, scatting, strutting and fancy dancing in a way few performers alive could match."[21] Another highlight came in May 1981, when Harold danced to "David Danced before the Lord" in *Salute to Duke*, a PBS-TV tribute to Duke Ellington broadcast from the Kennedy Center in Washington, D.C. In the opening solo, drummer Max Roach brushed a steady "and a ONE and a TWO" beat on the snare drum, the bassist plucked out a thumping walking beat, and the pianist fingered delicate running trills as Harold became the fourth instrument in the rhythm section with his taps. Whether tip-toeing daintily or skidding with controlled abandon across the space, Harold's softshoe dance ran the gamut of classic jazz dance steps. Circling crossbacks and crossovers, step-ball-changes, spin turns and grapevines, single turns and drops, rubberlegs, foot-dribbles, and full-bodied un-dulations: all were delivered with an attitude of capricious non-chalance, and with as much expressivity in the arms and hands as in the legs and feet. Slipping, sliding, and swiveling, Harold's shoes duplicated the whish sounds of Roach's wire brushes; it was as if sand were strewn across the floor as he was dancing.

The tempo changed, the rhythm section became more aggres-sive, and Harold jumped in succession onto each of three raised platforms in front of Roach's drum set. Then his rhythm dance, with its double wings, circling heel-toe clicks, and stamping rhythm breaks, became more emphatic. While continuing to pump the bass pedal, Roach threw his drumsticks to Harold, and they began to trade eights, with Roach beating the tom-tom and bass drums, and Harold drumming the edge of the platform with the sticks. Harold jumped back onto the platform and, with a swagger, jumped off it again, landing in a split-and-recover that was as smooth as his opening.[22]

This tour de force on television was but a warmup for Harold, who at age sixty moved on to conquer the theatre stage. In Febru-ary 1982, he starred with Honi Coles in a new tap musical, *Tappin'*

Uptown, at the Brooklyn Academy of Music. In August of that year, Harold assumed the lead role in the touring production of *Sophisticated Ladies*, a musical homage to Duke Ellington, which on Broadway (Lunt-Fontanne Theatre, March 1, 1981) had starred Gregory Hines. "There is no lessening of energy, enthusiasm or enjoyment," wrote Harvey Siders for the *Los Angeles Daily News* (17 September 1982) of Harold's opening. "The dancing is less spectacular but more sensual; Nicholas imbues his sexuality with humor. Hines was outgoing; Nicholas is outrageous . . . the show swings because Nicholas swings."

When the production moved to the Desert Inn in Las Vegas for ten months, Harold was performing twelve shows a week without injury. In a style described as "ageless," the *Las Vegas Review-Journal* (25 February 1983) reported, Harold "managed to

Harold Nicholas with Theresa Hayes in the Long Beach Civic Light Opera production of Sophisticated Ladies *in 1989 (photo by Craig Schwartz, courtesy of Harold Nicholas Archive).*

captivate millions of people throughout the world with his technical brilliance and the elegance of his style." The *Sentinel Voice* (6 January 1983) declared him a national treasure—"No one has ever and never will be able to dance the way he does with the ease he does . . . dancing with his timeless, enviable and impeccable style." And Rob Powers in the *Las Vegas Review Journal* (25 March 1983) wrote: "Those feet still sparkle the ground with the same ferocious machine-gun rat-tat-a-tat, and at times, the same measured delicateness that helped make the Nicholas Brothers one of the world's preeminent jazz dance teams."

The mid-eighties were stellar years for Harold as a soloist. In September 1983, he returned to Italy for four months to star in six *Il Paradiso* variety shows for RAI television in Rome. In one of these shows, we see "Harold Nicholas" in neon lights suspended over the orchestra. Harold chats in Italian to the host as he demonstrates tap steps. In English, he sings and dances to "It Don't Mean a Thing if It Ain't Got That Swing"; he ends by tapping up and down a flight of stairs.[23]

In June of 1984 Harold starred in Melvin Van Peebles's one-man musical comedy *Waltz of the Stork Boogie* off-Broadway at the New Federal Theatre. A year later, in August 1985, he embarked on the national tour of *The Tap Dance Kid*, the Tony Award-winning musical directed by Jerry Zaks and choreographed by Danny Daniels. After the show's opening at the Golden Theatre in San Francisco, one critic declared: "The most inspired performance comes from Harold Nicholas. If tap dancing is the rhythm of magic feet, Nicholas is one of the legendary musicians."[24]

The early eighties were productive years for Fayard, who, aside from performing with his brother, appeared as a soloist on the Shields and Yarnell television show and in several productions in the Louis B. Mayer Theatre in Los Angeles. But by the mid-eighties, Fayard's arthritic condition reached a critical point. "I was working with my brother doing a tour with Sammy Davis Jr.," Fayard remembers. "And my brother saw the trouble I was having. And he said, 'Don't do the splits, just let me do it. Just use your hands.'"[25] In 1985, Fayard underwent hip replacement surgery. Though he continued afterward to perform with Harold, he began devoting more of his time to teaching and choreographing.

By the mid-eighties, the Nicholas Brothers, riding on past performances and on Harold's most recent successes, were beginning to reach another peak in popularity. In August 1984, Harold met Fayard in Los Angeles, where the Nicholas Brothers were honored at the International Olympic Games Arts Festival. In December of that year, the brothers were back in New York, installed into the Wall of Fame at the world-famous Roseland Ballroom. The Nicholases were being asked to do so many public appearances that by the mid-eighties Rigmor Newman, the Nicholas Brothers' manager and agent, wrote a working script entitled "Nicholas Brothers Act." This sequence of songs and dances spanning the brothers' fifty-year career could be adapted and adjusted to a number of occasions and performance venues.

Fayard Nicholas with Lorraine Shields in the Shields and Yarnell Show, *broadcast on local television in Washington, D.C., in the early eighties (Harold Nicholas Archive).*

The suggested opening to the act was a film clip from the
"Jumpin' Jive" number from *Stormy Weather* (1943). The brothers
were introduced at the end of the sequence, walking out onstage
through the eight-by-ten-foot screen made up of vertical overlap-
ping strips. After chatting with the audience, they were to perform their first "Dance Specialty," an up-tempo tap dance
accompanied by the orchestra, then talk about the movies they
once made with Glenn Miller and his orchestra; singing and
dancing to "Chattanooga Choo Choo" (*Sun Valley Serenade*, 1941)
and "Kalamazoo" (*Orchestra Wives*, 1942) were to follow.

If the program was to be more than an hour in length, there
was the suggested introduction of a female jazz singer-dancer
who was versatile enough to perform her own material as well as
to sing and dance with the brothers. Harold would then sing
"Old Man River," with Fayard conducting the orchestra. Then the
brothers would perform a Latin American song-and-dance number. Harold would do a number from *Evolution of the Blues* (1978),
touching on such jazz legends as "King" Oliver, Louis Armstrong, Lester Young, and Charlie Parker; he would also dance to
"David Danced before the Lord," from *Salute to Duke* (1981).
Then Fayard would talk about the brothers' childhood and introduce a film clip from *Black Network* (1936); near the end of that
clip, the orchestra would pick up the music from the film track
and the brothers would dance, in synchrony with the film, before
their own giant images on the screen.[26]

In January 1985, when MGM released its third mega-musical
compilation, *That's Dancin'!*, Gene Siskel of the *Chicago Tribune*
(15 January 1985) declared that the film's single greatest moment
was a specialty act by "the hyperkinetic Nicholas Brothers" in
Down Argentine Way. In the *New Yorker* (7 January 1985), film
critic Pauline Kael confessed that when looking at that clip, "you
just about go crazy from the sheer aesthetic excitement of what
they are doing—they are flying."

In the late eighties, as mammoth discos in New York City like
the Ritz Ballroom were projecting the "Be a Clown" number
from *The Pirate* on their ceilings to excite their young patrons,[27]
the Nicholas Brothers continued to be showered with awards

such as the Apollo Theatre's Hall of Fame (1986), the Ebony Life-time Achievement Award (1987), and Harold's Dance Educators of America Award (1988). Ever more pleasing to the brothers were the accolades they were receiving from an entirely new generation of New York dance critics, who began to write about the Nicholas Brothers as though they were seeing their jazz tap dancing for the very first time.

In her review of the Brooklyn Academy of Music's *Gershwin Gala* in 1987, *New York Times* dance critic Anna Kisselgoff called Harold "a class unto himself, right down to his leg-splitting finale" (12 March 1987); one year after the performance, in another dance review, Kisselgoff recalled how Harold, at the *Gershwin Gala* the year before, had "suddenly burst on stage, and even in a brief moment illuminated—as other dancers that evening had not—the sense of style that Gershwin symbolized, and that the Nicholas Brothers embodied" (*New York Times*, 7 February 1988). In March 1988, when Harold appeared as guest artist with the Jazz Tap Ensemble at New York's Joyce Theatre, Jennifer Dunning of the *New York Times* (3 March 1988) reported than when Harold sidled out onto the stage for his performance, every inch and atom of his body seemed primed for entertainment: "He feathers the stage with his tap-dancing, which is of the light-footed fusillade school. . . . His old-style brand of total yet almost casual involvement in the entertaining of his audience is a little eerie at first, but while Mr. Nicholas is on stage, the evening sings." And in the film *Tap* (Hoofer Films/Tri-Star, 1988), Harold one-upped such veteran hoofers as Sammy Davis Jr., Bunny Briggs, Lon Chaney, and Steve Condos in a challenge dance.

But the single event that brought the Nicholas Brothers to the wide-eyed attention of New York critics was *Dance on Film: Dancin' in the Movies*, a five-week retrospective of dance in the movies, at New York's Film Forum 2 (15 January–18 February 1988). Curated by Program Director Bruce Goldstein, this dance-on-film festival included "Fascinating Rhythms," a culling of footage from the celebrated black dance archive of Ernie Smith, as well as an evening-long "Tribute to the Nicholas Brothers"

(18 February 1988), a gathering of film clips of the Nicholases from *Pie, Pie, Blackbird* (1932) to *Uptown Saturday Night* (1974). Writing in the *Village Voice* (1 March 1988) about the evening of tribute, dance critic Joan Acocella called the Nicholas Brothers "amazing artists—Harold, I think, the great virtuoso, Fayard the greater musician—and the sum was greater than its parts, for they fit together perfectly, and the dynamic between them—Harold's bravura presented like a gift to Fayard, Fayard's rhythmic mastery laid out like a net, or a blanket for the two of them—all that is still there years later, when they are both adults."

Bruce Goldstein, in his narration of the film clips, commented that because of the brothers' famous splits-down-the-stairs routine, they had been unjustly classed as a flash act—"That's just extra, that's not what they do. They're dancers." In response to Goldstein's remark, Acocella wrote, "Indeed they are, and for a sheer dance pleasure—the kind of joy that makes you feel that something is going to burst inside you, and you're going to die, and that's just fine—this show was the first-place winner of the series."

Writing about the Nicholases' tribute in *New York Magazine* (22 February 1988), dance critic Toby Tobias described, with particular clarity, the differences between this beautifully meshed pair: "Fayard's the rangier one, flyaway limbs flicking out from impossibly loose joints at rakish angles to create their own peculiar poetry. Physically, Harold is more compact and self-contained; his body reads as a single suave unit. . . . In both of them, from the very start, the charm is so potent it's scary, while the dancing, even at its most cultivated, seems to spring from a spontaneous impulse."

Wrote Anna Kisselgoff in the *New York Times* (7 February 1988): "Most of us tend to remember Fayard and Harold Nicholas as the superbly polished acrobatic tap team." She remembered seeing those "mind-boggling splits and tap rhythms that accompanied their elegance" in *Stormy Weather* (1943); she recalled the sheer exuberance of the brothers in "Chattanooga Choo Choo" from *Sun Valley Serenade* (1941), which became their trademark; and she thanked Goldstein for the compilation because it illustrated "the roots and range of the Nicholas Brothers' art." Kisselgoff was astute in her observation, moreover, that the "Be a Clown" routine in *The Pirate* was "more push-ups than taps," commenting that "Hollywood found room for Mr. Kelly, Fred Astaire, Ray Bolger, Donald O'Connor and others in the ensuing years. But not for the Nicholas Brothers." Noting that in *Black Network* (1936) the brothers demonstrated "exceptional speed and rhythmic intricacy even as adolescents," Kisselgoff also recognized the "clear sound and precision of their footwork" and their "willingness to create new shapes" in later films (especially, she thought, after the brothers worked with George Balanchine).

In their collaboration with Nick Castle on Twentieth Century-Fox films, Kisselgoff noticed, the "team's dancing takes on a wider dimension, looking suave but not slick, varying its acrobatic fluency through greater exploration of space." What struck her so forcibly about the Nicholas Brothers, Kisselgoff concluded, was "their utter generosity; how much they want to give you . . . digging hard into the rhythm with arms held high."

"Their virtuosity remains unrivalled," Arlene Croce wrote of the Nicholases in the *New Yorker* (15 February 1988). She added that although the film clips in the tribute were ripped from the contexts of the musicals they ornamented, the audiences at the Film Forum nevertheless saw something extraordinary—"two dancers of Astaire-like elegance, inventiveness, and originality who had somehow, despite the indignity of being typed as a novelty act, found an expressive language as memorable as any in American popular dance."

The Nicholas Brothers had survived the test of time for a new generation of dancers and critics. Through the medium of film, audiences would discover the rhythmic brilliance, the musicality, the eloquent footwork, and the full-bodied expressiveness of these two twentieth-century drum dancers, who had absorbed and embodied a three-hundred-year-old percussive dance tradition and had transformed it into classical American jazz dance.

A recent candid portrait of Harold and Fayard Nicholas (Harold Nicholas Archive).

Conclusion

To Fayard and Harold Nicholas:

Whose creativity and pioneering innovation have produced strikingly original work which has enriched our heritage;

Whose dazzling talent and unstoppable desire have taught the world to remember its spirit;

Whose choreography, daring technique, and extraordinary elegance have stretched the boundaries of dance, delighting and surprising audiences for more than half a century.

From vaudeville, Broadway, the great nightclubs, to television and films world-wide, they have danced into our hearts and history.

The Nicholas Brothers have challenged and inspired generations of dancers and choreographers, setting an unsurpassed standard to all who follow in their footsteps.

—1998 Samuel H. Scripps American Dance Festival Award, established to honor those great choreographers who have dedicated their lives and talents to the creation of our modern dance history, June 29, 1998.

When *Black and Blue*, the Broadway musical conceived and directed by Claudio Segovia and Hector Orezzoli, opened at the Minskoff Theatre on January 26, 1989, I noted in the dance review *Attitude* that "the feline ease of the blues found its match with the buck-and-bull fervor of tap dance."[1] *Black and Blue*, which bared the soul of the blues in all its expressive forms, starred the legendary blues singers Ruth Brown, Linda Hopkins, and Carrie Smith; the veteran hoofers Bunny Briggs, Ralph Brown, Lon Chaney, Jimmy Slyde, and Dianne Walker; and a group of young African-American dancers performing the swing and tap choreographies of Cholly Atkins, Henry LeTang, Frankie Manning, and Fayard Nicholas.

Up until *Black and Blue*, New York tap dancers, for the most part, were familiar with the jazz tap dancing and "vocal" Motown choreography of Cholly Atkins, the dance teachings of Henry LeTang, and the swing dancing of Frankie Manning. They were the least familiar, however, with the West Coast–based Fayard Nicholas—having at the time made only a vague connection between him and the fantastic spurts of tap dancing by the Nicholas Brothers seen on film. But Fayard's tap choreography in "I Want a Big Butter and Egg Man" in *Black and Blue*, created for dancers Kevin Ramsey, Ted Levy, and Eugene Fleming, made an indelible impression on members of the dance and general audience. Combining full-bodied rhythms and intricate gestures with witty splashes of acrobatics, it was a delightful and endearing work that earned Fayard, as one of the four co-choreographers of *Black and Blue*, a well-deserved Tony Award for Best Choreography in a Musical. "I Want a Big Butter and Egg Man," moreover, demonstrated the ease with which a new generation of dancers absorbed and embodied the signature Nicholas style of jazz tap dancing. The work represented a blueprint of sorts for succeeding generations of jazz artists who would continue to evolve this classic American jazz dance form.

"I want a butter and egg man/ From way out in the west," Carrie Smith croons at the opening of the number, bumping and grinding her hips to Louis Armstrong's thirty-two-bar blues tune. Sir Roland Hanna embellishes her sentiments on piano while

Jake Porter echoes them in counterpoint on trumpet. "I get so tired of working hard all day/ I want somebody who wants to play," Smith continues, and near the end of the chorus, in three-fold answer to her plea, Ramsey, Levy, and Fleming strut onstage in single file. Wearing black satin jackets, red-plaid pants and porkpie hats, they snap their fingers and flick out a "da da BOP di BOP di dada di BOP" break with their black patent-leather shoes, slipping into their tap dance.

As Smith proceeds to scat the tune, the dancers backstroke the floor with shim-sham slides that ricochet their legs into side-brushing, knee-high, leg extensions. Then they turn into profile and whip out lightly rippling skipping steps, as their hands circle smoothly over their chattering feet. The hands are an elegant complement to the feet. When the legs stroke backward cross-steps, the wrists circle baroque curlicues. When the feet shuffle to the front and side, the palms of the hands raised elbow-high rotate from face-up to face-down—all six palms in a row looking like a series of dashes.

In the second dancing chorus, Ramsey breaks from the trio with a light-skipping solo as he holds his hands out daintily, as if asking for them to be manicured. The dignified elegance of his stance is broken with double-time tapping and forward-leaning over-the-tops; he passes to Levy, who paddle-and-rolls in double time, then drops into a split-and-recover that he accents with a wink. Levy, in turn, passes to Fleming, whose frothy-light tap-ping quickly twists into rubber-legging in double time. Then all three dancers bob up and down, their bodies as straight as arrows while their splayed hands beat against invisible drums.

In the last chorus, the dancers rub their shiny black shoes into the ground in short-stroked pullbacks and long-stroked trenches, and then lunge into a straight-forward bow, snapping their fingers under Smith's wail: "I want a butter and egg man," she moans, and the men break out with stomps and slip-sliding back-steps. "I want a butter and egg man," she repeats, and the men respond to her high-pitched squeals with little skipping steps that balance them daintily on the tips of their toes. "I want to get me a butter and egg man," she bellows, to the men's softly shuffled "she BOP BOP da didalee BOP" beat, "and I hope a butter and egg man wants me." And she struts smoothly, her men in line behind her, off the stage.

Synchronous movement and the repetition and variation of rhythmic patterns; the use of call-and-response dialoguing, and the forward drive of the challenge; the rooting of rhythm in full-bodied movement and gestural detail; and the shaping of rhythm into beautiful corporeal forms—all employed to create a musically swinging tap choreography that was aimed to please an audience and to titillate them into relinquishing the thought process for an experience of pure, visceral pleasure: these are the salient ingredients of jazz tap performance that were bequeathed to the dancers of "I Want a Big Butter and Egg Man" by the Nicholas Brothers.

Cab Calloway, in the documentary *We Sing and We Dance*, summed up the career of the Nicholas Brothers when he stated: "They started out at the Cotton Club, and it was nothing other than that they were a great act. People loved them. They established themselves there, and they maintained it over a period of sixty to seventy years, and that's a remarkable thing." It is indeed remarkable, not only that the Nicholases have managed and maintained their career as musical artists for more than sixty years, but that they played a significant role in evolving this classic American jazz dance form.

The 1920s, when jazz music and dance entered the cultural American mainstream, set the foundation of the Nicholas Brothers' career. It was during this decade that improvised jazz music flowered, played and recorded by such artists as Louis Armstrong and Duke Ellington; that the maturation and Americanization of the Broadway musical theatre occurred, through such producers and musical artists as Florenz Ziegfeld and Sissle and Blake; that the explosion in the arts was experienced and celebrated by the Harlem Renaissance; and that the musical creativity of a whole range of composers and songwriters was showcased, including George and Ira Gershwin, Jerome Kern, Rodgers and Hart, Vernon Duke, and Harold Arlen.

While New York became the center of the jazz explosion in the twenties, it was at the Standard Theatre in Philadelphia, where Ulysses and Viola Nicholas led a jazz pit orchestra, that Fayard and Harold Nicholas received their thorough orientation to jazz. The smooth-dancing class act of Reed and Bryant, the rhythm tap dancing of Buck and Bubbles, the flash acrobatics of the Four Covans, and the dozens of black comedy dance teams—each of whom used their fine sense of timing to edge themselves apart from their competitors—these were the models from which Fayard and Harold Nicholas shaped their own complex and integrated jazz performance style.

If the Nicholases' style of jazz tap dancing was largely drawn from two seemingly disparate African-American performance traditions, black comedy dance and the class act, these two traditions were already creatively conjoined by the brothers by the time they came to New York in the early thirties to perform at the Cotton Club. Then, dancing with the Duke Ellington and Cab Calloway orchestras in this Harlem nightclub, which served up hot "jungle" music with cool sophistication, the brothers forged their streamlined style of jazz dancing. It was distinguished by lightness and speed, angularity and swinging rhythms. Their dancing was also informed by working on Broadway with George Balanchine and in London in the thirties with Clarence "Buddy" Bradley; both these choreographers reinforced a more vertical and downward drive of rhythm, combined with an inventiveness in playing the body as a percussive instrument.

In the postwar forties, as the steady, smooth, danceable rhythms of swing gave way to the dissonant harmonies and frenzied rhythmic shifts of late-1940s bebop, a radical transformation occurred in American jazz dance. Jazz tap rhythms, previously reserved for the feet, were to become absorbed and reshaped in the body, and a new style of "modern jazz dance"—minus the taps and less polyrhythmic—became popular. The "modern" styles, with the new sped-up tempos, and the fading of "old-fashioned" swing bands resulted in the virtual disappearance of traditional tap dancing from the musical stage. But the Nicholases endured this cataclysmic musical transition. Resisting the trend that relegated rhythm to the torso or the toes, they continued to evolve a style of jazz dance that was as rhythmically nuanced in the feet as in the body.

By the late forties, and after a five-year contract with Twentieth Century-Fox that enriched them immeasurably through their collaboration with Hollywood choreographer Nick Castle, Fayard and Harold had created their own uniquely modern style of jazz tap dancing that was distinguished for its eloquent footwork and full-bodied expressiveness. Their style of jazz dancing did not fall out of fashion in the fifties and sixties, and through the seventies and eighties it continued to impress audiences, which became ever more hungry for the Nicholases' style. Writing about a performance of Harold's in 1989, Chip Deffaa (*New York Post*, 23 December 1989) commented: "Whether singing or just moving about, Nicholas is a class act—a veteran nightclub pro whose savvy puts to shame most of the other over-hyped, soon-to-be-forgotten cabaret artists around town." Harold, at the time, was sixty-eight years old.

That the Nicholas Brothers received the prestigious Kennedy Center Honors award in 1991, were honored on National Tap Dance Day in New York with a FLO-BERT Award in 1992, received the Dance Magazine Award in 1995, and in 1998 were honored with the American Dance Festival's Samuel Scripps Award is testament to the worldwide recognition of their masterful dance artistry.

Several themes recur in the works of the Nicholas Brothers through their sixty-year career. The first is the profound musicality of their dancing, which makes them jazz musicians as much as tap dancers. Unlike conservatory-trained musicians well grounded in formal theory and instrumental technique, the Nicholases, like the jazzmen of the twenties, received their training in a "school" that the African-American author Ralph Ellison described as one of "apprenticeship, ordeals, initiation ceremonies, of rebirth." Ellison writes that it was only after a jazzman learned the fundamentals of his instrument and the traditional techniques of jazz, which included "the intonation, the mute work, manipulation of timbre, the body of traditional styles," that he then set out to "find, as it were, his soul."[2] As jazz musicians, the Nicholases made a subtle identification between their "instrument" and their deepest drives, which allowed them to express their own unique ideas, their own unique voice, or soundings.

The insistent exploration of rhythm that treated the body, from the feet up, as a percussion instrument is but one example of the brothers' supreme musicianship. Further proof is offered by jazz drummer Max Roach, who commented that "tap dancing is so close to jazz drumming" and added: "And I was fascinated with the things I heard from their [the Nicholas Brothers'] feet. Tap dancing to us had a sound to it, which was emphasized by them being so visual. They did some very intricate things that the drummers imitated."[3]

Writing about the interrelationship of sound and motion, critic Margo Jefferson astutely observed: "All music connects us to time and motion, which we experience in our bodies. The pulse beats when we listen; the senses fluctuate as we hear; the mind finds its meter as it takes in pitch, speed, and dynamics.... For dance and music, all one needs is a body attuned to the uses of time, space, and sound."[4] The Nicholas Brothers may be cited as one example of Jefferson's theory, for they were the very embodiment of sound, their jazz tap dancing an aural, visual, and visceral physicalization of music.

A second theme that can be traced through the Nicholas Brothers' career is their conception of tap dance as both a popular entertainment and an art. Musicality, beautiful movement form, and the use of repetition, synchrony, and call-and-response dialoguing to engage the audience in a rhythmic conversation comprised the discipline of their art—all for the ultimate goal, to please an audience. Fayard and Harold had taken to heart their father's words—"Don't look at your feet. You're entertaining the audience, not yourself."

By simultaneously drawing on black comedy dance and the class act, and blending comic quips and bizarre acrobatic feats with technically virtuosic rhythm tapping, the brothers were able to both titillate and impress their first audiences with a precocious sophistication that was entirely charming and disarming. This fusion of opposites remained key to the Nicholases' "art." By making it the highest form of entertainment, they managed to make rhythm dancing a *transformative* experience—and here, the word takes on more than one meaning for the Nicholases. They wanted their dancing to transcend racial barriers. They wanted audiences to see them not as *black dancers*, playing stereotyped roles, but as artists, expanding the form and meaning of dance. They wanted their dancing to make the spectator relinquish the thought process for an experience of pure sensory pleasure. And this they did. Sammy Davis Jr., for example, never forgot the experience of sitting in the Roxy Theatre and watching the Nicholas Brothers in *Orchestra Wives*. He saw the entire movie-house audience make the unprecedented move of standing up and cheering the brothers' special number.[5] Transfixed by Harold's "jaunty, effortlessly bold dancing" in a 1988 performance, Deborah Jowitt (*Village Voice*, 12 April 1988) described that evening of "first-class tap dancing" as having exerted a specific benevolent influence: "You leave the theatre feeling toned up, brightened: the rapid, clever, sly conversation by rhythm has challenged your sensibilities without exhausting you (as challenging conversations couched in words often do)." In the documentary film *Nicholas Brothers: We Sing and We Dance*, jazz and Broadway dancer Maurice Hines declared: "When they dance together it's magical. And anybody who's got any emotion or any feeling, and are true to themselves, will react truthfully to that and give them the standing ovation they deserve."

If exquisite rhythmic technique and a people-centered perfor-mance aesthetic were the salient features of the Nicholases' tap dancing, it was their brotherhood that gave them a heart-connec-tion with their audiences. "They were hardly ever allowed to appear with women partners, and so their dancing became a fra-ternal rather than a romantic metaphor—full of shared secrets and also of a certain friendly, slam-dunking competitiveness," dance critic Arlene Croce observed in the *New Yorker* (15 February 1988), adding, "Their progeny seems to include not just Michael Jackson but Michael Jordan."

As two male dancers, the brothers neither feminized their tap dancing nor emphasized the machismo in it. Instead they celebrated a positive male energy, which Robert Bly describes as being "irreverent . . . vital, sensuous, effervescent, full of feeling but not maudlin, and deeply connected to the earth and the collective history of . . . male ancestors."[6] Perhaps it was their natural athleticism, combined with their strong drawing from the stream of black comedy and eccentric dance, that fueled the stereotype of the Nicholas Brothers as flash dancers, which they were not. "To me, they were never flash," said Maurice Hines, "because they did close floor work too. They could do everything. To put them in the category of flash trivializes them."[7]

The uniqueness of the Nicholas Brothers is that they drew both from a two-hundred-year African-American performance tradition and from a three-hundred-year percussive dance tradition in America; the two were merged with ragtime and early jazz music at the turn of the twentieth century, and an apotheosis was reached in the swing era of the thirties and forties. This process resulted in the evolution of tap dance into a classical American form of jazz dance. In this context, the word "classical" has several connotations. First, when used in reference to the Nicholas Brothers' style of jazz tap dance, it invites a comparison with Western classical ballet. The element of vertical bodily alignment is what the two have in common. Margo Jefferson observed that in coming out of their splits the Nicholas Brothers "literally conduct themselves upward, with a bandleader's sweep of the arms."[8] Verticality is not specific to Western classical dance: "Line is something that all dancers want to have—and it doesn't have to be European line in terms of ballet. In that case there wouldn't have been a Martha Graham, or a Katherine Dunham," Maurice Hines commented. "The Nicholas Brothers had their own line. It might have looked like ballet line, but it was their line, and it was unique."[9]

In the documentary film *In a Jazz Way* (1986), Mura Dehn's statement that the Savoy Ballroom in Harlem was "the seat of classical dance" brings new meaning to the word "classical" with respect to the Nicholases' dance. Dehn, in making the connection between jazz music and dance, was suggesting that Swing as played by big-band orchestras was the "classic" jazz, and that the Lindy Hop—which everyone danced at the Savoy—was the classical dance counterpart to Swing. Dehn did not include jazz tap dancing as a form of swing dancing, though it is remarkable how the line dances performed by such lindy-hoppers as Al Minns and Pepsi Bethel, in Dehn's documentary film *The Spirit Moves* (1955), so accurately resemble (without the taps) the precision tap dancing of class-act dancers in the thirties, such as Pete, Peaches, and Duke or the Cotton Club Boys. Jazz tap dance, like the Lindy Hop, was performed to big-band swing music; it evolved, both musically and technically, while being performed by the swing bands of the thirties and forties, thus justifying its classification as a classic jazz dance form.

The Nicholas Brothers established their own form of "classical tap," to use Fayard's term, or classic jazz dancing, if we accept a Webster's dictionary definition of "classic" as being "time-honored, well-established, and superior in model shaping, that influences succeeding forms." This is most easily confirmed by the dozens of jazz dance artists who claim to have been profoundly influenced by the Nicholases' jazz artistry. "The first time I was aware of the Nicholas Brothers was when I was about seven years old," revealed Maurice Hines, when his tap dance teacher Henry LeTang brought him and his brother Gregory to the Apollo Theatre.

> And I saw them and they literally changed my life. I never saw anybody or any two people dance like that. They inspired me to be the dancer I became. I was very attracted to what is now called "line" in tap dancing and I knew it wasn't going to be just about the feet, I wanted it to be more. And Fayard was more—he was the ultimate to me, the ultimate. And so I think from then on I began to use my upper body more. I used my hands more . . . and I loved the camaraderie between the two of them, I loved the way Fayard looked at Harold with such pride, which is exactly how I used to look at my brother.[10]

Gregory Hines—who with his brother Maurice made up the young tap dance team of Hines and Hines—said he first became aware of the Nicholases at age nine. At that time he and his brother had been a dance team for about five or six years, and everywhere the Hineses performed, people said they reminded them of the Nicholas Brothers—or that they would *be* the next Nicholas Brothers. "I think, in my little mind, I figured they must have been great because I thought we were pretty good, so I thought we were gonna be the next Nicholas Brothers," revealed Hines. But then he saw them at the Apollo Theatre:

> When they came on, a roar went up, like a bullfighter made a great pass. . . . It was a very dramatic introduction, they both came in from opposite sides of the stage and did a great step, and my heart was beating so fast, just to see them in person. I remember the ease with which they did the act, which is what I was really looking for—cause on film you can take a whole lot of takes. But live, they just were so relaxed, and seemed to do everything effortlessly. I realized then that, er, nobody was gonna be the next Nicholas Brothers, least of all my brother and me.[11]

Gregory Hines has proclaimed the brothers as innovators who made the dancing seamless: "The flip or the split or the leap made so much sense to the dance, and the leap was a step, the split was a step. Then they would come up without using their hands and go right into another step—it was acrobatics, it was all part of the dance." He adds that what was different about their rhythm tapping was that they would "attack a step, pause between steps, and start on an upbeat."[12]

"Practically every move in break dancing, however new it may look, is not just foreshadowed but completely expressed in what the Nicholas Brothers did," said the dance critic Arlene Croce in the *New Yorker* (15 February 1988), adding that the real glory of their work lay in their simplest dancing and in their gift for counterpoint. "Harold, bending forward, tails flying," she wrote, "will rip off a cascade of quick rocking steps and gestures, and Fayard, beside him, will suddenly paraphrase Harold's movement as a series of quicksilver slurs and slides."

Ballet dancer Mikhail Baryshnikov has said that the accomplishments of the Nicholas Brothers lie beyond technique: "They opened so many doors for so many entertainers, black and white, with their own freedom and daring interpretations of the music." Baryshnikov considered the Nicholases among "the most amazing dancers I have ever seen in my life . . . ever. What is extraordinary about them is that you recognize their style in break dancing. You recognize their style in rap. . . . They have opened doors for so many people. They are the chain—that's why they are so important." Baryshnikov has further observed that even the elements of acrobatics in their dancing were never used "to punch the audience" but were all emotionally attached to the dance: "They knew exactly, where is the climax of the dance, where they can dance easy, when to smack the audience in the face, and when they can tease—that's the sign of a true choreographic mind."[13]

While the Nicholas Brothers have influenced, and been imitated by, other dancers of their generation, African-American musical artists of their generation believe, moreover, that the Nicholases were influential as role models for the black community. "You showed me the way, you showed me what I wanted to become, not only the sight but the sound," declared tap dancer Jimmy Slyde to the Nicholas Brothers at their Carnegie Hall tribute in 1996.[14] "Back in the Depression days when they got their start, many performers yearned to be the Nicholas Brothers," professed jazz singer Bobby Short. "They were role models," said drummer Max Roach. "And when you talk to people from that period I grew up with, we knew it, whether the world outside knew it or not. They are really geniuses. What they brought to the world of show business, quotes around that, or entertainment, still exists today. They went outside the art for us."[15]

A younger generation of African-American musical artists speaks with less nostalgia about the opportunities afforded the Nicholas Brothers. "When they talk about Fred Astaire and Gene Kelly, why don't they say something about Harold and Fayard Nicholas? That bubbles inside of me," choreographer Clarke Peters asked.

"The fact one black was making it at the time—Sammy Davis, Jr.—does not change the fact there was no room for the Nicholas

Brothers," rap artist M. C. Hammer declared. "There was room for Fred Astaire and Gene Kelly and Ginger Rogers, and a host of others, but only one black. The Nicholas Brothers would have been a threat to Astaire because, if I can walk on air, it's great, if no one else can do it. But if two guys walk in here, and they can do it—and lift their leg a little higher in the air—what I do isn't fantastic anymore."[16]

"Imagine what the Nicholas Brothers could have done if they had the opportunity," Maurice Hines mused. "Well, maybe that's why they weren't given the opportunity." Said Peters: "If they had all of that now, all that imagination and that creativity, God knows what they'd be doing—they'd be levitating!" Hammer said: "They'd be number one right now if they could rap or sing along with their incredible dancing. There's no doubt in my mind they'd be the biggest drawing act in the world."[17]

If tomorrow they were offered the right opportunity to perform together again, the Nicholas Brothers would jump at it. As Harold often declared, "Don't call me a legend. Just give me some work!"[18] While, at the ages of eighty-six and seventy-nine, Fayard and Harold are not able to leap down staircases over each other, they nevertheless have faith in each other's capabilities. Says Fayard about Harold: "You talk about your Donald O'Connors, Sammy Davis Juniors, and many of the other entertainers. But he has it. He does everything, only he does it better." Says Harold about Fayard: "People say Fred Astaire was a natural dancer because he danced from head-to-toe. I say that if my brother got together with Fred Astaire, there would be one Fred Astaire or one Fayard Nicholas. I think they were that close."

When the Nicholas Brothers were interviewed together in their 1992 documentary film *Nicholas Brothers: We Sing and We Dance*, Fayard was asked jokingly if he would trade Harold in for another brother. He immediately answered, "No way! No! We're so lucky to be together, and we'll never separate as brothers, as an act, 'cause we love each other. We love each other, even though it doesn't show sometimes. But it's there—you can't hide that even though everything is inside." Sitting next to his brother, Harold said, "Yeah, right. He's my brother, he's my teacher, and no matter what we do separately or how big we make it separately we're always together, always brothers. And nothing can split that in half, wives or nobody. 'Cause this is my brother. He needs me, I have to be there."

Fayard was then caught in a moment of reminiscing: "We did vaudeville, we did movies, we did TV. Like I've said before to anyone who's interviewed us, we've done everything in show business except opera." Harold, sitting next to his brother, turned to him and asked, "Did you ever want to do opera?" Fayard answered, "Oh yes, I wanted to do opera—a tap dancing opera."

Harold, too, wished for something he had not yet done: "I would still like to have had my own show, my own movie, featuring me, Harold Nicholas."

"'Harold Nicholas,'" Fayard repeated, adding with emphasis, "*and* His Brother. See—I was speaking for *both* of us!" Harold paused and slowly turned to Fayard. "Now the thing is, you have to speak for *yourself*, and I'll speak for *myself*," he said gently. "But that doesn't mean we're not brothers!"

Notes

Introduction

1. Brenda Dixon Stowell in Lynne Fauley Emery, *Black Dance from 1619 to Today* (Princeton, N.J.: Dance Horizons, 1988), 360.
2. James Lincoln Collier, "Jazz," in Barry Kernfeld, ed., *New Grove Dictionary of Jazz* (New York: St. Martin's Press, 1988), 580; Marshall Stearns, *The Story of Jazz* (New York: Oxford University Press, 1956), 3.
3. LeRoi Jones, *Blues People: The Negro Experience in White America and the Music That Developed from It* (New York: William Morrow, 1963), 111.
4. Gunther Schuller, *The Swing Era: The Development of Jazz* (New York: Oxford University Press, 1989), 729.
5. Houston A. Baker Jr., *Blues, Ideology, and Afro-American Literature: A Vernacular Theory* (Chicago: University of Chicago Press, 1984), 2.
6. Jahn Janheinz, *Muntu: An Outline of New African Culture* (New York: Grove, 1961), 164.
7. Kathy J. Ogren, *The Jazz Revolution: Twenties America and the Meaning of Jazz* (New York: Oxford University Press, 1989), 12–13.

Chapter One

1. Carl Van Vechten in Modris Ekstein, *Rites of Spring: The Great War and the Birth of the Modern Age* (New York: Houghton Mifflin, 1989), 14.
2. R.W.S. Mendl, *The Appeal of Jazz* (London: Philip Alland, 1927), 186.
3. Ralph Ellison, *Shadow and Act* (New York: Random House, 1964), 55.
4. Chris Goddard, *Jazz away from Home* (London: Paddington, 1979), 12.
5. Colonel William Heywood in Samuel B. Charters and Leonard Kunstadt, *Jazz: A History of the New York Scene* (New York: Da Capo, 1962), 65.
6. Goddard, *Jazz Away from Home*, 13; Charters and Kundstadt, *Jazz*, 66. While both Goddard and Charters and Kunstadt cite Bill Robinson's appointment as drum major in the 369th Regiment Band, there is no substantiation of this fact in either the Bill Robinson biography by Jim Haskins and N. R. Mitgang, *Mr. Bojangles* (New York: William Morrow, 1988), or Reid Badger's biography of James Reese Europe, *A Life in Ragtime* (New York: Oxford University Press, 1995).
7. Noble Sissle, "Ragtime by U.S. Army Band Gets Everyone over There," *St. Louis Dispatch*, 10 June 1918.
8. Gunther Schuller, *Early Jazz: Its Roots and Musical Development* (New York: Oxford University Press, 1968), 247.
9. Jean Cocteau in Lynn Garafola, *Diaghilev's Ballets Russes* (New York: Oxford University Press, 1989), 104.

10. Chevalier in Tyler Stovall, "Paris in the Age of Anxiety, 1919–39," in *Anxious Visions: Surrealist Art*, ed. Sidra Stich (New York: Regents of the University of California-Berkeley and Abbeville Press, 1990), 208.

11. *Variety* in Marshall Stearns, *The Story of Jazz* (New York: Oxford University Press, 1956), 155.

12. Marshall Stearns and Jean Stearns, *Jazz Dance: The Story of American Vernacular Dance* (New York: Macmillan, 1968), 22.

13. J. A. Rogers, "Jazz at Home," *Survey Graphic 6*, no. 6 (March 1925): 666.

14. James Lincoln Collier, *Louis Armstrong: An American Genius* (New York: Oxford University Press, 1983), 51–52.

15. Irene Castle, *Castles in the Air* (reprint, New York: Da Capo, 1980), 79.

16. James Reese Europe, "Castle Walk" (1914), Victor 17533; Schuller, *Early Jazz*, 248; Charters and Kunstadt, *Jazz*, 38.

17. Joe "King" Oliver, "Dippermouth Blues" (1923), *The Smithsonian Collection of Classic Jazz*, vol. 1; Lawrence Gushee, "New Orleans Jazz," in Barry Kernfeld, ed., *New Grove Dictionary of Jazz* (New York: St. Martin's Press, 1988), 836–37; J. Bradford Robinson, "Johnny Dodds," ibid., 294; Martin Williams, *The Jazz Tradition* (New York: Oxford University Press, 1993), 38.

18. Fletcher Henderson, "Sugarfoot Stomp" (1925), *Fletcher Henderson 1924–1927*, Jazz Archives No. 33 (1991); Thomas J. Hennessey, *From Jazz to Swing* (Detroit: Wayne State University Press, 1994), 83.

19. Houston A. Baker Jr., *Blues Ideology and Afro-American Literature: A Vernacular Theory* (Chicago: University of Chicago Press, 1984), 5.

20. Schuller, *Early Jazz*, 227.

21. W. C. Handy, *Father of the Blues* (New York: Macmillan, 1951), 144.

22. Bessie Smith, "St. Louis Blues" (1925), *Smithsonian Collection of Classic Jazz*, vol. 1.

23. Albert Murray, *Stomping the Blues* (New York: Da Capo, 1976), 138.

24. Nathan Huggins, ed., *Voices from the Harlem Renaissance* (New York and Oxford: Oxford University Press, 1976), 3.

25. Nathan Huggins, *The Harlem Renaisance* (New York: Oxford University Press, 1971), 5, 72–83.

26. Robert A. Bone, "The Background of the Harlem Renaissance," in Melvin Drummer, ed., *Black History: A Reappraisal* (Garden City, N.Y.: Doubleday, 1968), 420.

27. Handy, *Father of the Blues*, 187–188.

28. Huggins, *Harlem Renaissance*, 10–12; John Graziano, "Black Musical Theatre and the Harlem Renaissance Movement," in Samuel A. Floyd Jr., ed., *Black Music in the Harlem Renaissance: A Collection of Essays* (Westport, Conn.: Greenwood, 1990), 87–89.

29. Lawrence Levine, *The Unpredictable Past: Explorations in American Cultural History* (New York: Oxford University Press, 1993), 174.

30. Huggins, *Voices*, 339–340.

31. Kathy J. Ogren, *The Jazz Revolution: Twenties America and the Meaning of Jazz* (New York: Oxford University Press, 1989), 117.

32. Langston Hughes in Bone, "Background of the Harlem Renaissance," 408.

33. R. D. Darrell, "Black Beauty," *Disques* (June 1932): 153.
34. Duke Ellington, "The Duke Steps Out," *Rhythm* (March 1931): 20.
35. Delores Kirton Cayou, "The Origins of Modern Jazz Dance," *Black Scholar* 1, no. 8 (June 1970); John Miller Chernoff, *African Rhythm and African Sensibility* (Chicago: University of Chicago Press, 1979); James Lincoln Collier, "Jazz," in Kernfeld, *New Grove Dictionary*; Barbara Englebrecht, "Swinging at the Savoy," *Dance Research Journal* 15, no. 2 (1983); Gus Giordano, *Anthology of American Jazz Dance* (Evanston, Ill.: Orion, 1975); Katrina Hazzard-Gordon, *Jookin': The Rise of Social Dance Formations in African-American Culture* (Philadelphia: Temple University Press, 1990); Ben Sidran, *Black Talk* (New York: Da Capo, 1971); Stearns, *Story of Jazz*.
36. Collier, "Jazz"; Lynne Fauley Emery, *Black Dance from 1619 to Today* (Princeton, N.J.: Dance Horizons, 1972); Leroi Jones, *Blues People: The Negro Experience in White America and the Music That Developed from It* (New York: William Morrow, 1963); Stearns and Stearns, *Jazz Dance*; Robert Farris Thompson, *African Art in Motion: Icon and Act* (Berkeley and Los Angeles: University of California Press, 1974).
37. Cayou, "Origins of Modern Jazz Dance"; Constance Valis Hill and Sally Sommer, "Tap Dance," in Jack Salzman, David Lionel Smith, and Cornel West, eds., *Encyclopedia of African-American Culture and History* (New York: Macmillan Library Reference USA, 1996); Stearns and Stearns, *Jazz Dance*, 1968.
38. Will Marion Cook, "Clorindy, the Origin of the Cakewalk," *Theatre Arts* 31 (September 1947): 65.
39. Jones, *Blues People*, 81.
40. Stearns and Stearns, *Jazz Dance*, 117.
41. Carl Van Vechten, "The Negro Theatre" (1920), in *The Dance Writings of Carl Van Vechten* (New York: Dance Horizons, 1974), 36.
42. Virgil Thompson, "Swing Music," *Modern Music* 13 (May 1936): 12.
43. Van Vechten, "Negro Theatre," 38.
44. Ibid.
45. James Welson Johnson, *Black Manhattan* (New York: Knopf, 1930), 174.
46. Van Vechten, "Negro Theatre," 38.
47. Constance Valis Hill, "Jazz Modernism," in Gay Morris, ed., *Moving Words: Re-Writing Dance* (London: Routledge, 1996), 239.
48. Alan Dale in Phyllis Rose, *Jazz Cleopatra* (New York: Doubleday, 1989), 55.
49. John Graziano, interview with author, 30 May 1995.
50. Stearns and Stearns, *Jazz Dance*, 133–134.
51. Rose, *Jazz Cleopatra*, 55.
52. Stearns and Stearns, *Jazz Dance*, 146.
53. Gerald M. Bordman, *American Musical Theatre: A Chronicle* (New York: Oxford University Press, 1978), 382.
54. *New York Sun* in Alan Woll, *Black Musical Theatre* (New York: Da Capo, 1989), 103.
55. Ibid., 110.
56. Stearns and Stearns, *Jazz Dance*, 140.
57. Ibid., 187.

58. Langston Hughes, *Famous Negro Music Makers* (New York: Dodd, Mead, 1957), 49.
59. Mary Austin in Johnson, *Black Manhattan*, 214.
60. Ibid.
61. Alain Locke, *The Negro and His Music* (Washington, D.C.: Associates in Negro Folk Education, 1936), 135.

Chapter Two

1. Leonard Reed, interview by Bruce Goldstein, 1991.
2. Harold Nicholas, interview by author, 1995.
3. Dorothy Nicholas Morrow, interview by author, 29 November 1995.
4. Harold Nicholas, interview by Bruce Goldstein, 1991.
5. Dorothy Nicholas Morrow, interview by author, 1995.
6. Leonard Reed, interview by Goldstein.
7. Harold Nicholas, interview by author, 1996; Fayard Nicholas, interview by author, 1995.
8. Dorothy Nicholas Morrow, interview by author, 1995.
9. James Lincoln Collier, *Duke Ellington* (New York: Oxford University Press, 1987), 85.
10. Dorothy Nicholas Morrow, interview by Bruce Goldstein, 1991.
11. James Lincoln Collier, "Jazz," in Barry Kernfeld, ed., *New Grove Dictionary of Jazz* (New York: St. Martin's Press, 1988), 585.
12. Thomas J. Hennessey, *From Jazz to Swing: African-American Jazz Musicians and Their Music, 1890–1935.* (Detroit: Wayne State University Press, 1994), 36.
13. Collier, "Jazz," 585.
14. Viola Nicholas, interview by Marshall Stearns, 7 Feb. 1965.
15. Fayard Nicholas, interview by author, 1995.
16. Collier, "Jazz," 585.
17. Hennessey, *From Jazz to Swing*, 70.
18. *Winston-Salem Journal*, 4 March 1921, 21.
19. Fayard Nicholas, interview by Bruce Goldstein, 1991.
20. Fayard Nicholas, interview by author, 1995.
21. Marshall Stearns and Jean Stearns, "Vernacular Dance in Musical Comedy," *New York Folklore Quarterly* 22, no. 4 (December 1966): 243; Marshall Stearns and Jean Stearns, *Jazz Dance: The Story of American Vernacular Dance* (New York: Macmillan, 1968), 110.
22. Dorothy Nicholas Morrow, interview by Bruce Goldstein, 1991.
23. Fayard Nicholas, interview by author, 1995.
24. Fayard Nicholas, interview by Marshall Stearns and Jean Stearns, 6 Feb. 1965.
25. Dorothy Nicholas Morrow, interview by Bruce Goldstein, 1991.
26. Dorothy Nicholas Morrow, interview by author, 1995.
27. Leonard Reed, interview by Bruce Goldstein, 1991.
28. Ibid.
29. "Standard to Celebrate 14th Anniversary," *Philadelphia Tribune*, 12 January 1928, 6.
30. Ibid.

31. *Philadelphia Tribune,* 20 September 1928, 6.
32. *New York Amsterdam News,* 18 May 1932, 6–7.
33. Leonard Reed, interview by Bruce Goldstein, 1991.
34. *Philadelphia Tribune,* 5 September 1929, 6; 3 October 1929, 6.
35. *Philadelphia Tribune,* 16 January 1930, 6.
36. Leonard Reed, interview by Bruce Goldstein, 1991.
37. *Philadelphia Tribune,* 27 February 1926, 3; 10 November 1927, 6.
38. *Philadelphia Tribune,* 10 November 1927, 6; 22 July 1929, 6.
39. *Philadelphia Tribune,* 17 November 1927, 6.
40. *Philadelphia Tribune,* 23 January 1928, 6; 21 June 1928, 6.
41. *Philadelphia Tribune,* 19 December 1929, 6.
42. *Philadelphia Tribune,* 7 February 1929, 6; 26 June 1930, 6.
43. Louis Armstrong, "When It's Sleepy Time Down South" (1928), *Satchmo the Great,* Columbia 42259; "Louis Armstrong," James Lincoln Collier in Barry Kernfeld, ed., *New Grove Dictionary of Jazz,* 27–31; Martin Williams, *The Jazz Tradition* (New York: Oxford University Press, 1993), 51–53; Gunther Schuller, *Early Jazz: Its Roots and Musical Development* (New York: Oxford University Press, 1968), 89–133.
44. Leonard Reed in Rusty E. Frank, *Tap! The Greatest Tap Dance Stars and Their Stories, 1900–1955* (New York: William Morrow, 1990), 40.
45. Stearns and Stearns, *Jazz Dance,* 152.
46. *Philadelphia Tribune,* 31 December 1931, 7.
47. Fayard Nicholas, interview by author, 1995.
48. Frank, *Tap,* 66.
49. *Philadelphia Tribune,* 3 March 1927, 6.
50. *Philadelphia Tribune,* 16 July 1931, 6.
51. *Philadelphia Tribune,* 27 February 1926, 7; 30 March 1928, 6; 27 March 1930, 6.
52. *Philadelphia Tribune,* 8 March 1928, 6; 16 February 1928, 3.
53. Leonard Reed in Frank, *Tap,* 45.
54. Fayard Nicholas in *Nicholas Brothers: We Sing and We Dance,* video documentary cowritten and coproduced by Bruce Goldstein and Rigmor Newman, directed by Chris Boulder (New York: Picture Music International, 1992).
55. Fayard Nicholas, interview by author, 1996.
56. Dorothy Nicholas Morrow, interview by author, 1995.
57. Fayard Nicholas, interview by author, 1996.
58. Harold Nicholas, interview by Bruce Goldstein, 1991.
59. Harold Nicholas, interview by author, 1995.
60. Fayard Nicholas, interview by author, 1995.
61. Ibid.
62. *Philadelphia Tribune,* 14 February 1929, 6.
63. *Philadelphia Tribune,* 29 October 1931, 6.
64. Fayard Nicholas in Frank, *Tap,* 67.
65. Fayard Nicholas, interview by Bruce Goldstein, 1991.

Chapter Three

1. *Buck Dance* in *Crazy Feet*, ed. and comp. Ernie Smith (New York: Ernie Smith Black Dance Films, 1990), videocassette.
2. Marshall Stearns and Jean Stearns, *Jazz Dance: The Story of American Vernacular Dance* (New York: Macmillan, 1968), 176.
3. James Barton in the 1929 film *After Seben*, in video compilation *Crazy Feet*.
4. Ernie Smith, interview by author, 15 August 1995.
5. Barbara Englebrecht, "Swinging at the Savoy," *Dance Research Journal* 15, no. 2 (1983): 7.
6. LeGon's recollection of the bus trip with the Nicholases relayed by Rigmor Newman, interview by author, 28 November 1995; Viola Nicholas, interview by Marshall Stearns, 7 Feb. 1965.
7. Jervis Anderson, *This Was Harlem: A Cultural Portrait, 1900–1950* (New York: Farrar Straus Giroux, 1981), 339–341.
8. Alan Pomerance, *Repeal of the Blues: How Black Entertainers Influenced Civil Rights* (Secaucus, N.J.: Citadel, 1988), 6–7; Gerald M. Bordman, *American Musical Theatre: A Chronicle* (New York: Oxford University Press, 1978), 474.
9. James Weldon Johnson, *Black Manhattan* (New York: Knopf, 1930), 3–4.
10. Carl Van Vechten, "Letter to James Weldon Johnson" (25 February 1934), in *The Letters of Carl Van Vechten*, ed. Bruce Kellner (New Haven: Yale University Press, 1987), 134. The theory that the Harlem Renaissance extended past the 1920s and beyond New York has been put forward by a number of cultural historians in the past several decades; for example, Holland Cotter's "A 1920s Flowering That Didn't Disappear," *New York Times* (24 May 1998): 32, 34.
11. Houston A. Baker Jr., *Modernism and the Harlem Renaissance* (Chicago: University of Chicago Press, 1989), 92.
12. Gunther Schuller, *The Swing Era: The Development of Jazz* (New York: Oxford University Press, 1989), 201.
13. J. Bradford Robinson, "Swing," in Barry Kernfeld, ed., *New Grove Dictionary of Jazz* (New York: St. Martin's Press, 1988), 1176; Ted Fox, *Showtime at the Apollo* (reprint, New York: Da Capo, 1983), 82.
14. Stanley Dance, *The World of Swing* (New York: Charles Scribner's Sons, 1974), 404–5.
15. Leonard Reed, interview by Bruce Goldstein, 1991.
16. *New York Amsterdam News*, 6 March 1932, 7.
17. Viola Nicholas, interview by Marshall Stearns, 1965.
18. Fayard Nicholas, interview by author, 1995.
19. Thomas Cripps, *Slow Fade to Black: The Negro in American Film, 1900–1942* (New York: Oxford University Press, 1977), 219.
20. *Variety* in Klaus Stratemann, *Duke Ellington: Day by Day, Film by Film* (Copenhagen: JazzMedia, 1992), 8.
21. Ibid.
22. The Nicholas Brothers filmed the "China Boy" number in *Pie, Pie, Blackbird* with their tap shoes, as was the practice in the first years of talkies, when tap dances were recorded for sound during the filming of the scene. It was not

until around 1933 that new "dubbing" techniques of recording the sound of the taps in a sound studio were developed and brought into common use.

23. *New York Amsterdam News*, 21 September 1932, 8.
24. *New York Amsterdam News*, 20 April 1932, 7.
25. Viola Nicholas, interview by Marshall Stearns, 7 February 1965.
26. Fayard Nicholas, interview by author, 1995.
27. Anderson, *This Was Harlem*, 175.
28. Duke Ellington, *Music Is My Mistress* (Garden City, N.Y.: Doubleday, 1973), 80.
29. Edward Jablonski, *Harold Arlen: Happy with the Blues* (Garden City, N.Y.: Doubleday, 1961), 57.
30. Cab Calloway and Bryant Rollins, *Of Minnie the Moocher and Me* (reprint, New York: Crowell, 1976), 90.
31. Jim Haskins, *The Cotton Club* (New York: Random House, 1977), 30.
32. Jimmy Durante and Jack Kofoed, *Night Clubs* (New York: Knopf, 1931), 11.
33. Calloway, *Of Minnie the Moocher and Me*, 90.
34. Ibid.
35. Schuller, *Swing Era*, 332.
36. Fayard Nicholas, interview by author, 1995.
37. Ibid.
38. A tuxedo, sometimes called a dinner jacket, is a short, black (white in the summer) jacket that is worn with a black tie and regarded as evening wear; a tailcoat is a cutaway black jacket with tails that is worn with a white tie and a top hat, donned for formal occasions. Performers changed and mixed up the elements of evening clothes. Cab Calloway was known for wearing a white tailcoat (and played a white piano); he may have invented that variation.
39. Harold Nicholas in *Nicholas Brothers: We Sing and We Dance*, video documentary cowritten and coproduced by Bruce Goldstein and Rigmor Newman, directed by Chris Boulder (New York: Picture Music International, 1992).
40. *Stoopnocracy*, short subject film directed by Dave Fleisher, Paramount, 1933.
41. Eileen Southern, "Eubie Blake," in Barry Kernfeld, ed., *New Grove Dictionary of Jazz* (New York: St. Martin's Press, 1988), 115.
42. Schuller, *Swing Era*, 330.
43. Calloway, *Of Minnie the Moocher and Me*, 91.
44. Burt Korall, *Drummin' Men: The Heartbeat of Jazz, the Swing Years* (New York: Schirmer, 1990), 307–9.
45. Schuller, *Swing Era*, 48.
46. Fayard Nicholas, interview by author, 1995.
47. Fayard Nicholas, interview by author, 1995, 1996.
48. Spike Hughes, "The Duke—In Person," *Melody Maker* (May 1933): 353, 355.
49. Stratemann, *Duke Ellington*, 60.
50. Harold Nicholas, interview by author, 1995; Fayard Nicholas, interview by Bruce Goldstein, 1991.
51. Harold Nicholas, interview by Bruce Goldstein, 1991; Fayard Nicholas, interview by author, 1995.
52. Dexter in Koral, *Drummin' Men*, 24.

53. Susan Robeson, *The Whole World in His Hands: A Pictorial Biography of Paul Robeson* (Secaucus, N.J.: Citadel, 1981), 68.
54. Harold Nicholas in *Nicholas Brothers: We Sing and We Dance* (see note 39 above).

Chapter Four

1. LeRoi Jones, *Blues People: The Negro Experience in White America and the Music That Developed from It* (New York: William Morrow, 1963), 86.
2. Robert Toll, *Blacking Up: The Minstrel Show in Nineteenth-Century America* (New York: Oxford University Press, 1974), 36.
3. Jones, *Blues People*; Thomas Lawrence Riis, "Black Musical Theatre in New York: 1890–1915," Ph.D. diss., University of Michigan, 1981; Thomas Lawrence Riis, *More than Just a Minstrel Show: The Rise of Black Musical Theatre at the Turn of the Century* (Brooklyn: Institute of Studies in American Music, 1992); Marshall Stearns and Jean Stearns, *Jazz Dance: The Story of American Vernacular Dance* (New York: Macmillan, 1968); Toll, *Blacking Up*.
4. Harold Nicholas, interview by Bruce Goldstein, 1991; Fayard Nicholas, interview by author, 1995.
5. The Nicholases performed and recorded their tap dance in *Kid Millions* prior to filming the actual musical scene. In 1933, new techniques of filming and recording the sound of the taps began to be developed. When the Nicholases filmed the musical scene, they performed without tap shoes, listening to the sounds and rhythms of the taps that had been previously recorded.
6. Houston A. Baker Jr., *Modernism and the Harlem Renaissance* (Chicago: University of Chicago Press, 1989), xiv, 17.
7. Paul Laurence Dunbar, "We Wear the Mask," in Abraham Chapman, ed., *Black Voices: An Anthology of Afro-American Literature* (New York: Mentor, 1981), 355.
8. Marshall Stearns and Jean Stearns, "Frontiers of Humor: American Vernacular Dance," *Southern Folklore Quarterly* (September 1966): 227.
9. Thomas Cripps, *Slow Fade to Black: The Negro in American Film* (New York: Oxford University Press, 1977), 120.
10. Henry Louis Gates, *The Signifying Monkey: A Theory of African-American Literary Criticism* (New York: Oxford University Press, 1988), 25.
11. Harold Nicholas, interview by Bruce Goldstein, 1991.
12. Cripps, *Slow Fade to Black*, x.
13. In *The Big Broadcast of 1936* (1935), *The All-Colored Vaudeville Show* (1935), and *Black Network* (1936), the Nicholases recorded the sounds of their taps simultaneously with the filming of the musical scenes.
14. Baker, *Modernism and the Harlem Renaissance*, xv, 22.
15. Cripps, *Slow Fade to Black*, 112.

Chapter Five

1. John Hammond, *Josephine Baker* (Boston: Little, Brown, 1988), frontispiece.
2. Fayard Nicholas, interview by author, 1993.
3. Fayard Nicholas, interview by Marshall Stearns and Jean Stearns, 6 February 1965.
4. Program, *The Ziegfeld Follies of 1936*, Boston Opera House, 30 December 1935.

5. Harold Nicholas, interview by author, 1993.
6. Program, *The Ziegfeld Follies of 1936*, Forrest Theatre, Philadelphia, 20 January 1936.
7. Lew Leslie in Alan Woll, *Black Musical Theatre: From "Coontown" to "Dreamgirls"* (reprint, New York: Da Capo, 1989), 125.
8. Program, *Blackbirds of 1936*, Gaiety Theatre, London, 9 July 1936.
9. Harold Nicholas, interview by author, 1996.
10. Constance Valis Hill, "Buddy Bradley: The 'Invisible' Man of Broadway Brings Jazz Tap to London," *Proceedings: Society of Dance History Scholars*, Fifteenth Annual Conference, Riverside, Calif. (14–15 Feb. 1992): 77–84.
11. Harold Nicholas in *Nicholas Brothers: We Sing and We Dance*, video documentary cowritten and coproduced by Bruce Goldstein and Rigmor Newman, directed by Chris Boulder (New York: Picture Music International, 1992).
12. Harold Nicholas in ibid.; Harold Nicholas scrapbooks, 1930–36.
13. Leonard Reed, interview by Bruce Goldstein, 1991.
14. Fayard Nicholas, interview by author, 1993.
15. *New York Herald Tribune*, 13 June 1937.
16. Fayard Nicholas, interview by author, 1993.
17. Ibid.
18. Fayard Nicholas, interview by Marshall Stearns and Jean Stearns, 6 February 1965.
19. Cyril Beaumont, *The Diaghilev Ballet in London* (London: Black, 1951), 269.
20. Sally Banes, "Balanchine and Black Dance," *Choreography and Dance* 3, no. 3 (1993): 65.
21. Fred Danieli in Selma Jeanne Cohen, "Celebrating the Four Temperaments— II," *Ballet Review* 15, no. 1 (March 1987): 43.
22. Edwin Denby, "Some Thoughts about Classicism and George Balanchine," in *Dance Writings* (New York: Knopf, 1986), 438.
23. Banes, "Balanchine and Black Dance," 59–60.
24. Ibid.
25. Brenda Dixon Gottschild, *Digging the Africanist Presence in American Performance: Dance and Other Contexts* (Westport, Conn.: Greenwood, 1996), 70.
26. Fayard Nicholas, interview by author, 1993.
27. Dorothy Nicholas Morrow in *Nicholas Brothers: We Sing and We Dance* (see note 11 above).

Chapter Six

1. Bobby Short, interview by Bruce Goldstein, 1991.
2. Robert Toll, *On with the Show: The First Century of Show Business in America* (New York: Oxford University Press, 1976), 99.
3. Alan Woll, *Black Musical Theatre: From "Coontown" to "Dreamgirls"* (reprint, New York: Da Capo, 1989), 119.
4. Robert Toll, *Blacking Up: The Minstrel Show in Nineteenth-Century America* (New York: Oxford University Press, 1974), 68–69.
5. Marshall Stearns and Jean Stearns, *Jazz Dance: The Story of American Vernacular Dance* (New York: Macmillan, 1968), 286.

6. Ibid., 295.

7. Bobby Short, interview by Bruce Goldstein, 1991.

8. Max Roach, interview by Bruce Goldstein, 1991.

9. Stearns and Stearns, *Jazz Dance*, 301.

10. Leonard Reed, interview by Bruce Goldstein, 1991.

11. Fayard Nicholas, interview by author, 1993.

12. Leonard Reed, interview by Bruce Goldstein, 1991.

13. Ibid.

14. *Variety*, 24 March 1937.

15. Leonard Reed, interview by Bruce Goldstein, 1991.

16. Jim Haskins, *The Cotton Club* (New York: Random House, 1977), 138.

17. Fayard Nicholas, interview by author, 1995.

18. Haskins, *Cotton Club*, 133.

19. Dorothy Dandridge and Earl Conrad, *Everything and Nothing: The Dorothy Dandridge Tragedy* (New York: Abelard-Schuman, 1970), 43.

20. Marion Coles, interview by author, 13 June 1996.

21. Ted Fox, *Showtime at the Apollo* (reprint, New York: Da Capo, 1993), 74.

22. Leonard Reed, interview by Bruce Goldstein, 1991.

23. LeRoi Jones, *Blues People: The Negro Experience in White America and the Music That Developed from It* (New York: William Morrow, 1963), 27; Stearns and Stearns, *Jazz Dance*, 322–23; Jervis Anderson, *This Was Harlem: A Cultural Portrait*, 1900–1950 (New York: Farrar Straus, Giroux, 1981), 169; Gunther Schuller, *Early Jazz: Its Roots and Musical Development* (New York: Oxford University Press, 1968), 5.

24. Charles "Honi" Coles, interview by author, 29 March 1991.

25. Leonard Reed, interview by Bruce Goldstein, 1991.

26. Ibid.

27. Stearns and Stearns, *Jazz Dance*, 276.

28. Nicholas home movies, 1938–40; Stearns and Stearns, *Jazz Dance*, 278.

29. Fayard Nicholas, interview by author, 1993.

30. *Reflections with the Nicholas Brothers*, television documentary, WGBH-TV, Boston, 15 June 1996.

31. Max Roach, Bobby Short, and Dorothy Nicholas Morrow, interviews by Bruce Goldstein, 1991; Dorothy Nicholas Morrow, interview by author, 1995.

Chapter Seven

1. J. Bradford Robinson, "Swing," in Barry Kernfeld, ed., *New Grove Dictionary of Jazz* (New York: St. Martin's Press, 1988), 1176.

2. Stanley Dance, *The World of Swing* (New York: Charles Scribner's Sons, 1974), 197.

3. William S. Dutton, "We've Got Rhythm," *American Magazine* (19 March 1935): 26.

4. David W. Stowe, *Swing Changes: Big Band Jazz in New Deal America* (Cambridge: Harvard University Press, 1994), 1–3.

5. Glenn Miller in ibid., 4.

6. Ibid., 10; Robinson, "Swing," 1176; Gunther Schuller, *Early Jazz: Its Roots and Musical Development* (New York: Oxford University Press, 1968); Gunther Schuller, *The Swing Era: The Development of Jazz* (New York: Oxford University Press, 1989); Marshall Stearns, *The Story of Jazz* (New York: Oxford University Press, 1956).

7. Schuller, *Swing Era*, 223–24; Benny Goodman and Irving Kolodin, *The Kingdom of Swing* (New York: Frederick Ungar, 1939), 11; Frank Froeba in "Fats Waller Demonstrates Swing, Even Defines It," *Metronome* 52 (February 1936): 19.

8. Cab Calloway, "The New Cab Calloway's Hepster's Dictionary," in *Of Minnie the Moocher and Me* (New York: Crowell, 1976), 251–74.

9. Norma Miller in *Dancing*, video documentary directed by Rhoda Grauer, British Broadcasting Company, 1993.

10. Schuller, *Swing Era*, 676.

11. Imperial Society of Teachers of Dancing, *The Revised Technique of Latin American Dancing* (London: Imperial Society, 1971), 3.

12. Leonard Reed, interview by Bruce Goldstein, 1991.

13. Frank Rose, *The Agency: William Morris and the Hidden History of Show Business* (New York: Harper Collins, 1995), 76–77.

14. Ben M. Hall, *The Best Remaining Seats: The Story of the Golden Age of the Movie Palace* (New York: Bramhall House, 1957), 128.

15. Rex Stewart, *Jazz Masters of the* 30s (New York: Da Capo, 1972), 84.

16. Burt Korall, *Drummin' Men: The Heartbeat of Jazz, the Swing Years* (New York: Schirmer, 1990), 123.

17. Joe Newman in Korall, *Drummin' Men*, 152.

18. Fayard Nicholas, interview by author, 1996.

19. Korall, *Drummin' Men*, 249–304.

20. Fayard Nicholas, interview by author, 1995.

21. *Carmen Miranda: Bananas Is My Business,* documentary film, International Cinema, 1994.

22. Even though the film is silent, the words to "Mama Yo Quiero" are distinctly mouthed; this was later confirmed by Harold Nicholas.

23. Nick Castle, *How to Tap Dance* (Hollywood: By the author, 1948), 11–18.

24. The tap sounds and rhythms in all of the Nicholas Brothers' films for Twentieth Century-Fox were dubbed on a sound stage after the filming of the musical scene. Some Hollywood dancers allowed other (and often more experienced) tap dancers to record their tap sounds, but Fayard and Harold conceived, staged, and dubbed their own tap dances.

25. Harold Nicholas in *Nicholas Brothers: We Sing and We Dance*, video documentary cowritten and coproduced by Bruce Goldstein and Rigmor Newman, directed by Chris Boulder (New York: Picture Music International, 1992).

26. *Reflections with the Nicholas Brothers*, television documentary, WGBH-TV, Boston, 15 June 1996.

27. Donald Bogle, *Blacks in American Film and Television: An Illustrated Encyclopedia* (New York: Garland, 1988), 205–6.

28. Thomas Cripps, *Making Movies Black: The Hollywood Message Movie from World War II to the Civil Rights Era* (New York: Oxford University Press, 1993), 85.

29. Rusty E. Frank, *Tap! The Greatest Tap Dance Stars and Their Stories,* 1900–1955 (New York: William Morrow, 1990).

30. Leonard Reed, interview by Bruce Goldstein, 1991.

Chapter Eight

1. Fayard Nicholas, interview by author, 1993; Rusty E. Frank, *Tap! The Greatest Tap Dance Stars and Their Stories,* 1900–1955 (New York: William Morrow, 1990), 72; *Nicholas Brothers: We Sing and We Dance,* video documentary cowritten and coproduced by Bruce Goldstein and Rigmore Newman, directed by Chris Boulder (New York: Picture Music International, 1992); Fayard and Harold Nicholas, interview by author, 1996.

2. A number of dance critics and historians have observed that the Nicholas Brothers looked classically trained. Lynn Garafola, for example, in requesting that I conduct a public interview with Fayard and Harold Nicholas for the "Rethinking the Balanchine Legacy: Balanchine, Jazz, and Popular Dance" conference at the New York Public Library at Lincoln Center in 1993, suggested that I ask the brothers to trace the influence of ballet on their style; and David Vaughan, upon commissioning me to write an entry on the Nicholas Brothers for the *International Encyclopedia of Dance* (Oxford University Press, 1996), was curious to know about the classical ballet training the Nicholases had received.

3. Geri (Pate Nicholas) Branton, interview by Bruce Goldstein, 1991.

4. Horst Koegler, ed., *The Concise Oxford Dictionary of Ballet* (London: Oxford University Press, 1982), 32.

5. Adrian Stokes, "The Classic Ballet," in Roger Copeland and Marshall Cohen, eds., *What Is Dance?* (New York: Oxford University Press, 1983), 244.

6. A. K. Volinsky, "The Vertical: The Fundamental Principle of Classic Dance," in ibid., 255.

7. Castile-Blaze in Alistair Macauley, "Notes on Dance Classicism," *Dance Theatre Journal* 5, no. 2 (June 1987): 7.

8. André Levinson, "The Spirit of the Classic Dance," in *André Levinson on Dance: Writings from Paris in the Twenties,* ed. and trans. Joan Acocella and Lynn Garofola (Hanover and London: Wesleyan University Press, 1991), 45.

9. Stokes, "Classical Ballet," 244.

10. Cage in Macauley, "Notes on Dance Classicism," 36.

11. Lincoln Kirstein, "Classic Ballet: Aria of the Aerial," in Copeland and Cohen, *What Is Dance?,* 239.

12. *Reflections with the Nicholas Brothers,* television documentary, WGBH-TV, Boston, 15 June 1996.

13. Brenda Dixon Gottschild, *Digging the Africanist Presence in American Performance: Dance and Other Contexts* (Westport, Conn.: Greenwood, 1996), xiv.

14. Kirstein, "Aria of the Aerial," 243.

15. Adele Astaire in Cecil Beaton, *The Wandering Years, Diaries:* 1922–1939 (Boston: Little, Brown, 1961), 215–16; Brenda Dixon-Stowell, "Dancing in the Dark: The Life and Times of Margot Webb in Aframerican Vaudeville of the Swing Era," Ph.D. diss., New York University, 1981, 2.

16. John Mueller, *Astaire Dancing: The Musical Films* (New York: Knopf, 1985), 3.

17. Honi Coles, interview by author, 29 March 1991; Coles in David Hinckley, "A Honey of a Hoofer," *New York Sunday News Magazine* (7 August 1983): 5.
18. Fayard Nicholas, interview by author, 1995; Geri (Pate Nicholas) Branton, interview by Bruce Goldstein, 1991.
19. Alain Locke, *The Negro and His Music* (Washington, D.C.: Associates in Negro Folk Education, 1936), 96.
20. Benny Goodman and Irving Kolodin, *The Kingdom of Swing* (New York: Stackpole Sons, 1939), 182.
21. Gama Gilbert, "Higher Soars the Swing Fever," *New York Times Magazine* (14 August 1938): 19.
22. Gottchild, *Digging the Africanist Presence*, 71.
23. Macauley, "Notes on Dance Classicism," 39.
24. Lillian Moore, *Echoes of American Ballet*, ed. Ivor Guest (New York: Dance Horizons, 1976).
25. Kirstein, "Aria of the Aerial," 243.
26. Houston A. Baker Jr., *Modernism and the Harlem Renaissance* (Chicago: University of Chicago Press, 1989), xiv–xviii, 15–17, 49–52.
27. Gottschild, *Digging the Africanist Prescence*, 75.
28. Marshall Stearns, *Jazz Dance* (New York: Macmillan, 1968), 140–41.
29. Sally Sommer, interview by author, 1 February 1997; David Michael Levin, "Balanchine's Formalism," in Copeland and Cohen, *What Is Dance?*, 124.
30. Nathan Huggins, ed., *Voices from the Harlem Renaissance* (New York: Oxford University Press, 1976), 3.

Chapter Nine

1. Donald Bogle, *Blacks in American Film and Television: An Illustrated Encyclopedia* (New York: Garland, 1988), 205.
2. William Chafe, *The Unfinished Journey: America since World War II*, 3d ed. (New York: Oxford University Press, 1995); William O'Neil, *Coming Apart: An Informal History of America in the 1960s* (Chicago: Quadrangle, 1971).
3. Thomas Cripps, *Making Movies Black: The Hollywood Message Movie from World War II to the Civil Rights Era* (New York: Oxford University Press, 1993), 83.
4. Walter White in Cripps, *Making Movies Black*, 85.
5. Dorothy Nicholas Morrow in *Nicholas Brothers: We Sing and We Dance*, video documentary cowritten and coproduced by Bruce Goldstein and Rigmor Newman, directed by Chris Boulder (New York: Picture Music International, 1992).
6. James Weldon Johnson, *Black Manhattan* (New York: Knopf, 1930), 93.
7. Thomas DeFrantz, "Simmering Passivity: The Black Male Dancer on the Concert Stage," in Gay Morris, ed., *Moving Words:Re-Writing Dance* (London and New York: Routledge, 1996), 108.
8. Harold Nicholas, interview by author, 1996; Fayard Nicholas, interview by author, 1997.
9. Harold Nicholas, interview by author, 1996.
10. Geri (Pate Nicholas) Branton, interview by Bruce Goldstein, 1991.
11. Ibid.
12. Ibid.

13. Max Roach in Ira Gitler, *Swing to Bop: An Oral History of the Transition in Jazz in the 1940s* (New York: Oxford University Press, 1985), 77.

14. Peter Watrous, "The Man Who Defined Modern Jazz," *New York Times*, 13 November 1988, H26.

15. James Lincoln Collier, *The Reception of Jazz in America* (City University of New York: Institute for Studies in American Music, 1988), 340.

16. Ralph Ellison, *Shadow and Act* (New York: Random House, 1964), 201.

17. Lennie Tristano in Marshall Stearns and Jean Stearns, *Jazz Dance: The Story of American Vernacular Dance* (New York: Macmillan, 1968), 164.

18. David W. Stowe, *Swing Changes: Big Band Jazz in New Deal America* (Cambridge and London: Harvard University Press, 1994), 11.

19. George T. Simon, *Simon Says: The Sights and Sounds of the Swing Era, 1935–1955* (New York: Arlington House, 1971), 18.

20. *The Spirit Moves: Volume I Part II (1950–1955)*, video documentary directed by Mura Dehn, New York, 1955.

21. Max Roach, interview by Bruce Goldstein, 1991.

22. Fayard Nicholas, interview by author, 1995.

23. Dizzy Gillespie with Al Fraser, *To Be, or Not ... to Bop* (Garden City, N.Y.: Doubleday, 1979), 223.

24. Fayard Nicholas, interview by author, 1995.

25. Max Roach, interview by Bruce Goldstein; Walter Fuller in Gillespie, *To Be*, 224; Dizzy Gillespie in ibid., 223; Fayard Nicholas in ibid., 229–30.

26. Fayard Nicholas in ibid., 229.

27. Max Roach, interview by Bruce Goldstein, 1991.

28. Fayard Nicholas, interview by author, 1995.

29. Ibid.

30. Fayard Nicholas in Gillespie, *To Be*, 227–28.

31. Max Roach, interview by Bruce Goldstein, 1991.

32. Ibid.

33. Honi Coles in Tom Russell, "Bippidy-Boom-Shaga-Daga," *Conoisseur* (November 1983): 57.

34. Fayard Nicholas, interview by author, 1995.

35. Gerald M. Bordman, *American Musical Theatre: A Chronicle* (New York: Oxford University Press, 1978), 534.

36. *Newark Evening News* 23 May 1946; program, *St. Louis Woman*, Martin Beck Theatre, New York, 30 March 1946.

37. Bordman, *American Musical Theatre*, 551.

38. Harold Nicholas, interview by author, 1997.

39. Fayard Nicholas, interview by author, 1995.

40. *Nicholas Brothers: We Sing and We Dance* (see note 5 above).

41. Fayard Nicholas, interview by author, 1995.

42. Geri (Pate Nicholas) Branton, interview by Bruce Goldstein, 1991.

43. Harold Nicholas, interview by Bruce Goldstein, 1991.

44. Chafe, *Unfinished Journey*, 111–28; *Encyclopedia Britannica*, 912B.

45. *All-Star Revue: The Ed Wynn Show*, NBC-TV, 10 November 1951, television broadcast.

46. *The Bob Hope Christmas Show*, NBC-TV, 21 December 1951, television broadcast.
47. *Colgate Comedy Hour*, NBC-TV, 14 December 1952, television broadcast.
48. Dorothy Nicholas Morrow, interview by Bruce Goldstein, 1991.

Chapter Ten

1. *Hollywood Palace*, WABC-TV, 31 July 1964, television broadcast.
2. Harold Nicholas, interview by Bruce Goldstein, Picture Music International.
3. Harold Nicholas, interview by author, 1997; Doris G. Worsham, "Dancer's Talents Tapped for New Musical," *San Francisco Tribune*, 13 February 1981, 1.
4. Dorothy Nicholas Morrow, interview by author, 1995; interview by Goldstein, 1991.
5. Charles Honi Coles, interview by author, 29 March 1991.
6. Marshall Stearns, "Is Jazz Dance Hopelessly Square?" *Dance Magazine* (June 1959): 30.
7. Jack Cole, "It's Gone Silly!," *Dance Magazine* (December 1963): 35.
8. Billie Mahoney, "Did Tap Ever Really Die?" *International Tap Association Newsletter* (November-December 1996): 4–6.
9. Leticia Jay, "The Wonderful Old-Time Hoofers at Newport," *Dance Magazine* (September 1963): 18.
10. Harold Nicholas, interview by author, 1997; Worsham, "Dancer's Talents Tapped for New Musical" 9.
11. Harriet Jackson, "American Dancer, Negro," *Dance Magazine* (September 1966): 42.
12. *Hollywood Palace*, ABC-TV, 27 February 1965, television broadcast.
13. *Hollywood Palace*, ABC-TV, 14 November 1964, television broadcast.
14. Mahoney, "Did Tap Ever Really Die?" 7.
15. Patrick O'Connor, "Tap Happening," *Dance Magazine* (August 1969): 41.
16. Dorothy Wassermann, "A Short History of Jazz Tap Festivals," *Attitude: The Dancers' Magazine* 7, no. 1 (September 1990): 21.
17. Jane Goldberg, "It's All in the Feet," *Quincy* (Mass.) *Patriot Ledger*, 24 April 1974, 48.
18. Unidentified television show, circa 1972, Harold Nicholas Archive.
19. Susan Reiter, "Steps in Time: A Tap Dance Festival," *Dance News* (March 1980): 10.
20. Sally Sommer, "Hearing Dance, Watching Film," *Dancescope* 14, no. 3 (1980): 60.
21. Philip Elwood, "'Savoy' Defeats a Showy Potential," *San Francisco Examiner*, 12 February 1981, E7.
22. *Salute to Duke*, PBS-TV, 1981, television broadcast.
23. *Il Paradiso*, RAI-TV, Rome, 1983, television broadcast.
24. *San Francisco Tribune*, 5 August 1985; *Tap Dance Kid* TG14-TV, San Francisco, 1985, television broadcast.
25. Fayard Nicholas, interview by author, 1997.
26. Rigmor Newman, unpublished script, "Nicholas Brothers Act," 1985, Harold Nicholas Archive.

27. Alan Pomerance, *Repeal of the Blues: How Black Entertainers Influenced Civil Rights* (Secaucus, N.J.: Citadel, 1988), 98.

Conclusion

1. Constance Valis Hill, "Black and Blue." *Attitude: The Dancer's Magazine* 5, no. 3 (Spring 1989): 5.
2. Ralph Ellison, *Shadow and Act* (New York: Random House, 1964), 207.
3. Max Roach, interview by Bruce Goldstein, 1991.
4. Margo Jefferson, "An Era for Movement," *Dance Ink* (September 1993): 20.
5. Alan Pomerance, *Repeal of the Blues: How Black Entertainers Influenced Civil Rights* (Secaucus, N.J.: Citadel, 1988), 98.
6. Robert Bly, *Iron John: A Book about Men* (Reading, Mass.: Addison-Wesley, 1990), n.p.
7. Maurice Hines, interview by Bruce Goldstein, 1991.
8. Jefferson, "Era for Movement," 23.
9. Maurice Hines, interview by Bruce Goldstein, 1991.
10. Ibid.
11. Gregory Hines, interview by Bruce Goldstein. This same story was more or less repeated by Gregory Hines at the 1995 Dance Magazine Awards at the Asia House in New York City.
12. Gregory Hines, interview by Bruce Goldstein, 1991.
13. *Nicholas Brothers: We Sing and We Dance*, video documentary cowritten and coproduced by Bruce Goldstein and Rigmor Newman, directed by Chris Boulder (New York: Picture Music International, 1992).
14. Jimmy Slyde, "A Tribute to the Nicholas Brothers," Carnegie Hall, 6 April 1996. Persons paying tribute to the Nicholas Brothers included Bill Cosby, Clark Terry, Lena Horne, Christian McBride, Kevin Mahogany, Ben Vereen, Maurice Hines, and Savion Glover.
15. Ibid.
16. Ibid.
17. Ibid.
18. Alex Witchel, "Black and Blues Brothers," *New York Magazine* (2 January 1989): 16.

Glossary

Accent   The stress or emphasis on a beat or sound.

Attitude   In ballet, the position of the body supported on one leg, with the other lifted behind, the knee bent at a ninety-degree angle higher than the foot.

Ball Change   Shifting the weight on the balls of the feet from one foot to the other.

Bar   The unit of music contained between two bar lines, also referred to as a measure.

Barrel Turn   A complete turn of the body, with torso and legs leaning into a forward diagonal position.

Beat   The regular, recurring, and periodically accented pulse that constitutes the unit of measurement in all measured music.

Bells   The clicking together of the toes or heels.

Boogie-Woogie   A percussive style of piano blues characterized by the use of blue chordal progressions combined with steady, repetitive, left-hand bass figures.

Break   In tap dance, a two-measure movement following a six-measure movement that ends or punctuates the eight-measure phrase; in music, a brief solo passage usually lasting one or two bars, and frequently appearing at the end of a phrase, particularly the last phrase in a structural unit.

Breakaway   In the Lindy-Hop, a move in which dancers spin away from each other to improvise a dance break.

Breakdown   A jigging competition performed by slaves on the plantation, which developed into stomping, competitive solos by riverboatsmen on the frontier.

Bridge   Normally the third set of eight measures of a thirty-two-measure chorus; the formal transition in a passage of music that provides a contrast with the opening section.

Brush   The striking of the ball of the foot in any one direction.

Buck Dancing An early, flat-footed stepping style that works the foot close to the ground with shuffling and sliding steps, the movement mostly from the hips down.

Buck-and-Wing An early style of clog dancing combining the buck (a simple time step) with a wing (a simple hop), with one foot flung out to the side).

Cakewalk A prancing or strutting dance originated by plantation slaves to imitate and satirize the manners of the white master.

Charleston The most popular social dance of the 1920s, danced to propulsive swing rhythms; one of its many steps consisted of crossing and swinging one leg in front of and behind the other.

Chassé In ballet, a gliding step in which one foot "chases" the other out of its position.

Chug The forced forward movement of the ball of the foot sliding along the floor, followed by the drop of the heel.

Clog A dance originating in the Lakeland region of England and performed in wooden-soled shoes; in America, it blended with the jig and evolved into the soft shoe, or song-and-dance.

Cooch A sinuous dance comprising eccentric moves, gyrations, and shakes of the body, usually performed by a woman.

Coupe Jeté In ballet, a springing step from the position of *sur le coup de pied*.

Cramproll A rippling tap step in which toes and heels are dropped in a specific rhythmic pattern.

Crossover Crossing one foot over or in front of the other.

Cubanola A Latin-tinged tap rhythm (that can be danced to the accompaniment of a 3/2 clave rhythm) consisting of a side-traveling shuffle, hop, and ball-change.

Dig The forced striking of the heel into the floor in any direction.

Double Time Double the tempo first established in the routine.

Draw The drawing in of the free foot on the floor with a sliding motion.

Eccentric Highly individual and inventive moves that follow no set pattern.

Essence A basic movement associated with softshoe dancing, performed in medium 4/4 time signature.

Falling Off a Log A twisting movement consisting of shuffles and the alternate crossing and recrossing of one foot over the other, the body leaning sideways.

Fill A short harmonic, rhythmic, or melodic figure played at points of inactivity or stasis.

Flap In tap dancing, a forward brush-and-step motion made with the ball of the foot; may be executed in any direction, but normally forward or backward.

Flat-foot Striking, rubbing, or sliding the entire foot on the floor.

Four-square In music, when all four main beats of a bar in 4/4 time are evenly accented.

Fox-trot A ballroom dance made popular in the 1920s, based on the Two-Step, but danced in 4/4 time to a broken rhythm of "slow, slow, quick-quick (two quick counts equaling one slow count).

Grapevine A side-traveling ballroom dance step, adapted to tap and musical theatre dancing, in which the trailing foot crosses behind and in front of the leading foot.

Half Time Half the tempo first established in a routine.

Heel Drop The forced dropping of the heel into the floor with the weight placed on the ball of the foot.

Hoofer A tap dancer who emphasizes movements from the waist down and concentrates on the percussive intricacies of the feet.

Hoofing A word for tap dancing prevalent in the 1920s.

Hop A spring into the air from one foot, landing on the same foot with no transfer of weight.

Jeté In ballet, a jump from one leg to the other in which the working, or moving, leg moves forward, sideways, or backward.

Jig A lively rhythm in 6/8 time, prevalent in northern England and associated with Ireland, that accompanies a distinct form of rhythmic stepping.

Jive Described as "Harlemese speech" by Cab Calloway; a special language that developed from the culture of swing music and dance in the 1930s and 1940s.

Jump A leap from one foot to the other foot in any direction.

Kazotsky Kick A Russian folk-style flash step, in which the dancer kicks out the legs in rapid alternation from a squatting position.

Legomania   Highly individual and unusual leg movements in jazz dancing, such as rubber-legging.

Lindy Hop   A syncopated two-step with the accent on the offbeat.

Maxie Ford   A leaping sideways step consisting of a shuffle, pullback, and toe-tip.

Measure   The group of beats made by the regular recurrence of the primary, or heavy, accents, the position of which is marked on the staff by bars.

Offbeat   The unaccented beat of a measure.

One-Step   A ragtime ballroom dance in 2/4 time, introduced in the 1910s by Vernon and Irene Castle, with a step executed simply on the beat.

Over the Top   A virtuosic tap step, usually in the finale of a routine, consisting of bending forward, springing up, and bringing each leg in turn around from the back and across the front of the other leg.

Paddle and Roll   A close-to-the-floor style of tap dancing alternating the heel and toe in a rhythm similar to the single-and-double-stroke roll of the drum.

Pas de Deux   A duet, or dance for two.

Pickup   In tap dance, a side-brushing hopping step that produces two sounds.

Pigeon Wing   A scraping movement from one foot to another, sometimes accompanied by the fluttering arm and hand motions of a bird.

Plié   In ballet, the bending of the legs.

Port de Bras   In ballet, the carriage and movement of the arms through various positions.

Pullback   In tap dance, a back-brushing hopping step that produces two sounds.

Renversé Turn   The bending of the body during a turn, from the waist, sideways and backward, with the head following the movement of the body.

Rhythm   In music, the pattern of regular or irregular pulses caused by the duration and stress of the beat.

Riff   In tap dance, a rippling step that combines a brush on the ball of the foot with a scuff of the heel.

Roll   A series of rapid, consecutive taps.

Rond de Jambe   In ballet, a circular movement of the leg, performed *a terre* (on the floor) or *en l'air* (in the air).

Routine   A complete dance, consisting of two or more choruses of music.

Rub   A percussive step that presses the foot into the floor in a continuous motion, sustaining or retarding the beat.

Scat   A technique of jazz singing in which percussive patterns are translated into vocal lines by assigning syllables to characteristic rhythms.

Scissors   Sliding the legs together scissorlike, from second to first position.

Seconde, à la   In ballet, having the arms or legs spread wide apart, in second position.

Shim Sham Shimmy   Created in the 1920s by Leonard Reed and Willie Bryant and also called "Goofus," a one-chorus routine to a thirty-two-bar tune, with eight bars each of the Double Shuffle, Crossover, Tack-Annie, and Falling Off a Log.

Shuffle   A front brush followed by a back brush; can be executed to the front, side, or back.

Sissonne   In ballet, a scissorlike movement of the legs.

Slide   Pushing the foot along the floor smoothly and continuously in any direction.

Softshoe   Or Song-and-Dance, an early dance on the minstrel stage combining clog and shuffle techniques, performed in slow 4/4 time; metal taps were later affixed to the "soft" shoe.

Stomp   Striking the floor with the entire foot.

Stop Time   The suspension of the normal flow of notes by musicians who instead repeat in rhythmic unison a chord every four or eight counts to keep the rhythm going; during this time, the tap dancer is featured without having to compete with the music.

Stride   A solo piano style associated with ragtime and the stride Harlem piano school, marked by fast tempos, the full use of the piano's range, and a wide array of pianistic devices, including those from the classical repertory.

Strut   A cocky stride created by plantation slaves, presumably to imitate and exaggerate the authoritative gait of the white master.

Sur le Coup de Pied   A ballet step in which one foot is placed on the ankle of the other foot.

Suzie-Q   A side-traveling jazz step popular in the 1930s in which the hands are clasped in front of the body as one foot slides over and across the other, which in turn slides to the side.

Syncopation   A temporary displacing or shifting of the regular metrical accent.

Tack-Annie   An up-and-back shuffle comprising one part of the Shim Sham Shimmy.

Tempo   The rate of speed at which a dance is executed, sometimes referred to as the metronome beat.

Time Step   An eight-measure movement placed at the beginning of a routine, used on the vaudeville stage and in tap dance as a means of setting the tempo of the routine.

Trenches   A stationary running step consisting of long, backward slides, alternating one foot with the other, with the body bent forward at the waist and arms swinging 180 degrees.

Two-Step   A ragtime dance in 2/4 time that formed the basis of the Fox-trot and consisted of the even rhythm of "quick-quick, slow" (two quick counts equal to one slow count).

Vamp   A short passage, simple in rhythm, normally played in preparation for the entrance of the soloist and repeated until the soloist is ready to perform.

Variation   The improvised reforming of a step or rhythmic phrase that mirrors, references, or departs entirely from the original to create something new.

Walkaround   The grand finale in the minstrel show in which performers promenade, prance, and strut in a circle, improvising on variations of the walking step while showing off their own specialties.

Walk-off   An exiting step from the vaudeville stage in which two or more dancers, one behind the other and pressed together, stride step-for-step off the stage.

Wing   In tap dance, a virtuosic step in which one foot executes a step rhythm on the floor while the other creates a circular movement in the air, the two opposing impulses in balance, achieving the illusion of flying.

Bibliography

Books, Articles, and Reviews

Adamczyk, Alice J. *Black Dance: An Annotated Bibliography*. New York: Garland, 1989.

"American Juvenile Star Shows English Theatregoers How Real Dancing Is Done." *Chicago Defender*, 15 August 1936.

Anderson, Jack. "From Jazz Tap Ensemble, a Happy-Go-Lucky Style." *New York Times*, 2 April 1988.

Anderson, Jervis. *This Was Harlem: A Cultural Portrait, 1900–1950*. New York: Farrar Straus Giroux, 1981.

Armstead-Johnson, Helen. "Blacks in Vaudeville: Broadway and Beyond." In *American Popular Entertainment: Papers and Proceedings of the Conference on American Popular Entertainment*, ed. Myron Matlaw, 77–86. Westport, Conn.: Greenwood, 1979.

Asante, K. W. *Commonalities in African Dance: An Aesthetic Foundation*. Trenton, N.J.: Africa World Press, 1985.

Astaire, Fred. *Steps in Time*. New York: Harper & Brothers, 1959.

Atkinson, Brooks. "Fannie Brice in the 1936 Edition of the 'Follies' under Shubert Management." *New York Times*, 31 June 1936.

Badger, Reid. *A Life in Ragtime: A Biography of James Reese Europe*. New York: Oxford University Press, 1995.

Baker, Houston A., Jr. *Blues, Ideology, and Afro-American Literature: A Vernacular Theory*. Chicago: University of Chicago Press, 1984.

———. *Modernism and the Harlem Renaissance*. Chicago: University of Chicago Press, 1989.

Balliett, Whitney. *Such Sweet Thunder*. New York: Bobbs-Merrill, 1966.

Banes, Sally. "Balanchine and Black Dance." *Choreography and Dance* 3, no. 3 (1993): 59–77.

Barnes, Clive. "Gershwin Gala: Up & Down." *New York Post*, 12 March 1987.

Barnes, Howard. "Without Diamond Rings." *New York Herald Tribune*, 1 April 1946.

Beaton, Cecil. *The Wandering Years, Diaries: 1922–1939*. Boston: Little, Brown, 1961.

Beaumont, Cyril. *The Diaghilev Ballet in London*. London: Black, 1951.

Berlin, Edward A. *Ragtime: A Musical and Cultural History*. Berkeley: University of California Press, 1980.

"Big Broadcast of 1936." *New York Times*, 19 September 1935.

Bilman, Larry. *Film Choreographers and Dance Directors: An Illustrated Biographical Encyclopedia, with a History and Filmographies, 1893–1995*. Jefferson, N.C., and London: McFarland, 1997.

"Blackbirds of 1936 at the Lyceum." *Play Pictorial* (London) 69, no. 411 (September 1936): 1–16.

Blake, Eubie, and Lawrence Carter. *Keys of Memory*. Detroit: Balamp, 1979.

Blum, Martin. "Black Music: Pathmaker of the Harlem Renaissance." *Missouri Journal of Research in Music Education* 3, no. 3 (1974): 72–79.

Bly, Robert. *Iron John: A Book about Men*. Reading, Mass.: Addison-Wesley, 1990.

Bogle, Donald. *Blacks in American Film and Television: An Illustrated Encyclopedia*. New York and London: Garland, 1988.

——. *Dorothy Dandridge*. New York: Boulevard, 1997.

——. *Toms, Coons, Mulattoes, Mammies, and Bucks: An Interpretive History of Blacks in American Films*. New York: Viking, 1973.

Bone, Robert A. "The Background of the Harlem Renaissance." In *Black History: A Reappraisal*, ed. Melvin Drummer, 408–21. Garden City, N.Y.: Doubleday, 1968.

Bontemps, Arna. *The Harlem Renaissance Remembered*. New York: Dodd, Mead, 1972.

Bordman, Gerald M. *American Musical Theatre: A Chronicle*. New York: Oxford University Press, 1978.

Breton, Marcela, ed. *Hot and Cool: Jazz Short Stories*. New York: Plume (Penguin), 1990.

Browning, Barbara. *Samba: Resistance in Motion*. Bloomington and Indianapolis: Indiana University Press, 1995.

Buckman, Peter. *Let's Dance*. New York and London: Paddington, 1978.

Burgett, Paul. "Vindication as a Thematic Principle in the Writings of Alain Locke on the Music of Black Americans." In *Black Music in the Harlem Renaissance*, ed. Samuel A. Floyd Jr., 29–40. Westport, Conn.: Greenwood, 1990.

Bushell, Garvin. *Jazz from the Beginning*. Ann Arbor: University of Michigan Press, 1988.

Calloway, Cab, and Bryant Rollins. *Of Minnie the Moocher and Me*. New York: Crowell, 1976.

——. "The New Cab Calloway Hepster's Dictionary, 1944 Edition." In Cab Calloway and Bryant Rollins, *Of Minnie the Moocher and Me*, 251–74. New York: Crowell, 1976.

Caspary, Vera. "The Black, Black Bottom of the Swanee River." *Dance* (March 1927): 15–16.

Castle, Irene. *Castles in the Air*. New York: Doubleday, 1958; reprint, New York: Da Capo, 1980.

Castle, Nick. *How to Tap Dance*. Hollywood, Calif.: By the author, 1948.

Cayou, Delores Kirton. "The Origins of Modern Jazz Dance." *Black Scholar* 1, no. 8 (June 1970): 26–30.

Chafe, William H. *The Unfinished Journey: America since World War II*. 3d ed. New York: Oxford University Press, 1995.

Chapman, John. "'St. Louis Woman' a Tuneful, Gay and Well-Staged Negro Musical." *New York Daily News*, 1 April 1946.

Charters, Ann. *Nobody: The Story of Bert Williams*. New York and London: Macmillan, 1970.

Charters, Samuel B., and Leonard Kunstadt. *Jazz: A History of the New York Scene*. Reprint, New York: Da Capo, 1962.

Chernoff, John Miller. *African Rhythm and African Sensibility*. Chicago: University of Chicago Press, 1979.

Cohen, Selma Jeanne. "Celebrating the Four Temperaments—II." *Ballet Review* 15, no. 1 (March 1987): 38–43.

Cole, Jack. "It's Gone Silly!" *Dance Magazine* (December 1963): 35–36.

Coleman, Robert. "'St. Louis Woman' Is Fast Musical." *New York Mirror*, 1 April 1946.

Collier, James Lincoln. *Duke Ellington*. New York: Oxford University Press, 1987.

——. "Jazz." In *New Grove Dictionary of Jazz*, ed. Barry Kernfeld, 580–606. New York: St. Martin's Press, 1988.

——. *Jazz: The American Theme Song*. New York: Oxford University Press, 1993.

——. "Louis Armstrong." In *New Grove Dictionery of Jazz*, ed. Barry Kernfeld, 27–31. New York: St Martin's Press, 1988.

——. *Louis Armstrong: An American Genius*. New York: Oxford University Press, 1983.

——. *The Making of Jazz*. New York: Dell, 1978.

——. *The Reception of Jazz in America*. City University of New York: Institute for Studies in American Music, 1988.

Cook, Will Marion. "Clorindy, the Origin of the Cakewalk." *Theatre Arts* 31 (September 1947): 61–65.

Copeland, Roger, and Marshall Cohen, eds. *What Is Dance? Readings in Theory and Criticism*. New York and Oxford: Oxford University Press, 1983.

Cotter, Holland. "A 1920s Flowering That Didn't Disappear." *New York Times*, 24 May 1998.

"Cotton Club Aims to Please Big Crowds." *Brooklyn Daily Eagle*, 8 October 1937.

"Cotton Club, N.Y." *Variety*, 12 October 1938.

"The Cotton Club Scores Again." *New York Sun*, 2 October 1937.

Crease, R. D. "Swing Story." *Authentic Jazz Dance Journal* 1 (1988): 5–10.

Cripps, Thomas. *Making Movies Black: The Hollywood Message Movie from World War II to the Civil Rights Era*. New York: Oxford University Press, 1993.

——. *Slow Fade to Black: The Negro in American Film, 1900–1942*. New York: Oxford University Press, 1977.

Croce, Arlene. "Flash Act." *New Yorker* (15 February 1988): 25–27.

——. *The Fred Astaire and Ginger Rogers Book*. New York: Vintage, 1977.

Cunard, Nancy, ed. *Negro*. London: Wishart, 1934.

Dabney, Thomas L. "Europe Afire with Craze for Jazz and Charleston." *Philadelphia Tribune*, 28 July 1927.

Dance, Stanley. *The Night People: Reminiscences of a Jazzman*. Boston: Crescendo, 1971.

——. *The World of Swing*. New York: Charles Scribner's Sons, 1974.

Dandridge, Dorothy, and Earl Conrad. *Everything and Nothing: The Dorothy Dandridge Tragedy*. New York: Abelard-Schuman, 1970.

Darrell, R. D. "Black Beauty." *Disques* (June 1932): 152–61.

Davis, Curt. "Half a Hoof Team Vocalizes." *New York Post*, 22 December 1984.

Deffaa, Chip. "Nicholas Displays His Class." *New York Post*, 23 December 1989.

DeFrantz, Thomas. "Simmering Passivity: The Black Male Dancer on the Concert Stage." In *Moving Words: Re-Writing Dance*, ed. Gay Morris, 107–20. London and New York: Routledge, 1996.

Delaney, Joe. "'Sophisticated Ladies' Dynamite." *This Is Las Vegas*, 7 January 1983.

Denby, David. "Movies." *New York Magazine* (28 January 1985): 75.

Denby, Edwin. *Dance Writings*, ed. Robert Cornfield and William Mackey. New York: Knopf, 1986.

"Desert Inn Showroom 'Sizzles' with 'Sophisticated Ladies.'" *Sentinel Voice*, 6 January 1983.

Dixon-Stowell, Brenda. "Dancing in the Dark: The Life and Times of Margot Webb in Aframerican Vaudeville of the Swing Era." Ph.D. diss., New York University, 1981.

Dodds, Warren "Baby," and Gara Farry. "The Baby Dodds Story." *Jazz Journal* 8, no. 7 (July 1955): 8.

Donahue, Jack. "Hoofing." *Saturday Evening Post* (14 September 1929): n.p.

Douglas, Ann. *Terrible Honesty: Mongrel Manhattan in the 1920s*. New York: Farrar, Straus & Giroux, 1995.

Duberman, Martin. *Paul Robeson*. New York: Knopf, 1988.

Dunbar, Paul Laurence. "We Wear the Mask." In *Black Voices: An Anthology of Afro-American Literature*, ed. Abraham Chapman, 355. New York: Mentor, 1981.

Duncan, Donald. "The Dance with the Noise." *Dance Magazine* (August 1961): 42–44.

Dunning, Jennnifer. "Light-Footed Fusillade School of Tap." *New York Times*, 31 March 1988.

——. "A Tap-Flamenco Union." *New York Times*, 28 May 1988.

——. "The Toes Are Tapping and the Bags Stay Packed." *New York Times*, 28 March 1988.

Durante, Jimmy, and Jack Kofoed. *Night Clubs*. New York: Knopf, 1931.

Dutton, William S. "We've Got Rhythm." *American Magazine*, (19 March 1935): 26–29, 52–53.

Ekstein, Modris. *Rites of Spring: The Great War and the Birth of the Modern Age*. New York: Houghton Mifflin, 1989.

Ellington, Edward Kennedy "Duke." "The Duke Steps Out." *Rhythm* (March 1931): 20–22.

——. *Music Is My Mistress*. Garden City, N.Y.: Doubleday, 1973.

"Ellingtonians." *Variety* (21 March 1928): 69.

Ellison, Ralph. *Shadow and Act*. New York: Random House, 1964.

——. "What Would America Be Like without Blacks?" *Time* 95 (6 April 1970): 55.

Elwood, Philip. "'Savoy' Defeats a Showy Potential." *San Francisco Examiner*, 12 February 1981.

Emery, Lynne Fauley. *Black Dance from 1619 to Today*. 2d rev. ed., with a foreword by Katherine Dunham. Princeton, N.J.: Dance Horizons, 1988.

Englebrecht, Barbara. "Swinging at the Savoy." *Dance Research Journal* 15, no. 2 (1983): 3–10.

Erenbery, Lewis A. *Steppin' Out: New York Nightlife and the Transformation of American Culture 1890–1930*. Westport, Conn.: Greenwood, 1944.

"Fats Waller Demonstrates Swing, Even Defines It." *Metronome* 52 (February 1936): 19, 33.

Feldman, Anita. *Inside Tap: Technique and Improvisation for Today's Tap Dancer*. Pennington, N.J.: Princeton Book Co., 1996.

Field, Rowland. "Nicholas Brothers Inseparable." *Newark Evening News*, 23 May 1946.

Flatow, Sheryl. "Flashy Tapper's Return." *New York Post*, 29 March 1988.

Fletcher, Tom. *100 Years of the Negro in Show Business*. New York: Burge, 1954.

Floyd, Samuel A., Jr., ed. *Black Music in the Harlem Renaissance: A Collection of Essays*. Westport, Conn.: Greenwood, 1990.

Fox, Ted. *Showtime at the Apollo*. Reprint, New York: Da Capo, 1983.

Francis, Robert. "Lives of Nicholas Brothers Run as Parallel as Their Dance Steps." *Brooklyn Daily Eagle*, 28 April 1946.

Frank, Rusty E. *Tap! The Greatest Tap Dance Stars and Their Stories, 1900–1955*. New York: William Morrow, 1990.

Garafola, Lynn. *Diaghilev's Ballets Russes*. New York: Oxford University Press, 1989.

Garland, Robert. "'St. Louis Woman' Opens at Martin Beck Theatre." *Journal American* (New York), 1 April 1946.

Gates, Henry Louis. *The Signifying Monkey: A Theory of African-American Literary Criticism*. New York: Oxford University Press, 1988.

"Gene Krupa Gives Swing 'Low Down.'" *The New York Times*, 12 July 1942.

Gilbert, Douglas. *American Vaudeville*. Reprint, New York: Dover, 1940.

Gilbert, Gama. "Higher Soars the Swing Fever." *New York Times Magazine* (14 August 1938): 6–7, 19.

———. "Swing." *The New York Times Magazine* (19 November 1939): 14.

Gillespie, Dizzy, with Al Fraser. *To Be, or Not . . . to Bop*. Garden City, N.Y.: Doubleday, 1979.

Giordano, Gus, ed. *Anthology of American Jazz Dance*. Evanston, Ill.: Orion, 1975.

Gitler, Ira. *Swing to Bop: An Oral History of the Transition in Jazz in the 1940s*. New York: Oxford University Press, 1985.

Goddard, Chris. *Jazz away from Home*. London: Paddington, 1979.

Goldberg, Jane. "It's All in the Feet." *Quincy* (Mass.) *Patriot Ledger*, 24 April 1974.

Goodman, Benny, and Irving Kolodin. *The Kingdom of Swing*. New York: Frederick Ungar, 1939.

Goodman, Benny, and Ted Shane. "Now Take the Jitterbug." *Collier's* 103 (25 February 1939): 11–13, 60.

Gottschild, Brenda Dixon. *Digging the Africanist Presence in American Performance: Dance and Other Contexts*. Westport, Conn. and London: Greenwood, 1996.

Grant, Gail. *Technical Manual and Dictionary of Classical Ballet*, 3d rev. ed. New York: Dover, 1967.

Graziano, John. "Black Musical Theatre and the Harlem Renaissance Movement." In *Black Music in the Harlem Renaissance: A Collection of Essays*, ed. Samuel A. Floyd Jr., 87–110. Westport, Conn.: Greenwood, 1990.

Green, Blake. "Tapping into a Rich Legacy." *Newsday*, 30 December 1989.

Gushee, Lawrence. "New Orleans Jazz." In *New Grove Dictionary of Jazz*, ed. Barry Kernfeld, 836–37. New York: St. Martin's Press, 1988.

Haley, Charles T. "To Do Good and Do Well: Middle-Class Blacks and the Depression, Philadelphia, 1929–1941." Ph.D. diss., State University of New York at Binghamton, 1980.

Hall, Ben M. *The Best Remaining Seats: The Story of the Golden Age of the Movie Palace*. New York: Bramhall House, 1957.

Hamlin, Jesse. "Harold Nicholas: Time Off from Tapping to Sing." *New York Times*, 21 December 1984.

——. "Tap Master in the Spotlight Again." *San Francisco Chronicle*, 6 June 1989.

Hammond, Bryan, and Patrick O'Connor. *Josephine Baker*. Boston, Toronto, and London: Little, Brown, 1988.

Hammond, John. "The King of Swing." *Crisis* 44 (April 1937): 110–11, 123–24.

Handy, W. C. *Father of the Blues*. New York: Macmillan, 1951.

Haskins, Jim. *The Cotton Club*. New York: Random House, 1977.

Hazzard-Gordon, Katrina. *Jookin': The Rise of Social Dance Formations in African-American Culture*. Philadelphia: Temple University Press, 1990.

Hennessey, Thomas J. *From Jazz to Swing: African-American Jazz Musicians and Their Music, 1890–1935*. Detroit: Wayne State University Press, 1994.

Hill, Constance Valis. "Bill 'Bojangles' Robinson." In *Encyclopedia of African-American Culture and History*, ed. Jack Salzman, David Lionel Smith, and Cornel West, n.p. New York: Macmillan Library Reference USA, 1996.

——. "Black and Blue." *Attitude: The Dancers' Magazine* 5, no. 3 (Spring 1989): 4–5.

——. "Bring in the Praise." *Village Voice* (17 April 1998): 91.

——. "Buddy Bradley: The 'Invisible' Man of Broadway Brings Jazz Tap Dance to London." *Proceedings: Society of Dance History Scholars*, Fifteenth Annual Conference Riverside, Calif. (14 February 1992): 77–84.

——. "Jazz Modernism." In *Moving Words: Re-Writing Dance*, ed. Gay Morris, 227–42. London: Routledge, 1996.

——. "Nicholas Brothers." In *International Encyclopedia of Dance*, ed. Selma Jeanne Cohen, n.p. New York: Oxford University Press, 1998.

Hill, Constance Valis, and Sally Sommer. "Tap Dance." In *Encyclopedia of African-American Culture and History*, ed. Jack Salzman, David Lionel Smith, and Cornel West, 2605–10. New York: Macmillan Library Reference USA, 1996.

Hinckley, David. "A Honey of a Hoofer." *New York Sunday News Magazine* (7 August 1983): 5.

Holden, Stephen. "Grapelli, 80, Stars at His Tribute." *New York Times*, 16 April 1988.

Horricks, Raymond. *Dizzy Gillespie and the Be-Bop Revolution*. New York: Hippodrome, 1984.

"House Reviews: Apollo Theatre, N.Y." *Variety* (9 December 1953), 67–68.

Huggins, Nathan Irvin. *The Harlem Renaissance*. New York: Oxford University Press, 1971.

——, ed. *Voices from the Harlem Renaissance*. New York and Oxford: Oxford University Press, 1976.

Hughes, Langston. *Famous Negro Music Makers*. New York: Dodd, Mead, 1957.

Hughes, Langston, and Milton Meltzer. *Black Magic: A Pictorial History of the*

African-American in the Performing Arts. Reprint, with a new foreword by Ossie Davis. New York: Da Capo, 1967.

Hughes, Spike. "The Duke—In Person." *Melody Maker* (May 1933): 353, 355.

Hurston, Zora Neale. "Characteristics of Negro Expression." In *Voices from the Harlem Renaissance*, ed. Nathan Irvin Huggins, 224–50. New York and Oxford: Oxford University Press, 1995.

Hyatt, Marshall, ed. *The Afro-American Cinematic Experience*. Wilmington, Del.: Scholarly Resources, 1983.

Imperial Society of Teachers of Dancing. *The Revised Technique of Latin American Dancing*. London: Imperial Society, 1971.

Isaacs, Edith J. R. *The Negro in the American Theatre*. New York: Theatre Arts, 1947.

Islan, Richard. *Hoofing on Broadway*. New York: Prentice Hall, 1987.

Jablonski, Edward. *Harold Arlen: Happy with the Blues*. Garden City, N.Y.: Doubleday, 1961.

Jackson, Harriet. "American Dancer, Negro." *Dance Magazine* (September 1966): 35–42.

Janheinz, Jahn. *Muntu: An Outline of New African Culture*. New York: Grove, 1961.

Jay, Leticia. "The Wonderful Old-Time Hoofers at Newport." *Dance Magazine* (September) 1963, 8–19.

Jefferson, Margo. "An Era for Movement." *Dance Ink* (September 1993): 18–24.

"Jeni LeGon Likes London, but Not Its Race Prejudice." *Norfolk* (Va.) *Journal and Guide*, 1 February 1936.

"The Jive Language." *Metronome* 55 (June 1939): 20.

Johnson, James Weldon. *Black Manhattan*. New York: Knopf, 1930.

Johnson, Malcolm. "Good News from Hollywood." *New York Sun*, 20 November 1937.

Jones, LeRoi. *Blues People: The Negro Experience in White America and the Music That Developed from It*. New York: William Morrow, 1963.

Jowitt, Deborah. "Foot Conversations." *Village Voice* (2 April 1988):n.p.

Kael, Pauline. "'Cotton Club.'" *New Yorker* (7 January 1985): n.p.

Keepnews, Orrin, and Bill Graur Jr., eds. *A Pictorial History of Jazz: People and Places from New Orleans to Modern Jazz*. New York: Crown, 1955.

Kenney, William Howland. *Chicago Jazz: A Cultural History, 1904–1930*. New York and Oxford: Oxford University Press, 1993.

——. "The Influence of Black Vaudeville on Early Jazz." *The Black Perspective in Music* 14, no. 3 (Sept. 1986): 232–48.

Kernfeld, Barry, ed. *New Grove Dictionary of Jazz*. New York: St. Martin's Press, 1988.

"Kid Millions." *New York Times*, 17 November 1934.

Kimble, Robert, and William Bolcolm. *Reminiscing with Sissle and Blake*. New York: Viking, 1973.

Kirstein, Lincoln. "Aria of the Aerial." In *What Is Dance?*, ed. Roger Copeland and Marshall Cohen, 238–43. New York and Oxford: Oxford University Press, 1983.

Kisselgoff, Anna. "Dance: Tap of 30s and 40s." *New York Times*, 12 March 1987.

——. "Dance View." *New York Times*, 7 February 1997.

Kobal, John. *Gotta Sing, Gotta Dance: A Pictorial History of Film Musicals.* London and New York: Hamlyn, 1971.

Koegler, Horst, ed. *The Concise Oxford Dictionary of Ballet.* 2d ed. London: Oxford University Press, 1982.

Korall, Burt. *Drummin' Men: The Heartbeat of Jazz, the Swing Years.* New York: Schirmer Books, 1990.

Leavy, Walter. "The Mystery and Real-Life Tragedy of Dorothy Dandridge." *Ebony* (December 1993): 36–43.

Levin, David Michael. "Balanchine's Formalism." In *What Is Dance?*, ed. Roger Copeland and Marshall Cohen, 123–45. New York and Oxford: Oxford University Press, 1983.

Levine, Lawrence W. *Black Culture and Black Consciousness.* Oxford and New York: Oxford University Press, 1977.

———. *The Unpredictable Past: Explorations in American Cultural History.* New York: Oxford University Press, 1993.

Levinson, André. "The Spirit of the Classic Dance." In *Andre Levinson on Dance: Writings from Paris in the Twenties*, ed. and trans. Joan Acocella and Lynn Garafola , 42–48. Hanover and London: Wesleyan University Press, 1991.

Lewis, David Levery. *When Harlem Was in Vogue.* New York: Knopf, 1981.

Locke, Alain. *The Negro and His Music.* Washington, D.C.: Associates in Negro Folk Education, 1936.

Macauley, Alistair. "Notes on Dance Classicism." *Dance Theatre Journal* 5, no. 2 (June 1987): 6–9, 36–39.

Mahoney, Billie. "Did Tap Ever Really Die?" *International Tap Association Newsletter* (November-December 1996): 3–7, 18–20.

———. "What We Tap Dancers Were Doing in the 1950s." *International Tap Association Newsletter* (March-April 1995): 3–7.

Malnig, Julie. *Dancing till Dawn: A Century of Exhibition Ballroom Dance.* New York and London: New York University Press, 1992.

Malone, Jacqui. *Steppin' on the Blues: The Visible Rhythms of African American Dance.* Urbana and Chicago: University of Illinois Press, 1996.

McDowell, Roddy. *Double Exposure.* New York: William Morrow, 1991.

Mendl, R. W. S. *The Appeal of Jazz.* London: Philip Alland, 1927.

Miller, Paul Edward. *Downbeat's Yearbook of Swing.* Chicago: Downbeat, 1939.

Mitgang, N. R. *Mr. Bojangles: The Biography of Bill Robinson.* New York: William Morrow, 1988.

Moore, Lillian. *Echoes of American Ballet*, ed. Ivor Guest. New York: Dance Horizons, 1976.

Morris, Gay, ed. *Moving Words: Re-Writing Dance.* London and New York: Routledge, 1996.

Mueller, John. *Astaire Dancing: The Musical Films.* New York: Knopf, 1985.

Murray, Albert. *Stomping the Blues.* New York: Da Capo, 1976.

"New Cotton Club Show." *New York Herald-Tribune*, 2 October 1937.

Newman, Rigmor. *The Nicholas Brothers Act.* New York: Harold Nicholas Archive, 1985.

———. *The Nicholas Brothers' Philadelphia Connection*. New York: Harold Nicholas Archive, 1990.

"Nicholas Brothers Biggest Split; Harold, Fayard are 7000 Apart." *Ebony* (May 1960): 77–80.

"Nicholas Brothers: Our Three Gravy Years in Europe." *Our World* (January 1952): 24–27.

"The Nicholas Brothers Still a Team in 'St. Louis Woman.'" *Brooklyn Daily Eagle*, 24 March 1946.

"Nicholas Brothers Steppin' High with 50 Years of Success." *Jet* (25 June 1981): 56–57.

Noble, Peter. *The Negro in Films*. London: British Yearbooks, 1949.

Null, Gary. *Black Hollywood: The Black Performer in Motion Pictures*. New York: Citadel, 1975.

O'Connor, Patrick. "Tap Happening." *Dance Magazine* (August 1969): 40–42.

Ogren, Kathy J. *The Jazz Revolution: Twenties America and the Meaning of Jazz*. New York: Oxford University Press, 1989.

Oliver, Paul. "Boogie-Woogie." In *New Grove Dictionary of Jazz*, ed. Barry Kernfeld, 135–36. New York: St. Martin's Press, 1988.

O'Neil, William L. *Coming Apart: An Informal History of America in the 1960s*. Chicago: Quadrangle, 1971.

"Part of the Plot of This Show Comes from the Show Itself." *New York Herald Tribune*, 13 June 1937.

"The Passing of Gibson." *New York Amsterdam News*, 18 May 1932.

"Pathe's 'Get Out and Get Under.'" *Winston-Salem Journal*, 3 April 1921.

Perry, Dave. *Jazz Greats*. London: Phaidon, 1996.

Pollak, Max. "The Real Jimmy Slyde." *International Tap Association Newsletter* (May-June 1997): 3–10.

Pomerance, Alan. *Repeal of the Blues: How Black Entertainers Influenced Civil Rights*. Secaucus, N.J.: Citadel, 1988.

Posner, Lee (Harlemania). "Harlem More Like Heaven to Negro Artists Now." *New York Amsterdam News*, 21 September 1932.

Powers, Rob. "Harold Nicholas Adds Sparkle to 'Ladies.'" *Las Vegas Review-Journal*, 25 March 1983.

Rascoe, Burton. "'St. Louis Woman' Delightful Musical." *New York World-Telegram*, 2 April 1946.

Regan, Kate. "Old-Timers Out-Tap the Kids." *San Francisco Chronicle*, 12 June 1989.

Reiter, Susan. "Steps in Time: A Tap Dance Festival." *Dance News* (March 1980): 10.

Rhapsodies in Black: Art of the Harlem Renaissance. Berkeley, Los Angeles, and London: University of California Press, 1997.

Rice, Vernon. "'St. Louis Woman' Arrives—Fast-Paced and Never Dull." *New York Post*, 1 April 1946.

Richardson, James. "Blame It on Jazz: King Fox Trot." *Dance* (March 1927): 30–31, 51.

Riis, Thomas Lawrence. "Black Musical Theatre in New York: 1890–1915." Ph.D. diss., University of Michigan, 1981.

———. *More than Just a Minstrel Show: The Rise of Black Musical Theatre at the Turn of the Century*. Brooklyn: Institute of Studies in American Music at Brooklyn College, 1992.

Robeson, Susan. *The Whole World in His Hands: A Pictorial Biography of Paul Robeson*. Secaucus, N.J.: Citadel, 1981.

Robinson, J. Bradford. "Johnny Dodds" (294), "Scat Singing" (1093–94), "Swing" (1176), and "Chick Webb" (1273). In *New Grove Dictionary of Jazz*, ed. Barry Kernfeld. New York: St. Martin's Press, 1988.

Rogers, J. A. "Jazz at Home." *Survey Graphic* 6, 6 (March 1925): 665–68.

Rose, Frank. *The Agency: William Morris and the Hidden History of Show Business*. New York: Harper Collins, 1995.

Rose, Phyllis. *Jazz Cleopatra*. New York: Doubleday, 1989.

Russell, Tom. "Bippidy-Boom-Shaga-Daga." *Connoisseur* (November 1983): 57–59.

Sampson, Henry T. *Blacks in Blackface: A Sourcebook on Early Black Musical Shows*. Metuchen, N.J.: Scarecrow, 1980.

Santosuosso, Ernie. ". . . And the great sounds of jazz." *Boston Globe*, 22 June 1987.

Schiffman, Jack. *Uptown: The Story of Harlem's Apollo Theatre*. New York: Cowles, 1971.

Schoener, Allon, ed. *Harlem on My Mind: Culture Capital of Black America, 1900–1968*. New York: Random House, 1968.

Schuller, Gunther. *Early Jazz: Its Roots and Musical Development*. New York: Oxford University Press, 1968.

——. *The Swing Era: The Development of Jazz*. New York: Oxford University Press, 1989.

Scott, Nancy. "'Tap Dance Kid': A Hit in Spite of Itself." *San Francisco Examiner*, 5 August 1985.

Sennett, Ted. *Hollywood Musicals*. New York: Abrams, 1981.

Shipley, Glenn. *Modern Tap Dancing*. Los Angeles: Action Marketing Group, 1963.

Siders, Harvey. "New Kid in Class: Sophisticated Ladies." *Daily News* (Los Angeles), 17 September 1982.

Sidran, Ben. *Black Talk*. New York: Da Capo, 1971.

Simon, George T. *Simon Says: The Sights and Sounds of the Swing Era, 1935–1955*. New York: Arlington House, 1971.

Siskel, Gene. "'That's Dancing.'" *Chicago Tribune*, 18 January 1985.

Sissle, Noble. "Ragtime by U.S. Army Band Gets Everyone over There." *St. Louis Post-Dispatch*, 10 June 1918.

Sommer, Sally. "Hearing Dance, Watching Film." *Dancescope* 14, no. 3 (1980): 52–62.

Southern, Eileen. "Conversation with Eubie Blake: A Legend in His Own Lifetime." *Black Perspectives in Music* 1 (1973): 50–59.

——. "Eubie Blake." In *New Grove Dictionary of Jazz*, ed. Barry Kernfeld, 115. New York: St. Martin's Press, 1988.

——. *The Music of Black Americans*. New York: Norton, 1971.

"Standard to Celebrate 14th Anniversary." *Philadelphia Tribune*, 12 January 1928.

Stearns, Marshall. "Is Jazz Dance Hopelessly Square?" *Dance Magazine* (June 1959): 30, 35.

——. *The Story of Jazz*. New York: Oxford University Press, 1956.

Stearns, Marshall, and Jean Stearns. "Frontiers of Humor: American Vernacular Dance." *Southern Folklore Quarterly* (September 1966): 227–35.

——. *Jazz Dance: The Story of American Vernacular Dance*. New York: Macmillan, 1968.

——. "Vernacular Dance in Musical Comedy." *New York Folklore Quarterly* 22, no. 4 (December 1966): 251–61.

Stewart, Rex. *Jazz Masters of the 30s*. New York: Da Capo, 1972.

Stich, Sidra. *Anxious Visions: Surrealist Art*. New York: Regents of the University of California-Berkeley, and Abbeville Press, 1990.

Stokes, Adrian. "The Classic Ballet." In *What Is Dance?*, ed. Roger Copeland and Marshall Cohen, 244–54. Oxford and New York: Oxford University Press, 1983.

Stovall, Tyler. "Paris in the Age of Anxiety, 1919–39." In *Anxious Visions: Surealist Art*, ed. Sidra Stich, 201–21. New York: Regents of the University of California, Berkeley, and Abbeville Press, 1990.

Stowe, David W. *Swing Changes: Big Band Jazz in New Deal America*. Cambridge and London: Harvard University Press, 1994.

Stratemann, Klaus. *Duke Ellington: Day by Day, Film by Film*. Copenhagen: JazzMedia, 1992.

Sullivan, Ed. "Hi-De-Ho Mark Set by Cotton Club Express." *New York Daily News*, 18 March 1937.

Supin, Charles. "An Ageless Harold Nicholas." *Las Vegas Review-Journal*, 25 February 1983.

"Swing, Swing, Oh Beautiful Swing!" *Metronome* 52 (February 1936): 19, 33.

Szwed, John F., and Roger D. Abraham. *Afro-American Folk Culture: An Annotated Bibliography of Materials from North, Central, and South America and the West Indies*. Parts 1 and 2. Philadelphia: Institute for the Study of Human Issues, 1978.

This Fabulous Century, vol. 4, *1930–1940* New York: Time-Life, 1969.

Thompson, Robert Farris. "An Aesthetic of the Cool." *African Arts* 7, no. 1 (September 1983): 41–42, 64–67, 89–92.

——. *African Art in Motion: Icon and Act*. Berkeley and Los Angeles: University of California Press, 1974.

——. "Dance and Culture, an Aesthetic of the Cool: West African Dance." *African Arts* (September 1989): 41–67.

Thompson, Virgil. "Swing Again." *Modern Music* 15 (March 1938): 160–66.

——. "Swing Music." *Modern Music* 13 (May 1936): 12–17.

Tobias, Tobi. "Dance." *New York Magazine* (30 March 1987): n.p.

——. "Dance." *New York Magazine* (22 February 1988): n.p.

Toll, Robert C. *Blacking Up: The Minstrel Show in Nineteenth-Century America*. New York: Oxford University Press, 1974.

——. *On with the Show: The First Century of Show Business in America*. New York: Oxford University Press, 1976.

Tucker, Mark. "The Renaissance Education of Duke Ellington." In *Black Music in the Harlem Renaissance*, ed. Samuel A. Floyd Jr., 111–27. Westport, Conn.: Greenwood, 1990.

——, ed. *The Duke Ellington Reader*. New York: Oxford University Press, 1993.

Ulanov, Barry. "The Films, Phony and Otherwise." *Metronome* (July 1943): 15.

Van Dam, Theodore. "The Influence of the West African Song of Derision in the New World." *African Music* 1 (1954): 53–56.

Van Vechten, Carl. *The Dance Writings of Carl Van Vechten*. New York: Dance Horizons, 1974.

———. *The Letters of Carl Van Vechten*, ed. Bruce Kellner. New Haven and London: Yale University Press, 1987.

———. "The Negro Theatre." In *In the Garrett*. New York: Knopf, 1920.

Volinsky, A. K. "The Vertical: The Fundamental Principle of Classic Dance," trans. Seymour Barofsky. In *What Is Dance?*, ed. Roger Copeland and Marshall Cohen, 255–56. New York and Oxford: Oxford University Press, 1983.

Walker, Dan. "Star Dancing Keeps Cotton Club at Top." *New York Daily News*, 26 September 1937.

Wassermann, Dorothy. "A Short History of Jazz Tap Festivals." *Attitude: The Dancers' Magazine* 7, no. 1 (September 1990): 21–25.

Watkins, Mel. *On the Real Side: Laughing, Lying, and Signifying—The Underground Tradition of African-American Humor That Transformed American Culture, from Slavery to Richard Pryor*. New York: Simon & Schuster, 1994.

Watrous, Peter. "The Man Who Defined Modern Jazz." *New York Times*, 13 November 1988.

Weber, Bruce. "Marquee Will Make a Comeback in Paramount's Restoration." *New York Times*, August 1990.

Williams, Martin. *Jazz Heritage*. New York: Oxford University Press, 1985.

———. *The Jazz Tradition*. 2d rev. ed. New York: Oxford University Press, 1993.

Willis, Cheryl M. "Tap Dance: Memories and Issues of African-American Women Who Performed between 1930–1950." Ph.D. diss., Temple University, 1991.

Wilson, John S. "A Brother Nicholas Evokes Astaire." *New York Times*, 22 December 1989.

Winz, Cory D. *Black Culture and the Harlem Renaissance*. Houston: Rice University Press, 1988.

Witchell, Alex. "Black and Blues Brothers." *New York Magazine* (2 January 1989): 16.

Woll, Allen. *Black Musical Theatre: From "Coontown" to "Dreamgirls."* Reprint, New York: Da Capo, 1989.

Wood, Peter. "'Gimme de Kneebone Bent': African Body Language and the Evolution of American Dance Forms." In *The Black Tradition in American Modern Dance*, ed. Gerald E. Myers, 7–9 American Dance Festival Program, 1988.

Worsham, Doris G. "Dancer's Talents Tapped for New Musical." *San Francisco Tribune*, 13 February 1981.

Zunser, Florence. "'Opera Must Die,' Says Galli-Curci! Long Live the Blues!" *New York Evening Graphic Magazine* (20 December 1930): n.p.

The Nicholas Brothers on Film, Television, and Video

The All-Colored Vaudeville Show. Directed by Roy Mack. Vitaphone/ Warner Brothers, 1935. Short subject musical film.

All-Star Revue: The Ed Wynn Show. NBC-TV, 10 November 1951. Television broadcast.

American Black Achievement Awards. ABC-TV, January 1988. Television broadcast.

American Film Institute: Salute to Gene Kelly. CBS-TV, 7 May 1985. Television broadcast.

Apollo 50th Anniversary. NBC-TV, May 1985. Television broadcast.

Bell Telephone Hour. "The Song and Dance Man." NBC-TV, 16 January 1966. Television broadcast.

The Big Broadcast of 1936. Directed by Norman Taurog, musical numbers staged by Leroy Prinz. Paramount Pictures, 1935. Motion picture.

Black and Blue. Directed by Claudio Segovia and Hector Orezzoli. Public Broadcasting Company: Dance in America, 1989. Videocassette.

Black Network. Directed by Roy Mack. Vitaphone/Warner Brothers, 1936. Short subject film.

The Bob Hope Christmas Show. NBC-TV, 23 December 1951. Television broadcast.

Botta e Riposta. Italy: Italia Pictures, 1951. Motion picture.

Cab Calloway: A Collection of Film Excerpts. Edited and compiled by Ernie Smith. New York: Ernie Smith Black Dance Films, 1985. Video compilation.

Calling All Stars. London: British Lion Films, 1937. Motion picture.

Carmen Miranda: Bananas Is My Business. Rio de Janeiro: International Cinema, 1994. Documentary film.

Carolina Blues. Directed by Leigh Jason. Columbia Pictures, 11 December 1944. Motion picture.

Colgate Comedy Hour. "The Abbot and Costello Show." NBC-TV, 14 December 1952. Television broadcast.

Coronado. Metro-Goldwyn-Mayer, 1936. Motion picture.

The Cotton Club Comes to the Ritz. London: BBC-TV, July 1985. Television broadcast.

Crazy Feet. Edited and compliled by Ernie Smith. New York: Ernie Smith Black Dance Films, 1990. Video compilation.

Dixieland Jamboree. Vitaphone/Warner Brothers, 24 April 1946. Short subject musical film.

Down Argentine Way. Directed by Irving Cummings, musical numbers staged by Nick Castle and Geneva Sawyer. Twentieth Century-Fox Films, 11 October 1940. Motion picture.

The Emperor Jones. Directed by Dudley Murphey. New York: United Artists, 1933. Motion picture.

Fascinatin' Rhythms. Edited and compiled by Ernie Smith. New York: Ernie Smith Black Dance Films, 1986. Video compilation.

The Five Heartbeats. Twentieth Century-Fox, 1990. Motion picture.

The Great American Broadcast. Twentieth Century-Fox, 1940. Motion picture.

The Harold Nicholas Show. Italy: RAI-TV, 1983. Television broadcast series.

Hollywood Palace. WABC-TV, 31 July 1964, 14 November 1964, and 27 February 1965. Television broadcast.

Jazzin' It Up: The Style of the Nicholas Brothers. Directed by Celia Ipiotis. New York: WNYC-TV Eye on Dance, 1988. Television broadcast.

The Kennedy Center Honors. NBC-TV, December 1987. Television broadcast.

Kid Millions. Directed by Roy Del Ruth, choreographed by Seymour Felix. Samuel Goldwyn, 1934. Motion picture.

L'Empire de la Nuit. France: UFA-Comacio, 1963. Motion picture.

The Liberation of L. B. Jones. Columbia, 1970. Motion picture.

My American Wife. Metro-Goldwyn-Mayer, 1936. Motion picture.

Nicholas Brothers: Flying High. Foxstar Productions and Van Ness Films. A&E Network's Biography Series, 23 Feb. 1999. Documentary film.

Nicholas Brothers: We Sing and We Dance. Cowritten and coproduced by Bruce Goldstein and Rigmor Newman, directed by Chris Boulder. New York: Picture Musical International, 1992. Documentary film.

Nicholas Home Movies. Unedited 16mm film taken by Viola, Fayard, and Harold Nicholas and Lorenzo Hill, 1935–45. New York: Harold Nicholas Archive.

Orchestra Wives. Directed by Archie Mayo. Twentieth Century-Fox, 4 September 1942. Motion picture.

Pie, Pie, Blackbird. Eubie Blake and His Band. Vitaphone/Warner Brothers, 1932. Short subject musical film.

The Pirate. Directed by Vicente Minelli, dance direction by Robert Alton and Gene Kelly. Metro-Goldwyn-Mayer, 1949. Motion picture.

The Reckless Age. Directed by Felix Feist. Universal Films, 26 October 1944. Motion picture.

Reflections with the Nicholas Brothers. Directed by Calvin Lindsay Jr. Boston: WGBH-TV, 15 June 1996. Television broadcast.

Salute to Duke. New York: PBS-TV, 1981. Television broadcast.

Show Stoppers. Nicholas Brothers Promotional. New York: Marabou Pictures, 1988. Videocassette.

Stoopnocracy. Directed by Dave Fleisher. New York: Max Fleisher/Paramount, 1933. Short subject film.

Stormy Weather. Directed by Andrew Stone, musical numbers staged by Nicholas Castle. Twentieth Century-Fox, 16 July 1943. Motion picture.

Sun Valley Serenade. Directed by H. Bruce Humberstone, choreographed by Hermes Pan. Twentieth Century-Fox, 29 August 1941. Motion picture.

Take It or Leave It. Twentieth Century-Fox, 1944. Motion picture.

Tap. Directed by Nick Castle Jr., choreographed by Henry LeTang. Hoofer Films/Tri-Star, 1988. Motion picture.

The Tap Dance Kid. San Francisco: WTGI, 4 December 1981. Television broadcast.

Tap Dancin'. Directed by Christian Blackwood. New York: Blackwood Films, 1980. Documentary film.

That's Dancing! Metro-Goldwyn-Mayer/United Artists, 1985. Motion picture.

That's Entertainment. Metro-Goldwyn-Mayer, 1974. Motion picture.

Tin Pan Alley. Twentieth Century Fox, 1940. Motion picture.

Uptown Saturday Night. Warner Brothers, 1974. Motion picture.

Interviews

Baryshnikov, Mikhail. Interview by Bruce Goldstein, produced by Rigmor Newman, New York, 1991; transcript, Picture Musical International, New York.

Branton, Geri (Pate Nicholas). Interview by Bruce Goldstein, produced by Rigmor Newman, Los Angeles, 1991; transcript, Picture Musical International, New York.

Coles, Charles Honi. Telephone interview by author, 29 March 1991, Queens, N.Y.

Coles, Marion. Telephone interview by author, 13 June 1996, Queens, N.Y.

Graziano, John. Telephone interview by author, 30 May 1995, New York.

Hines, Gregory. Interview by Bruce Goldstein, produced by Rigmor Newman, New York, 1991; transcript, Picture Musical International, New York.

Hines, Gregory. Telephone interview by author, 15 April 1991, New York.

Hines, Maurice. Interview by Bruce Goldstein, produced by Rigmor Newman, Los Angeles, 1991; transcript, Picture Musical International, New York.

Newman, Rigmor. Telephone interview by author, 28 Nov. 1995; 17 February 1997; 10 May 1997, New York.

Nicholas, Dorothy (Morrow). Telephone interview by author, 29 November 1995, Los Angeles.

Nicholas, Dorothy (Morrow). Interview by Bruce Goldstein, produced by Rigmor Newman, Los Angeles, 1991; transcript, Picture Musical International, New York.

Nicholas, Fayard. Telephone interview by author, 4 April 1993, 8 April 1993, 8 April 1995, 17 April 1995, 8 July 1995, 22 October 1995, 29 October 1995, 20 January 1996, 2 July 1996, 20 July 1996, 24 March 1997, 15 April 1997, 18 May 1997, 7 June 1997, 14 June 1997, 23 June 1997, 14 September 1997, Woodland Hills, Calif.

Nicholas, Fayard. Interview by author, 17 April 1995, Mayflower Hotel, New York.

Nicholas, Fayard. Unpublished interview by Marshall and Jean Stearns, 6 February 1965, Knickerbocker Hotel, Hollywood, Calif.; transcript, Harold Nicholas Archive, New York City.

Nicholas, Fayard and Harold. Interview by Bruce Goldstein, produced by Rigmor Newman, Los Angeles, 1991; transcript, Picture Musical International, New York.

Nicholas, Fayard and Harold. Public interview by author, "An Evening with the Nicholas Brothers," 16 April 1996, Harvard University, Cambridge, Mass.; videorecording.

Nicholas, Harold. Telephone interview by author, 1 December 1995, 30 June 1996, 21 May 1997, New York.

Nicholas, Harold. Public interview by author, "Rethinking the Balanchine Legacy: Balanchine, Jazz, and Popular Dance," 19 April 1993, Lincoln Center Library for the Performing Arts, New York; video recording, Dance Collection, Lincoln Center Library for the Performing Arts.

Nicholas, Harold. Interview by Bruce Goldstein, produced by Rigmor Newman, Los Angeles, 1991; transcript, Picture Musical International, New York.

Nicholas, Viola. Unpublished telephone interview by Marshall Stearns, 7 February 1965; transcript, Harold Nicholas Archive, New York.

Reed, Leonard. Interview by Bruce Goldstein, produced by Rigmor Newman, Los Angeles, 1991; transcript, Picture Musical International, New York.

Roach, Max. Interview by Bruce Goldstein, produced by Rigmor Newman, New York, 1991; transcript, Picture Musical International, New York.

Short, Bobby. Interview by Bruce Goldstein, produced by Rigmor Newman, New York, 1991: transcript, Picture Musical International, New York.

Smith, Ernie. Interview by author, 15 August 1995, Bolton Landing, N.Y.

Sommer, Sally. Telephone interview by author, 7 February 1997, New York.

Index

OTHER COOPER SQUARE PRESS TITLES OF INTEREST

STEPS IN TIME
An Autobiography
Fred Astaire
Foreword by Ginger Rogers
New introduction by
Jennifer Dunning
376 pp., 46 b/w photos
0-8154-1058-1
$19.95

A CENTURY OF DANCE
A Hundred Years of Musical
Movement, From Waltz to Hip Hop
Ian Driver
256 pp., 135 b/w, color photos
0-8154-1133-2
$29.95

THE BOYS FROM SYRACUSE
The Schuberts' Theatrical Empire
Foster Hirsch
374 pp., 24 b/w photos
0-8154-1103-0
$18.95

BLACKFACE
Reflections on African Americans
in the Movies
Expanded Edition
Nelson George
330 pp., 23 b/w photos
0-8154-1194-4
$16.95

HATTIE
The Life of Hattie McDaniel
Carlton Jackson
250 pp., 16 b/w photos
1-56833-004-9
$12.95

JOSEPHINE BAKER
The Hungry Heart
Jean-Claude Baker &
Chris Chase
592 pp., 84 b/w photos
0-8154-1149-9
$21.95

REMINISCING WITH
NOBLE SISSLE AND EUBIE BLAKE
Robert Kimball &
William Bolcom
256 pp., 244 b/w photos
0-8154-1045-X
$24.95

A SILENT SIREN SONG
The Aitken Brothers' Hollywood
Odyssey, 1905–1926
Al P. Nelson & Mel R. Jones
288 pp., 42 b/w photos
0-8154-1069-7
$25.95 cloth

WAITING FOR DIZZY
Fourteen Jazz Portraits
Gene Lees
Foreword by Terry Teachout
272 pp.
0-8154-1037-9
$17.95